SWORD ART ONLINE

mother's ROSARY

002

ART: TSUBASA HADUKI
ORIGINAL STORY: REKI KAWAHARA
CHARACTER DESIGN: abec

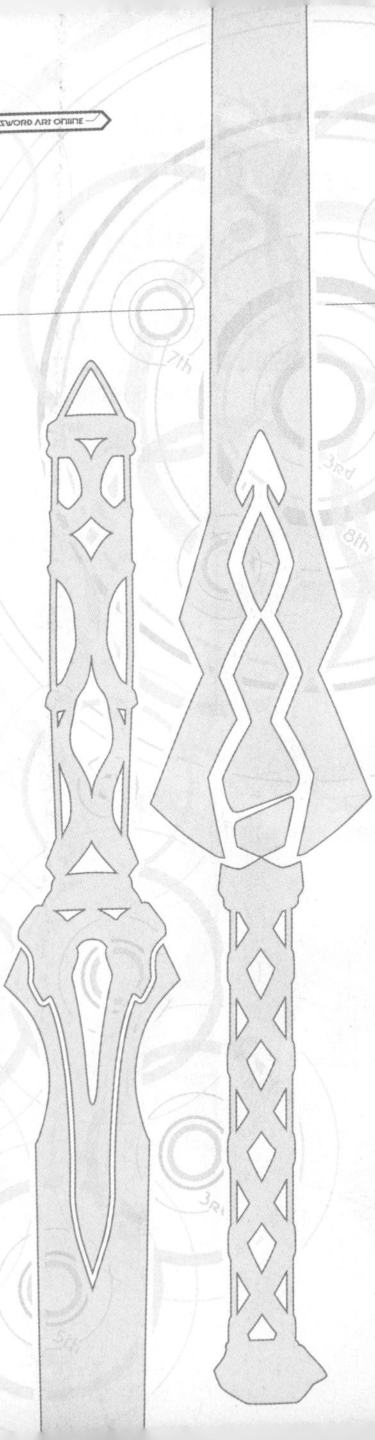

002

SWORD ART ONLINE mother's ROSARY

ART : tsubasa haduki
original story : REKI KAWAHARA
character design : abec

contents

date : 8 jan 2026 thu 13:00

YMIR ALfheim online

SWORD ART ONLINE
MOTHER'S ROSARY

002

SWORD ART ONLINE mother's rosary

art : tsubasa haduki
original story : reki kawahara
character design : abec

stage.004

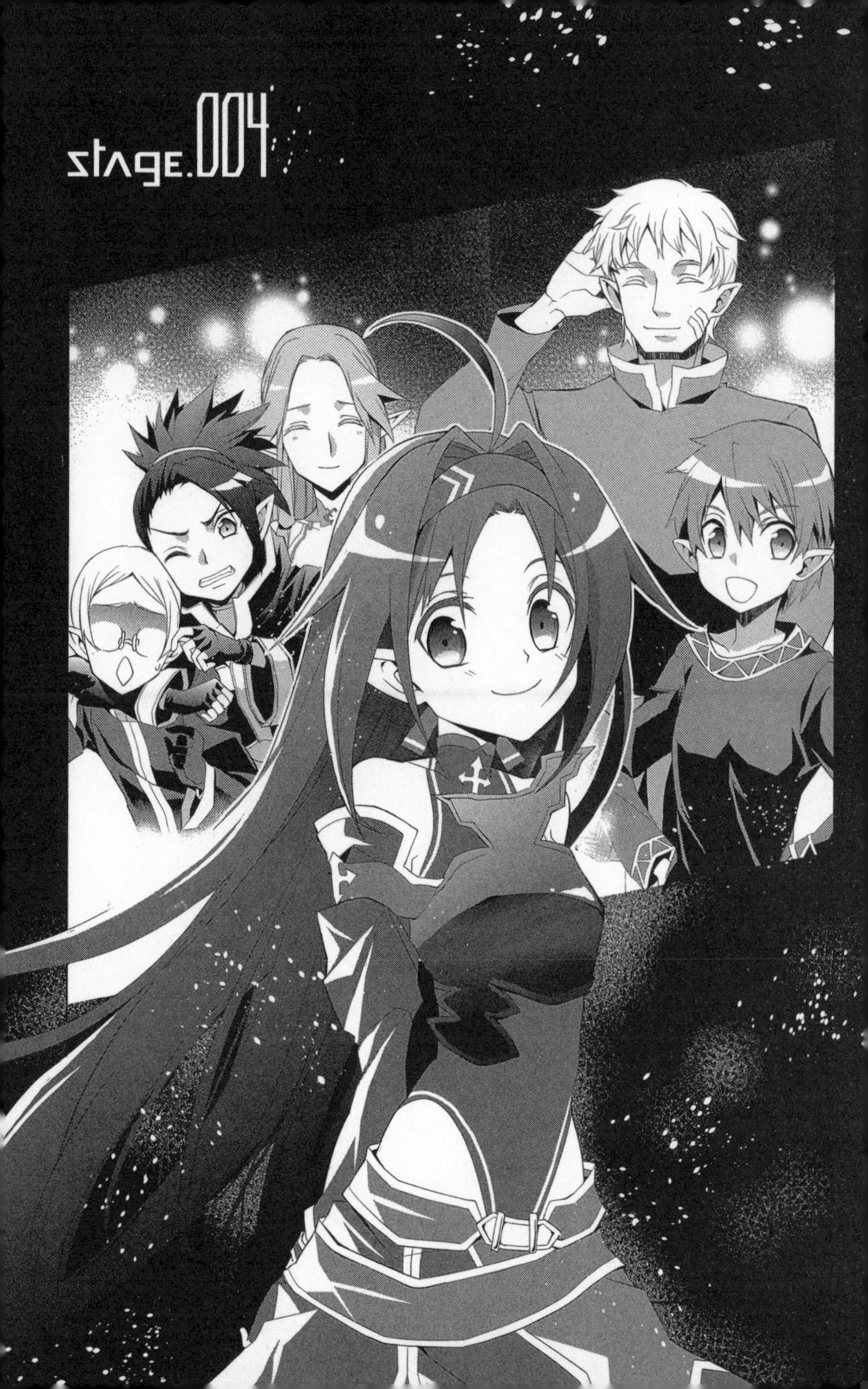

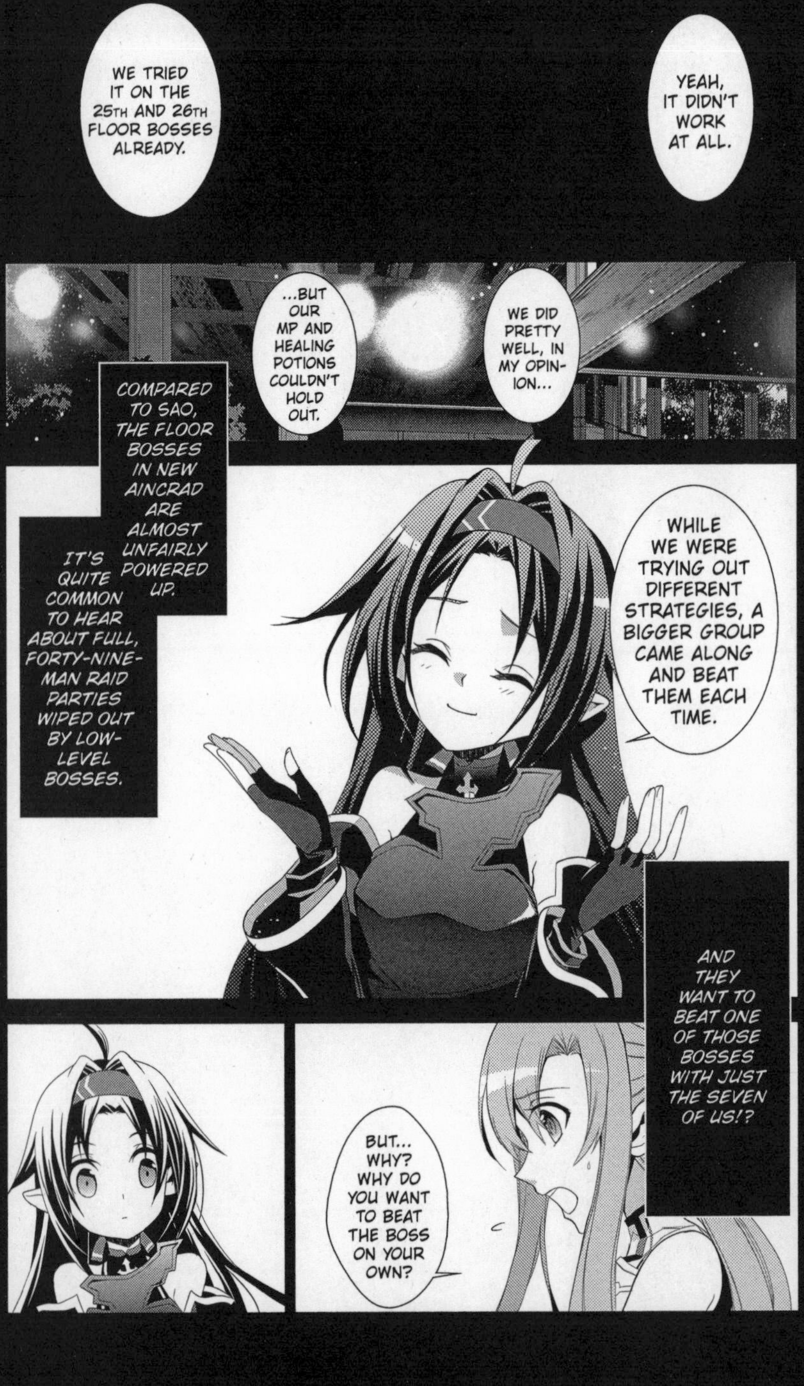

YEAH, IT DIDN'T WORK AT ALL.
WE TRIED IT ON THE 25TH AND 26TH FLOOR BOSSES ALREADY.
WE DID PRETTY WELL, IN MY OPIN-ION...
...BUT OUR MP AND HEALING POTIONS COULDN'T HOLD OUT.
WHILE WE WERE TRYING OUT DIFFERENT STRATEGIES, A BIGGER GROUP CAME ALONG AND BEAT THEM EACH TIME.
COMPARED TO SAO, THE FLOOR BOSSES IN NEW AINCRAD ARE ALMOST UNFAIRLY POWERED UP.
IT'S QUITE COMMON TO HEAR ABOUT FULL, FORTY-NINE-MAN RAID PARTIES WIPED OUT BY LOW-LEVEL BOSSES.
AND THEY WANT TO BEAT ONE OF THOSE BOSSES WITH JUST THE SEVEN OF US!?
BUT... WHY? WHY DO YOU WANT TO BEAT THE BOSS ON YOUR OWN?

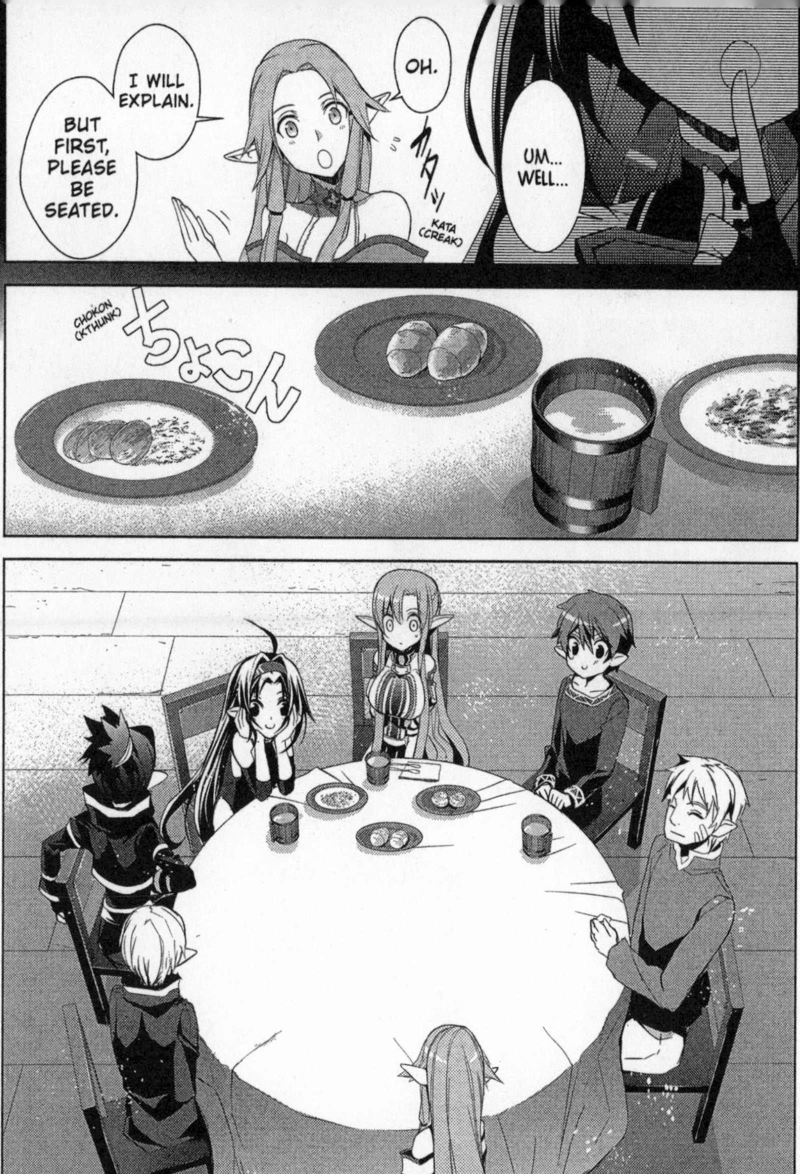
UM... WELL...
OH.
カタッ
KATA (CREAK)
I WILL EXPLAIN.
BUT FIRST, PLEASE BE SEATED.
ちょこん
CHOKON (KTHUNK)

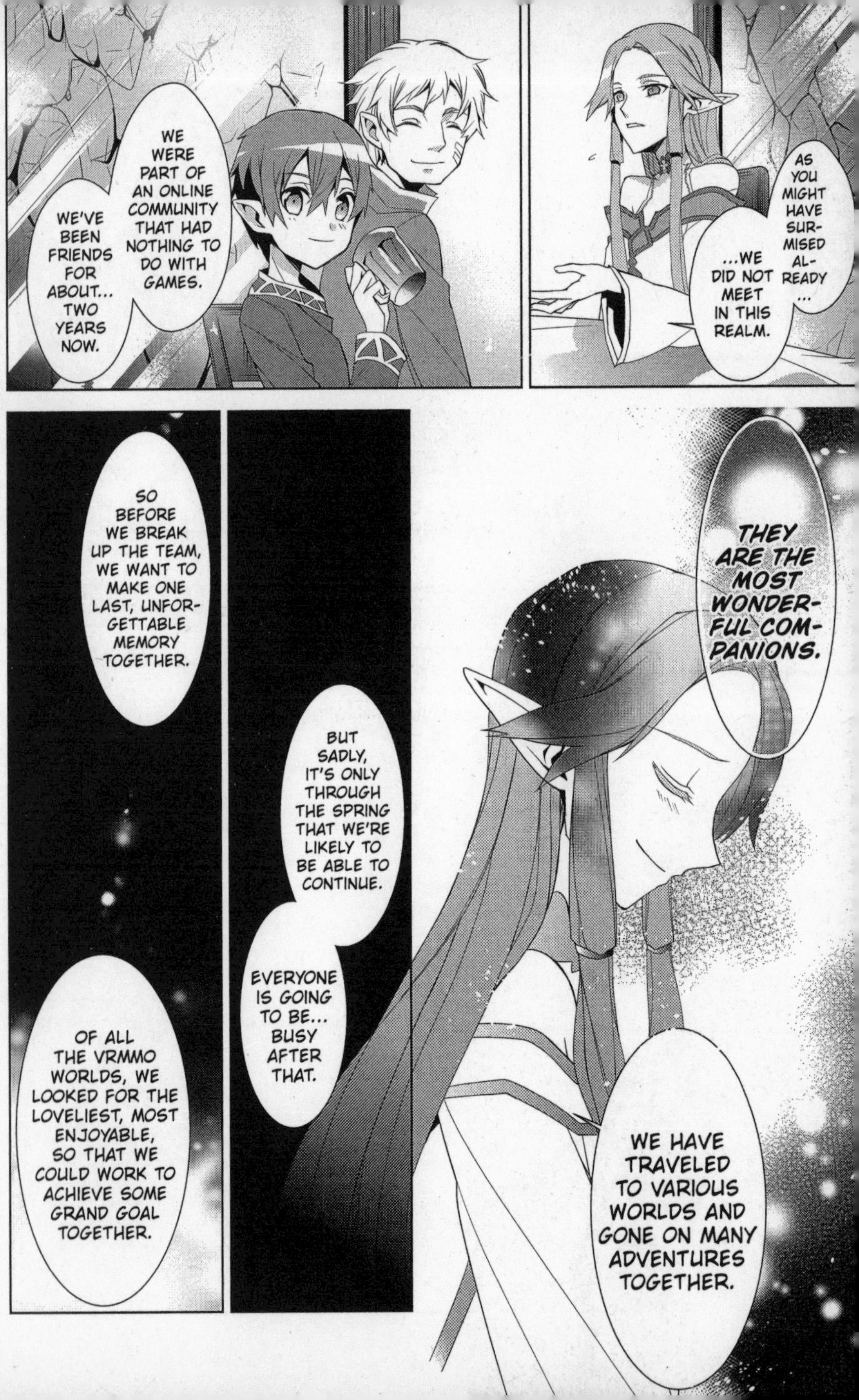
AS YOU MIGHT HAVE SURMISED ALREADY...
...WE DID NOT MEET IN THIS REALM.
WE WERE PART OF AN ONLINE COMMUNITY THAT HAD NOTHING TO DO WITH GAMES.
WE'VE BEEN FRIENDS FOR ABOUT... TWO YEARS NOW.
THEY ARE THE MOST WONDERFUL COMPANIONS.
WE HAVE TRAVELED TO VARIOUS WORLDS AND GONE ON MANY ADVENTURES TOGETHER.
BUT SADLY, IT'S ONLY THROUGH THE SPRING THAT WE'RE LIKELY TO BE ABLE TO CONTINUE.
EVERYONE IS GOING TO BE... BUSY AFTER THAT.
SO BEFORE WE BREAK UP THE TEAM, WE WANT TO MAKE ONE LAST, UNFORGETTABLE MEMORY TOGETHER.
OF ALL THE VRMMO WORLDS, WE LOOKED FOR THE LOVELIEST, MOST ENJOYABLE, SO THAT WE COULD WORK TO ACHIEVE SOME GRAND GOAL TOGETHER.

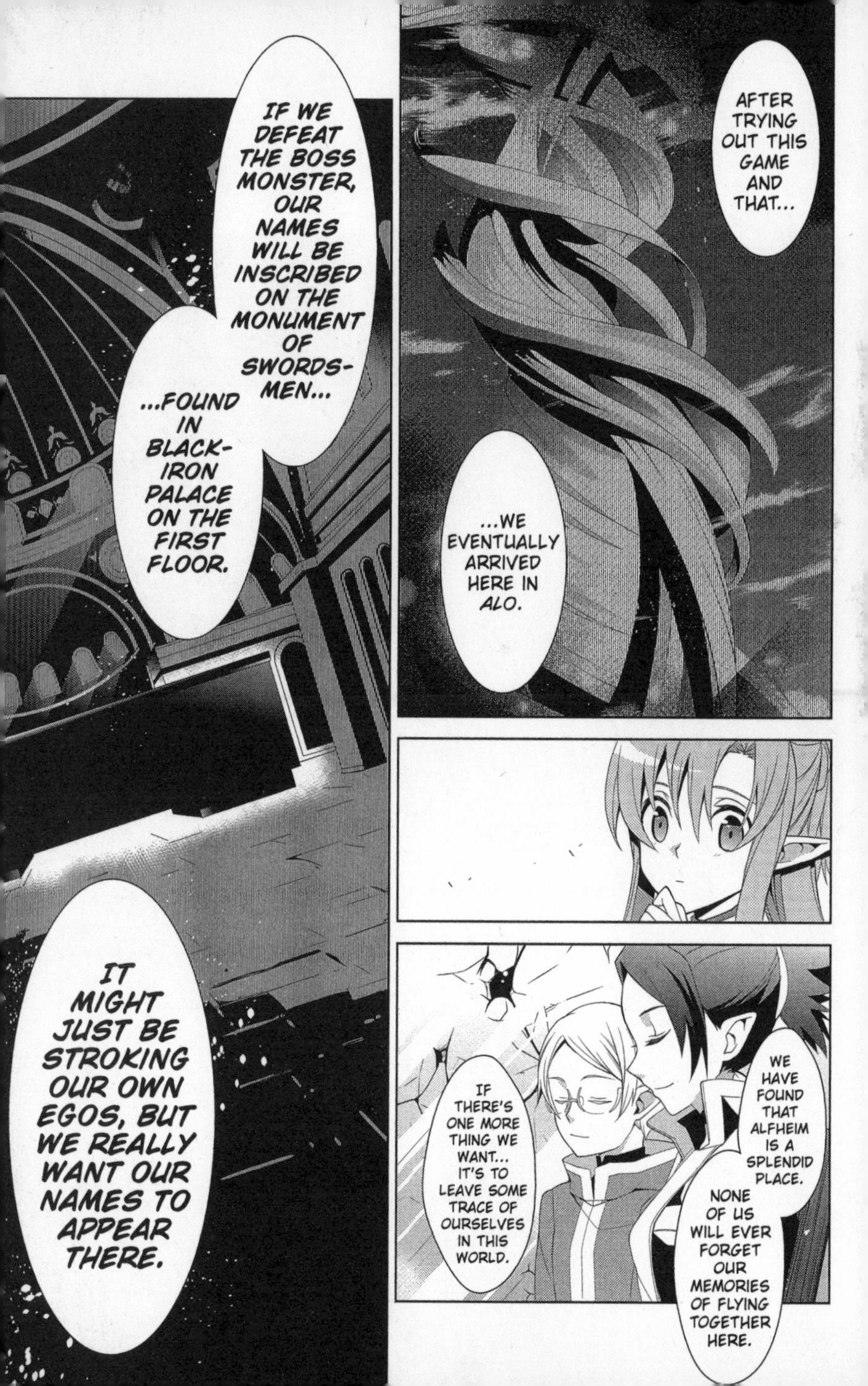
AFTER TRYING OUT THIS GAME AND THAT...
...WE EVENTUALLY ARRIVED HERE IN ALO.
WE HAVE FOUND THAT ALFHEIM IS A SPLENDID PLACE.
NONE OF US WILL EVER FORGET OUR MEMORIES OF FLYING TOGETHER HERE.
IF THERE'S ONE MORE THING WE WANT... IT'S TO LEAVE SOME TRACE OF OURSELVES IN THIS WORLD.
IF WE DEFEAT THE BOSS MONSTER, OUR NAMES WILL BE INSCRIBED ON THE MONUMENT OF SWORDS-MEN...
...FOUND IN BLACK-IRON PALACE ON THE FIRST FLOOR.
IT MIGHT JUST BE STROKING OUR OWN EGOS, BUT WE REALLY WANT OUR NAMES TO APPEAR THERE.

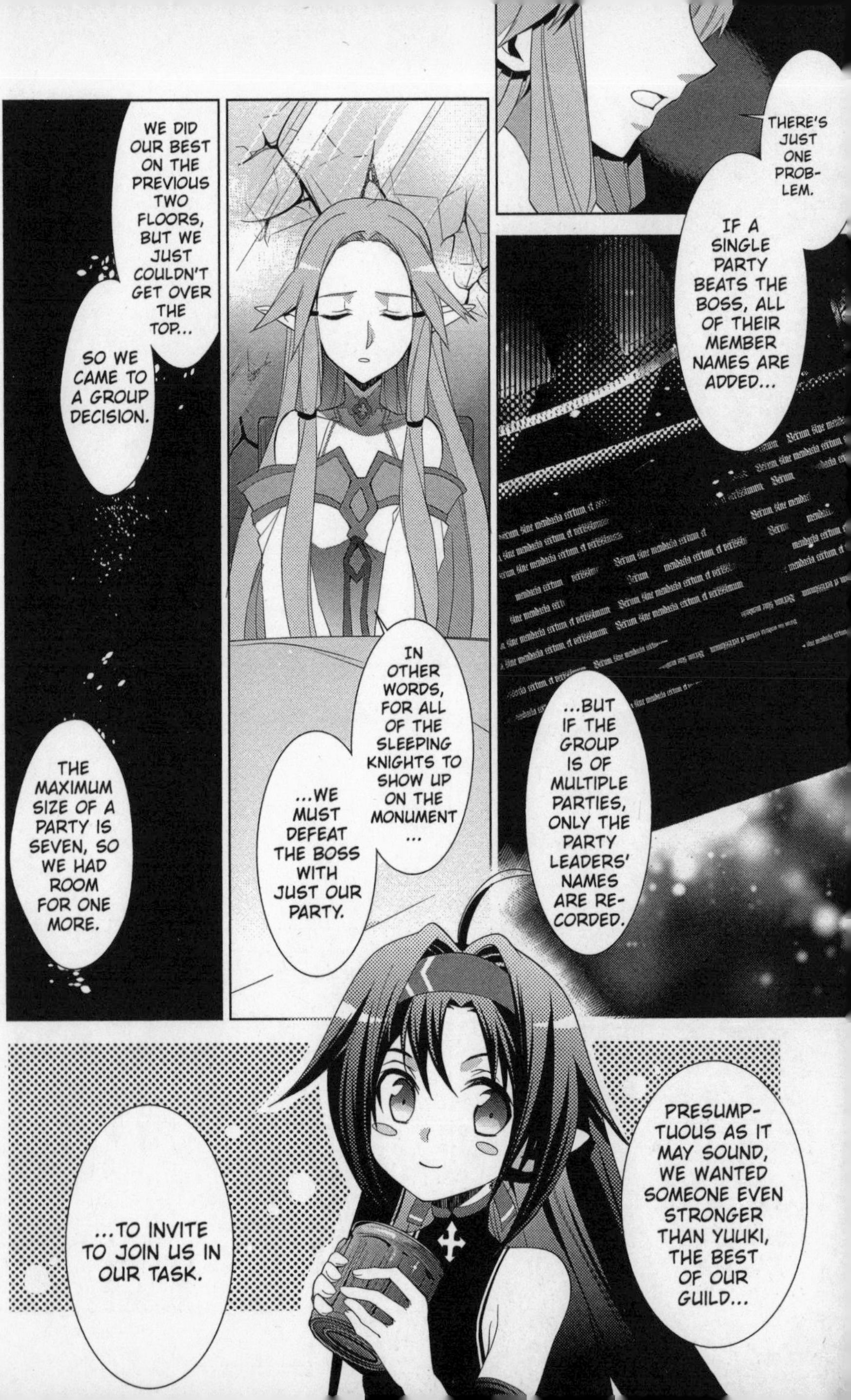
THERE'S JUST ONE PROB-LEM.
IF A SINGLE PARTY BEATS THE BOSS, ALL OF THEIR MEMBER NAMES ARE ADDED...
...BUT IF THE GROUP IS OF MULTIPLE PARTIES, ONLY THE PARTY LEADERS' NAMES ARE RE-CORDED.
IN OTHER WORDS, FOR ALL OF THE SLEEPING KNIGHTS TO SHOW UP ON THE MONUMENT...
...WE MUST DEFEAT THE BOSS WITH JUST OUR PARTY.
WE DID OUR BEST ON THE PREVIOUS TWO FLOORS, BUT WE JUST COULDN'T GET OVER THE TOP...
SO WE CAME TO A GROUP DECISION.
THE MAXIMUM SIZE OF A PARTY IS SEVEN, SO WE HAD ROOM FOR ONE MORE.
PRESUMP-TUOUS AS IT MAY SOUND, WE WANTED SOMEONE EVEN STRONGER THAN YUUKI, THE BEST OF OUR GUILD...
...TO INVITE TO JOIN US IN OUR TASK.

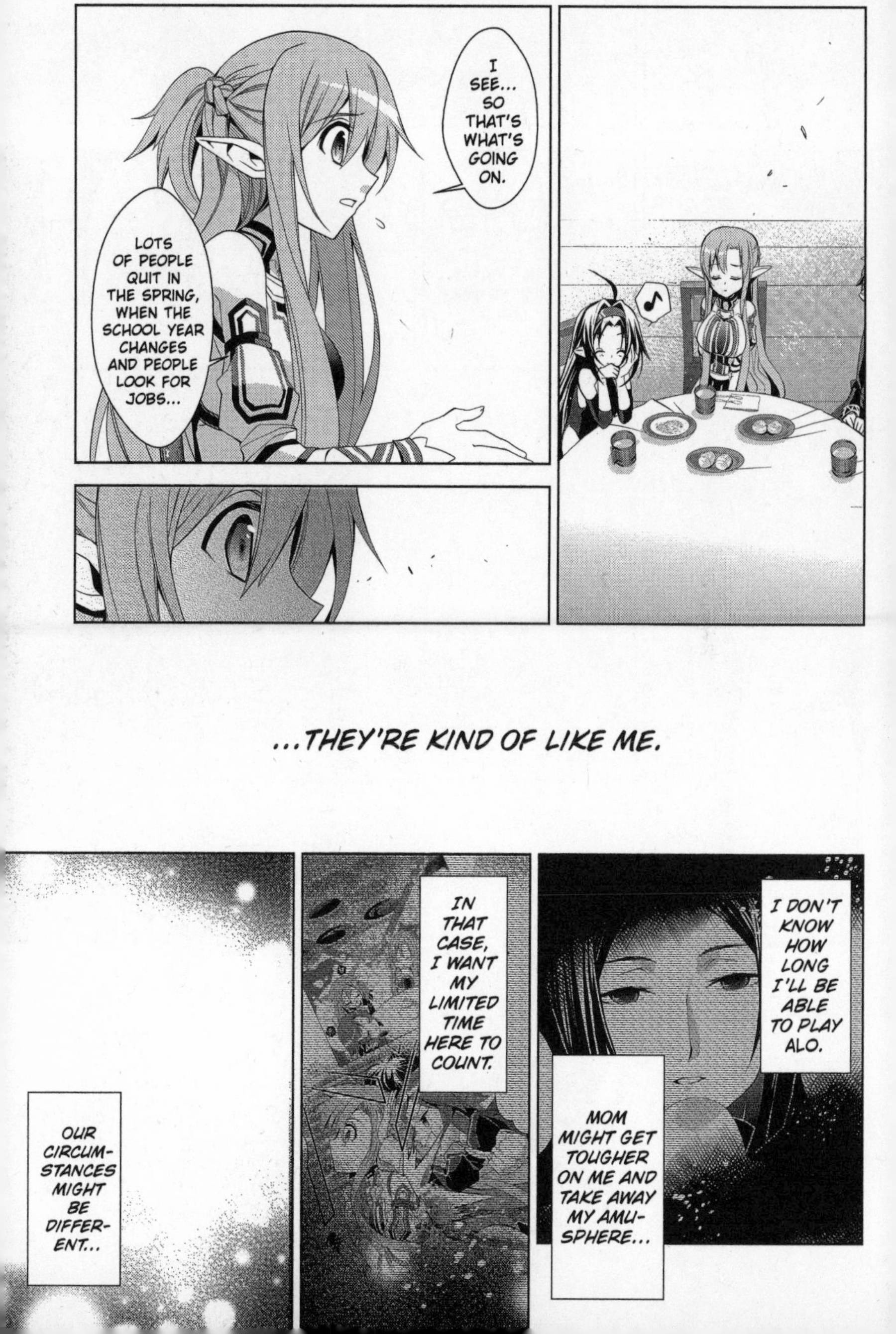
I SEE... SO THAT'S WHAT'S GOING ON.
LOTS OF PEOPLE QUIT IN THE SPRING, WHEN THE SCHOOL YEAR CHANGES AND PEOPLE LOOK FOR JOBS...
...THEY'RE KIND OF LIKE ME.
I DON'T KNOW HOW LONG I'LL BE ABLE TO PLAY ALO.
MOM MIGHT GET TOUGHER ON ME AND TAKE AWAY MY AMU-SPHERE...
IN THAT CASE, I WANT MY LIMITED TIME HERE TO COUNT.
OUR CIRCUM-STANCES MIGHT BE DIFFER-ENT...

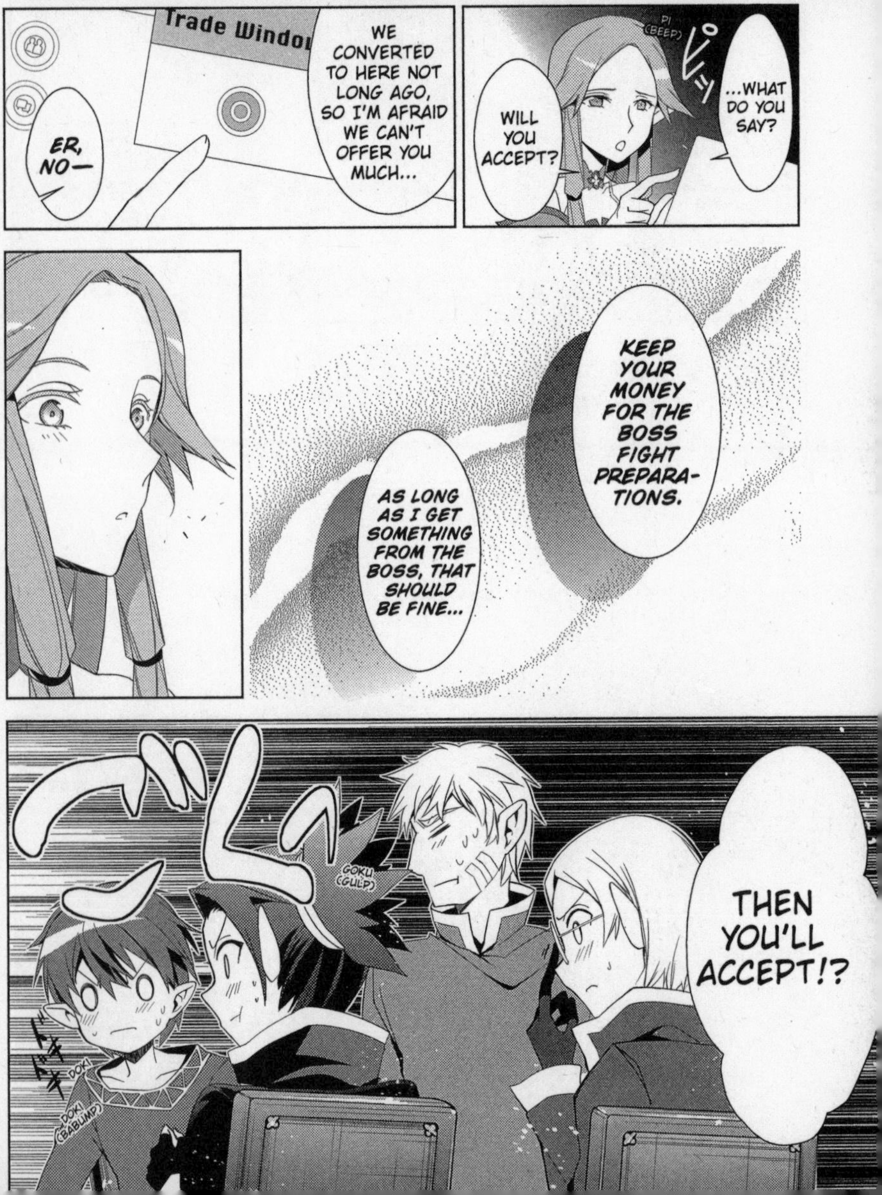
PI (BEEP)
...WHAT DO YOU SAY?
WILL YOU ACCEPT?
Trade Windo
WE CONVERTED TO HERE NOT LONG AGO, SO I'M AFRAID WE CAN'T OFFER YOU MUCH...
ER, NO—
KEEP YOUR MONEY FOR THE BOSS FIGHT PREPARATIONS.
AS LONG AS I GET SOMETHING FROM THE BOSS, THAT SHOULD BE FINE...
THEN YOU'LL ACCEPT!?
GOKU (GULP)
DOKI DOKI (BABUMP)

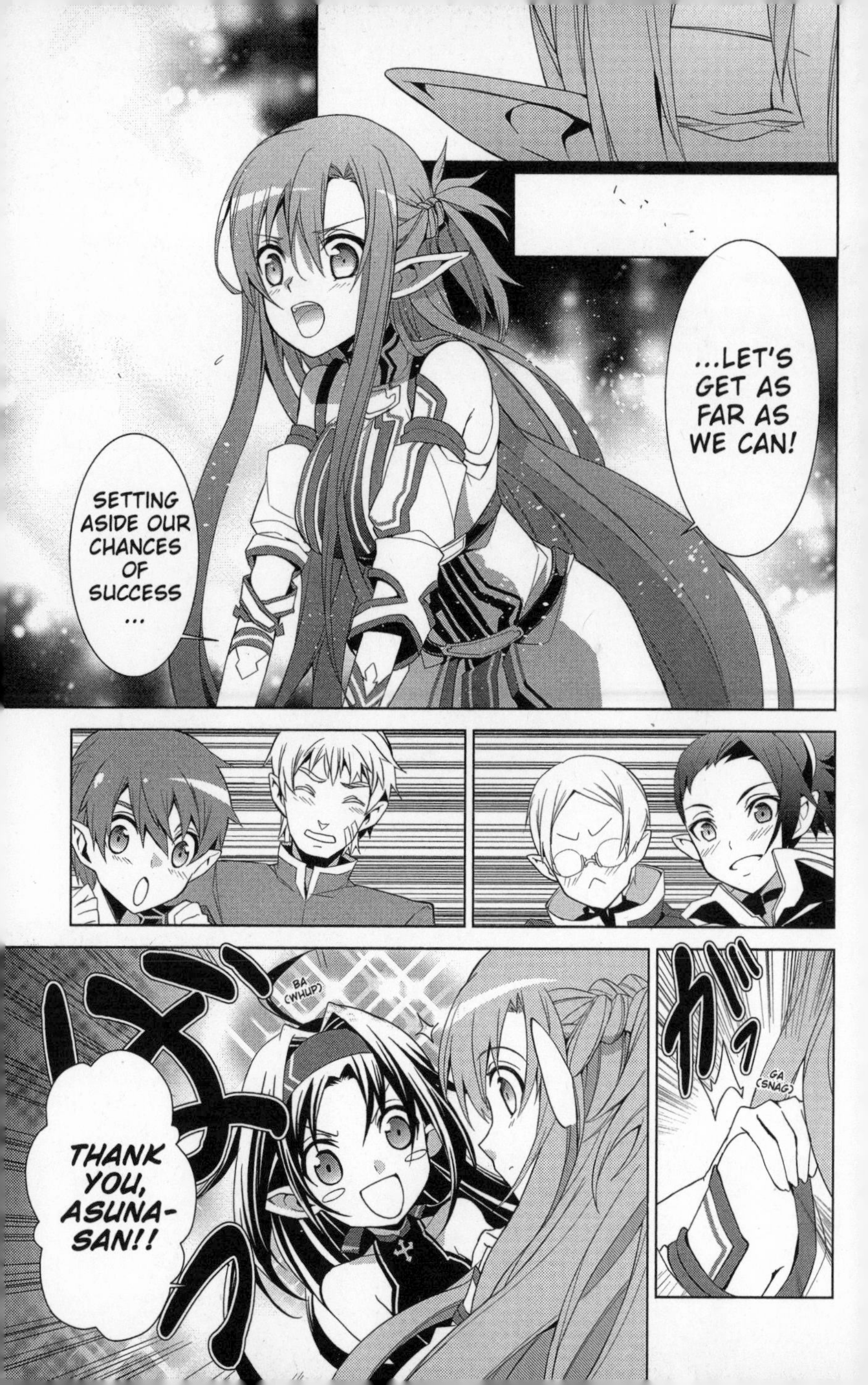
...LET'S GET AS FAR AS WE CAN!
SETTING ASIDE OUR CHANCES OF SUCCESS ...
GA (SNAG)
BA (WHUP)
THANK YOU, ASUNA-SAN!!

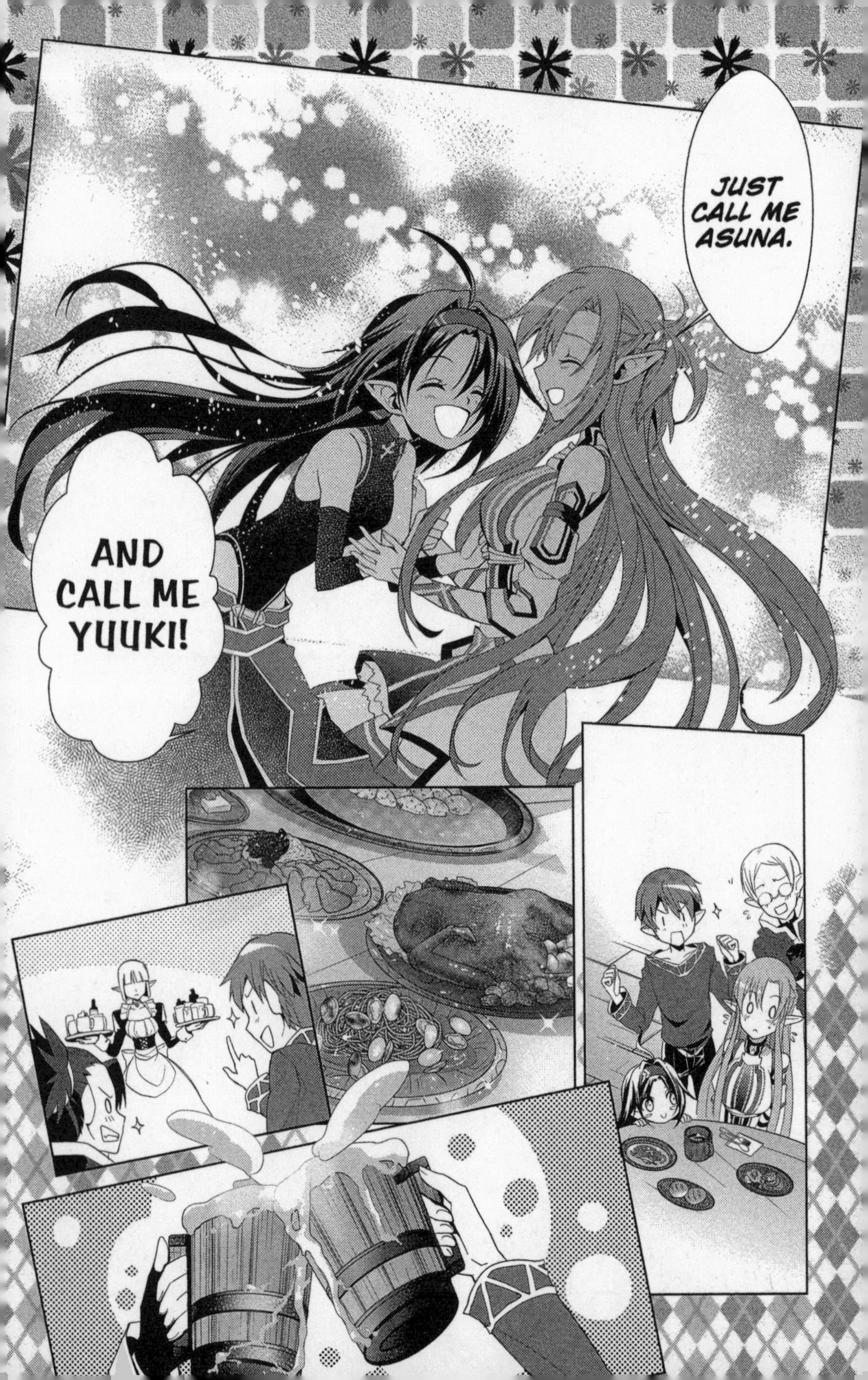
JUST CALL ME ASUNA.
AND CALL ME YUUKI!

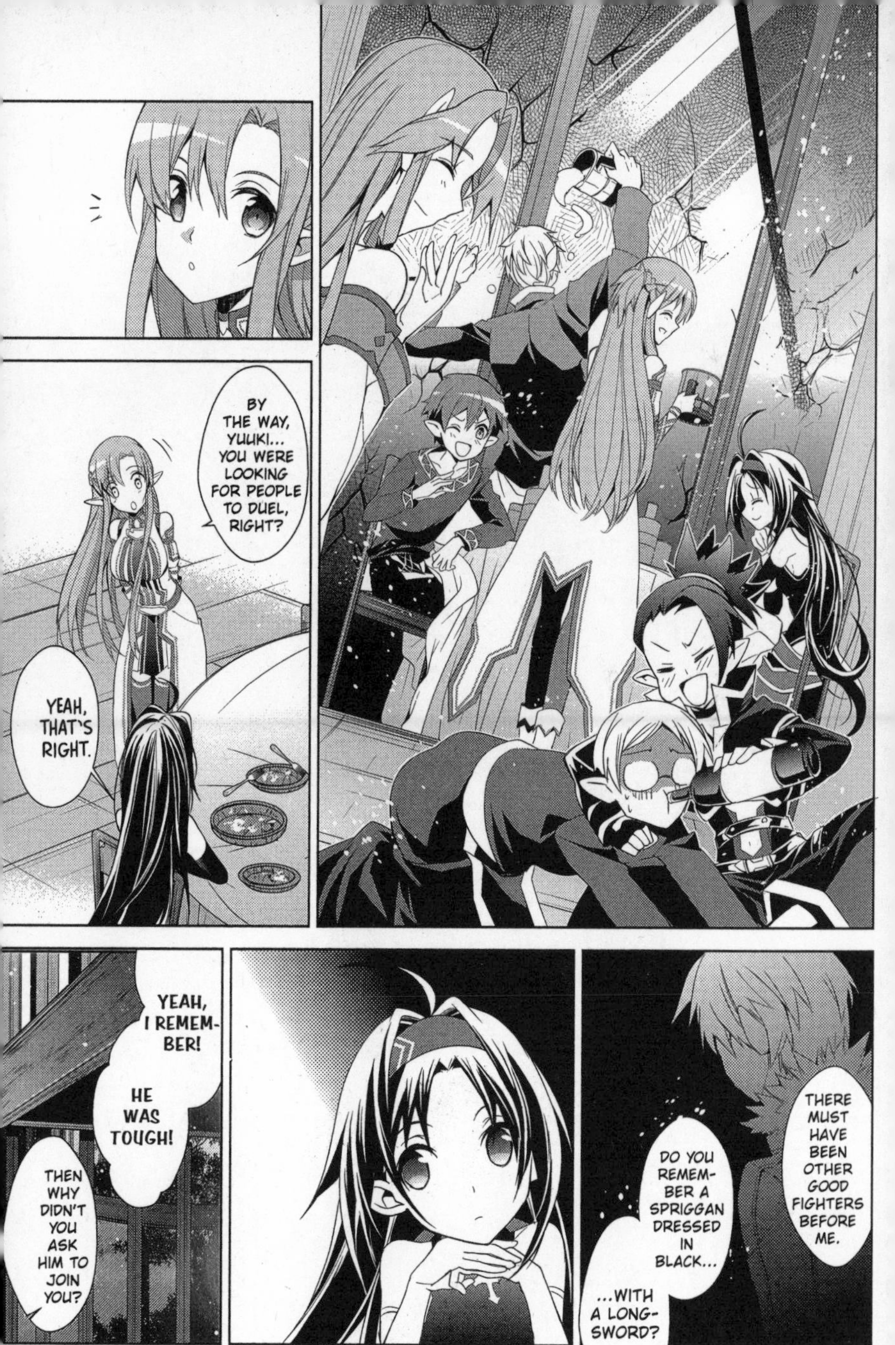
BY THE WAY, YUUKI... YOU WERE LOOKING FOR PEOPLE TO DUEL, RIGHT?
YEAH, THAT'S RIGHT.
THERE MUST HAVE BEEN OTHER GOOD FIGHTERS BEFORE ME.
DO YOU REMEMBER A SPRIGGAN DRESSED IN BLACK...
...WITH A LONG-SWORD?
YEAH, I REMEMBER!
HE WAS TOUGH!
THEN WHY DIDN'T YOU ASK HIM TO JOIN YOU?

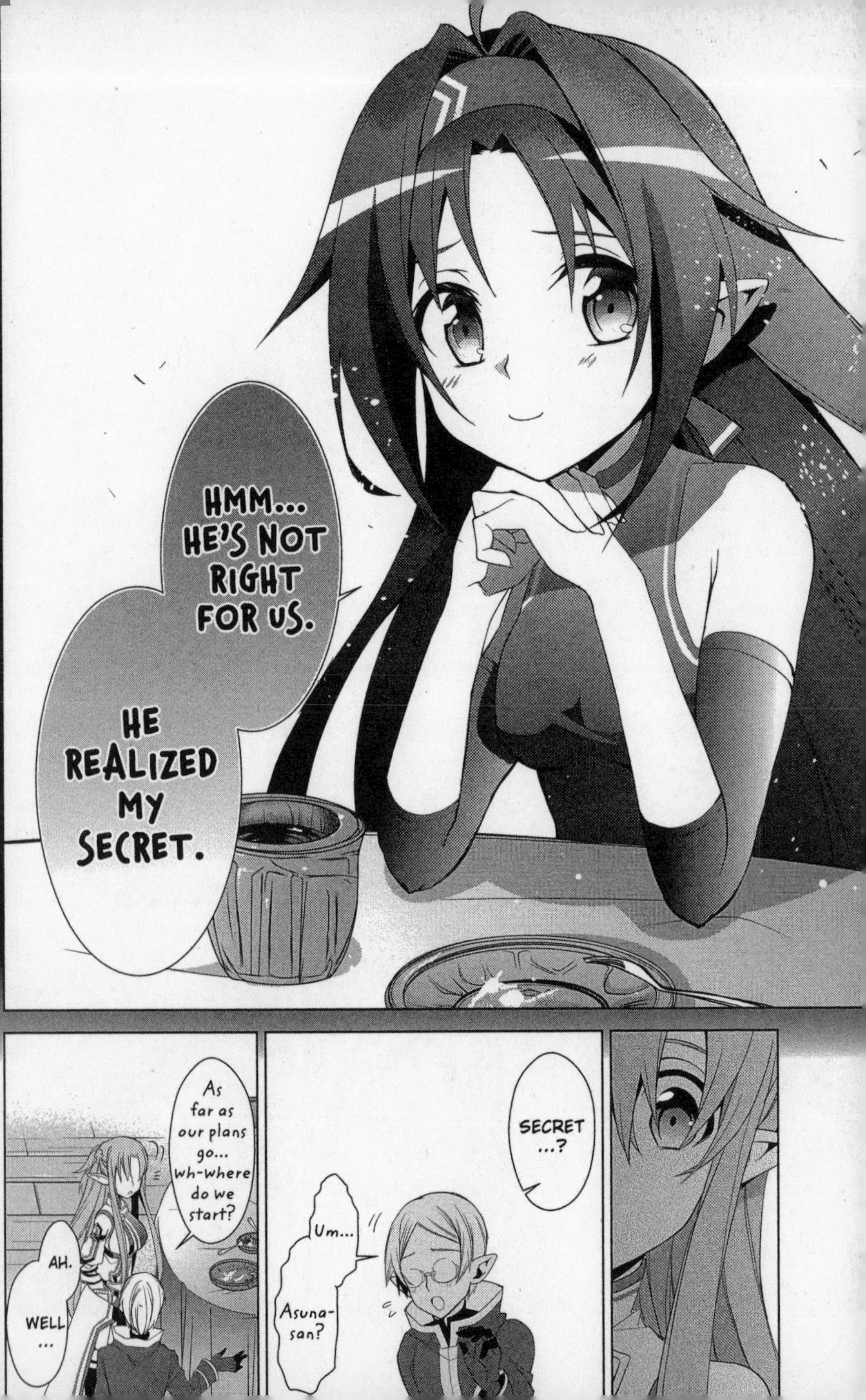
HMM... HE'S NOT RIGHT FOR US.
HE REALIZED MY SECRET.
SECRET ...?
Um...
Asuna-san?
As far as our plans go... wh-where do we start?
AH. WELL ...

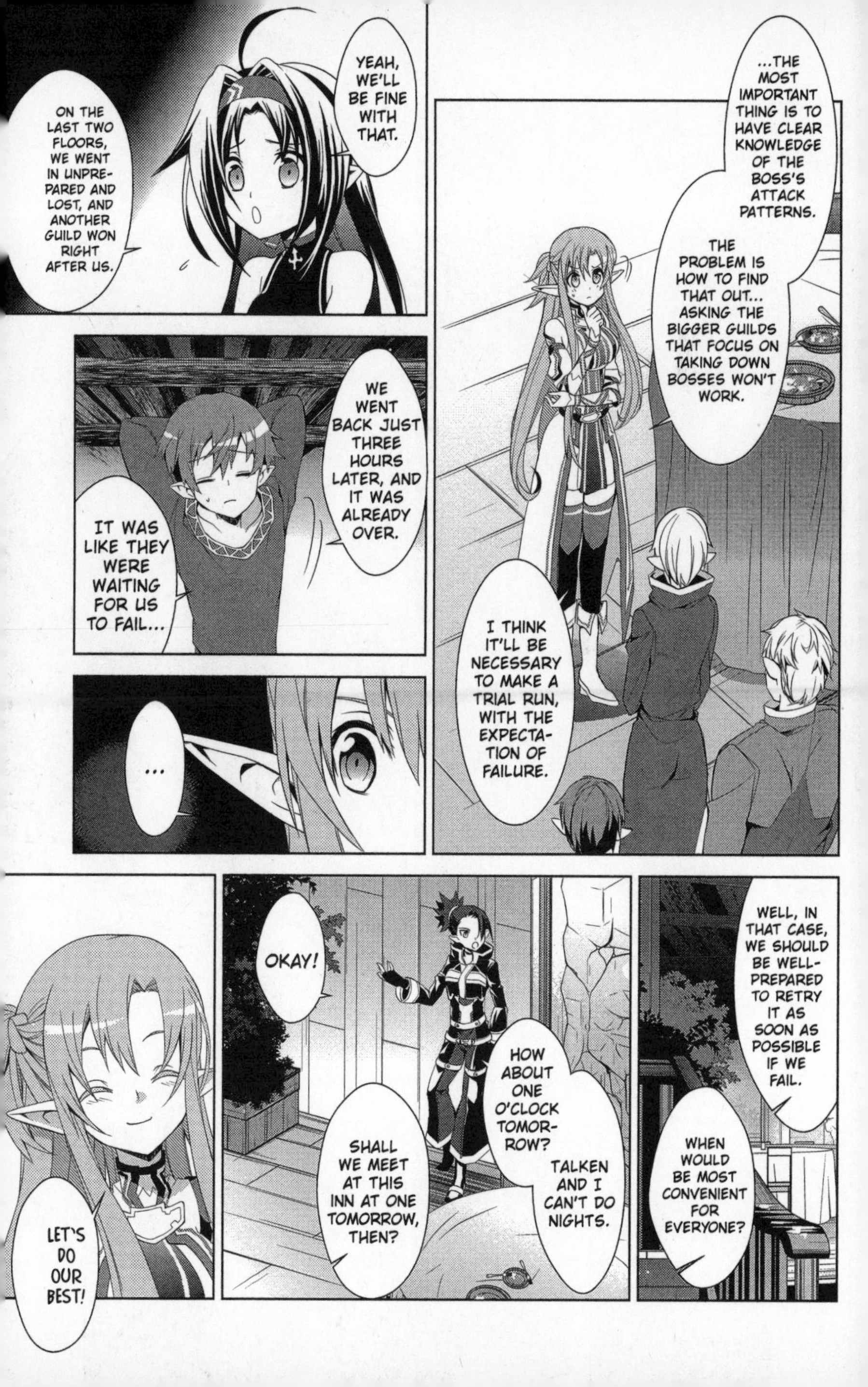
...THE MOST IMPORTANT THING IS TO HAVE CLEAR KNOWLEDGE OF THE BOSS'S ATTACK PATTERNS.
THE PROBLEM IS HOW TO FIND THAT OUT... ASKING THE BIGGER GUILDS THAT FOCUS ON TAKING DOWN BOSSES WON'T WORK.
I THINK IT'LL BE NECESSARY TO MAKE A TRIAL RUN, WITH THE EXPECTATION OF FAILURE.
YEAH, WE'LL BE FINE WITH THAT.
ON THE LAST TWO FLOORS, WE WENT IN UNPREPARED AND LOST, AND ANOTHER GUILD WON RIGHT AFTER US.
WE WENT BACK JUST THREE HOURS LATER, AND IT WAS ALREADY OVER.
IT WAS LIKE THEY WERE WAITING FOR US TO FAIL...
...
WELL, IN THAT CASE, WE SHOULD BE WELL-PREPARED TO RETRY IT AS SOON AS POSSIBLE IF WE FAIL.
WHEN WOULD BE MOST CONVENIENT FOR EVERYONE?
HOW ABOUT ONE O'CLOCK TOMORROW?
TALKEN AND I CAN'T DO NIGHTS.
SHALL WE MEET AT THIS INN AT ONE TOMORROW, THEN?
OKAY!
LET'S DO OUR BEST!

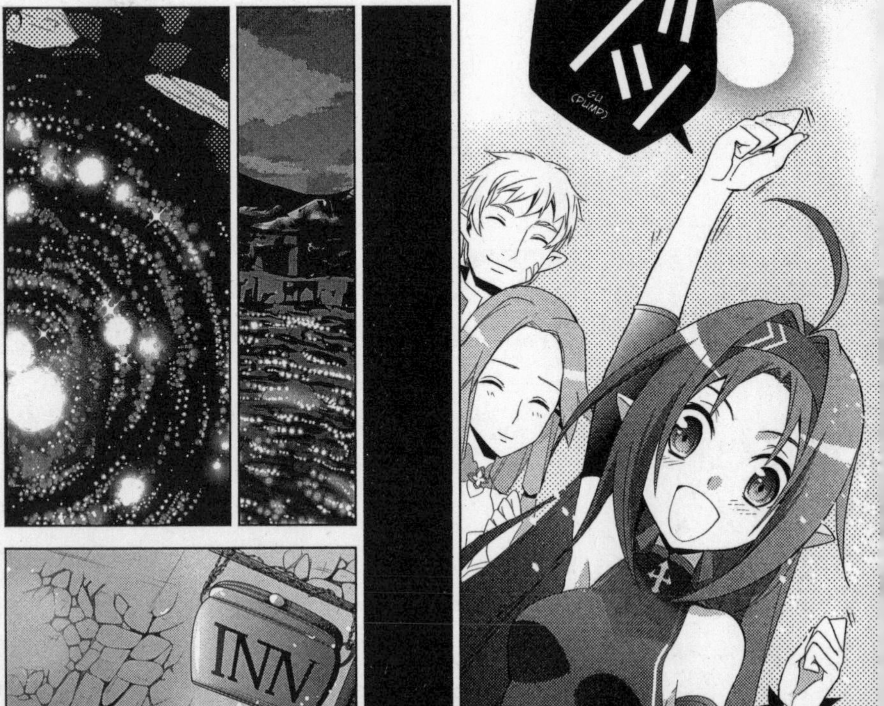
ググッ
GU (PUMP)
YEAH!

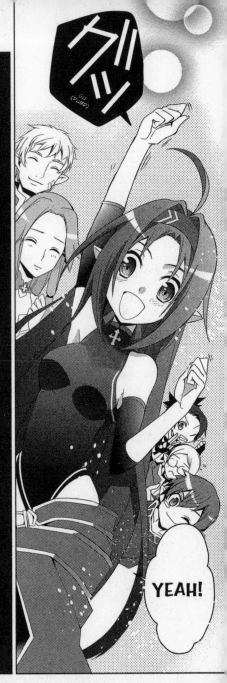

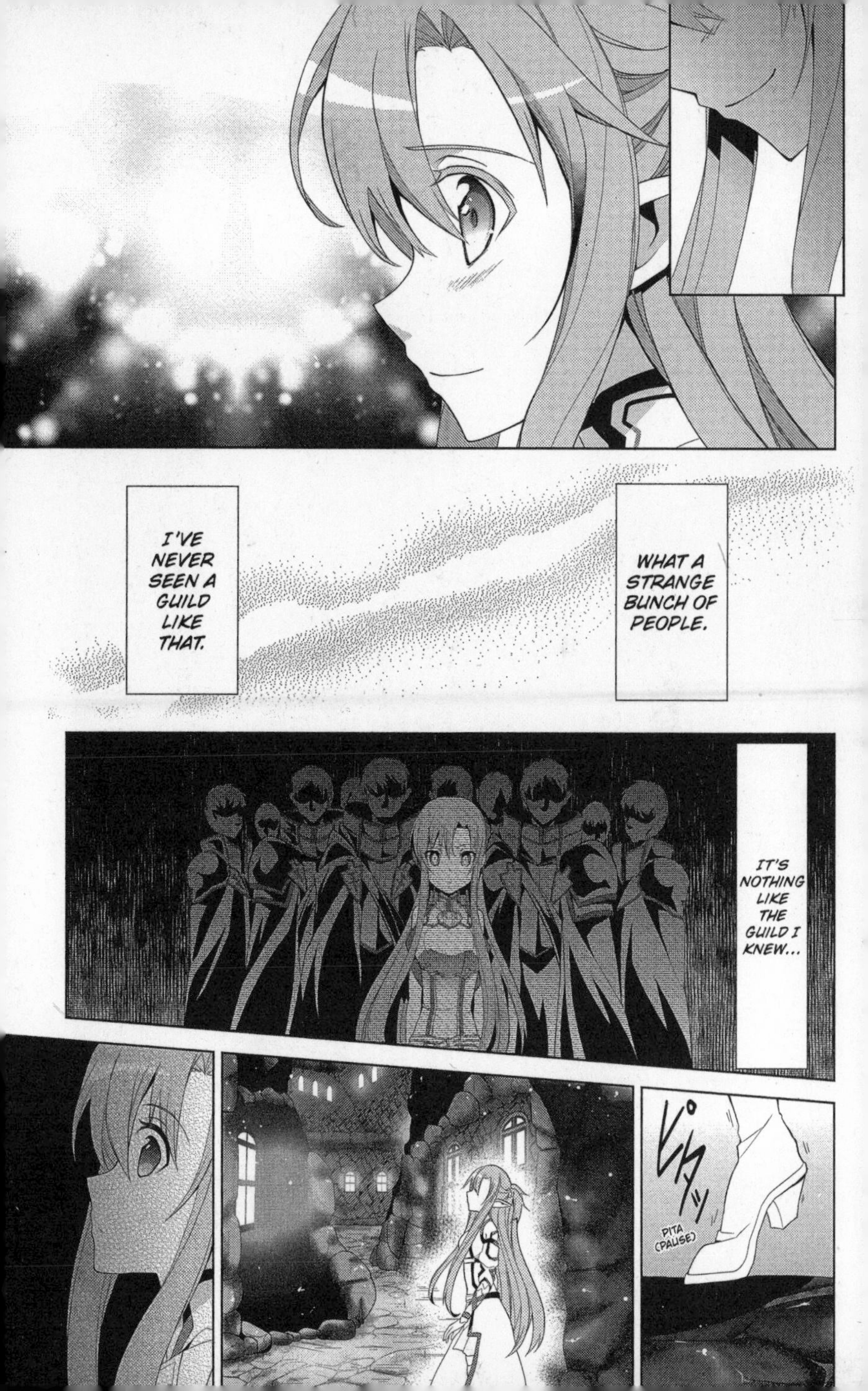
WHAT A STRANGE BUNCH OF PEOPLE.
I'VE NEVER SEEN A GUILD LIKE THAT.
IT'S NOTHING LIKE THE GUILD I KNEW...
ピタッ
PITA (PAUSE)

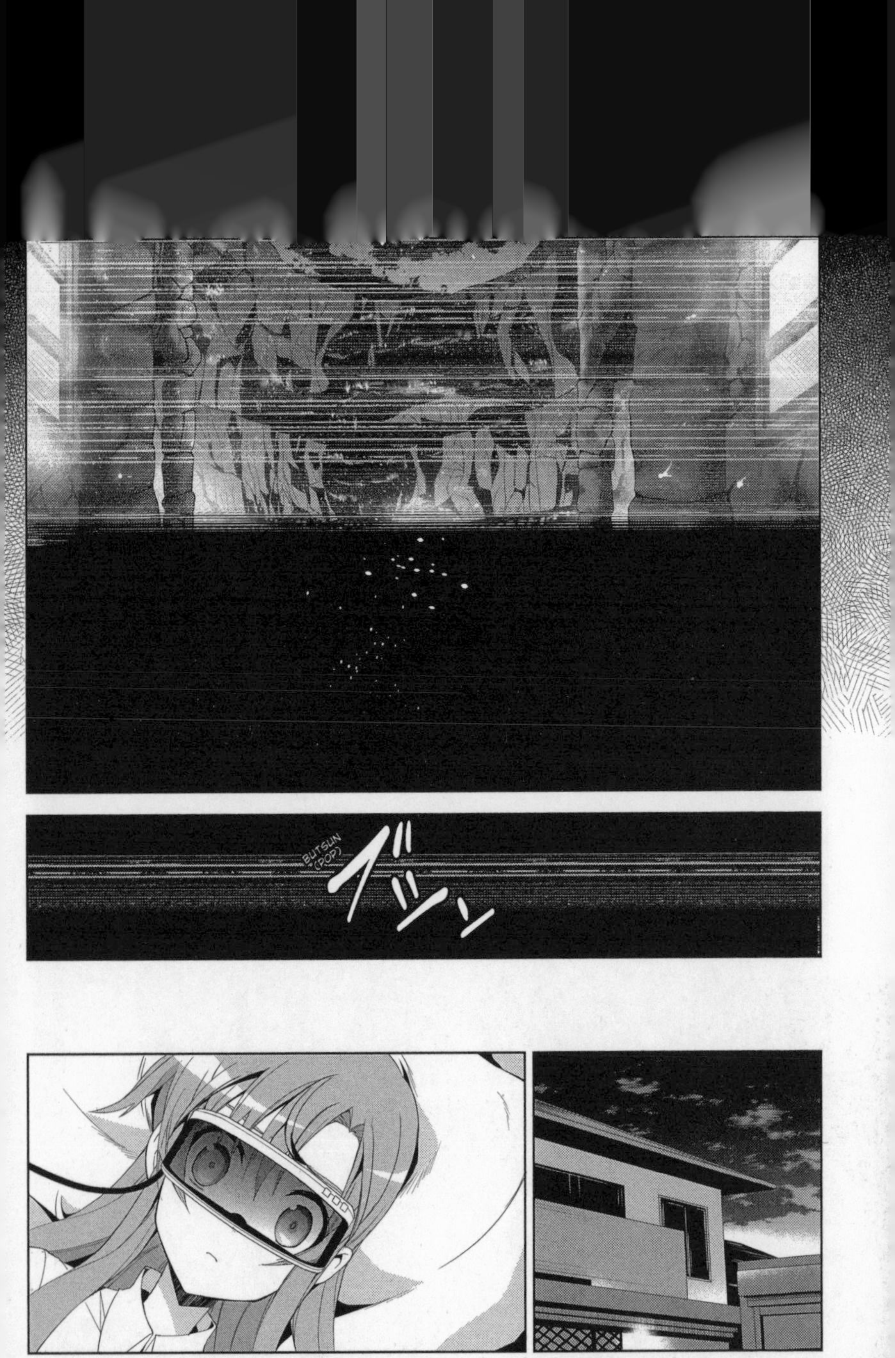
BUTSUN (POP)
ブツン

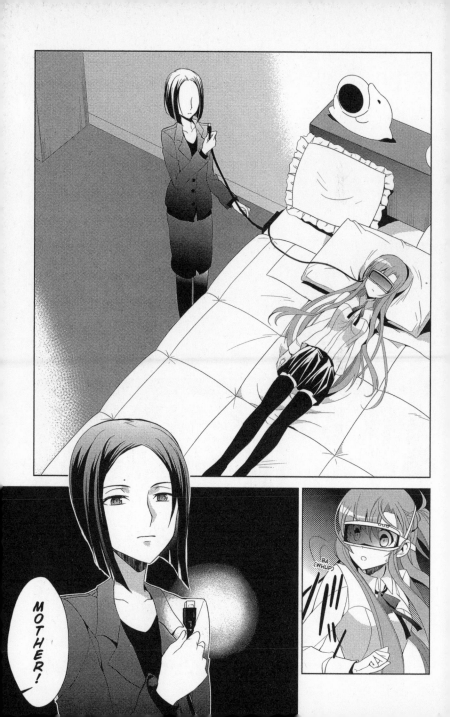

MOTHER!

BA
(WHUP)

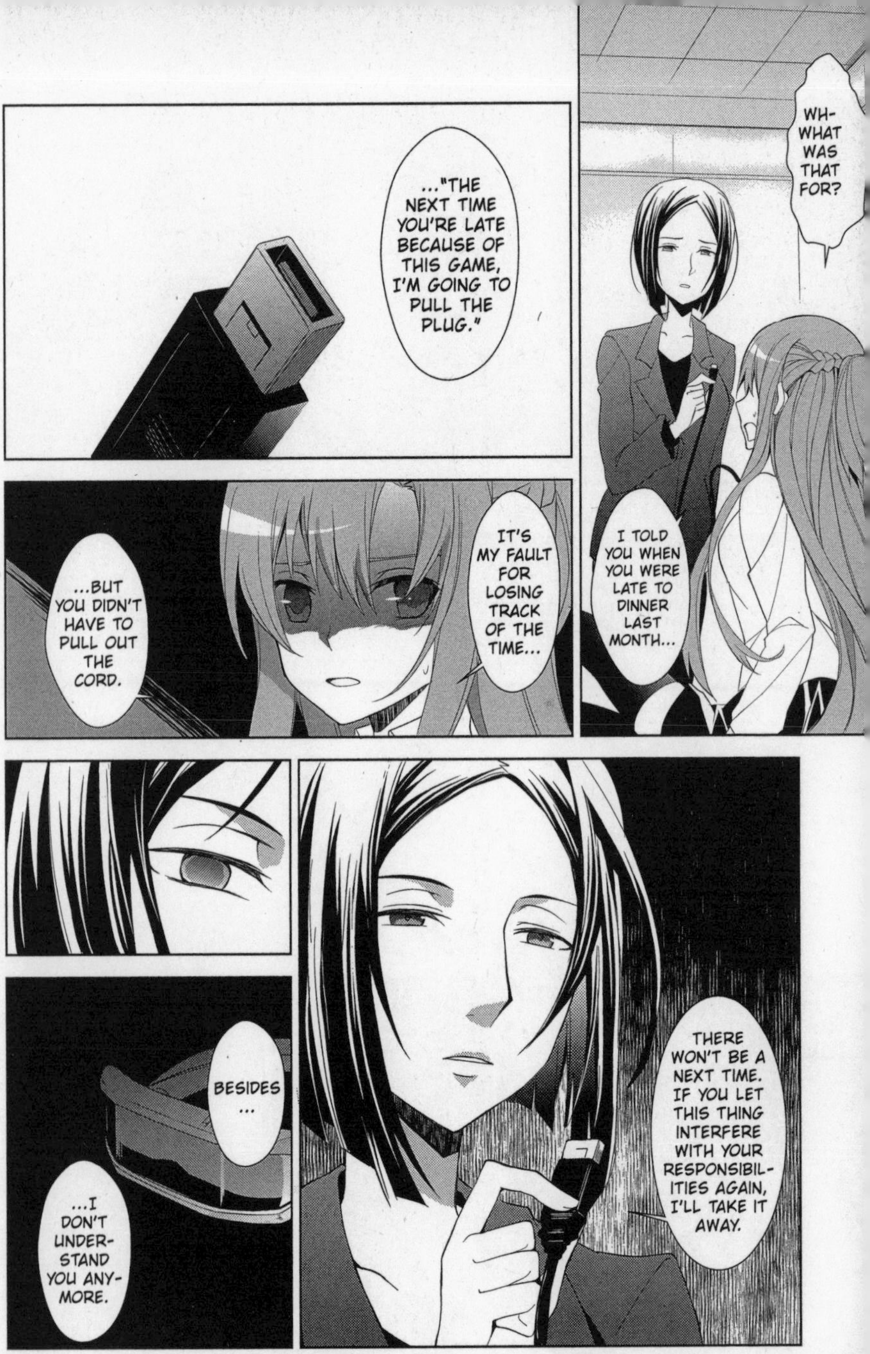
WH-WHAT WAS THAT FOR?
I TOLD YOU WHEN YOU WERE LATE TO DINNER LAST MONTH...
..."THE NEXT TIME YOU'RE LATE BECAUSE OF THIS GAME, I'M GOING TO PULL THE PLUG."
IT'S MY FAULT FOR LOSING TRACK OF THE TIME...
...BUT YOU DIDN'T HAVE TO PULL OUT THE CORD.
THERE WON'T BE A NEXT TIME. IF YOU LET THIS THING INTERFERE WITH YOUR RESPONSIBIL-ITIES AGAIN, I'LL TAKE IT AWAY.
BESIDES...
...I DON'T UNDER-STAND YOU ANY-MORE.

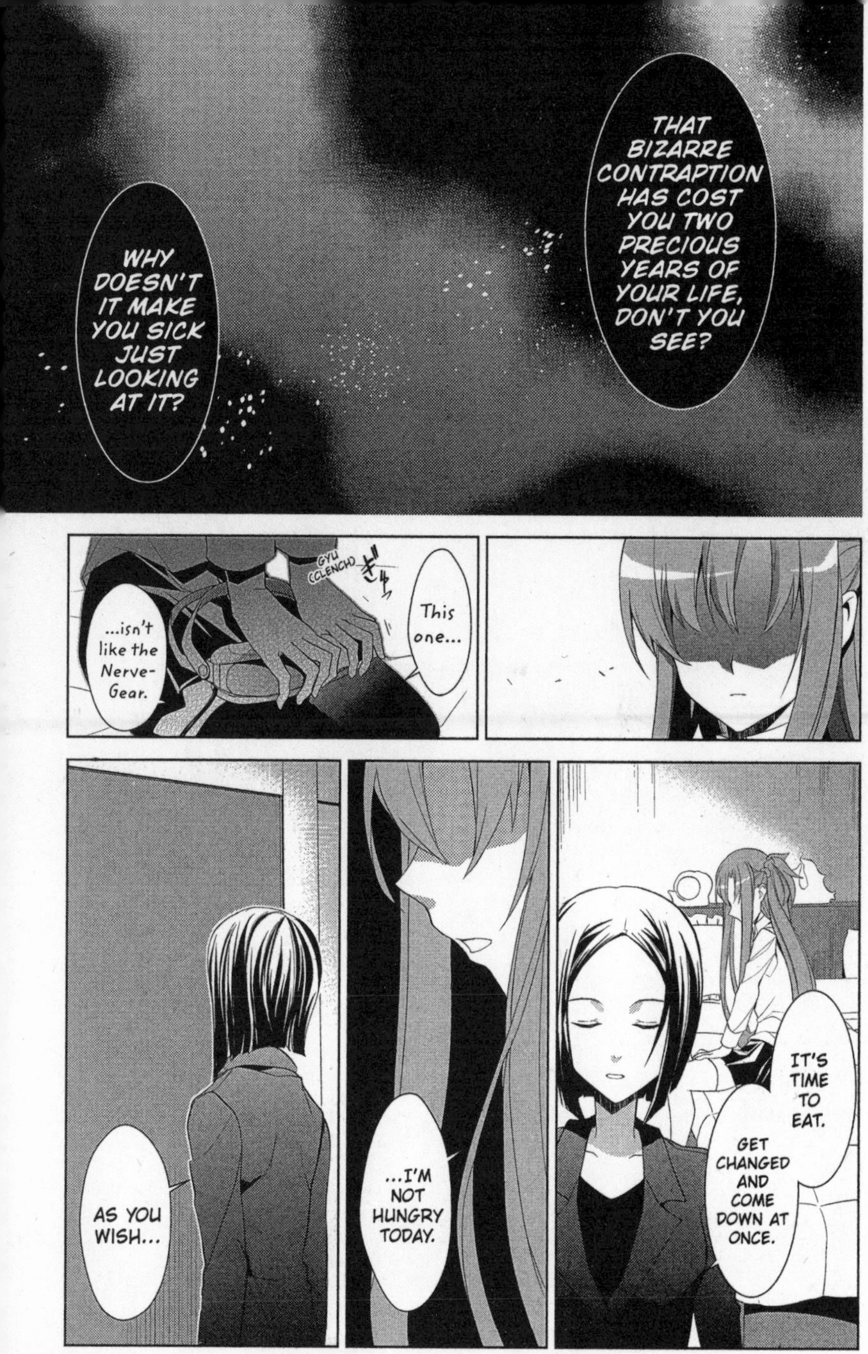
THAT BIZARRE CONTRAPTION HAS COST YOU TWO PRECIOUS YEARS OF YOUR LIFE, DON'T YOU SEE?
WHY DOESN'T IT MAKE YOU SICK JUST LOOKING AT IT?
This one...
GYU (CLENCH)
...isn't like the Nerve-Gear.
IT'S TIME TO EAT.
GET CHANGED AND COME DOWN AT ONCE.
...I'M NOT HUNGRY TODAY.
AS YOU WISH...

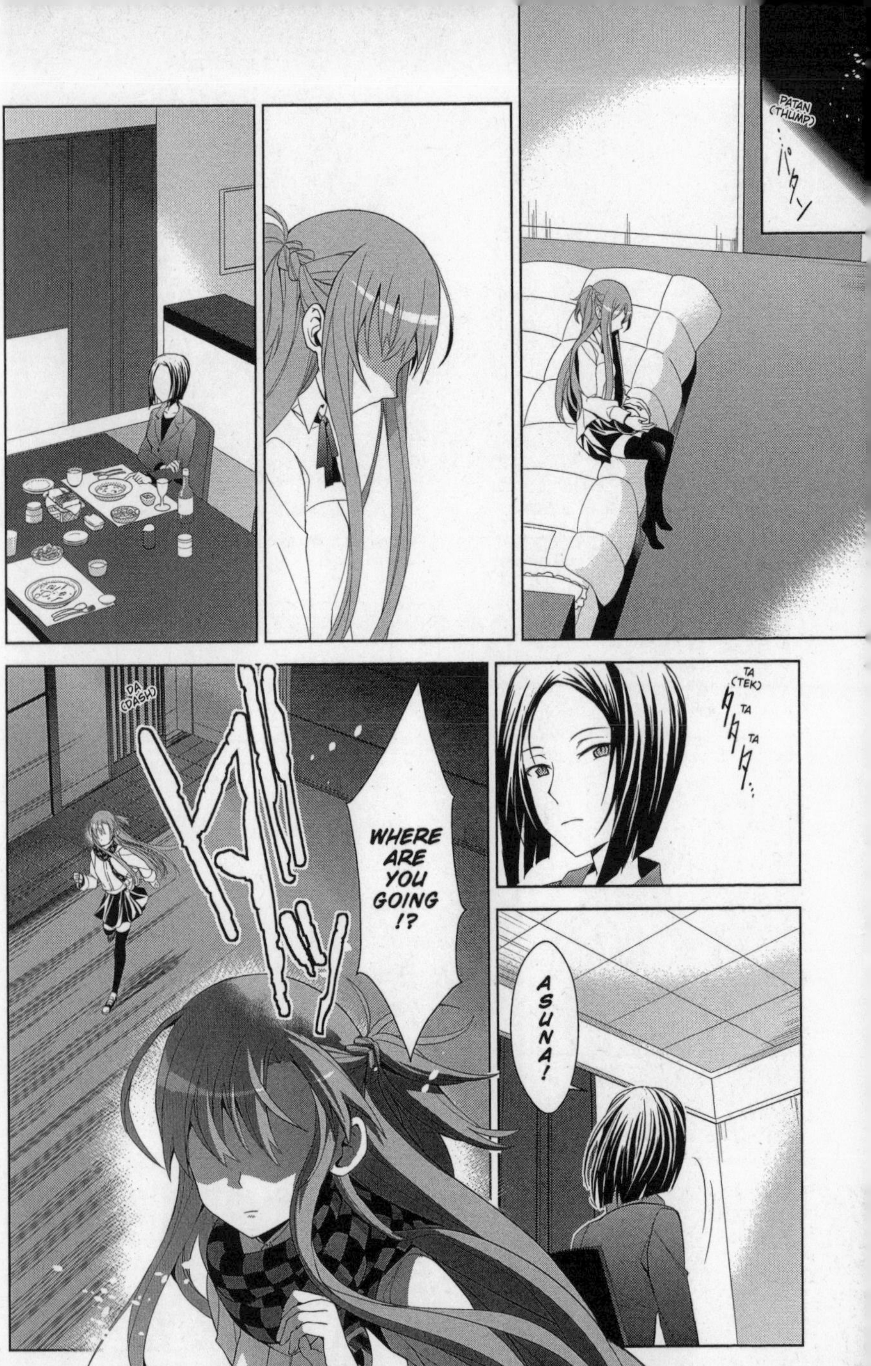
PATAN (THUMP)
…パタン
TA (TEK) TA TA
タタタ…
ASUNA!
DA (DASH)
ダッ
WHERE ARE YOU GOING!?

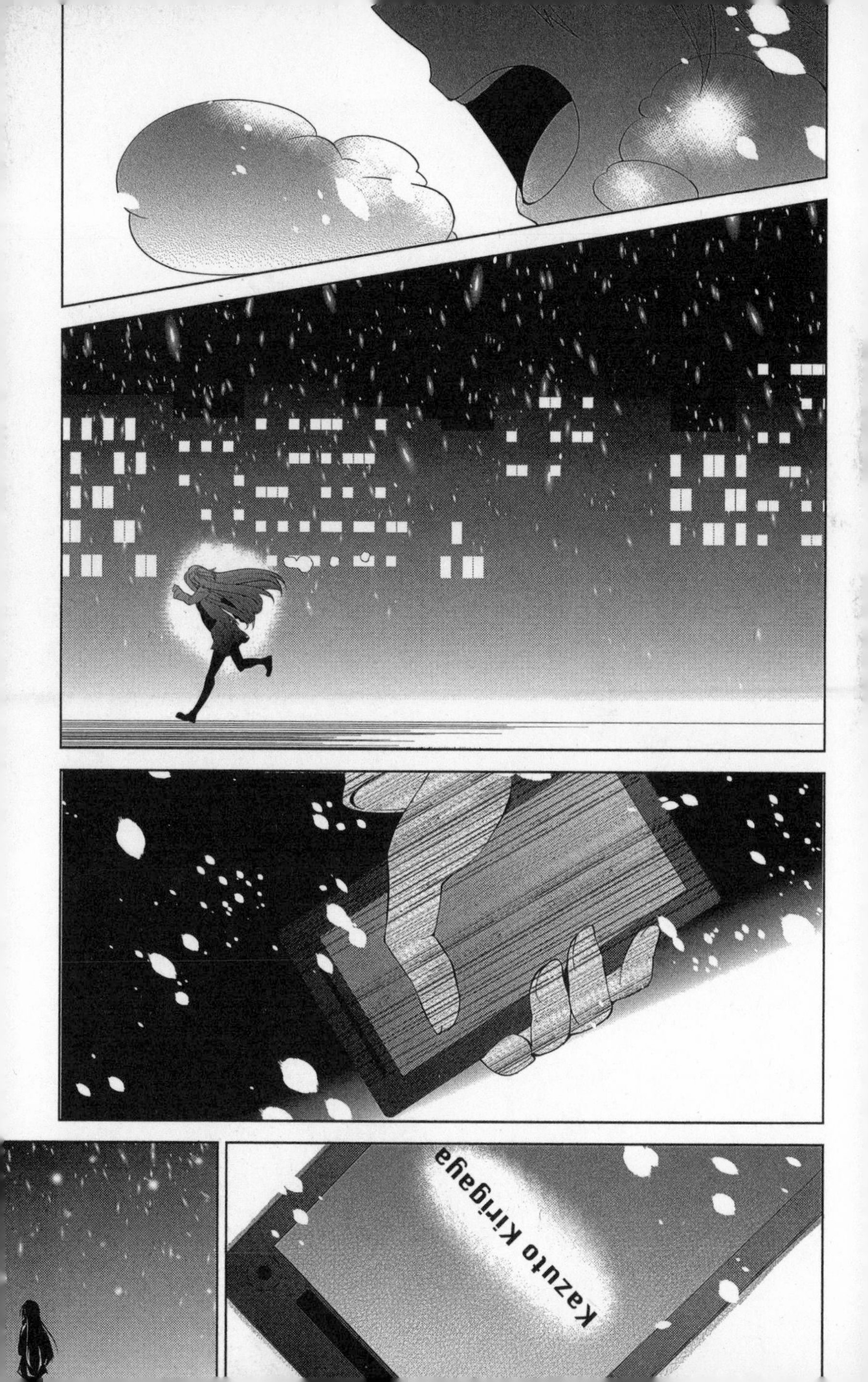
Kazuto Kirigaya

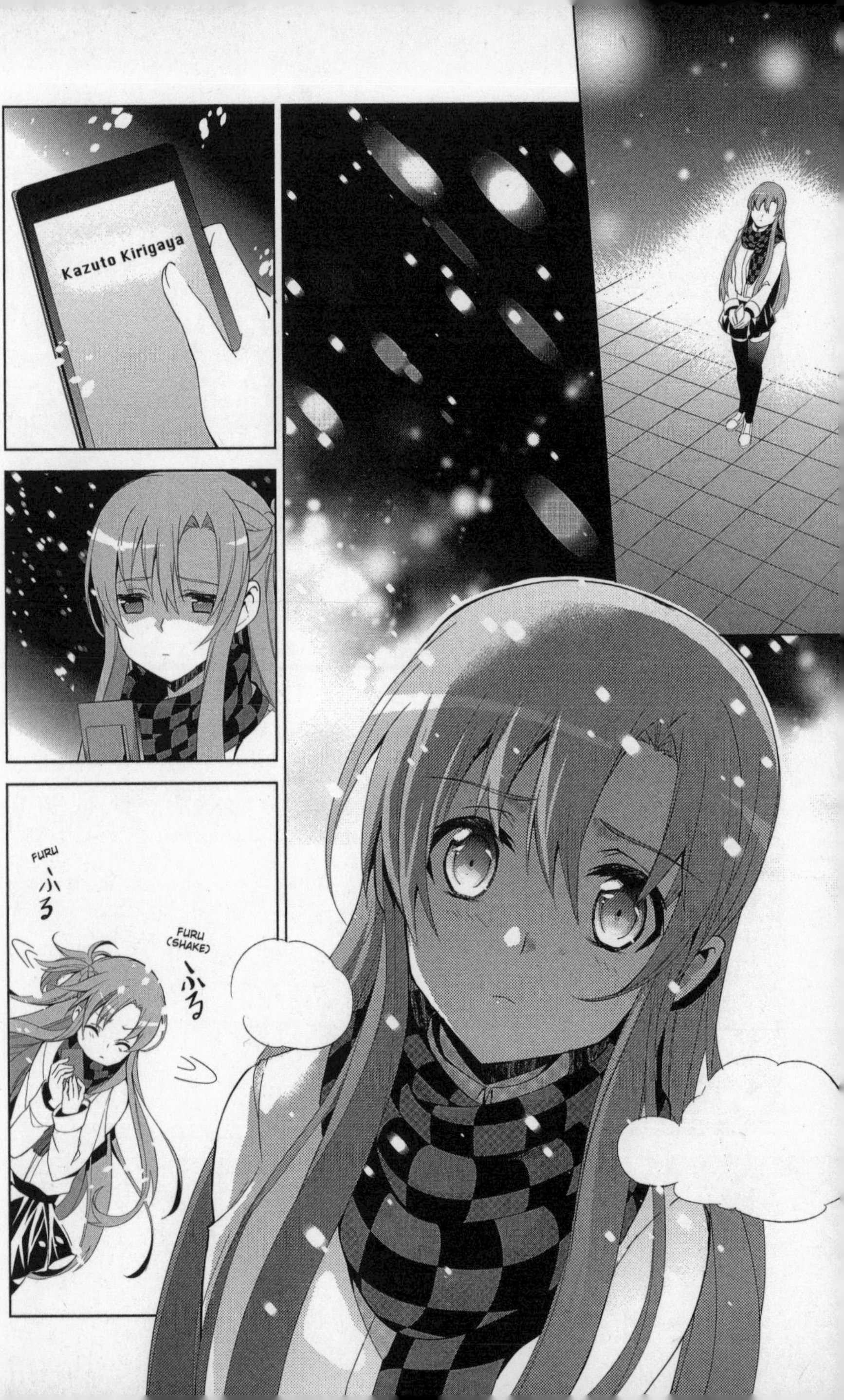
Kazuto Kirigaya
FURU
ふる
FURU (SHAKE)
ふる

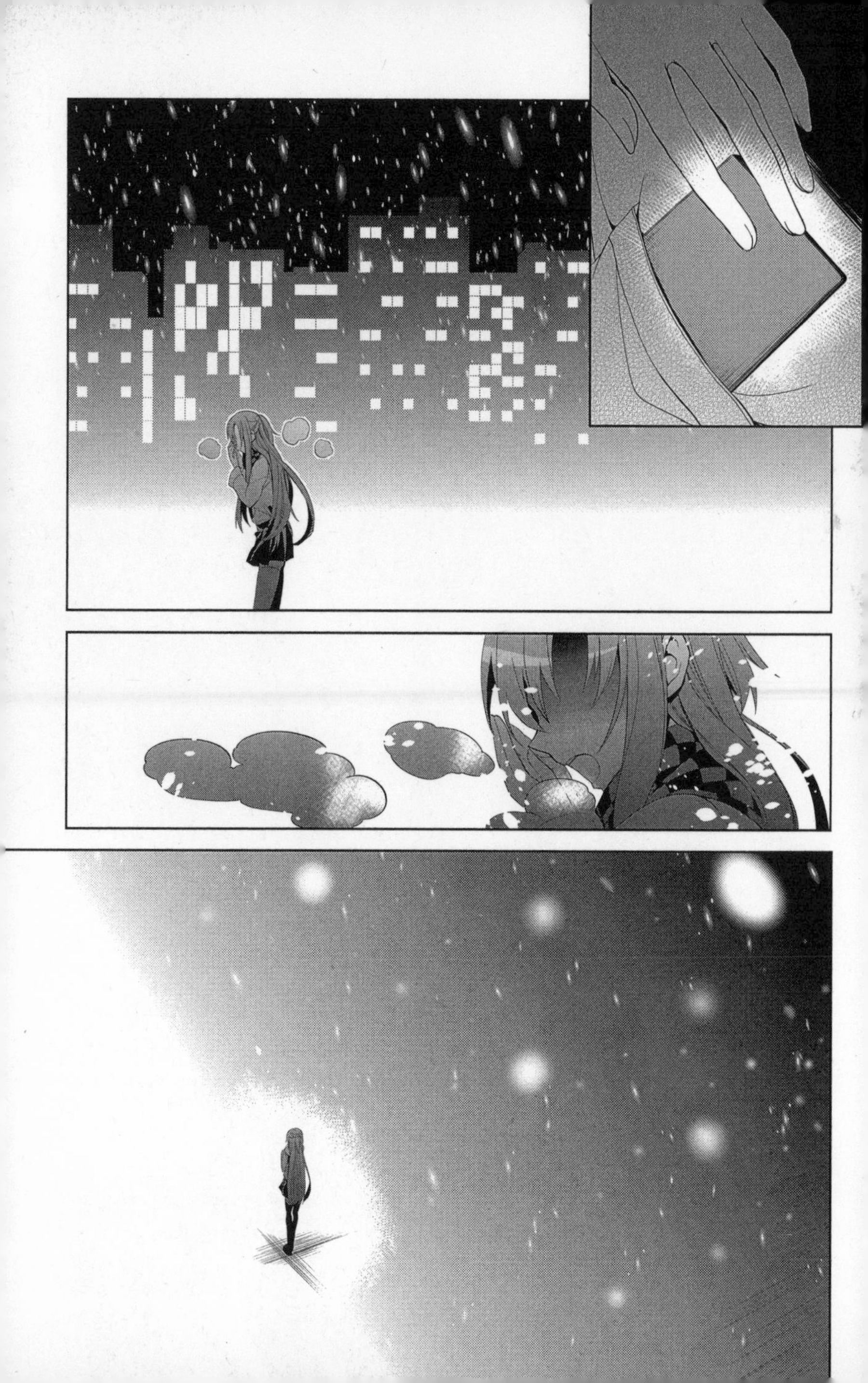

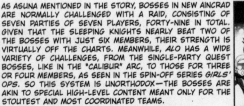

SWORD ART ONLINE mother's rosary **01**
BACKGROUND GUIDE

BOSSES AND RAID PARTIES IN NEW AINCRAD

AS ASUNA MENTIONED IN THE STORY, BOSSES IN NEW AINCRAD ARE NORMALLY CHALLENGED WITH A RAID, CONSISTING OF SEVEN PARTIES OF SEVEN PLAYERS, FORTY-NINE IN TOTAL. GIVEN THAT THE SLEEPING KNIGHTS NEARLY BEAT TWO OF THE BOSSES WITH JUST SIX MEMBERS, THEIR STRENGTH IS VIRTUALLY OFF THE CHARTS. MEANWHILE, *ALO* HAS A WIDE VARIETY OF CHALLENGES, FROM THE SINGLE-PARTY QUEST BOSSES, LIKE IN THE "CALIBUR" ARC, TO THOSE FOR THREE OR FOUR MEMBERS, AS SEEN IN THE SPIN-OFF SERIES *GIRLS' OPS*. SO THIS SYSTEM IS UNORTHODOX—THE BOSSES ARE AKIN TO SPECIAL HIGH-LEVEL CONTENT MEANT ONLY FOR THE STOUTEST AND MOST COORDINATED TEAMS.

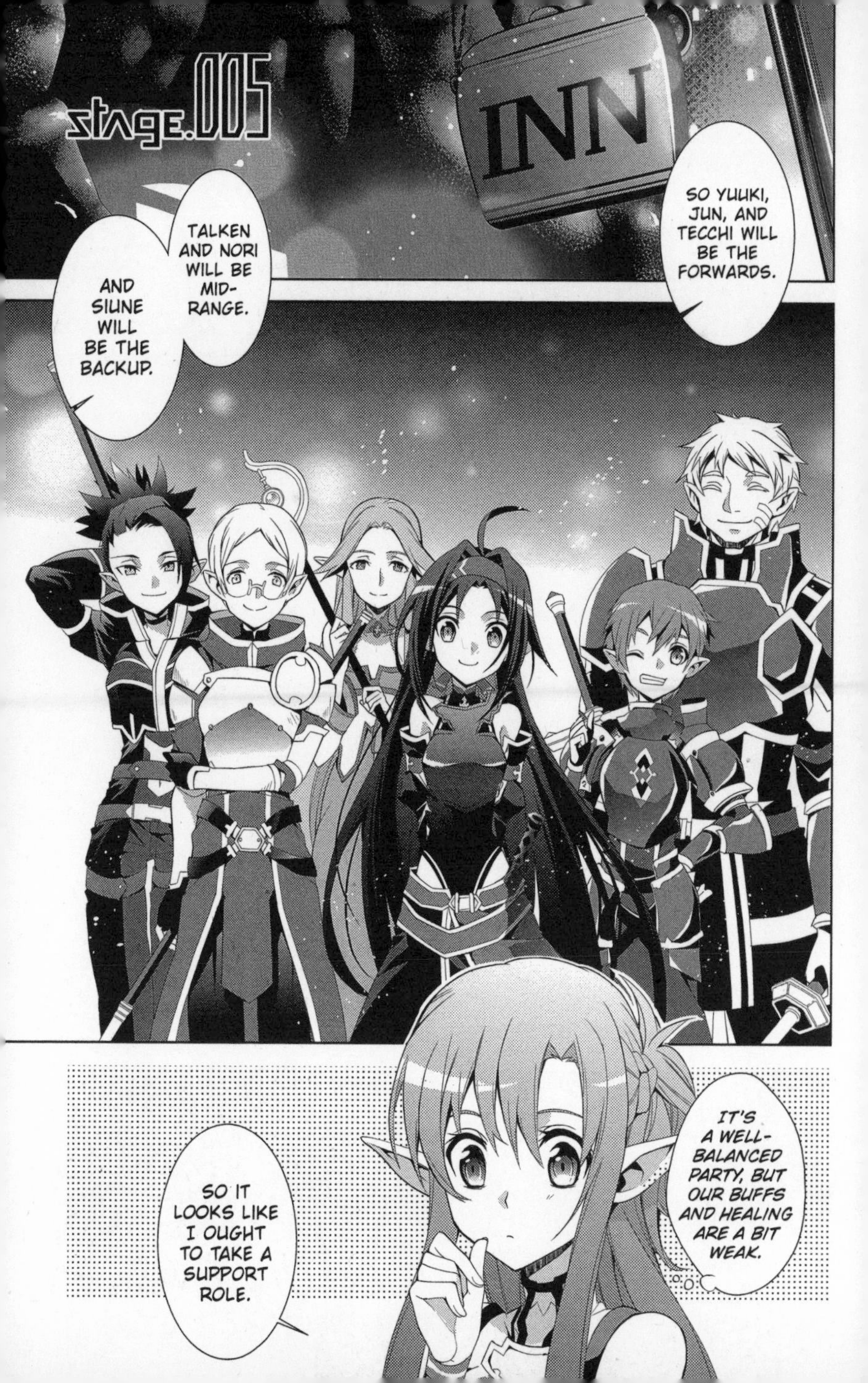
stage.005
INN
SO YUUKI, JUN, AND TECCHI WILL BE THE FORWARDS.
TALKEN AND NORI WILL BE MID-RANGE.
AND SIUNE WILL BE THE BACKUP.
IT'S A WELL-BALANCED PARTY, BUT OUR BUFFS AND HEALING ARE A BIT WEAK.
SO IT LOOKS LIKE I OUGHT TO TAKE A SUPPORT ROLE.

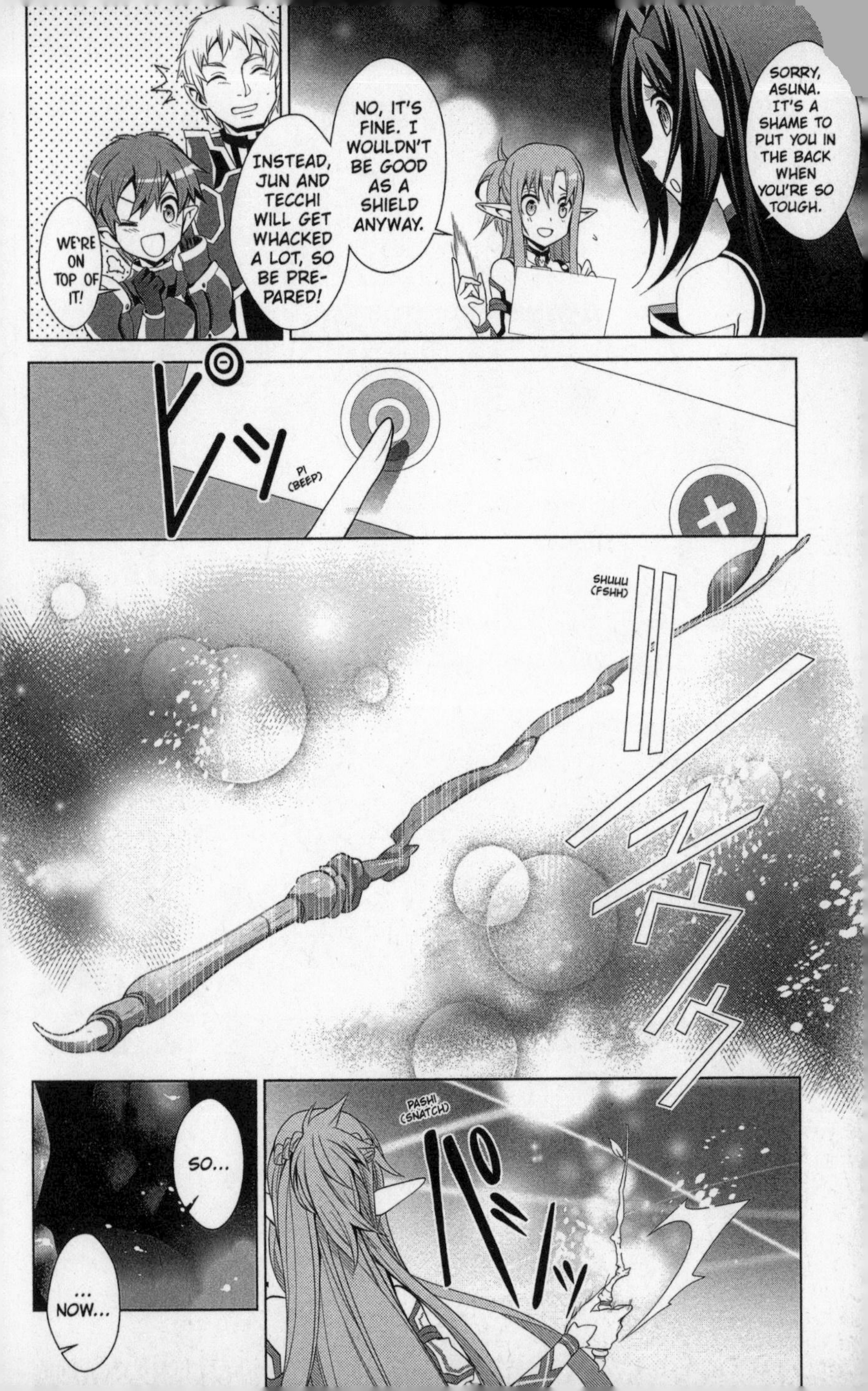
SORRY, ASUNA. IT'S A SHAME TO PUT YOU IN THE BACK WHEN YOU'RE SO TOUGH.
NO, IT'S FINE. I WOULDN'T BE GOOD AS A SHIELD ANYWAY.
INSTEAD, JUN AND TECCHI WILL GET WHACKED A LOT, SO BE PRE-PARED!
WE'RE ON TOP OF IT!
PI (BEEP)
SHUUU (FSHH)
PASHI (SNATCH)
SO...
...NOW...

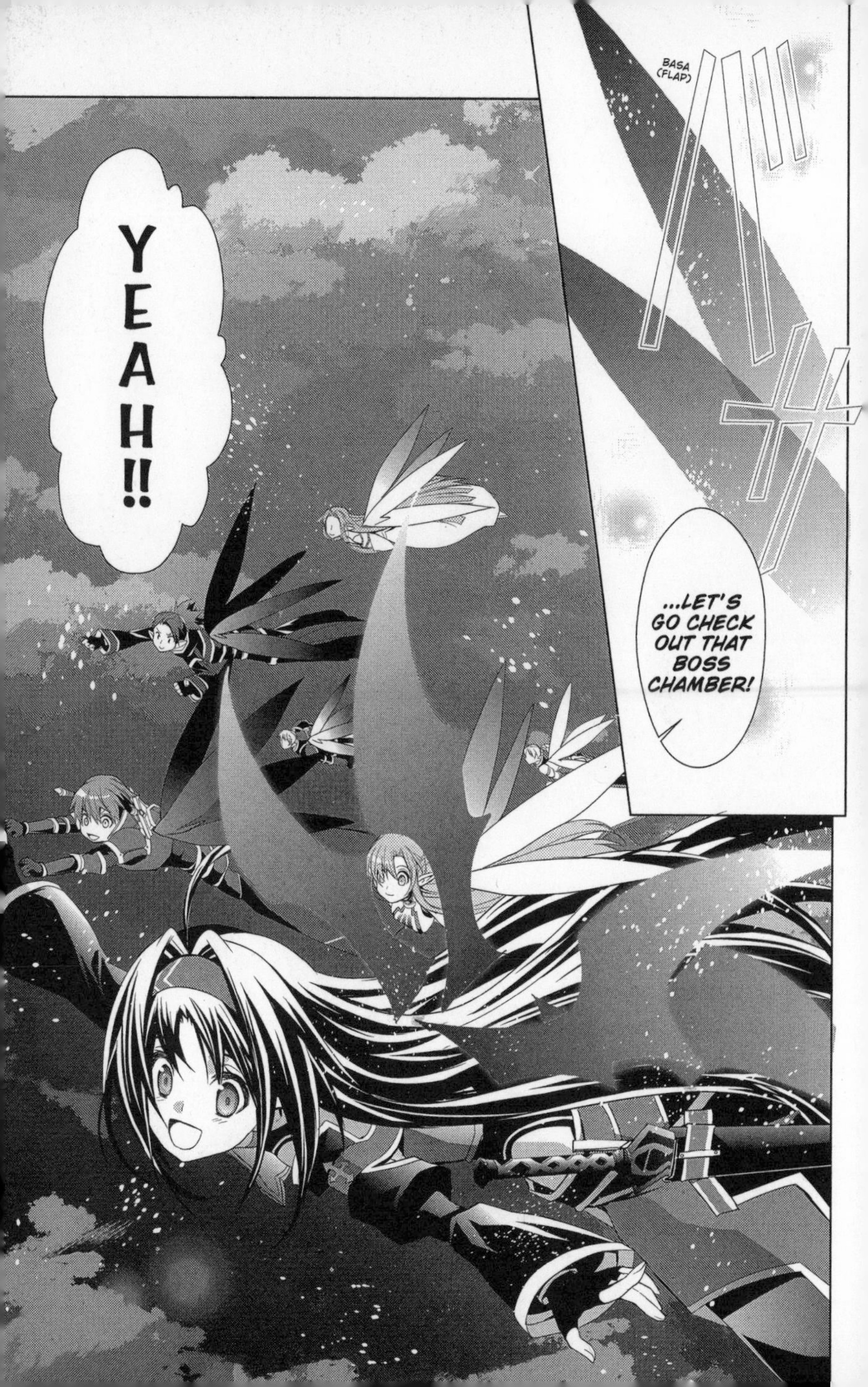
BASA (FLAP)
...LET'S GO CHECK OUT THAT BOSS CHAMBER!
YEAH!!

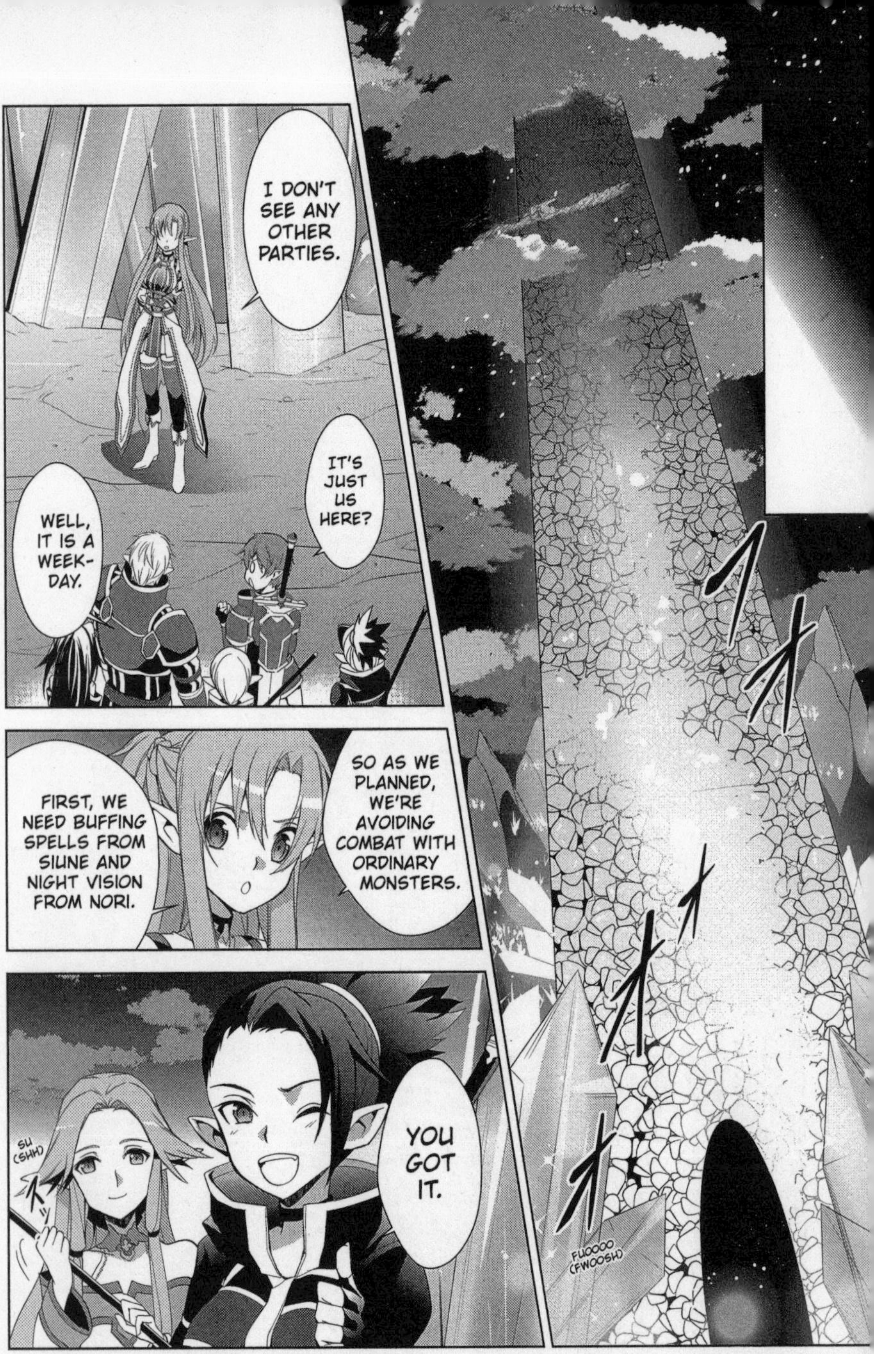
FUOOOO (FWOOSH)
I DON'T SEE ANY OTHER PARTIES.
IT'S JUST US HERE?
WELL, IT IS A WEEK-DAY.
SO AS WE PLANNED, WE'RE AVOIDING COMBAT WITH ORDINARY MONSTERS.
FIRST, WE NEED BUFFING SPELLS FROM SIUNE AND NIGHT VISION FROM NORI.
YOU GOT IT.
SU (SHH)

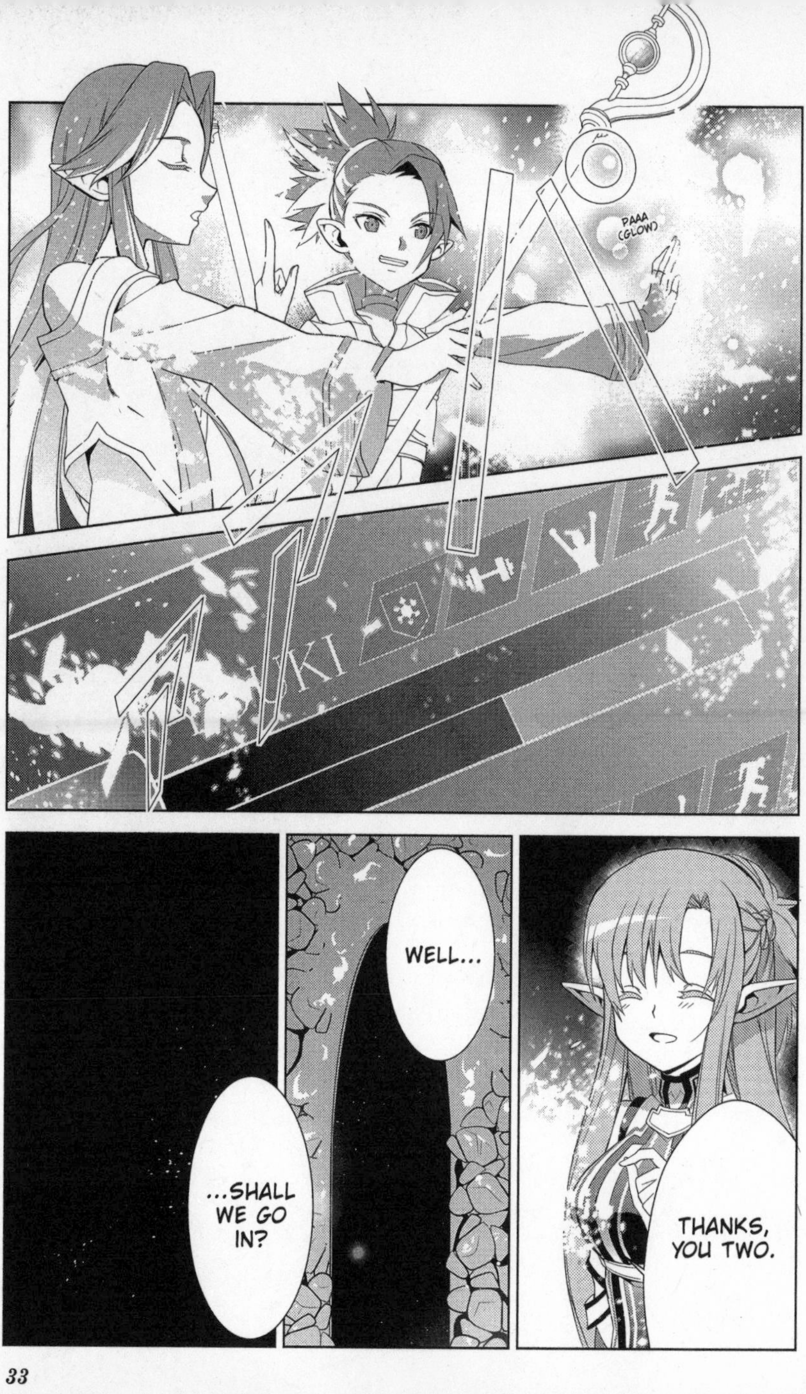
PAAA (GLOW)
THANKS, YOU TWO.
WELL...
...SHALL WE GO IN?

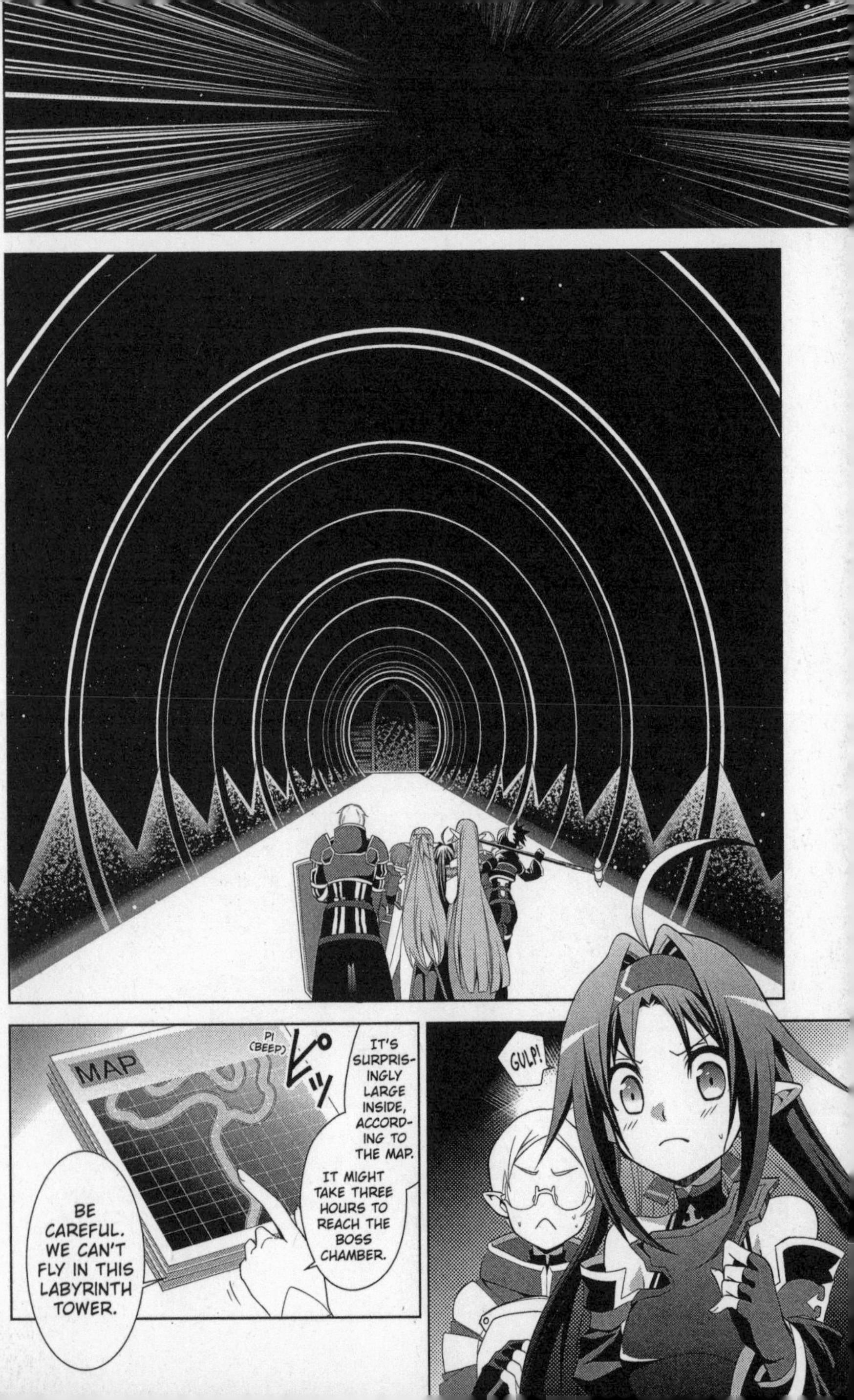
GULP!
PI (BEEP)
MAP
IT'S SURPRISINGLY LARGE INSIDE, ACCORDING TO THE MAP.
IT MIGHT TAKE THREE HOURS TO REACH THE BOSS CHAMBER.
BE CAREFUL. WE CAN'T FLY IN THIS LABYRINTH TOWER.

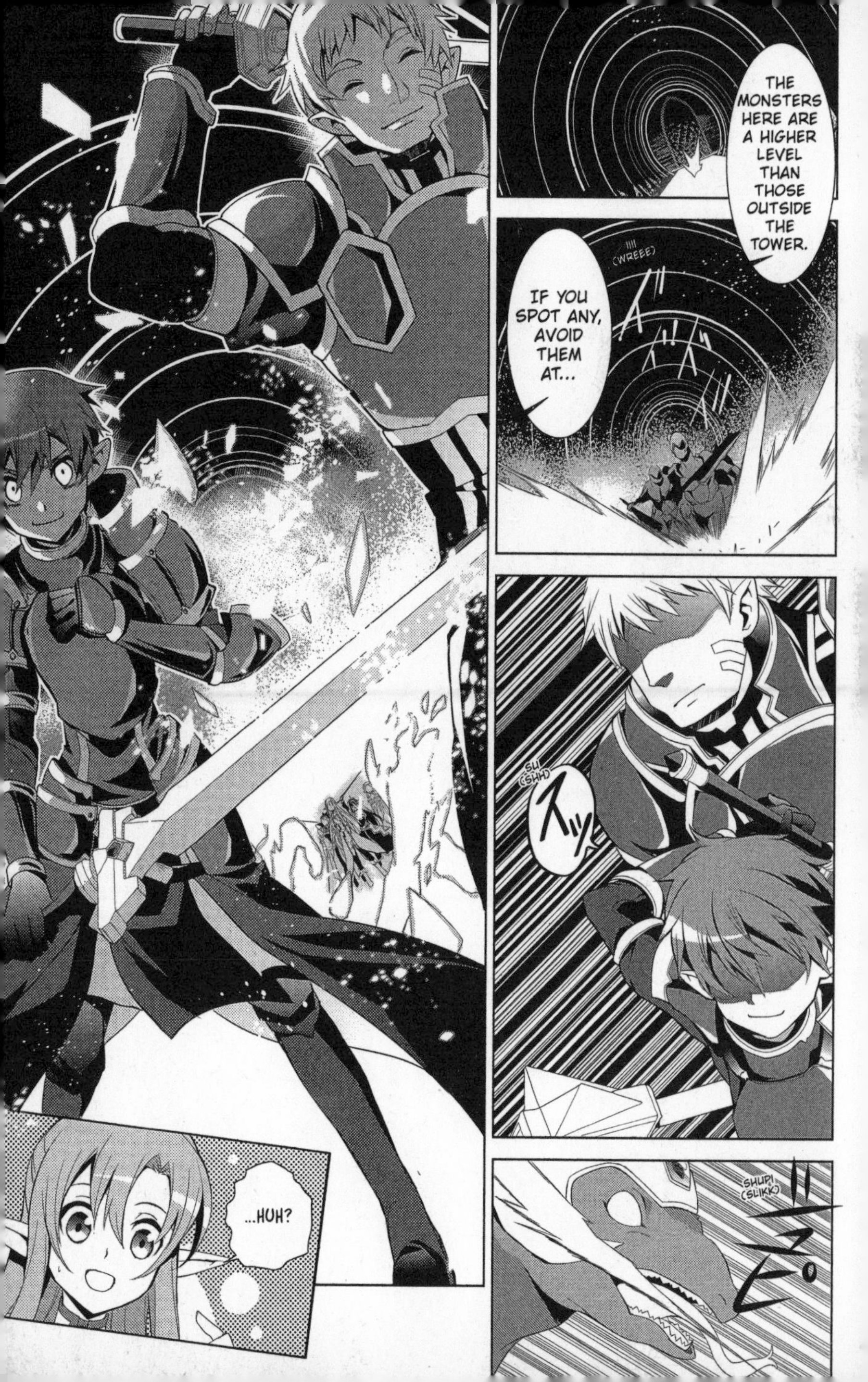
THE MONSTERS HERE ARE A HIGHER LEVEL THAN THOSE OUTSIDE THE TOWER.
(WREEE)
IF YOU SPOT ANY, AVOID THEM AT...
SU (SHH)
SHUPI (SLIKK)
...HUH?

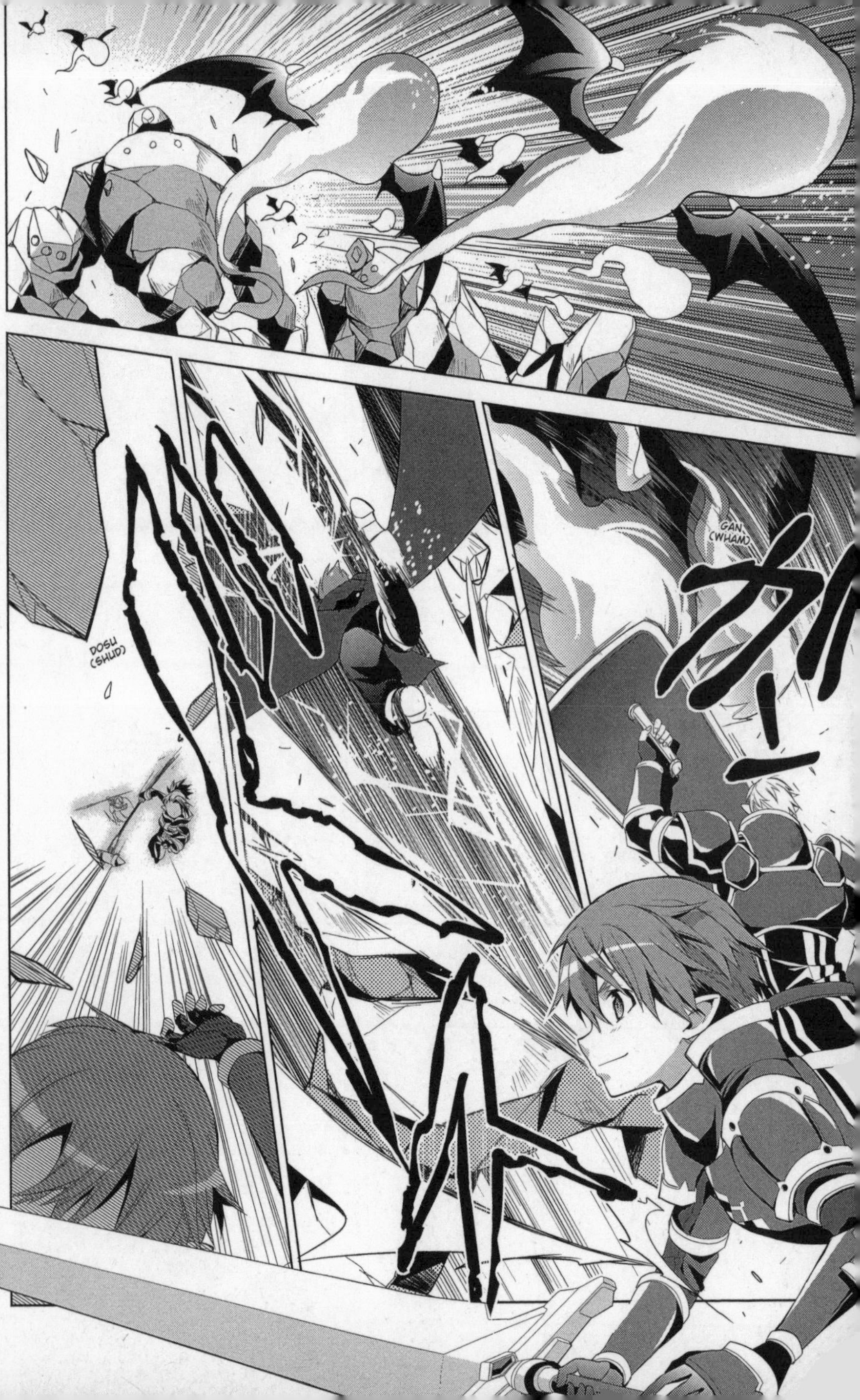
GAN (WHAM)
DOSU (SHUD)

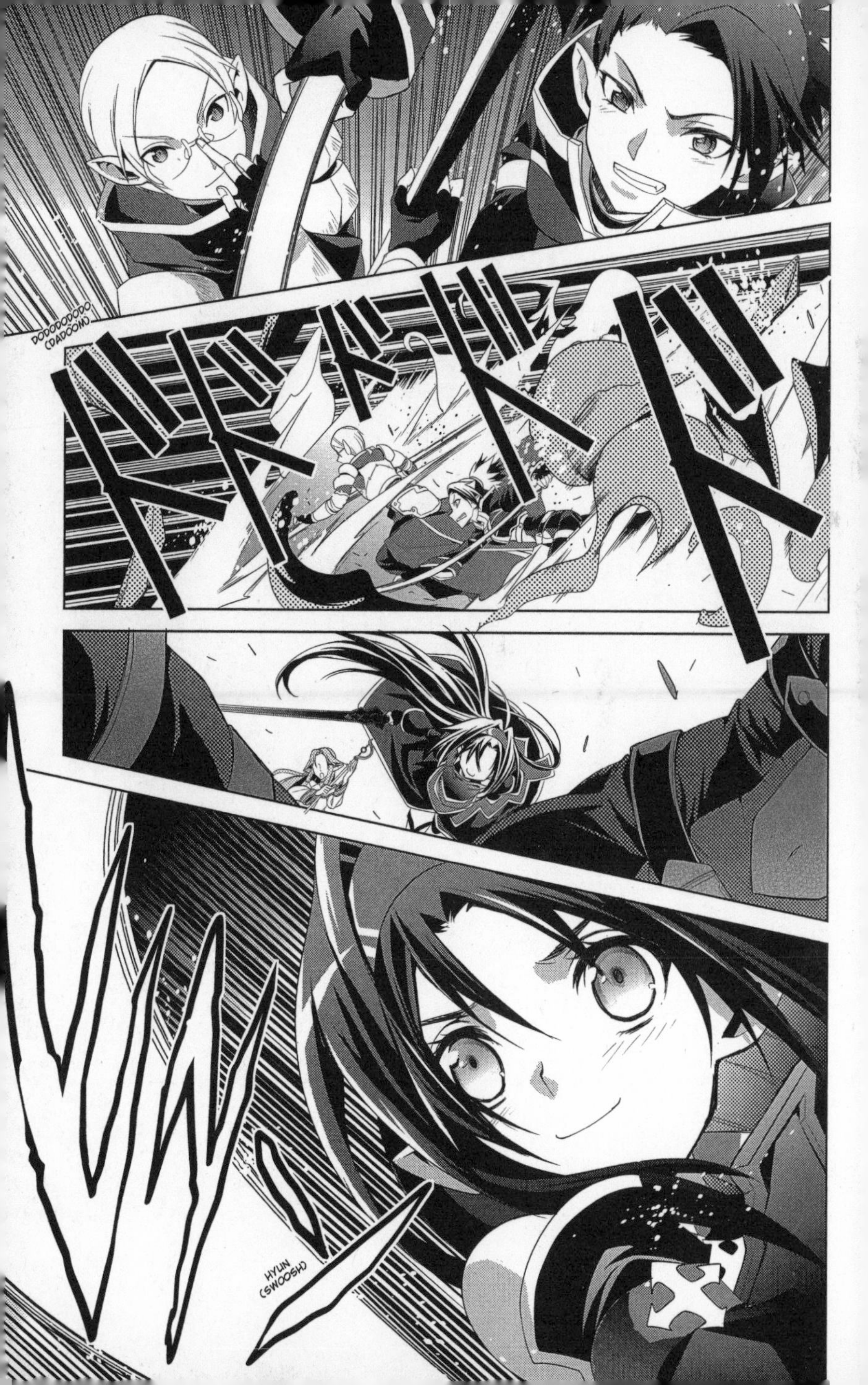
DODODODODO (DADOOM)
HYUN (SWOOSH)

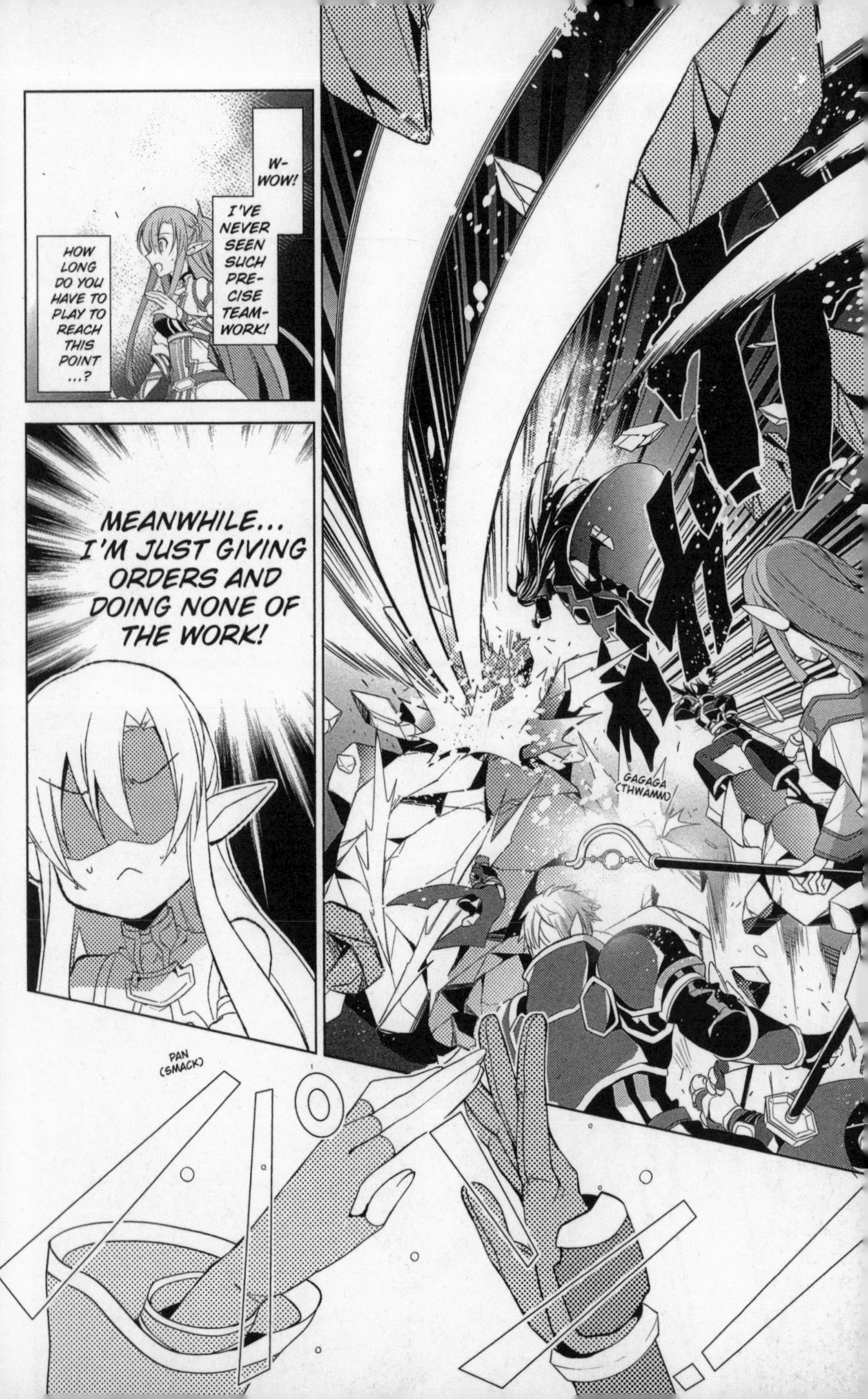
GAGAGA (THWAMM)
W-WOW!
I'VE NEVER SEEN SUCH PRECISE TEAM-WORK!
HOW LONG DO YOU HAVE TO PLAY TO REACH THIS POINT ...?
MEANWHILE... I'M JUST GIVING ORDERS AND DOING NONE OF THE WORK!
PAN (SMACK)

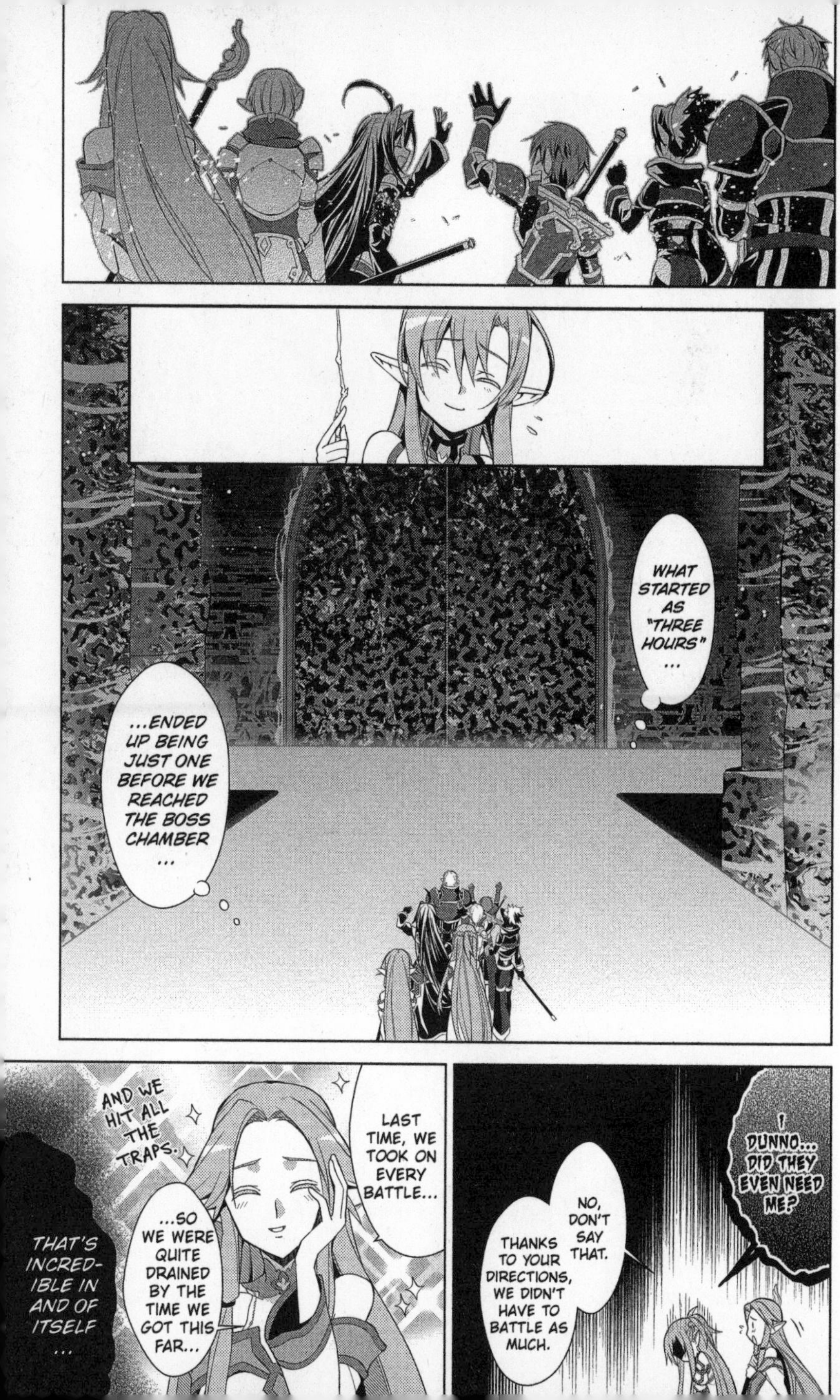
WHAT STARTED AS "THREE HOURS"...
...ENDED UP BEING JUST ONE BEFORE WE REACHED THE BOSS CHAMBER...
I DUNNO... DID THEY EVEN NEED ME?
NO, DON'T SAY THAT.
THANKS TO YOUR DIRECTIONS, WE DIDN'T HAVE TO BATTLE AS MUCH.
LAST TIME, WE TOOK ON EVERY BATTLE...
AND WE HIT ALL THE TRAPS.
...SO WE WERE QUITE DRAINED BY THE TIME WE GOT THIS FAR...
THAT'S INCREDIBLE IN AND OF ITSELF...

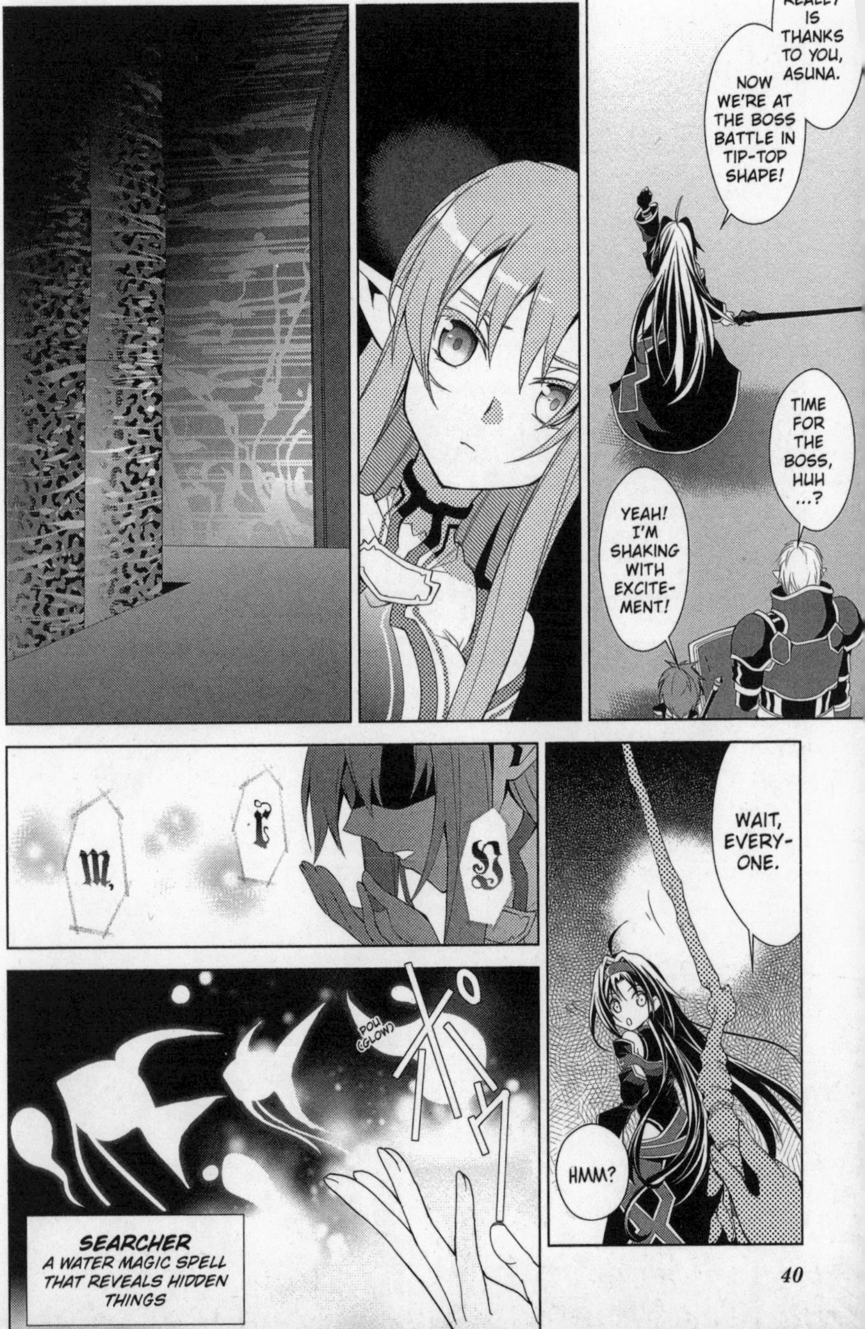
IT REALLY IS THANKS TO YOU, ASUNA.
NOW WE'RE AT THE BOSS BATTLE IN TIP-TOP SHAPE!
TIME FOR THE BOSS, HUH ...?
YEAH! I'M SHAKING WITH EXCITE-MENT!
WAIT, EVERY-ONE.
HMM?
POU (GLOW)
SEARCHER
A WATER MAGIC SPELL THAT REVEALS HIDDEN THINGS

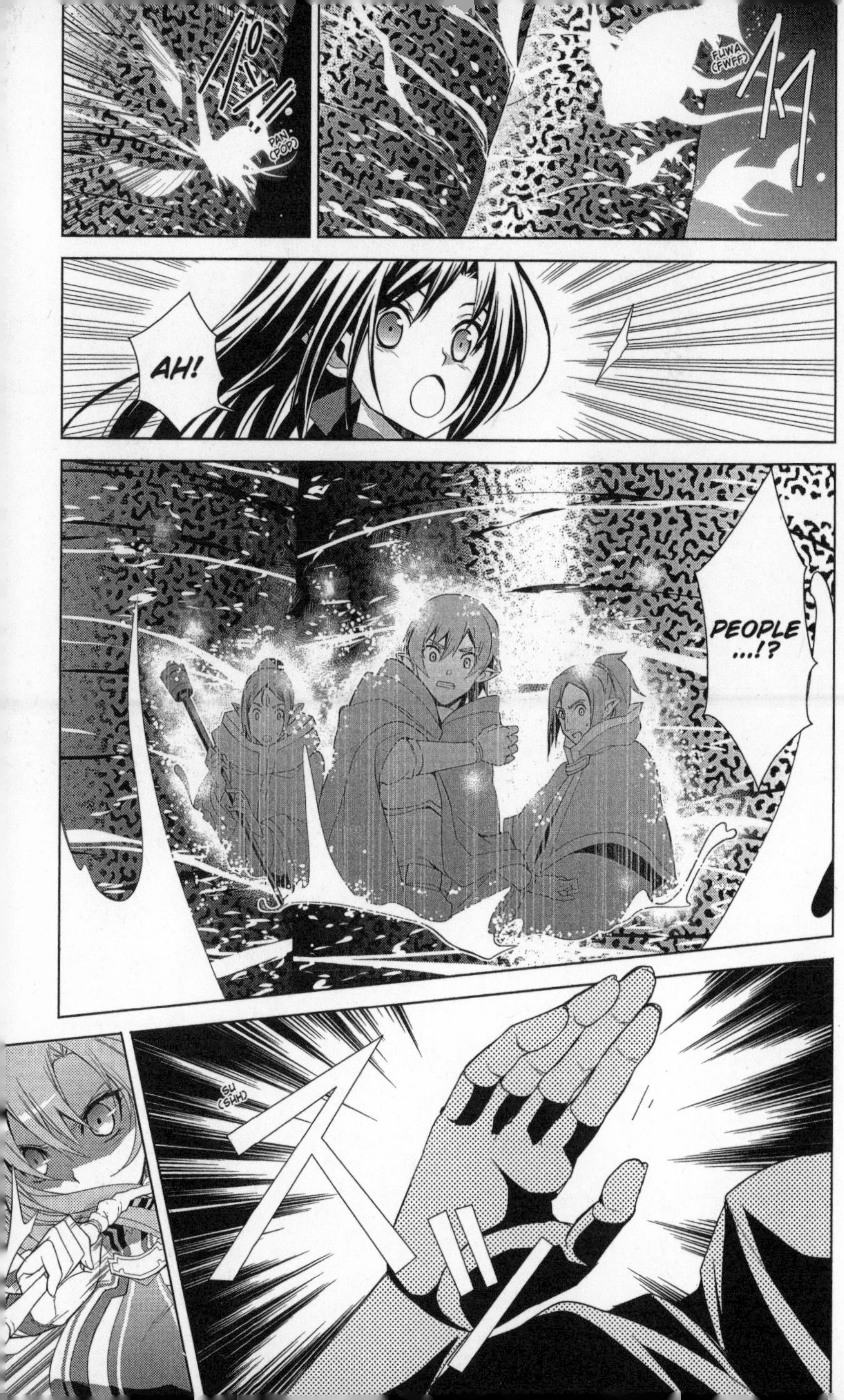
FUWA (FWFF)
PAN (POP)
AH!
PEOPLE ...!?
SU (SHH)

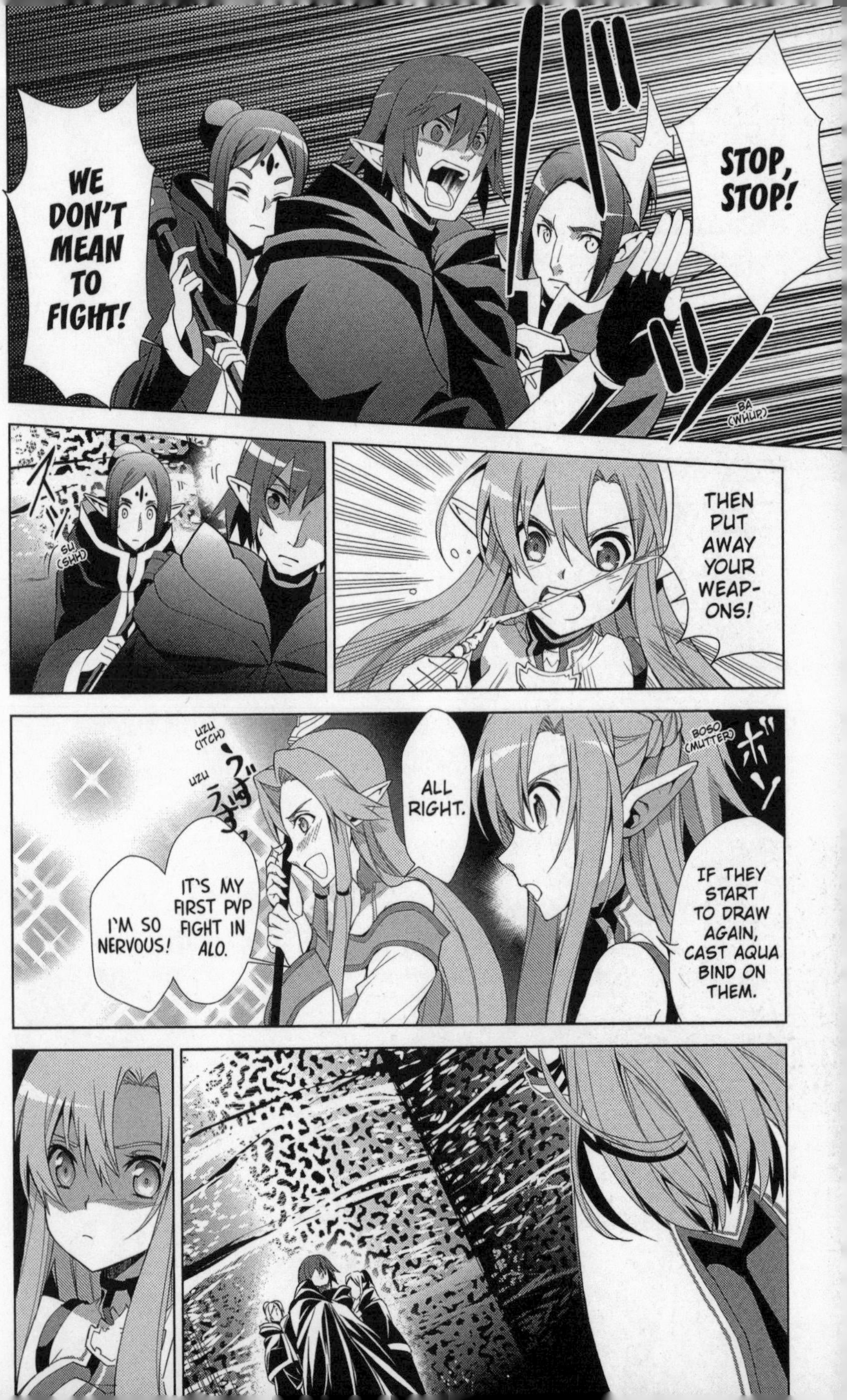
STOP, STOP!
BA (WHUP)
WE DON'T MEAN TO FIGHT!
THEN PUT AWAY YOUR WEAP-ONS!
SU (SHH)
BOSO (MUTTER)
IF THEY START TO DRAW AGAIN, CAST AQUA BIND ON THEM.
ALL RIGHT.
UZU (ITCH)
UZU
IT'S MY FIRST PVP FIGHT IN ALO.
I'M SO NERVOUS!

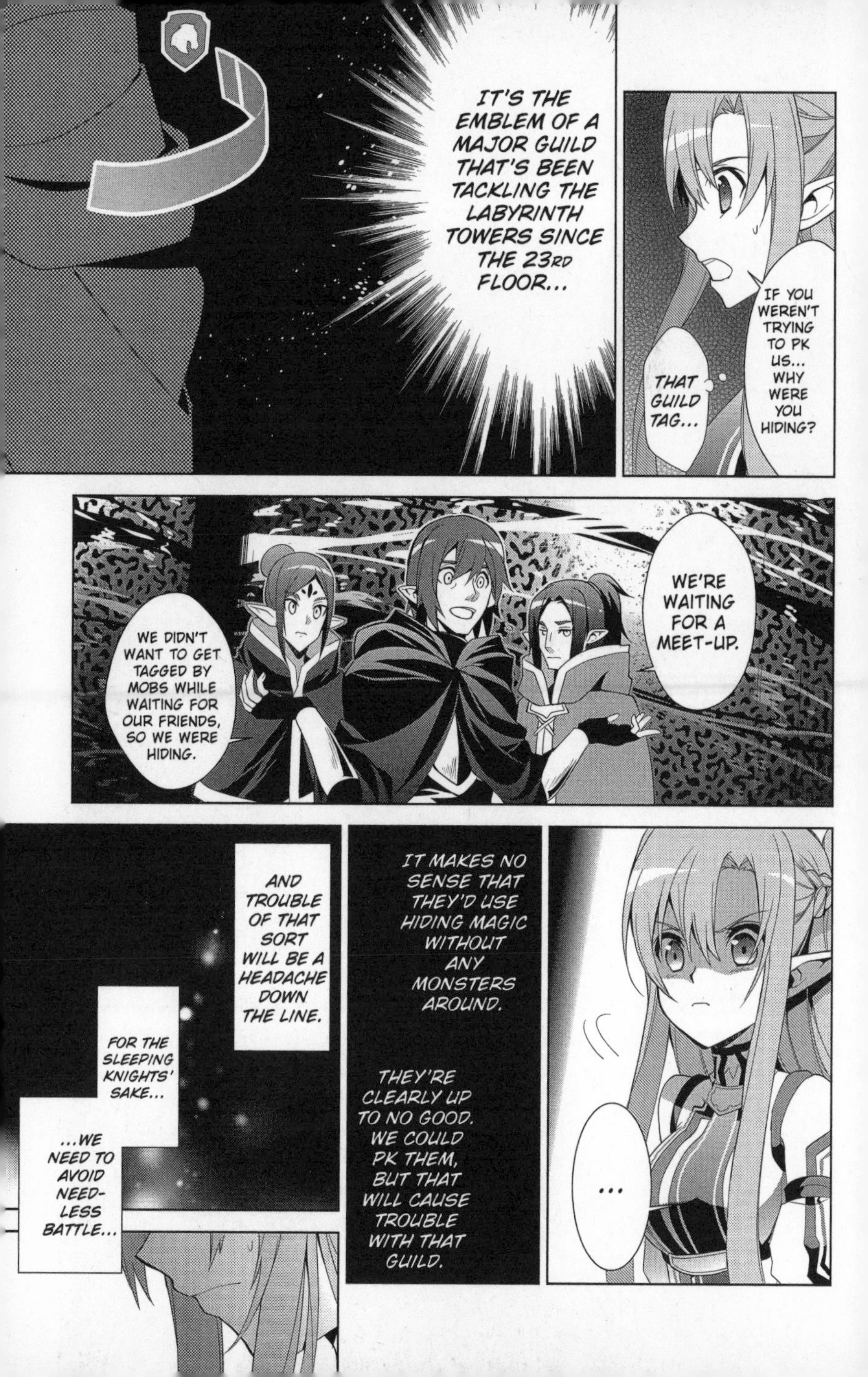
IF YOU WEREN'T TRYING TO PK US... WHY WERE YOU HIDING?
THAT GUILD TAG...
IT'S THE EMBLEM OF A MAJOR GUILD THAT'S BEEN TACKLING THE LABYRINTH TOWERS SINCE THE 23RD FLOOR...
WE'RE WAITING FOR A MEET-UP.
WE DIDN'T WANT TO GET TAGGED BY MOBS WHILE WAITING FOR OUR FRIENDS, SO WE WERE HIDING.
...
IT MAKES NO SENSE THAT THEY'D USE HIDING MAGIC WITHOUT ANY MONSTERS AROUND.
THEY'RE CLEARLY UP TO NO GOOD. WE COULD PK THEM, BUT THAT WILL CAUSE TROUBLE WITH THAT GUILD.
AND TROUBLE OF THAT SORT WILL BE A HEADACHE DOWN THE LINE.
FOR THE SLEEPING KNIGHTS' SAKE...
...WE NEED TO AVOID NEED-LESS BATTLE...

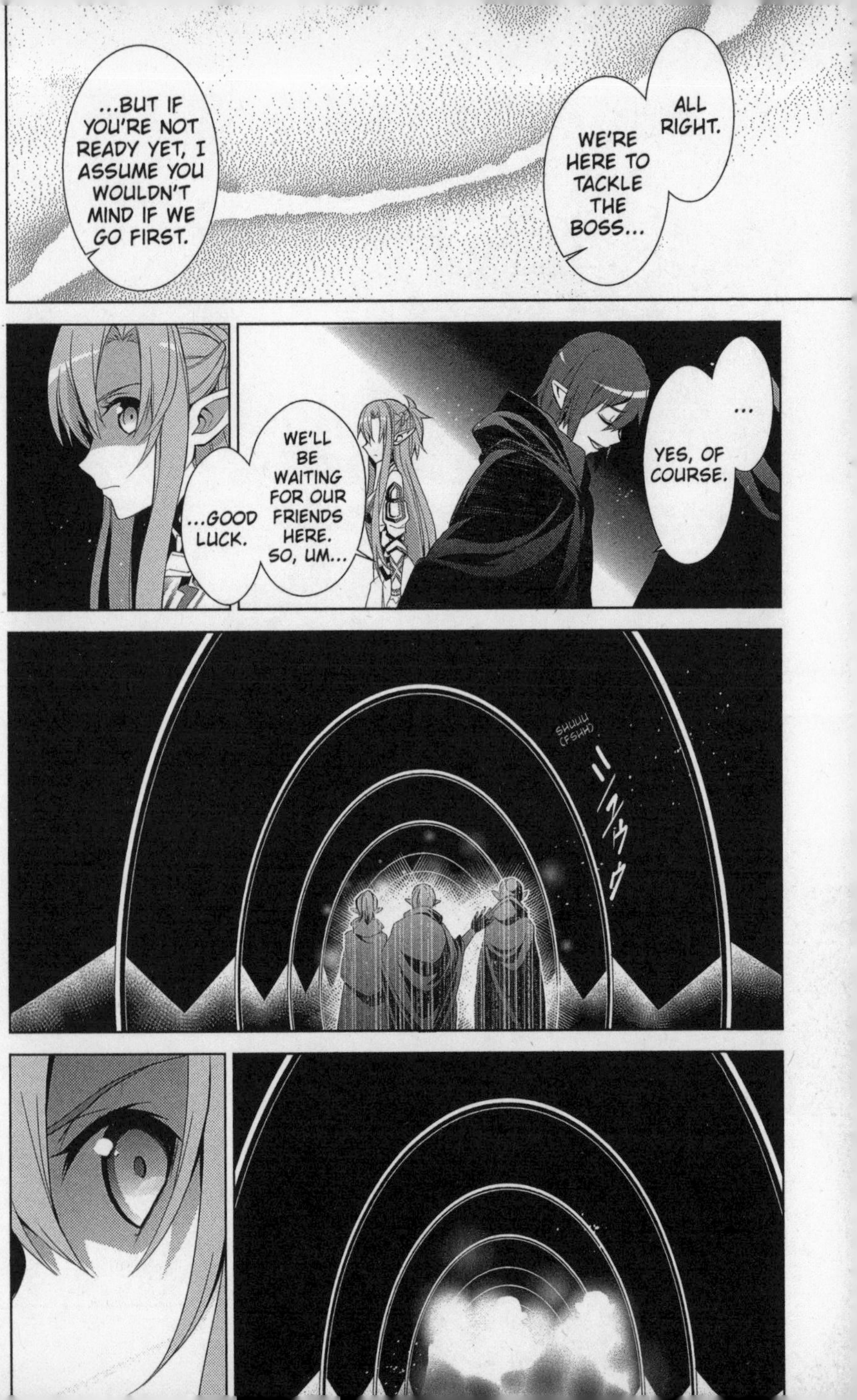
ALL RIGHT.
WE'RE HERE TO TACKLE THE BOSS...
...BUT IF YOU'RE NOT READY YET, I ASSUME YOU WOULDN'T MIND IF WE GO FIRST.
...
YES, OF COURSE.
WE'LL BE WAITING FOR OUR FRIENDS HERE. SO, UM...
...GOOD LUCK.
SHUUU (FSHH)

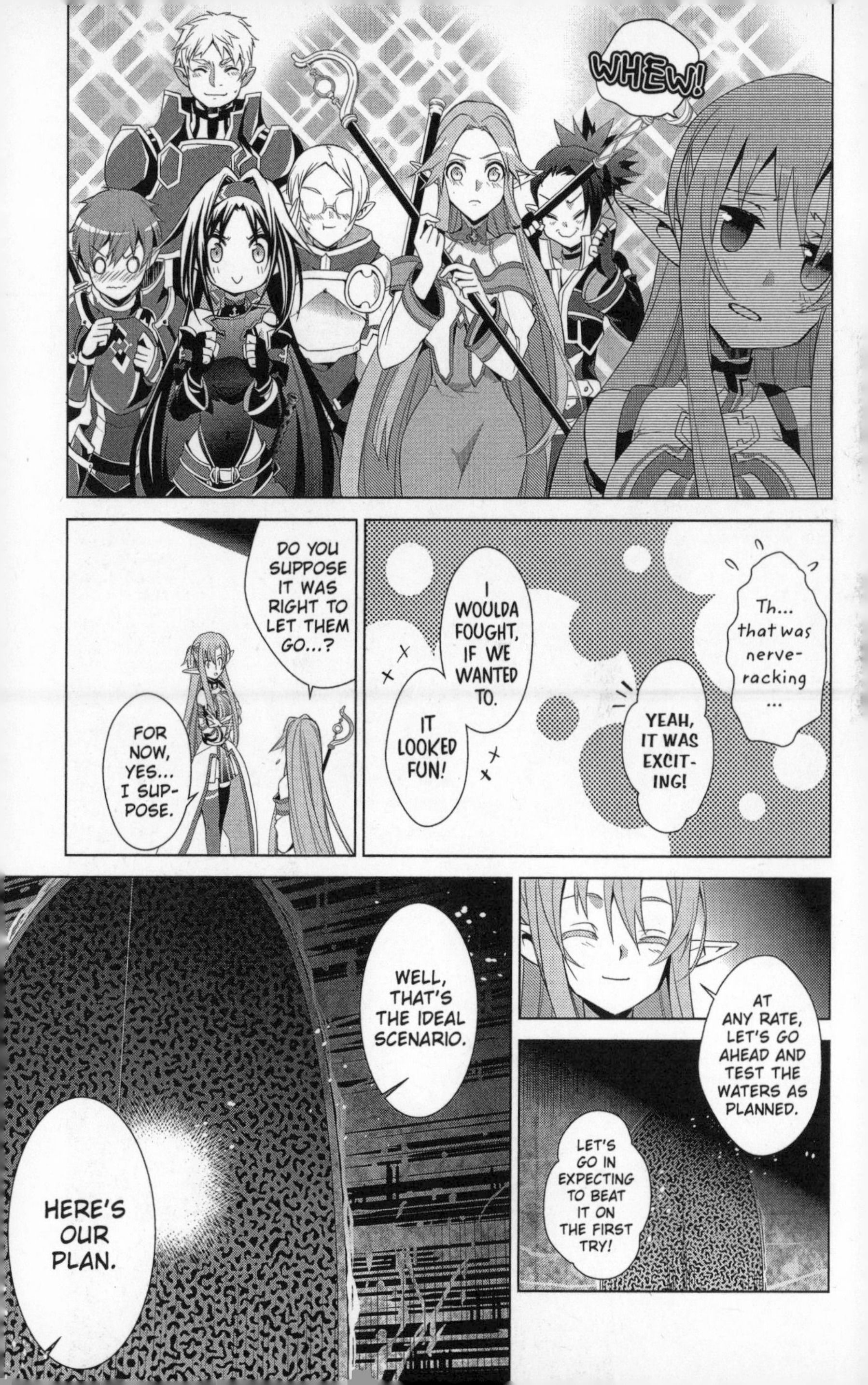
WHEW!
Th... that was nerve-racking...
YEAH, IT WAS EXCIT-ING!
I WOULDA FOUGHT, IF WE WANTED TO.
IT LOOKED FUN!
DO YOU SUPPOSE IT WAS RIGHT TO LET THEM GO...?
FOR NOW, YES... I SUP-POSE.
AT ANY RATE, LET'S GO AHEAD AND TEST THE WATERS AS PLANNED.
LET'S GO IN EXPECTING TO BEAT IT ON THE FIRST TRY!
WELL, THAT'S THE IDEAL SCENARIO.
HERE'S OUR PLAN.

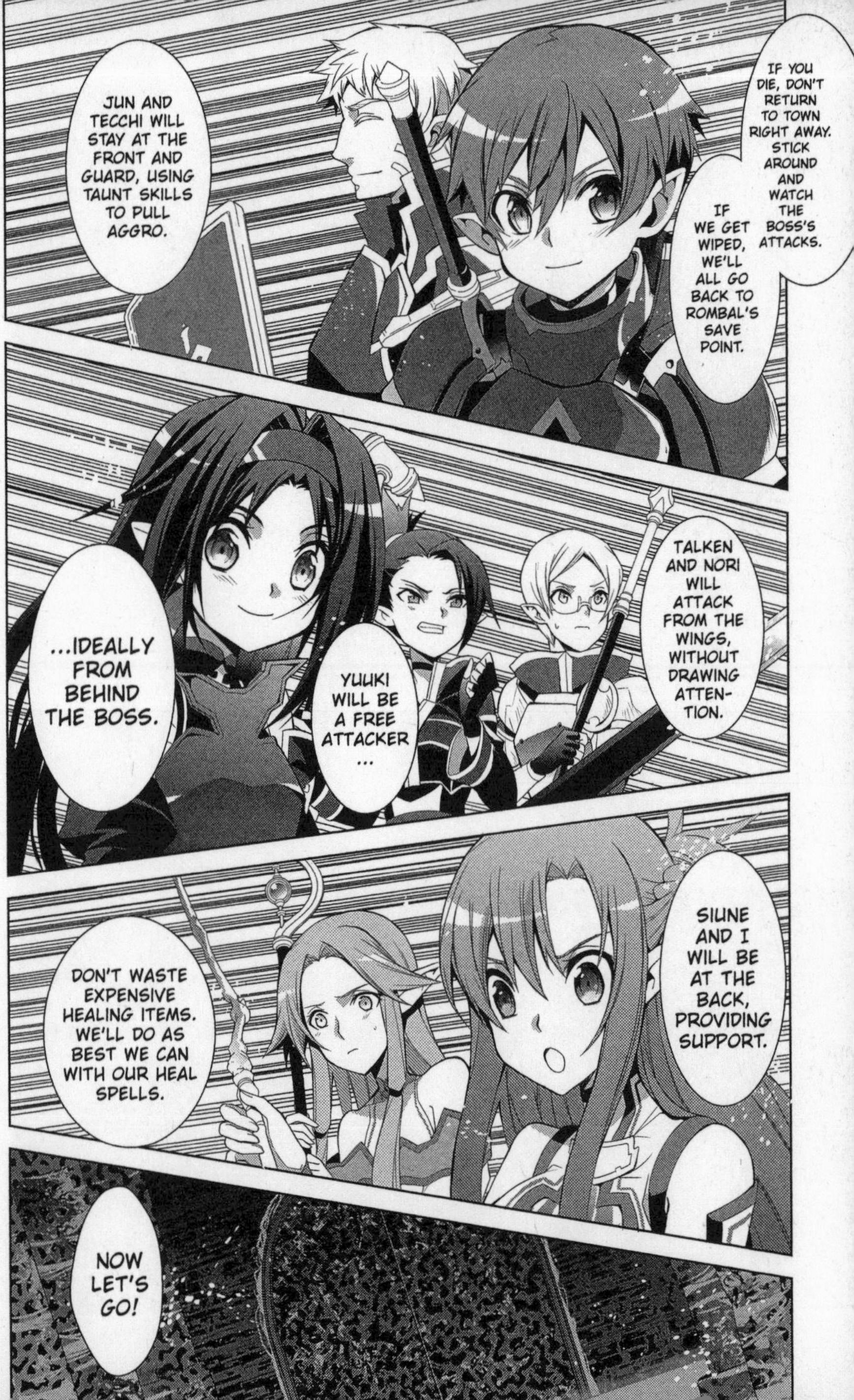
IF YOU DIE, DON'T RETURN TO TOWN RIGHT AWAY. STICK AROUND AND WATCH THE BOSS'S ATTACKS.
IF WE GET WIPED, WE'LL ALL GO BACK TO ROMBAL'S SAVE POINT.
JUN AND TECCHI WILL STAY AT THE FRONT AND GUARD, USING TAUNT SKILLS TO PULL AGGRO.
TALKEN AND NORI WILL ATTACK FROM THE WINGS, WITHOUT DRAWING ATTEN-TION.
YUUKI WILL BE A FREE ATTACKER ...
...IDEALLY FROM BEHIND THE BOSS.
SIUNE AND I WILL BE AT THE BACK, PROVIDING SUPPORT.
DON'T WASTE EXPENSIVE HEALING ITEMS. WE'LL DO AS BEST WE CAN WITH OUR HEAL SPELLS.
NOW LET'S GO!

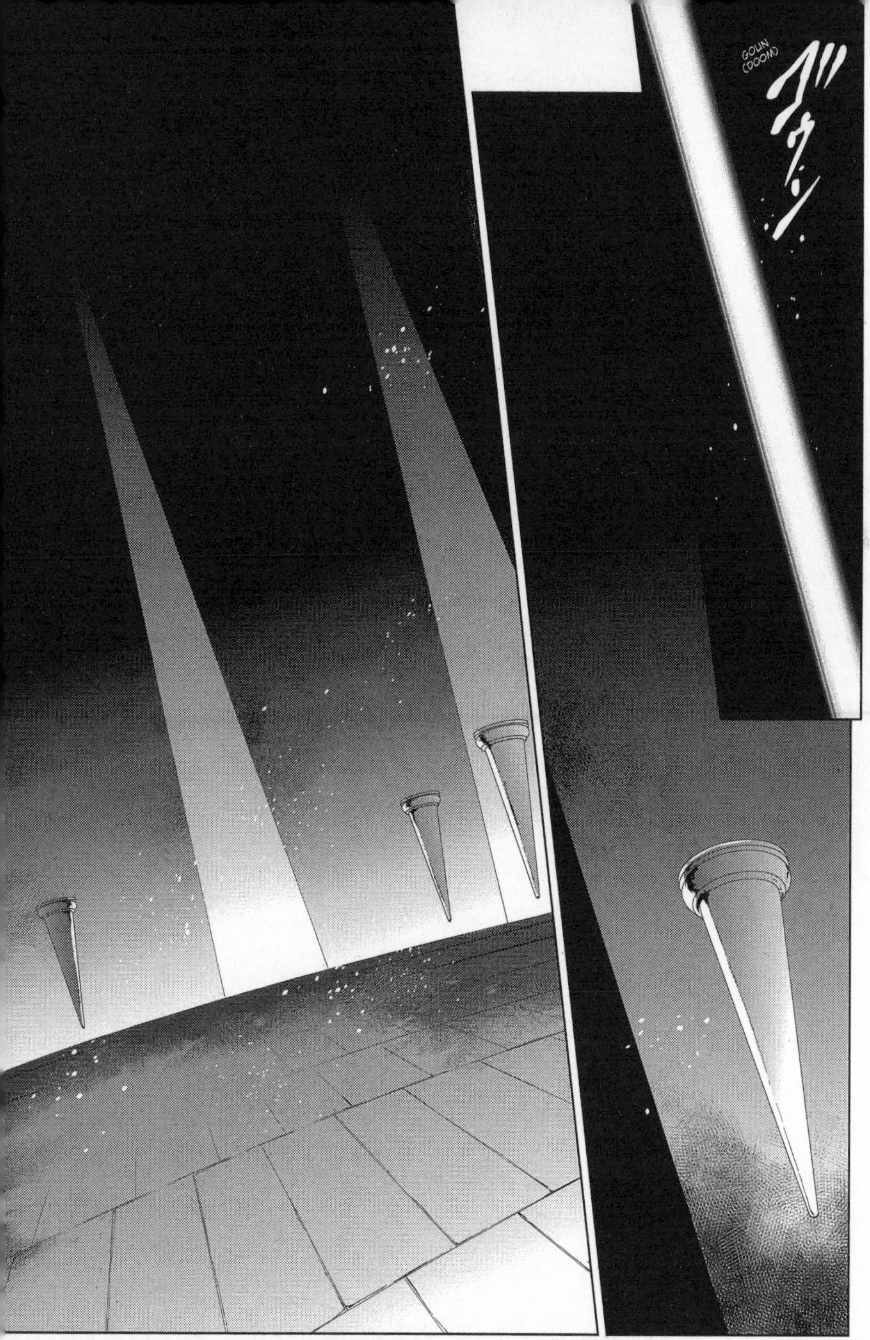
GOUN (DOOM)
ゴウン

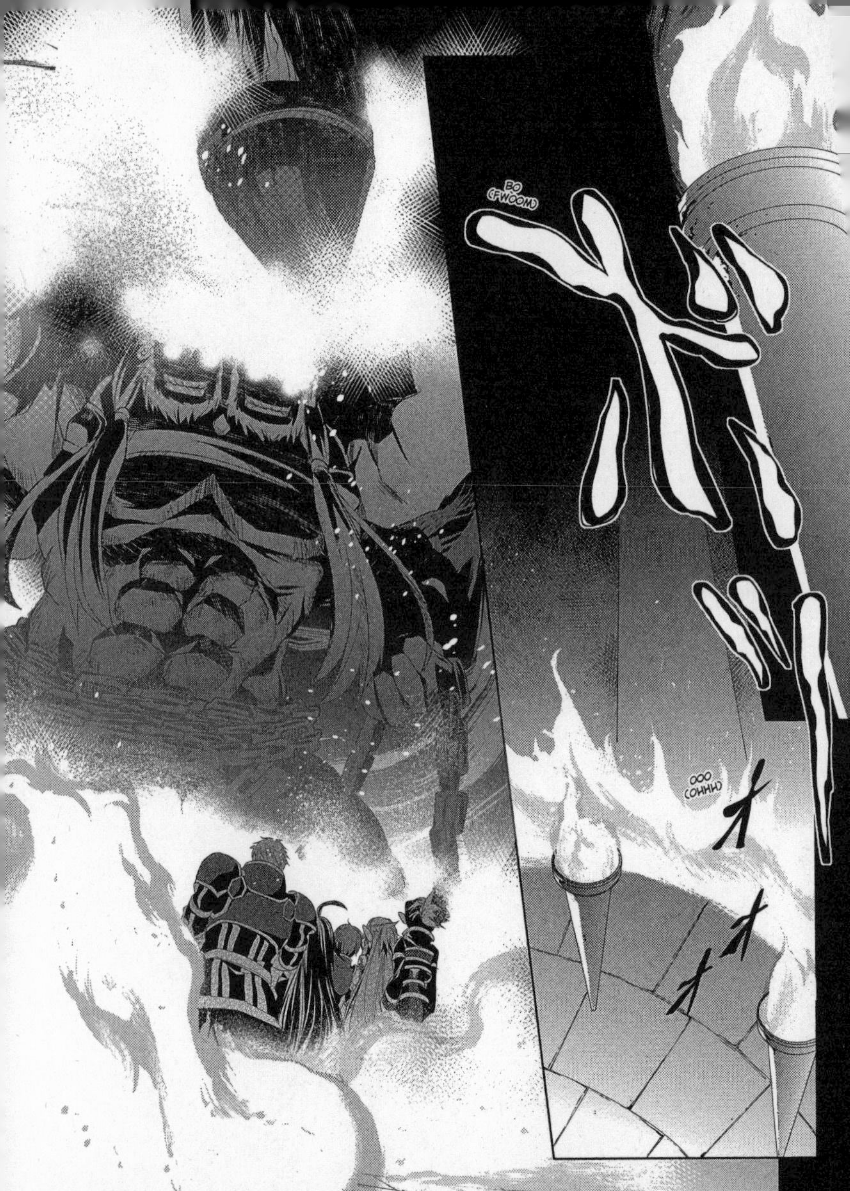
BO (FWOOM)
OOO (OHHH)

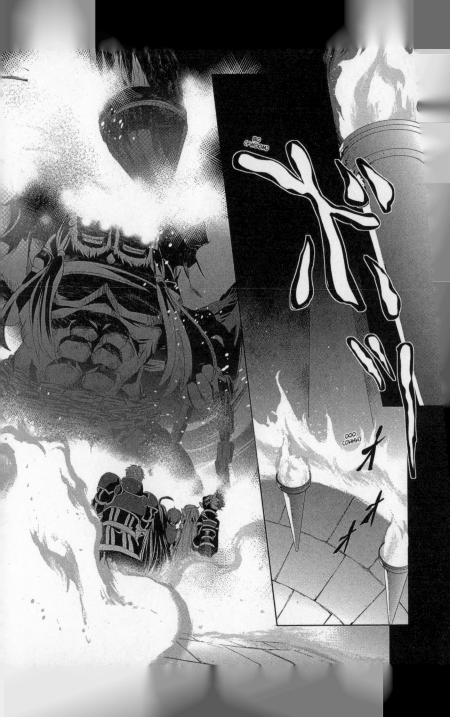

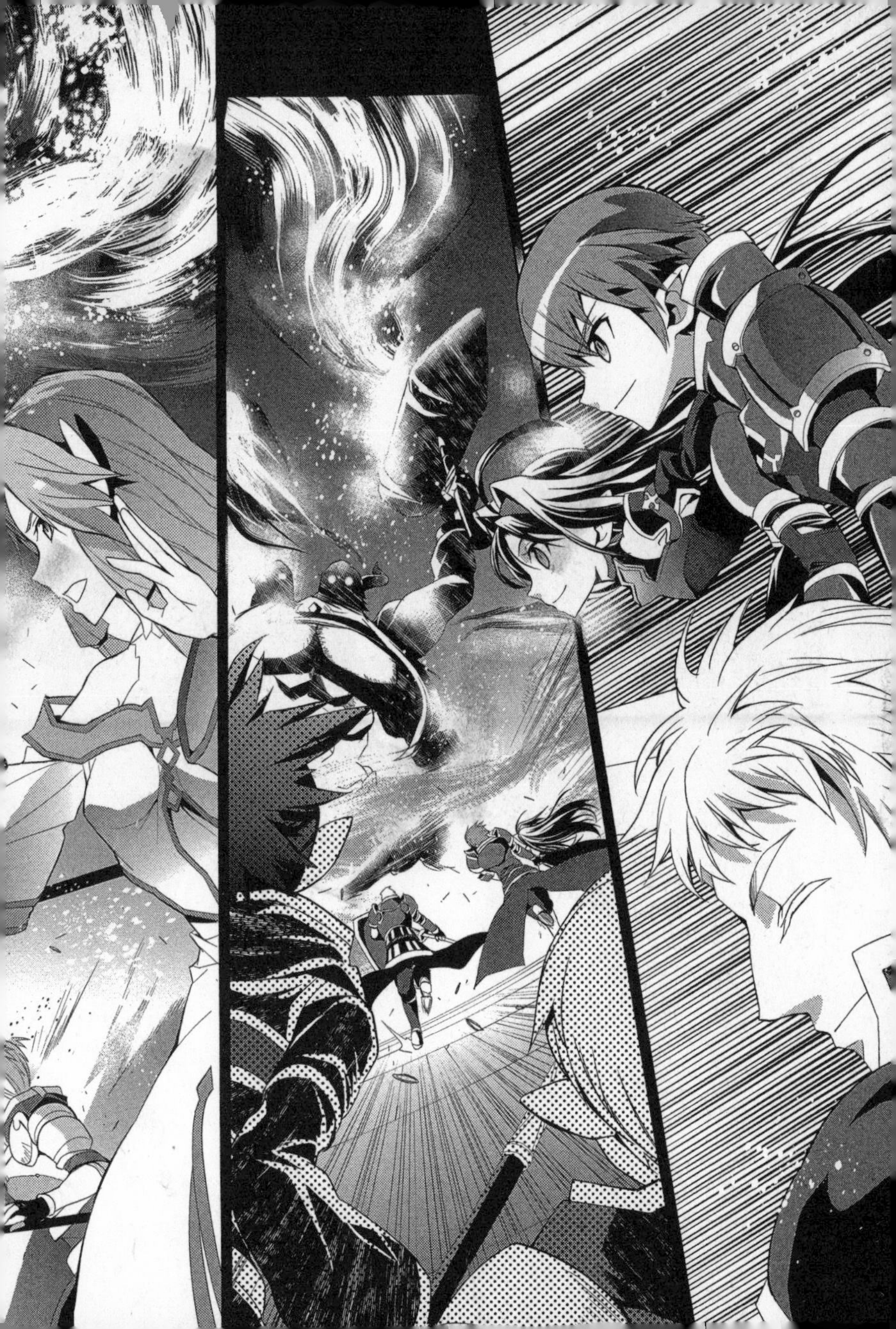

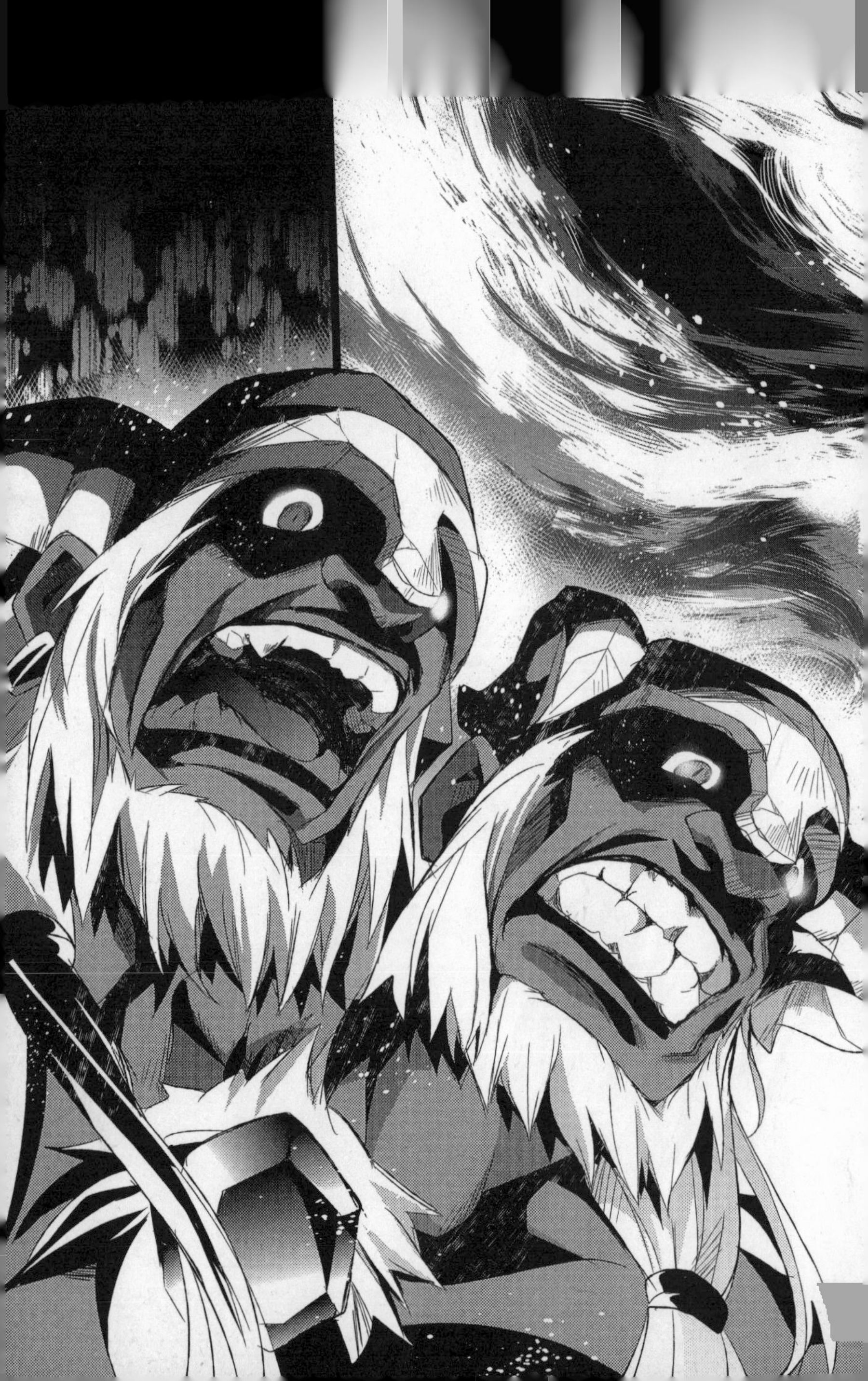

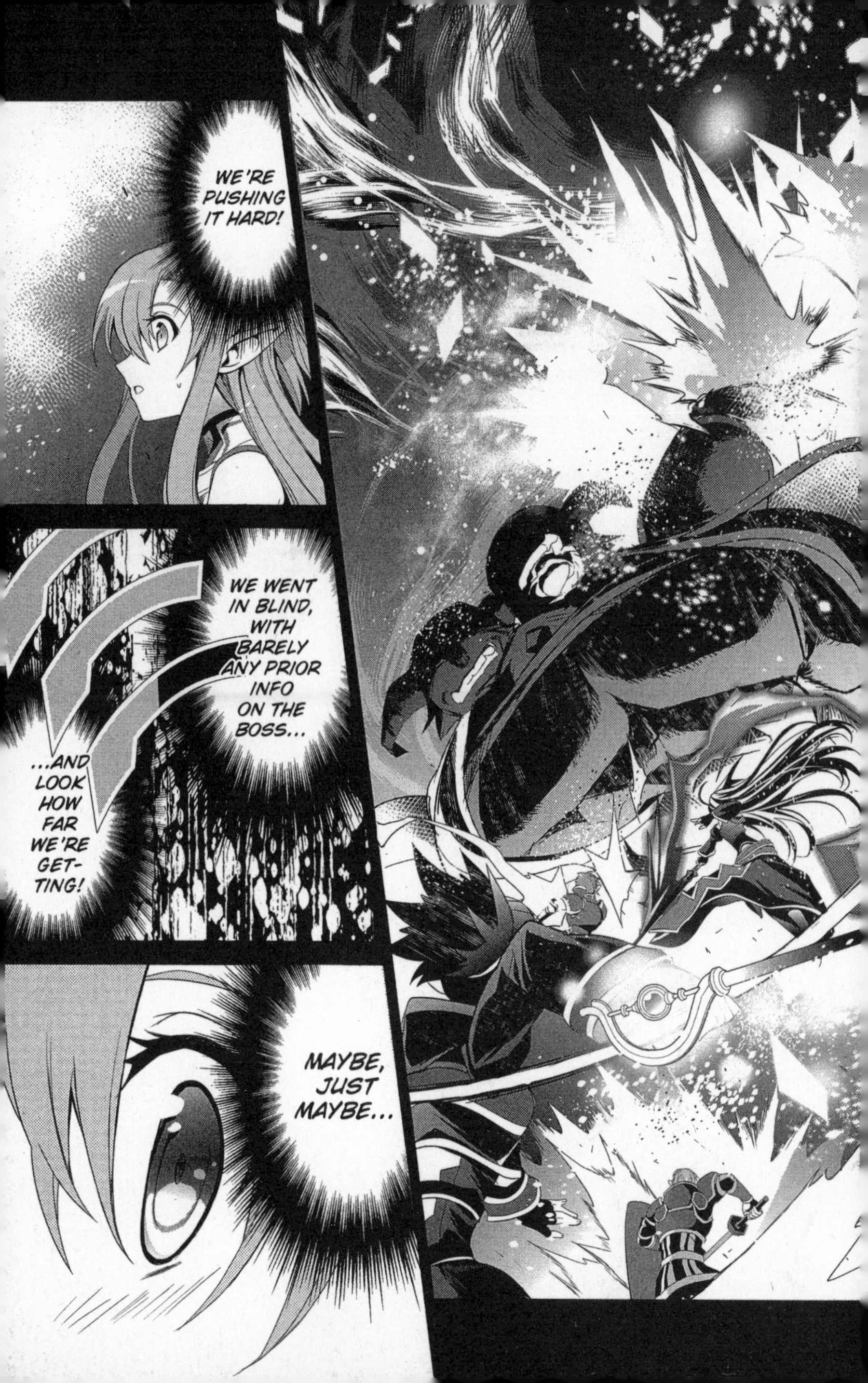
WE'RE PUSHING IT HARD!
WE WENT IN BLIND, WITH BARELY ANY PRIOR INFO ON THE BOSS...
...AND LOOK HOW FAR WE'RE GET-TING!
MAYBE, JUST MAYBE...

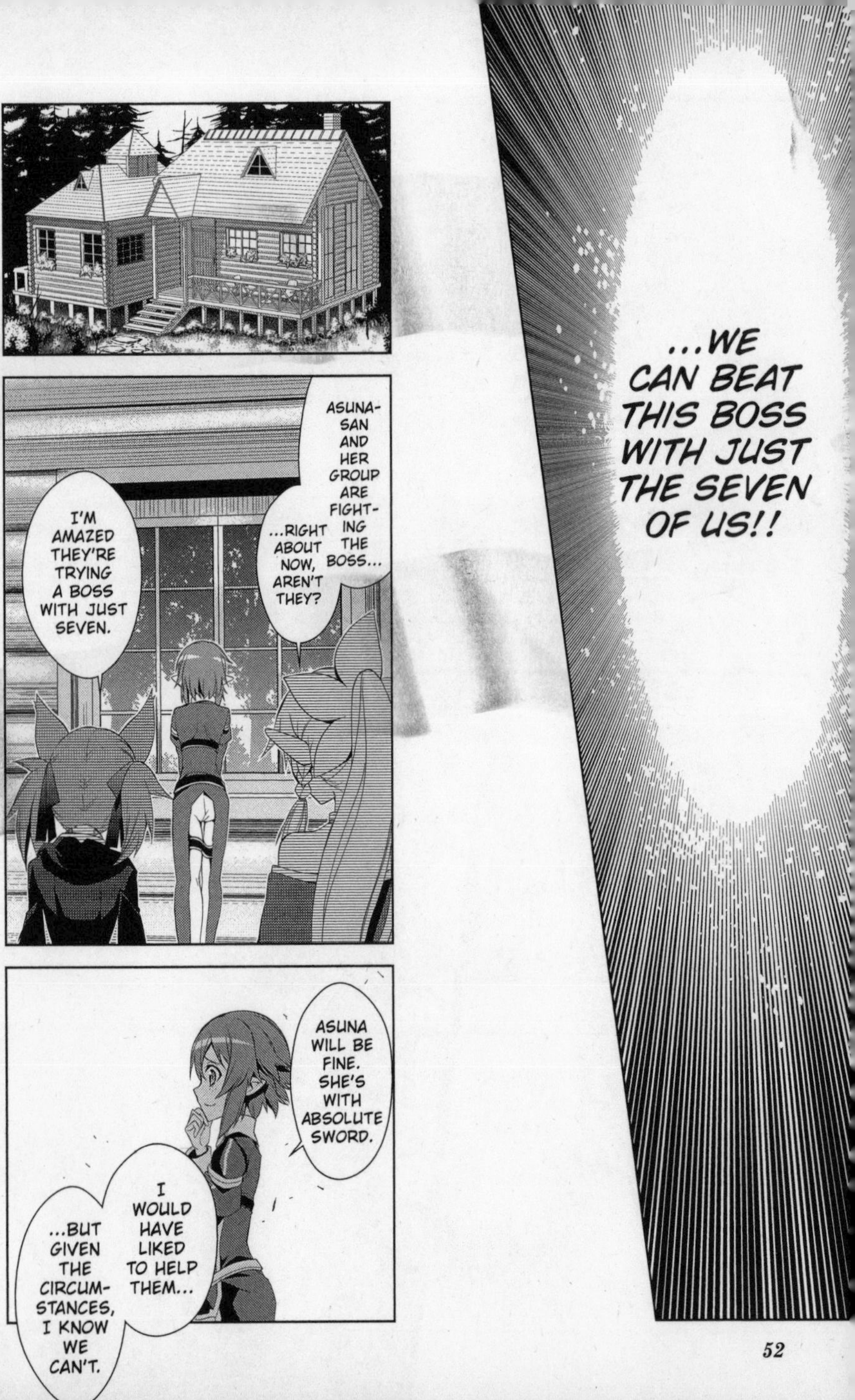
...WE CAN BEAT THIS BOSS WITH JUST THE SEVEN OF US!!
ASUNA-SAN AND HER GROUP ARE FIGHTING THE BOSS...
...RIGHT ABOUT NOW, AREN'T THEY?
I'M AMAZED THEY'RE TRYING A BOSS WITH JUST SEVEN.
ASUNA WILL BE FINE. SHE'S WITH ABSOLUTE SWORD.
I WOULD HAVE LIKED TO HELP THEM...
...BUT GIVEN THE CIRCUMSTANCES, I KNOW WE CAN'T.

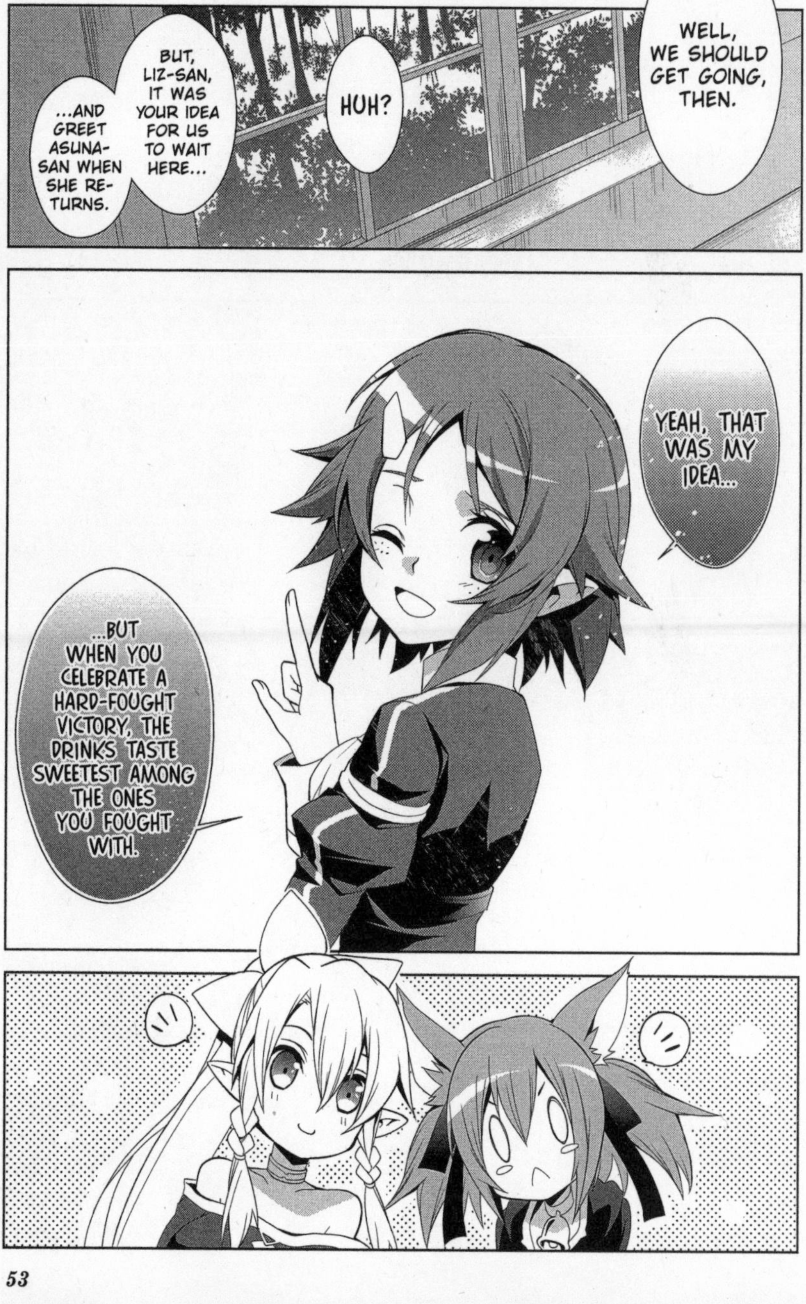
WELL, WE SHOULD GET GOING, THEN.
HUH?
BUT, LIZ-SAN, IT WAS YOUR IDEA FOR US TO WAIT HERE...
...AND GREET ASUNA-SAN WHEN SHE RE-TURNS.
YEAH, THAT WAS MY IDEA...
...BUT WHEN YOU CELEBRATE A HARD-FOUGHT VICTORY, THE DRINKS TASTE SWEETEST AMONG THE ONES YOU FOUGHT WITH.

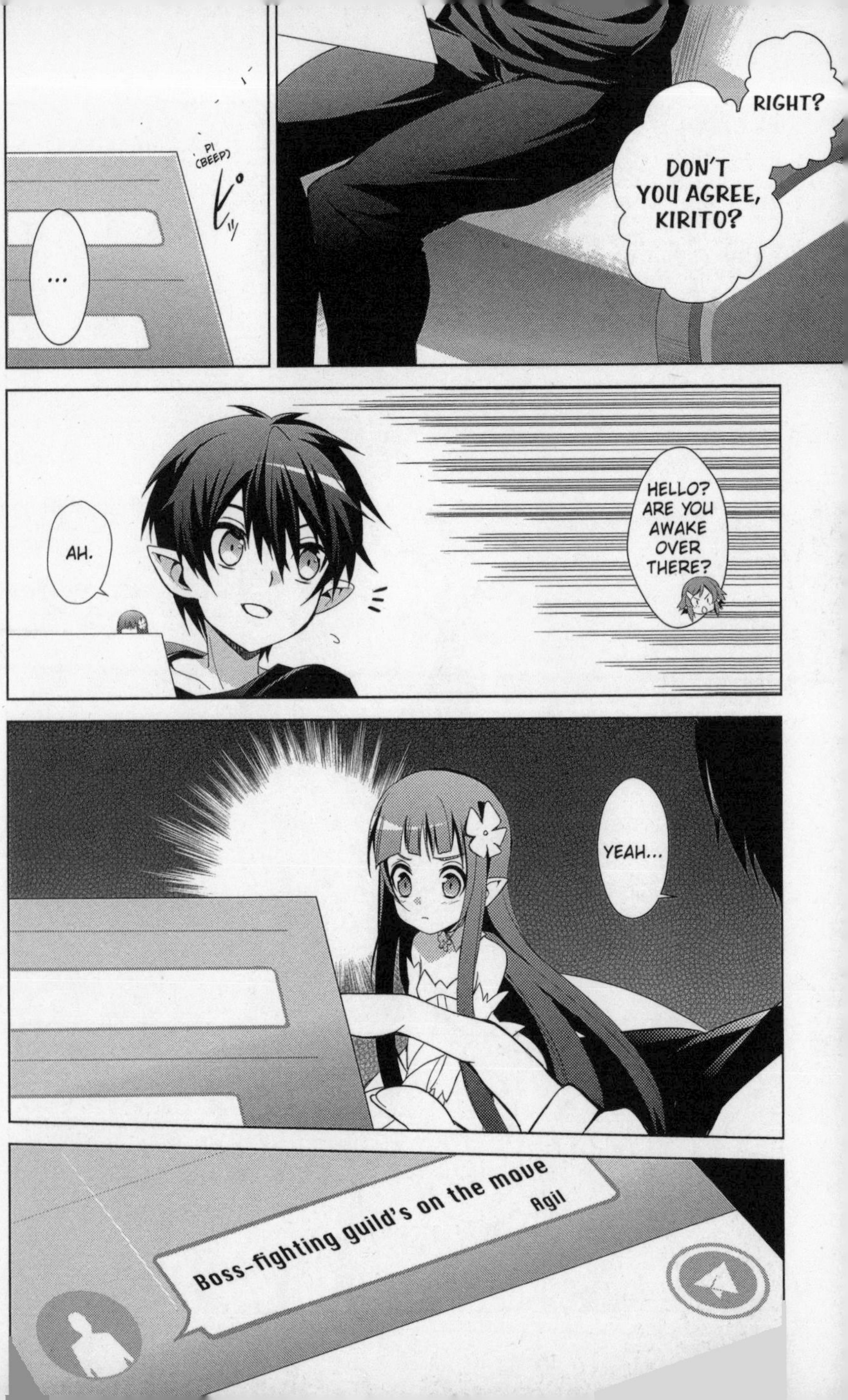
RIGHT?
DON'T YOU AGREE, KIRITO?
PI (BEEP)
...
HELLO? ARE YOU AWAKE OVER THERE?
AH.
YEAH...
Boss-fighting guild's on the move
Agil

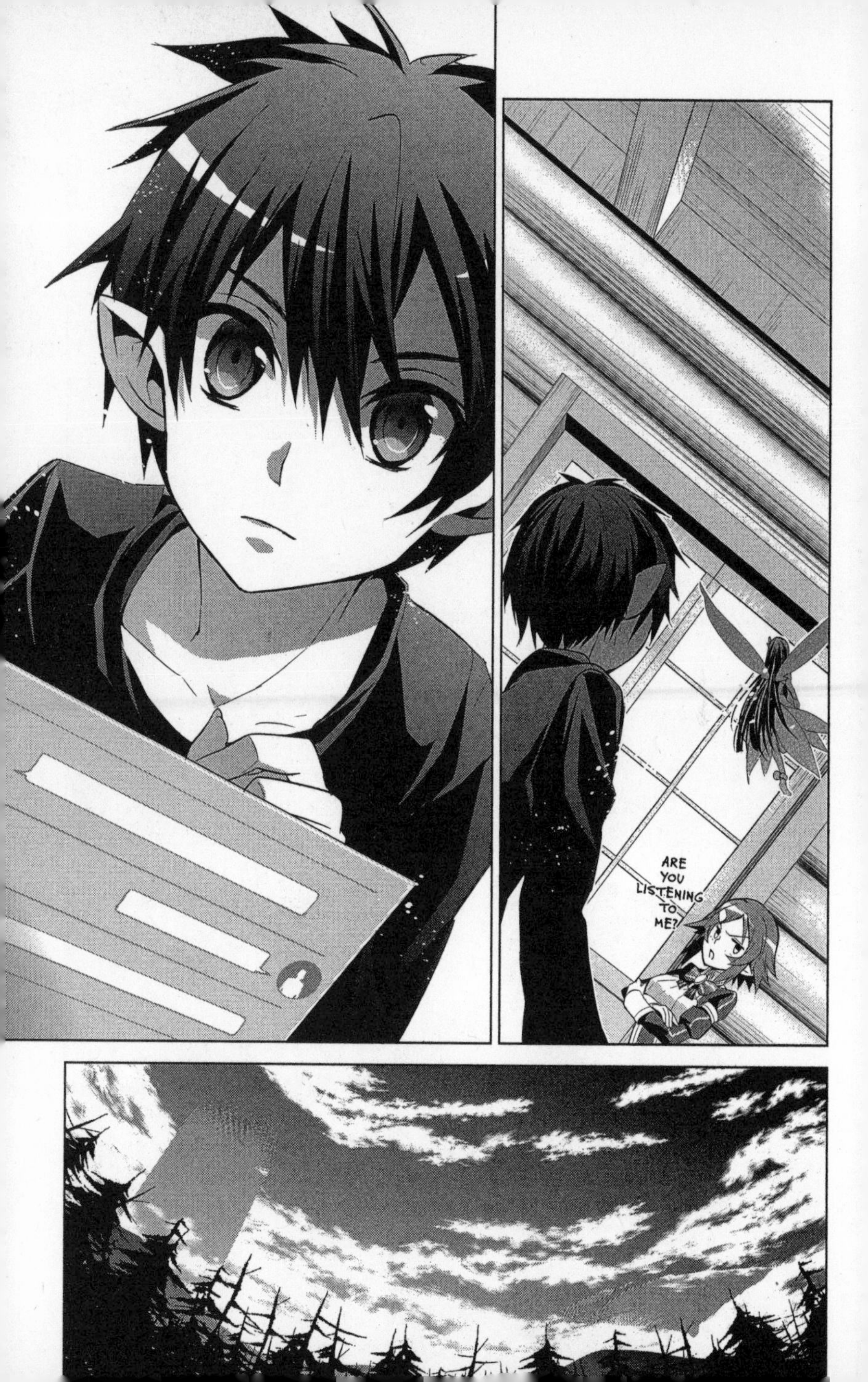
ARE YOU LISTENING TO ME?

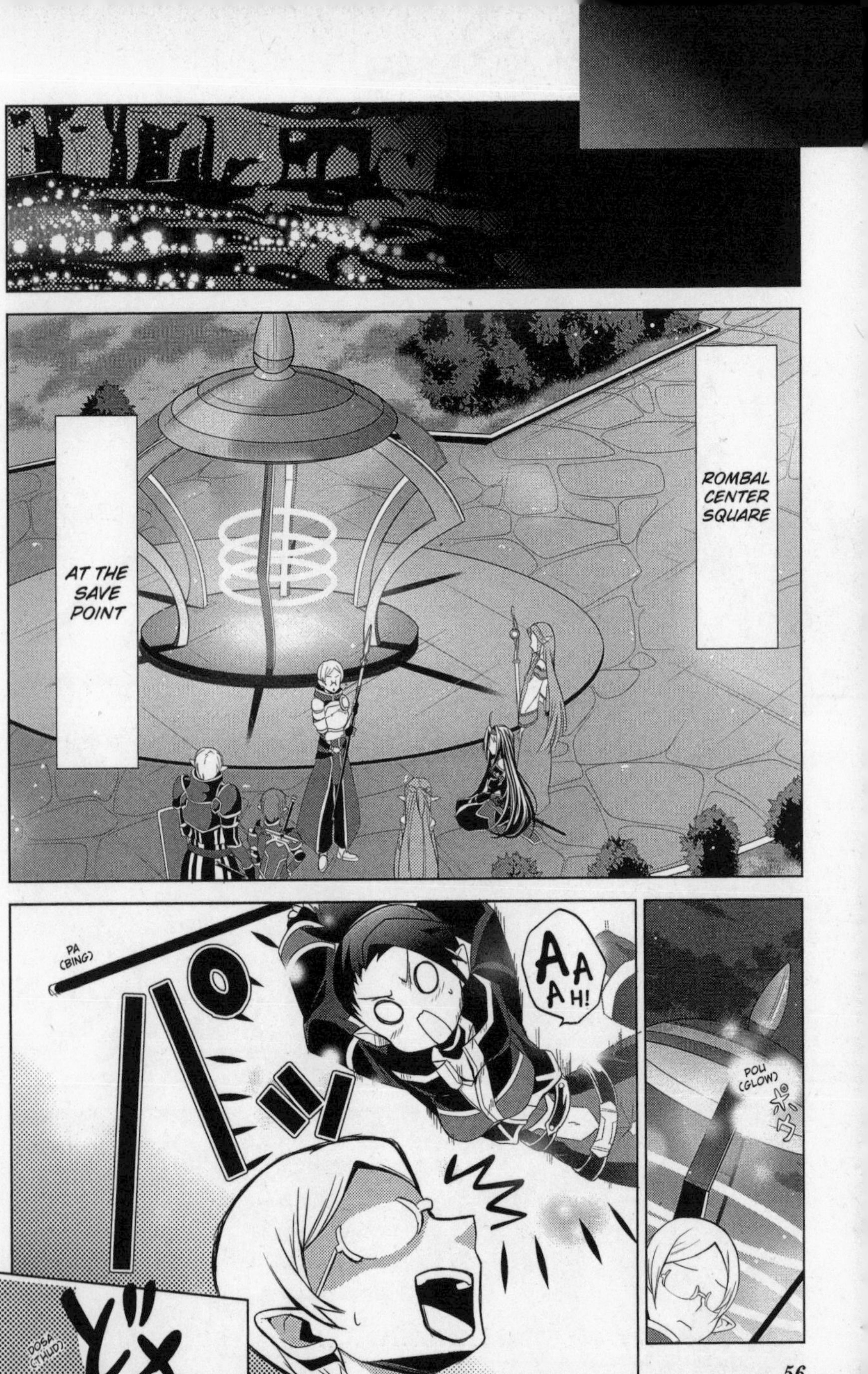
ROMBAL CENTER SQUARE
AT THE SAVE POINT
POU (GLOW)
PA (BING)
AAAH!
DOSA (THUD)

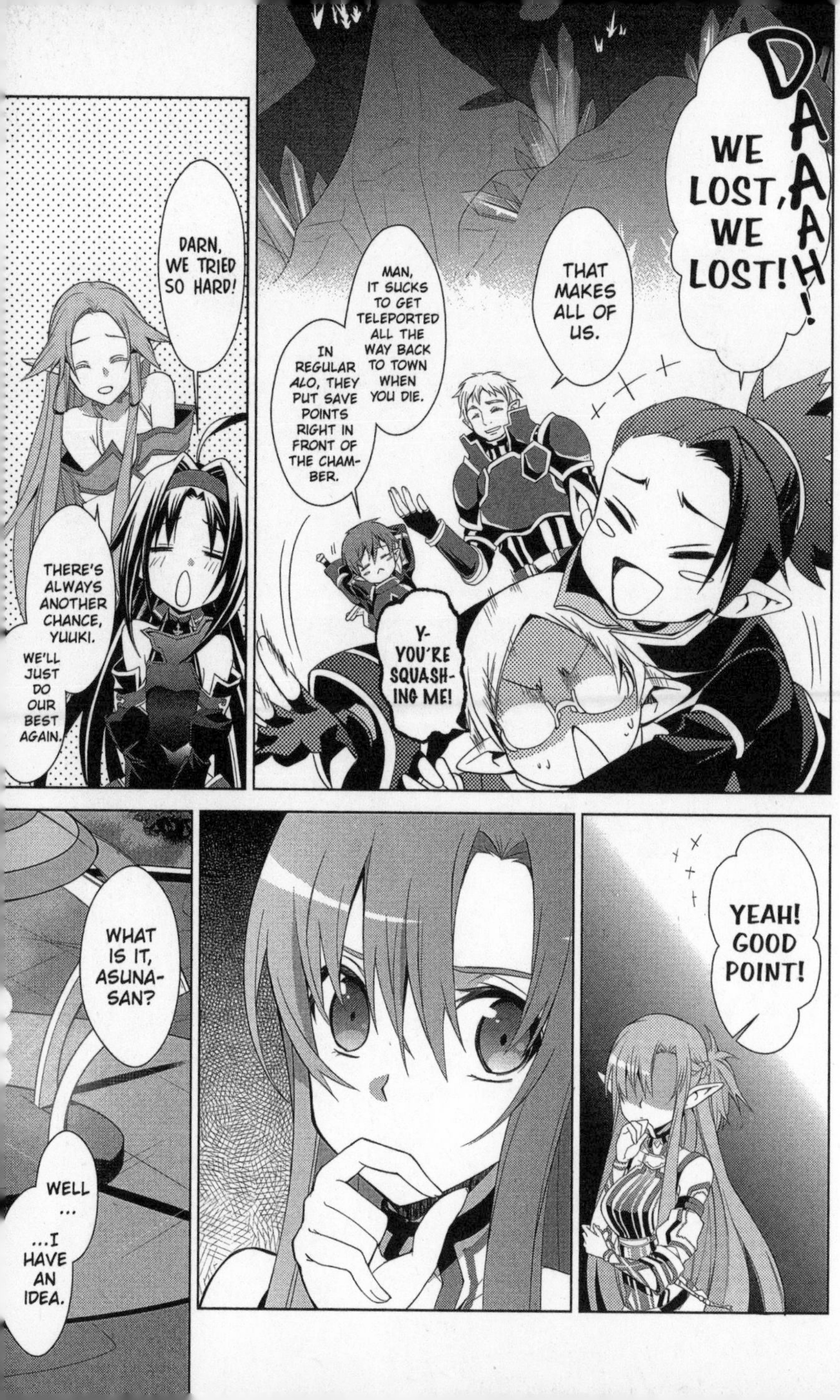
DAAAAH!
WE LOST, WE LOST!
THAT MAKES ALL OF US.
MAN, IT SUCKS TO GET TELEPORTED ALL THE WAY BACK TO TOWN WHEN YOU DIE.
IN REGULAR ALO, THEY PUT SAVE POINTS RIGHT IN FRONT OF THE CHAMBER.
Y-YOU'RE SQUASHING ME!
DARN, WE TRIED SO HARD!
THERE'S ALWAYS ANOTHER CHANCE, YUUKI.
WE'LL JUST DO OUR BEST AGAIN.
YEAH! GOOD POINT!
WHAT IS IT, ASUNA-SAN?
WELL...
...I HAVE AN IDEA.

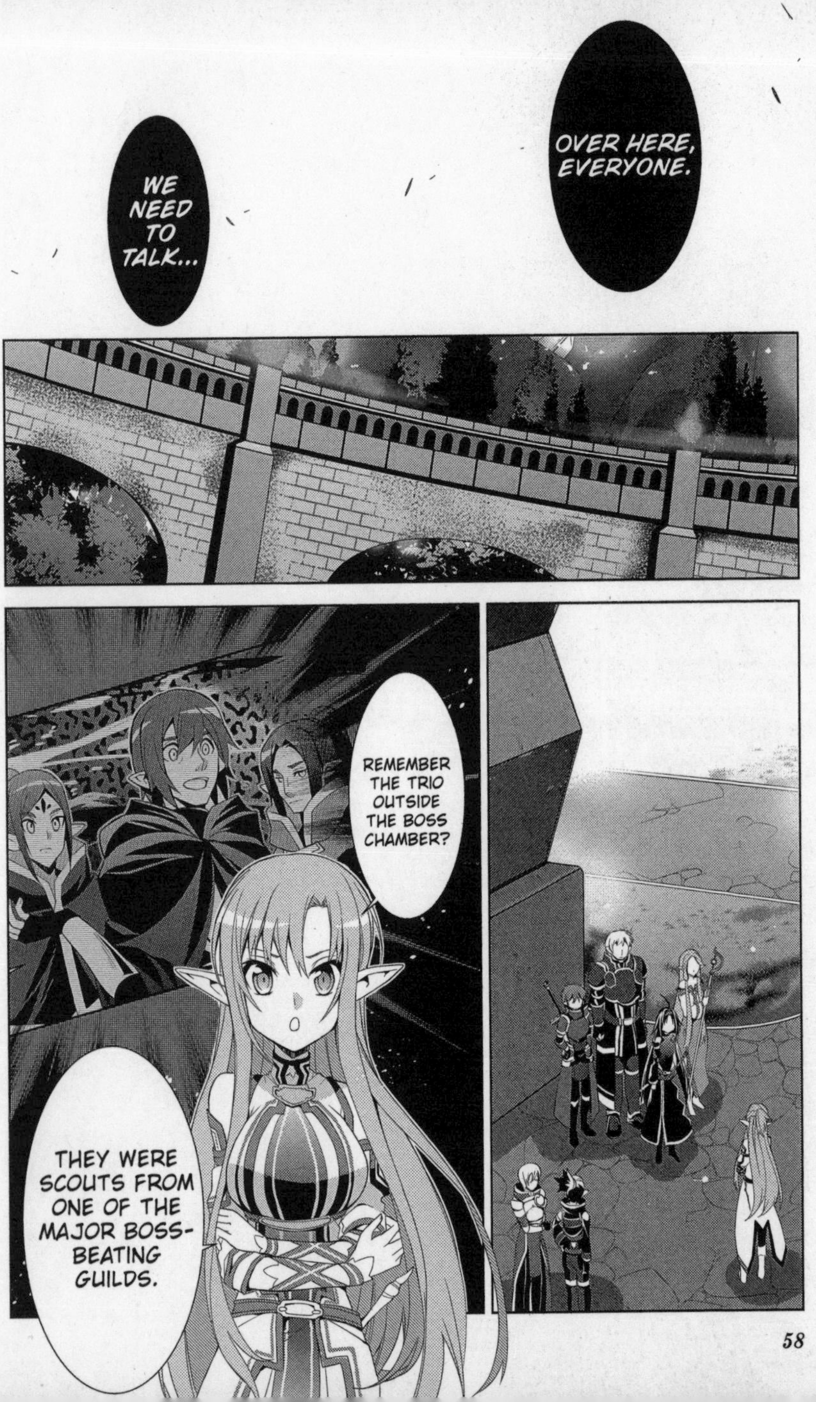
OVER HERE, EVERYONE.
WE NEED TO TALK...
REMEMBER THE TRIO OUTSIDE THE BOSS CHAMBER?
THEY WERE SCOUTS FROM ONE OF THE MAJOR BOSS-BEATING GUILDS.

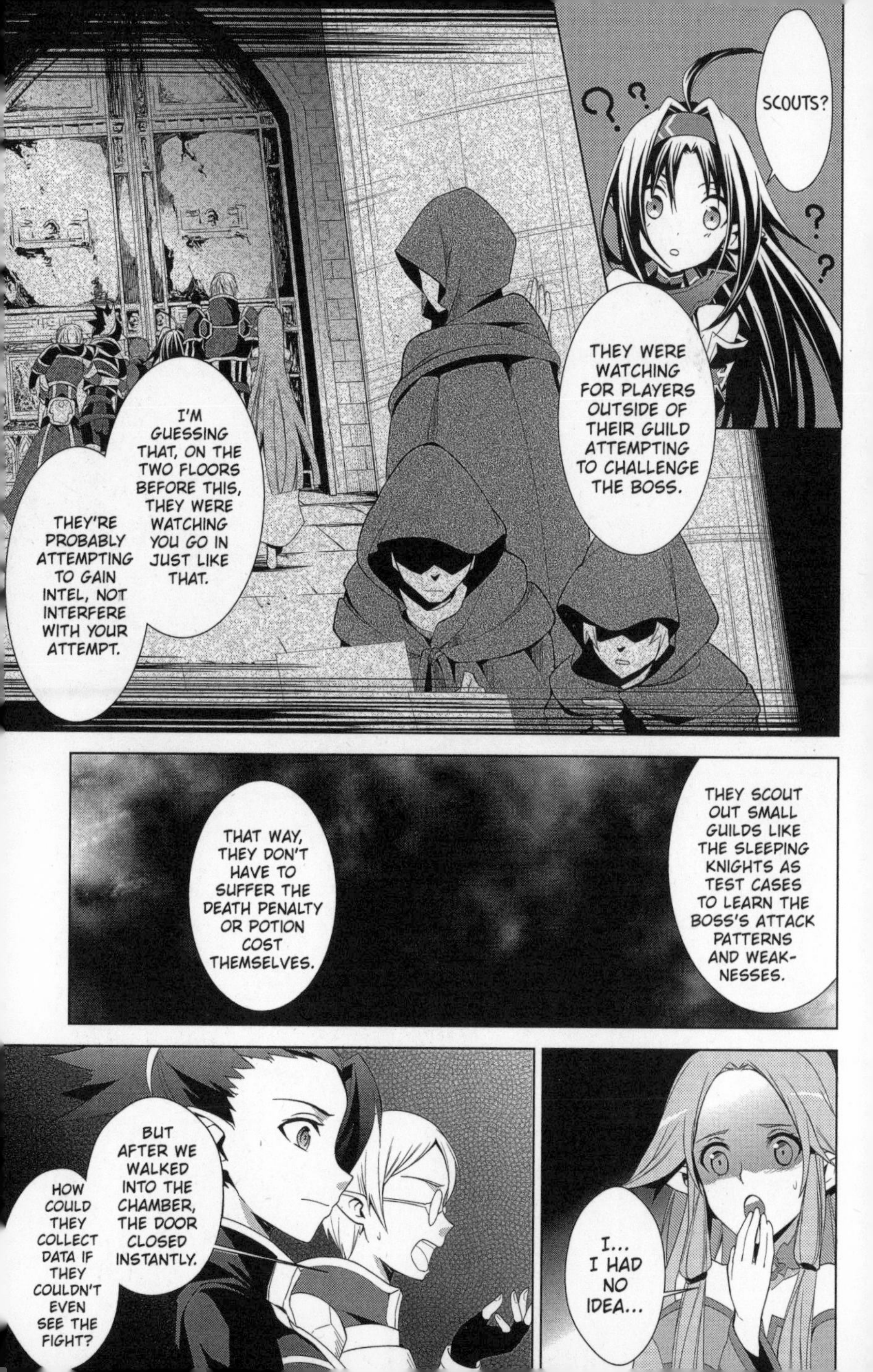
SCOUTS?
THEY WERE WATCHING FOR PLAYERS OUTSIDE OF THEIR GUILD ATTEMPTING TO CHALLENGE THE BOSS.
I'M GUESSING THAT, ON THE TWO FLOORS BEFORE THIS, THEY WERE WATCHING YOU GO IN JUST LIKE THAT.
THEY'RE PROBABLY ATTEMPTING TO GAIN INTEL, NOT INTERFERE WITH YOUR ATTEMPT.
THEY SCOUT OUT SMALL GUILDS LIKE THE SLEEPING KNIGHTS AS TEST CASES TO LEARN THE BOSS'S ATTACK PATTERNS AND WEAK-NESSES.
THAT WAY, THEY DON'T HAVE TO SUFFER THE DEATH PENALTY OR POTION COST THEMSELVES.
I... I HAD NO IDEA...
BUT AFTER WE WALKED INTO THE CHAMBER, THE DOOR CLOSED INSTANTLY.
HOW COULD THEY COLLECT DATA IF THEY COULDN'T EVEN SEE THE FIGHT?

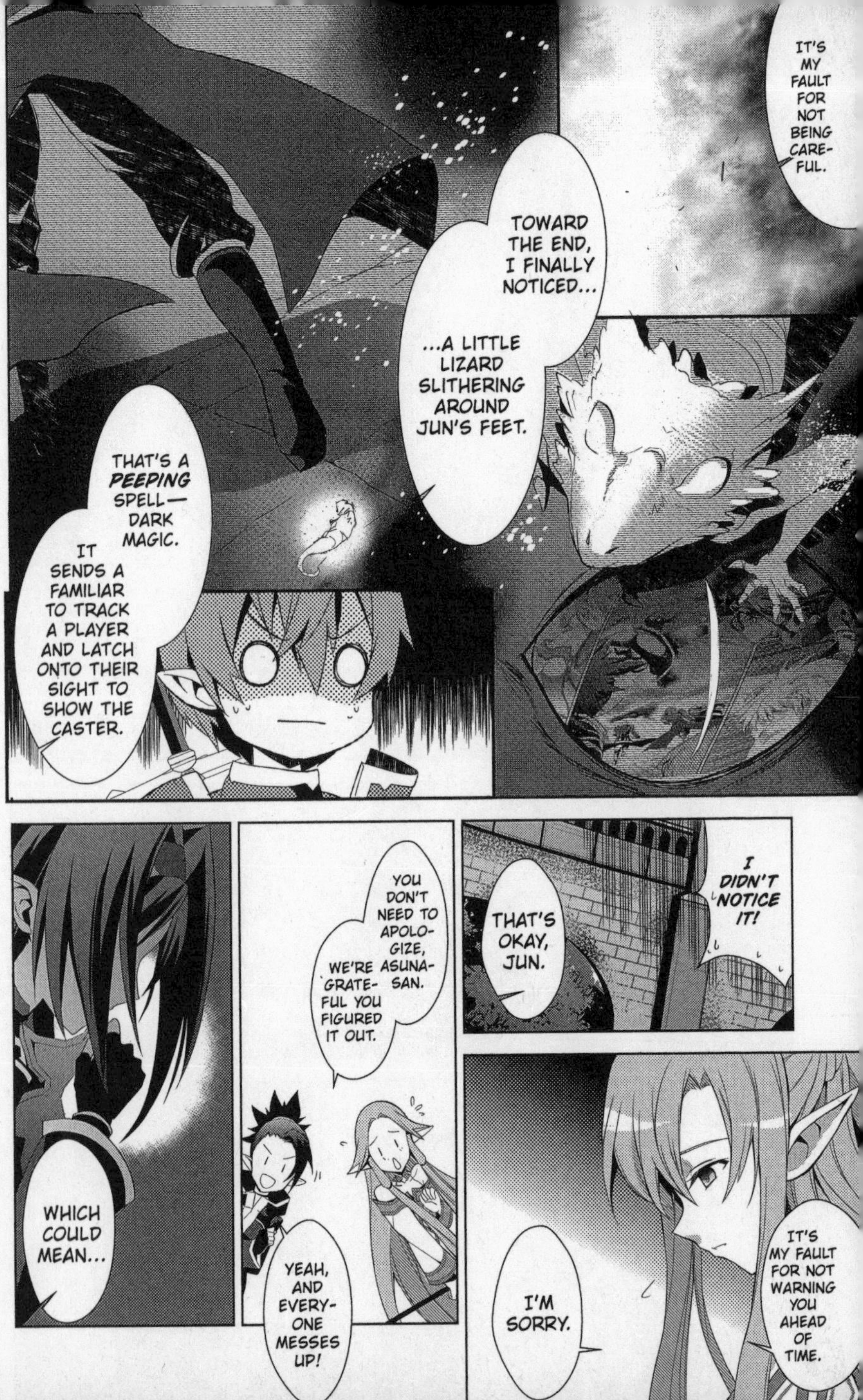
IT'S MY FAULT FOR NOT BEING CARE-FUL.
TOWARD THE END, I FINALLY NOTICED...
...A LITTLE LIZARD SLITHERING AROUND JUN'S FEET.
THAT'S A *PEEPING* SPELL—DARK MAGIC.
IT SENDS A FAMILIAR TO TRACK A PLAYER AND LATCH ONTO THEIR SIGHT TO SHOW THE CASTER.
I DIDN'T NOTICE IT!
THAT'S OKAY, JUN.
IT'S MY FAULT FOR NOT WARNING YOU AHEAD OF TIME.
I'M SORRY.
YOU DON'T NEED TO APOLO-GIZE, ASUNA-SAN.
WE'RE GRATE-FUL YOU FIGURED IT OUT.
YEAH, AND EVERY-ONE MESSES UP!
WHICH COULD MEAN...

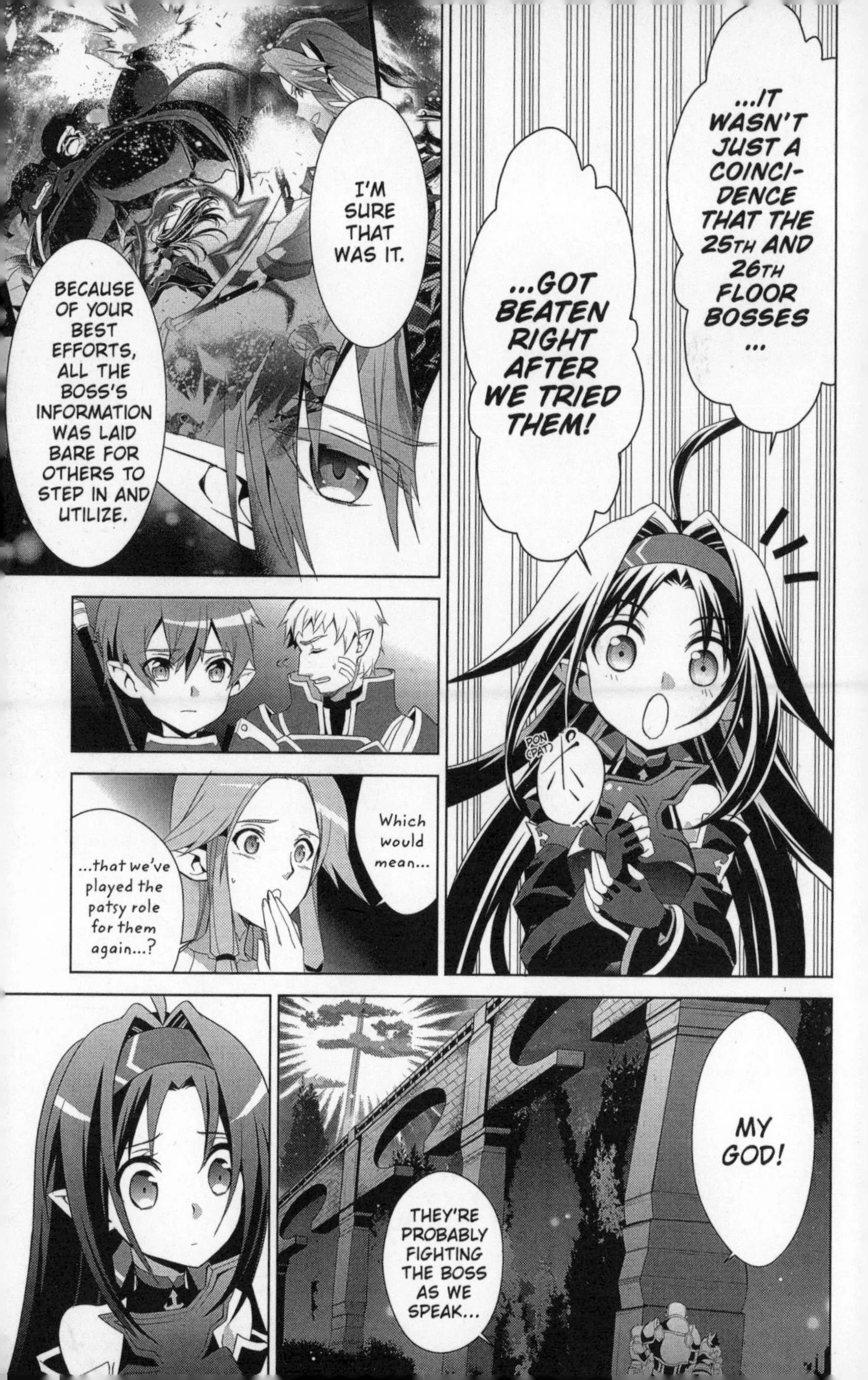
...IT WASN'T JUST A COINCI-DENCE THAT THE 25TH AND 26TH FLOOR BOSSES...
...GOT BEATEN RIGHT AFTER WE TRIED THEM!
PON (PAT)
I'M SURE THAT WAS IT.
BECAUSE OF YOUR BEST EFFORTS, ALL THE BOSS'S INFORMATION WAS LAID BARE FOR OTHERS TO STEP IN AND UTILIZE.
Which would mean...
...that we've played the patsy role for them again...?
MY GOD!
THEY'RE PROBABLY FIGHTING THE BOSS AS WE SPEAK...

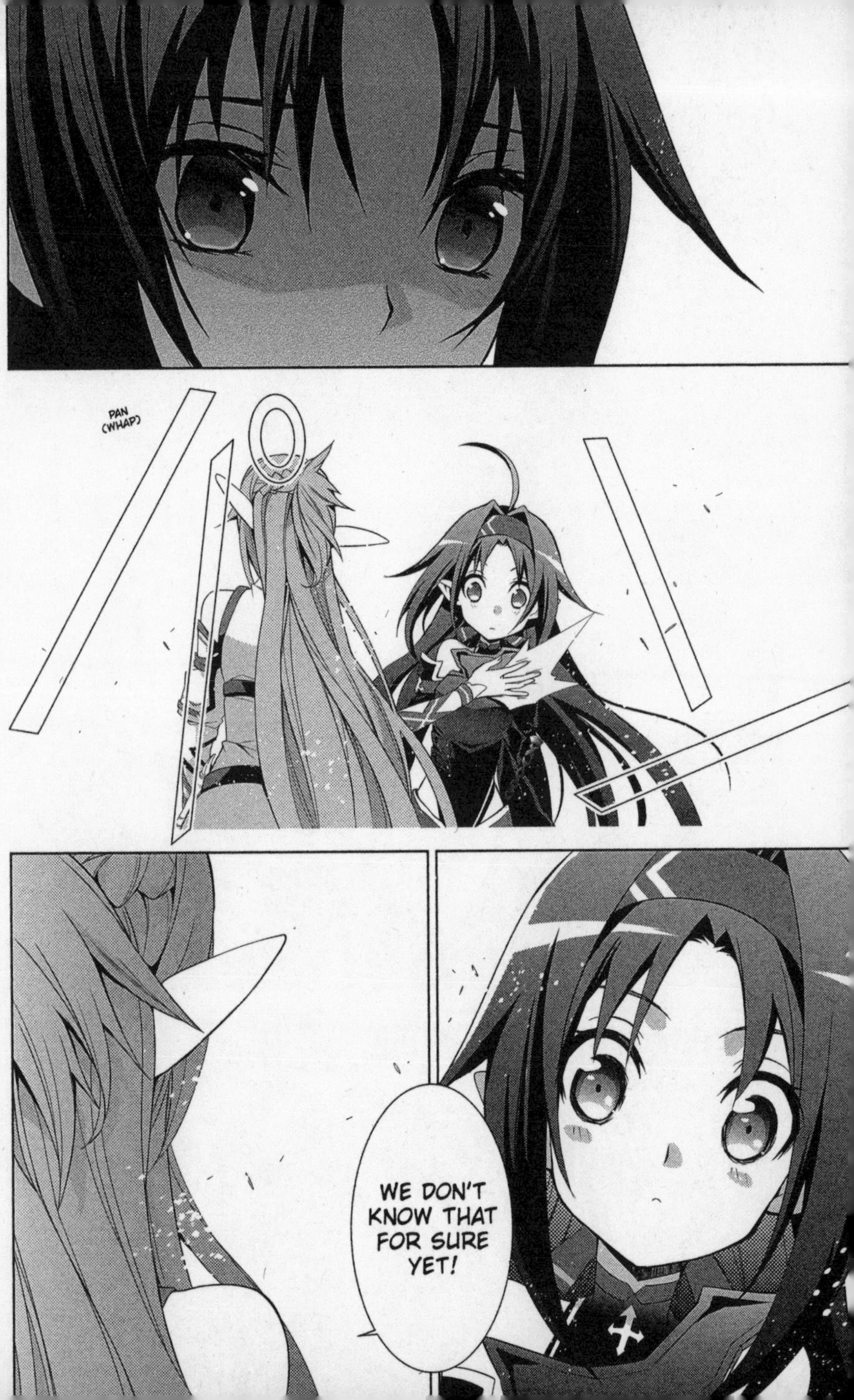
PAN (WHAP)
WE DON'T KNOW THAT FOR SURE YET!

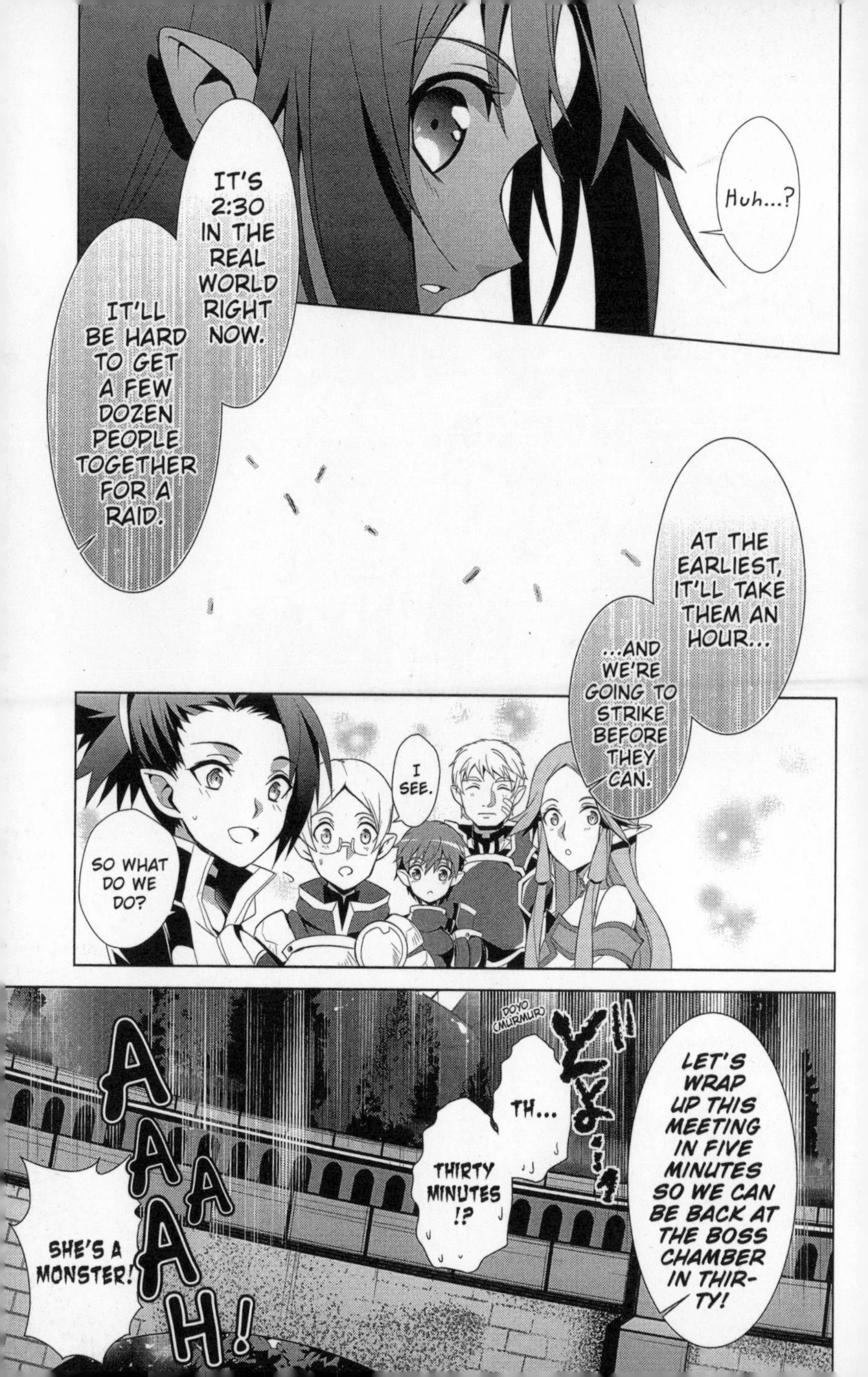
Huh...?
IT'S 2:30 IN THE REAL WORLD RIGHT NOW.
IT'LL BE HARD TO GET A FEW DOZEN PEOPLE TOGETHER FOR A RAID.
AT THE EARLIEST, IT'LL TAKE THEM AN HOUR...
...AND WE'RE GOING TO STRIKE BEFORE THEY CAN.
I SEE.
SO WHAT DO WE DO?
LET'S WRAP UP THIS MEETING IN FIVE MINUTES SO WE CAN BE BACK AT THE BOSS CHAMBER IN THIRTY!
DOYO (MURMUR)
TH...
THIRTY MINUTES!?
AAAAH!
SHE'S A MONSTER!

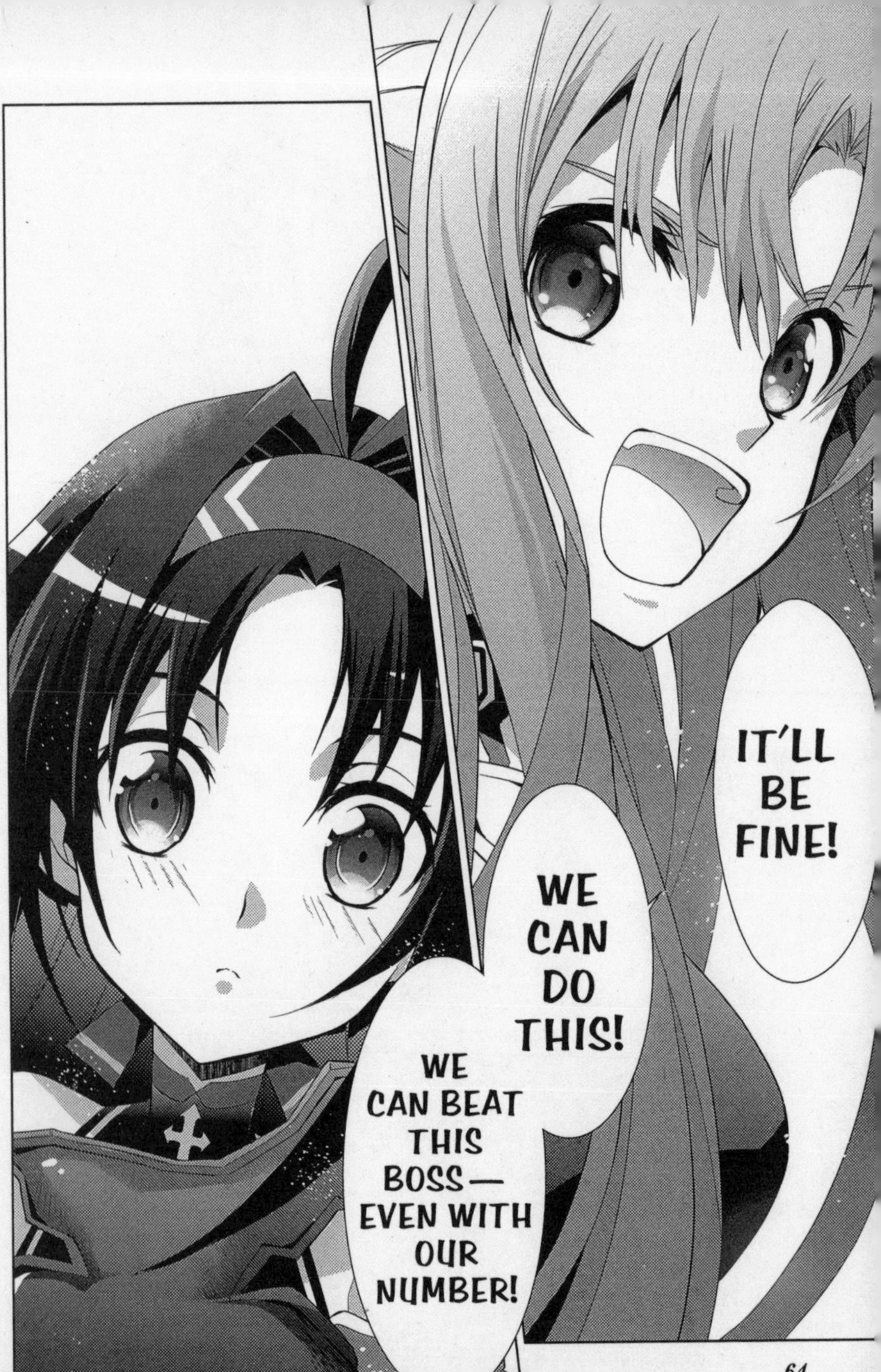
IT'LL BE FINE!
WE CAN DO THIS!
WE CAN BEAT THIS BOSS—EVEN WITH OUR NUMBER!

SWORD ART ONLINE
MOTHER'S ROSARY

SWORD ART ONLINE mother's rosary
BACKGROUND GUIDE 02

VRMMORPG MANNERS

THE SPYING DEPICTED IN THIS BOSS BATTLE—AND BY THE
LARGE GROUP "MONOPOLY," SEEN LATER IN THE VOLUME—
INVOLVES THE COMMON MANNERS OF VRMMORPGS, AS
SEEN THROUGHOUT THE SAO SERIES, NOT JUST *MOTHER'S
ROSARY*. THERE'S A HARASSMENT CODE THAT CUTS DOWN
ON UNWANTED CONTACT BETWEEN AVATARS OF THE OPPOSITE
SEX, AS WELL AS SYSTEM-ENACTED METHODS OF MAINTAIN-
ING BEHAVIOR, BUT IT'S COMMONLY AGREED THAT CERTAIN
RULES MUST BE UPHELD FOR EVERYONE TO ENJOY THE GAME
TOGETHER. READING SAO WITH AN EYE OUT FOR THESE
EXAMPLES OF "MANNERS IN A FUTURISTIC GAME" MIGHT GIVE
YOU A NEWFOUND APPRECIATION FOR THE STORY.

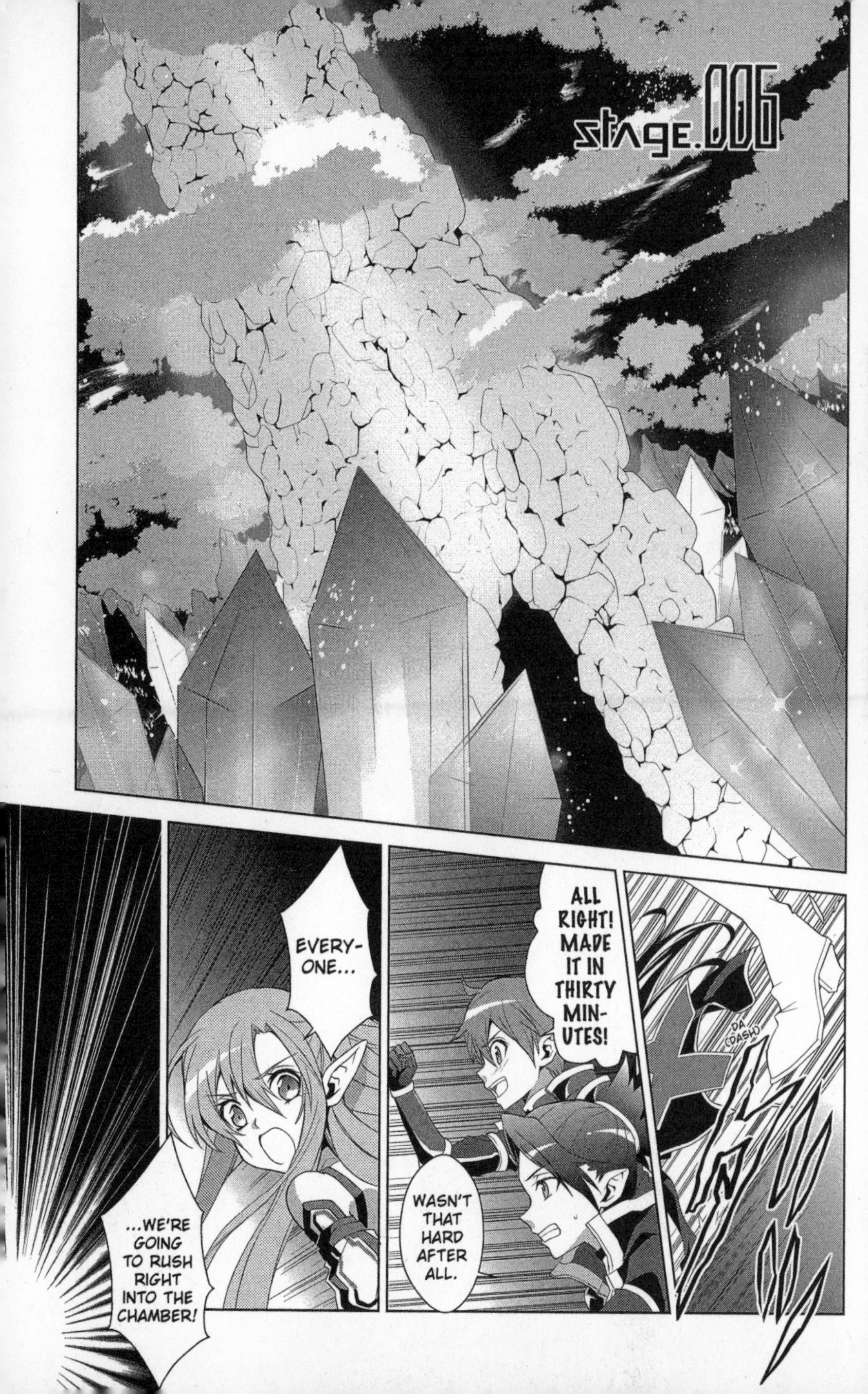
stage.006
DA (DASH)
ALL RIGHT! MADE IT IN THIRTY MIN-UTES!
WASN'T THAT HARD AFTER ALL.
EVERY-ONE...
...WE'RE GOING TO RUSH RIGHT INTO THE CHAMBER!

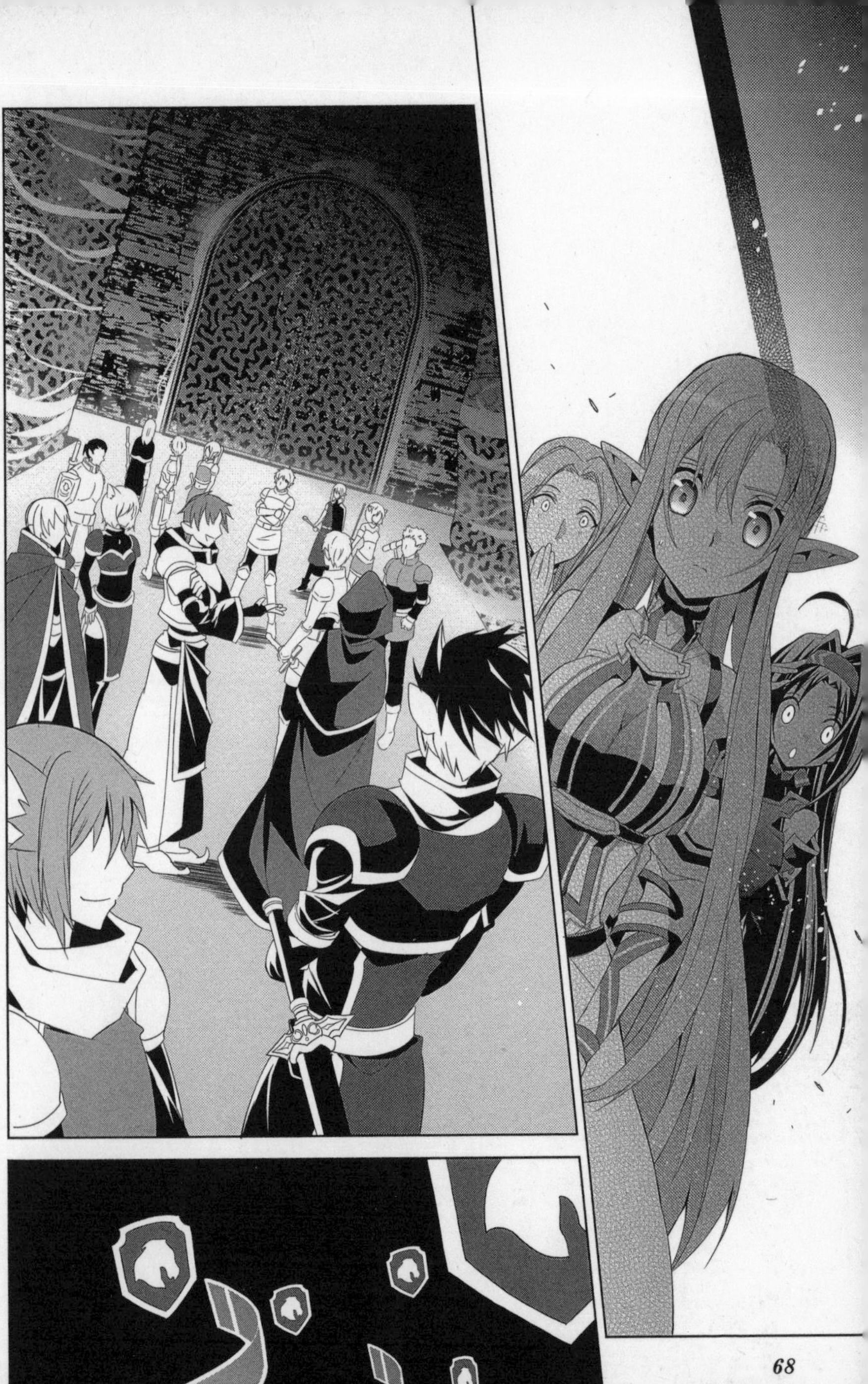

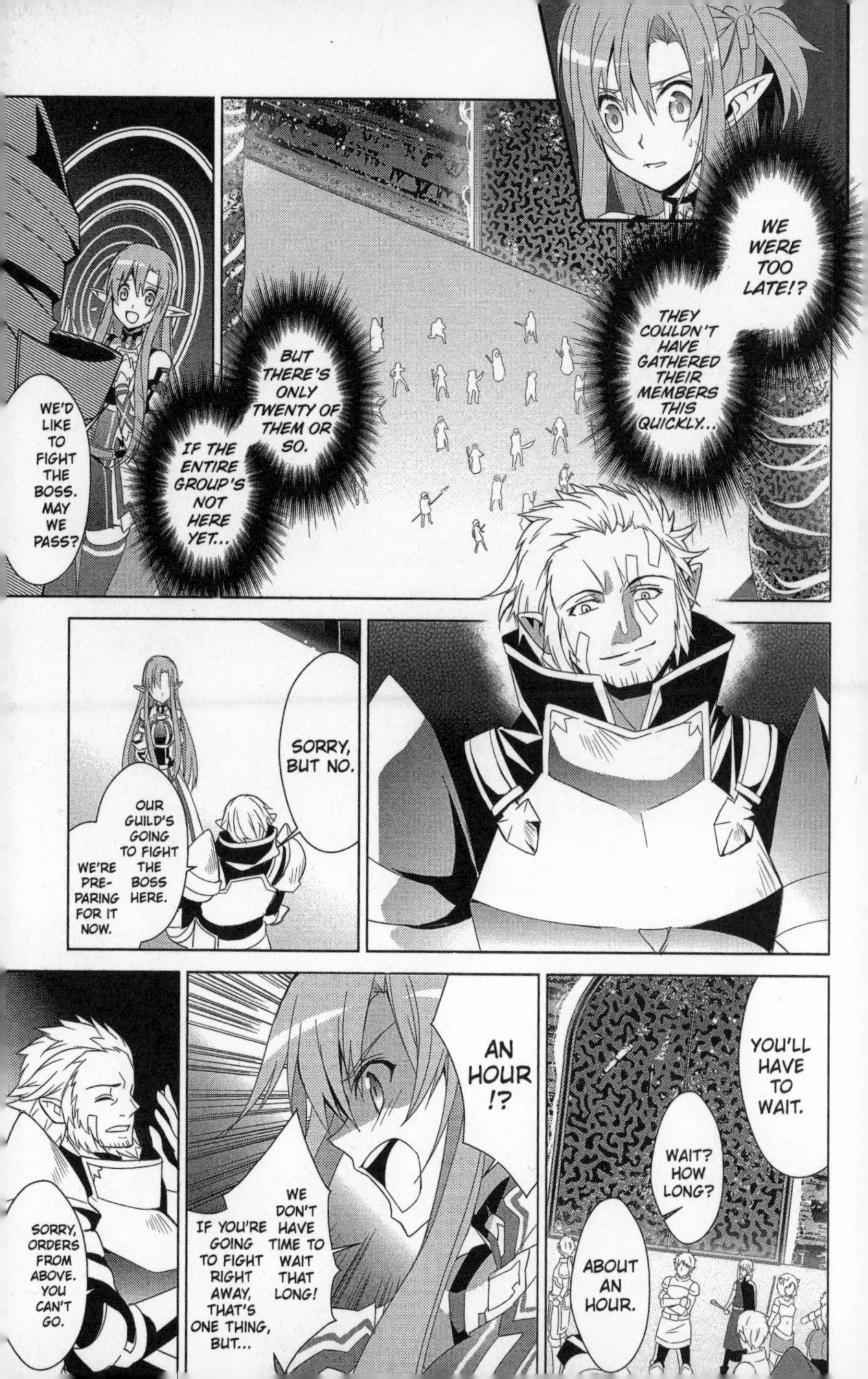
WE WERE TOO LATE!?
THEY COULDN'T HAVE GATHERED THEIR MEMBERS THIS QUICKLY...
BUT THERE'S ONLY TWENTY OF THEM OR SO.
IF THE ENTIRE GROUP'S NOT HERE YET...
WE'D LIKE TO FIGHT THE BOSS. MAY WE PASS?
SORRY, BUT NO.
OUR GUILD'S GOING TO FIGHT THE BOSS HERE.
WE'RE PRE-PARING FOR IT NOW.
YOU'LL HAVE TO WAIT.
WAIT? HOW LONG?
ABOUT AN HOUR.
AN HOUR!?
WE DON'T HAVE TIME TO WAIT THAT LONG!
IF YOU'RE GOING TO FIGHT RIGHT AWAY, THAT'S ONE THING, BUT...
SORRY, ORDERS FROM ABOVE. YOU CAN'T GO.

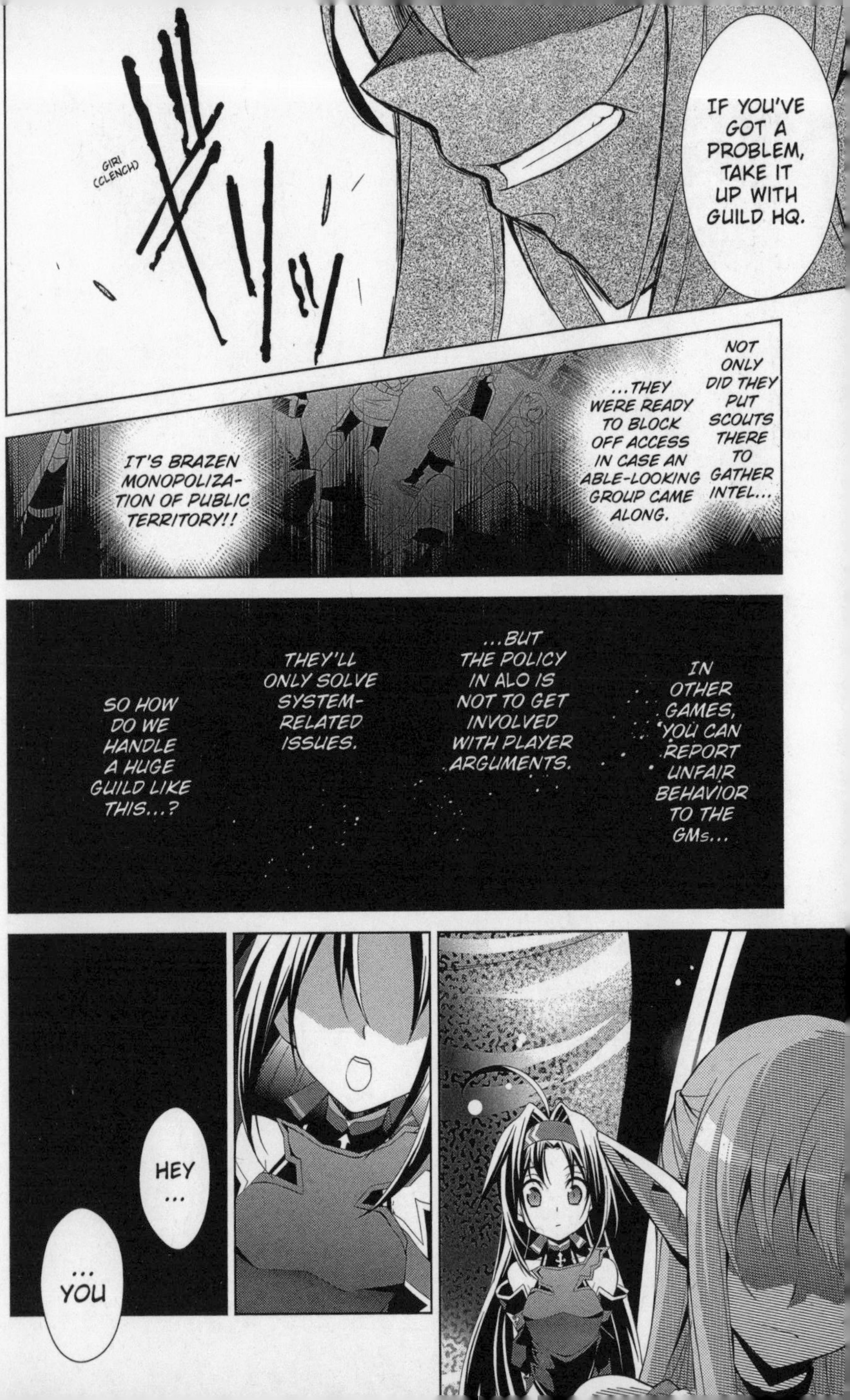
IF YOU'VE GOT A PROBLEM, TAKE IT UP WITH GUILD HQ.
GIRI (CLENCH)
NOT ONLY DID THEY PUT SCOUTS THERE TO GATHER INTEL...
...THEY WERE READY TO BLOCK OFF ACCESS IN CASE AN ABLE-LOOKING GROUP CAME ALONG.
IT'S BRAZEN MONOPOLIZATION OF PUBLIC TERRITORY!!
IN OTHER GAMES, YOU CAN REPORT UNFAIR BEHAVIOR TO THE GMs...
...BUT THE POLICY IN ALO IS NOT TO GET INVOLVED WITH PLAYER ARGUMENTS.
THEY'LL ONLY SOLVE SYSTEM-RELATED ISSUES.
SO HOW DO WE HANDLE A HUGE GUILD LIKE THIS...?
HEY...
...YOU

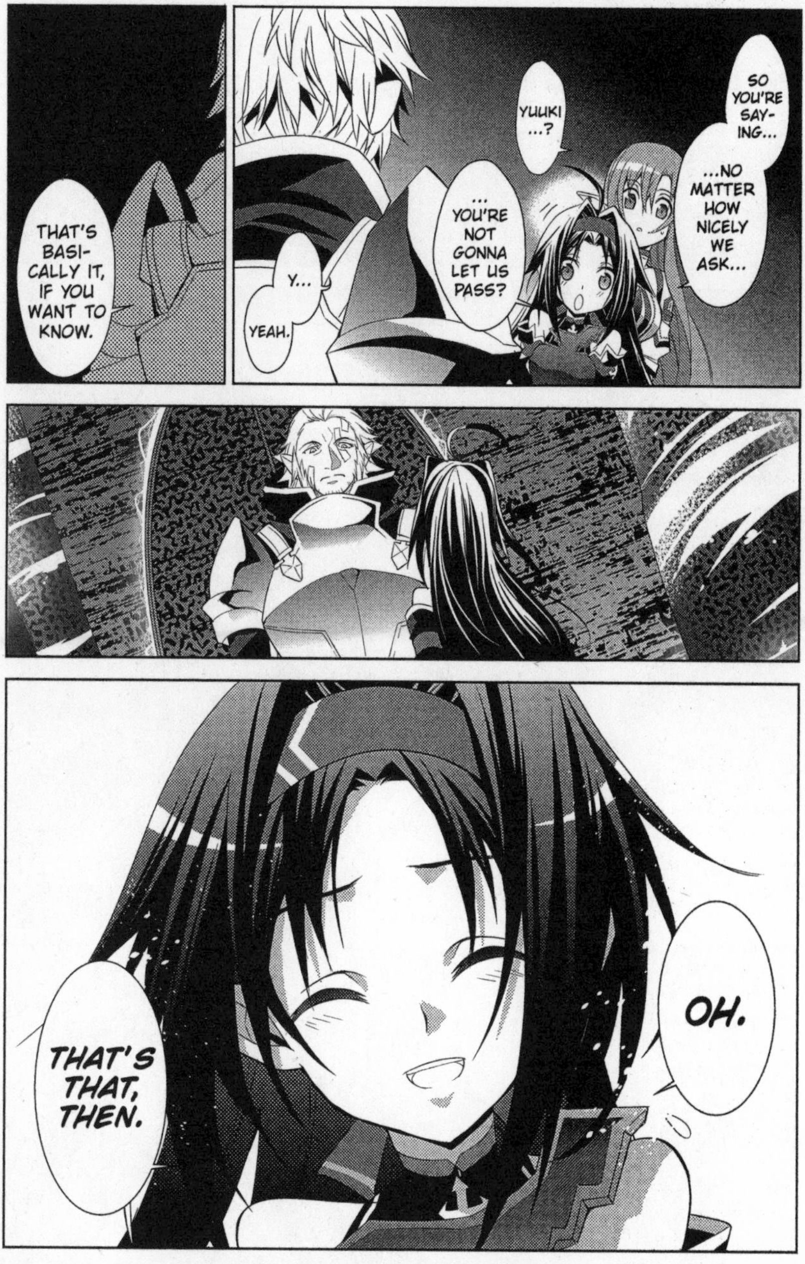
SO YOU'RE SAY-ING...
...NO MATTER HOW NICELY WE ASK...
YUUKI ...?
... YOU'RE NOT GONNA LET US PASS?
Y...
YEAH.
THAT'S BASI-CALLY IT, IF YOU WANT TO KNOW.
OH.
THAT'S THAT, THEN.

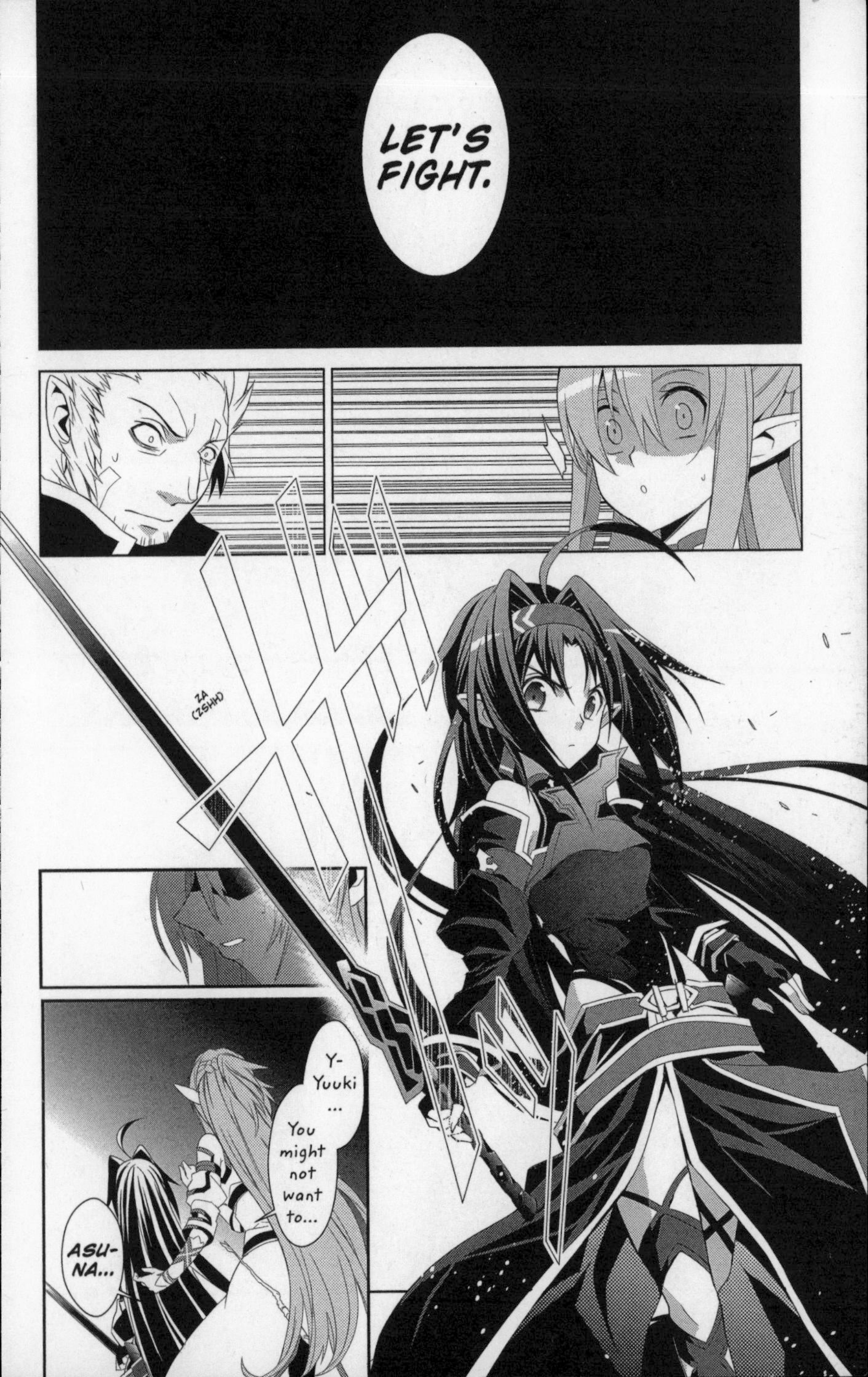
LET'S FIGHT.
ZA (ZSHH)
Y-Yuuki... You might not want to...
ASUNA...

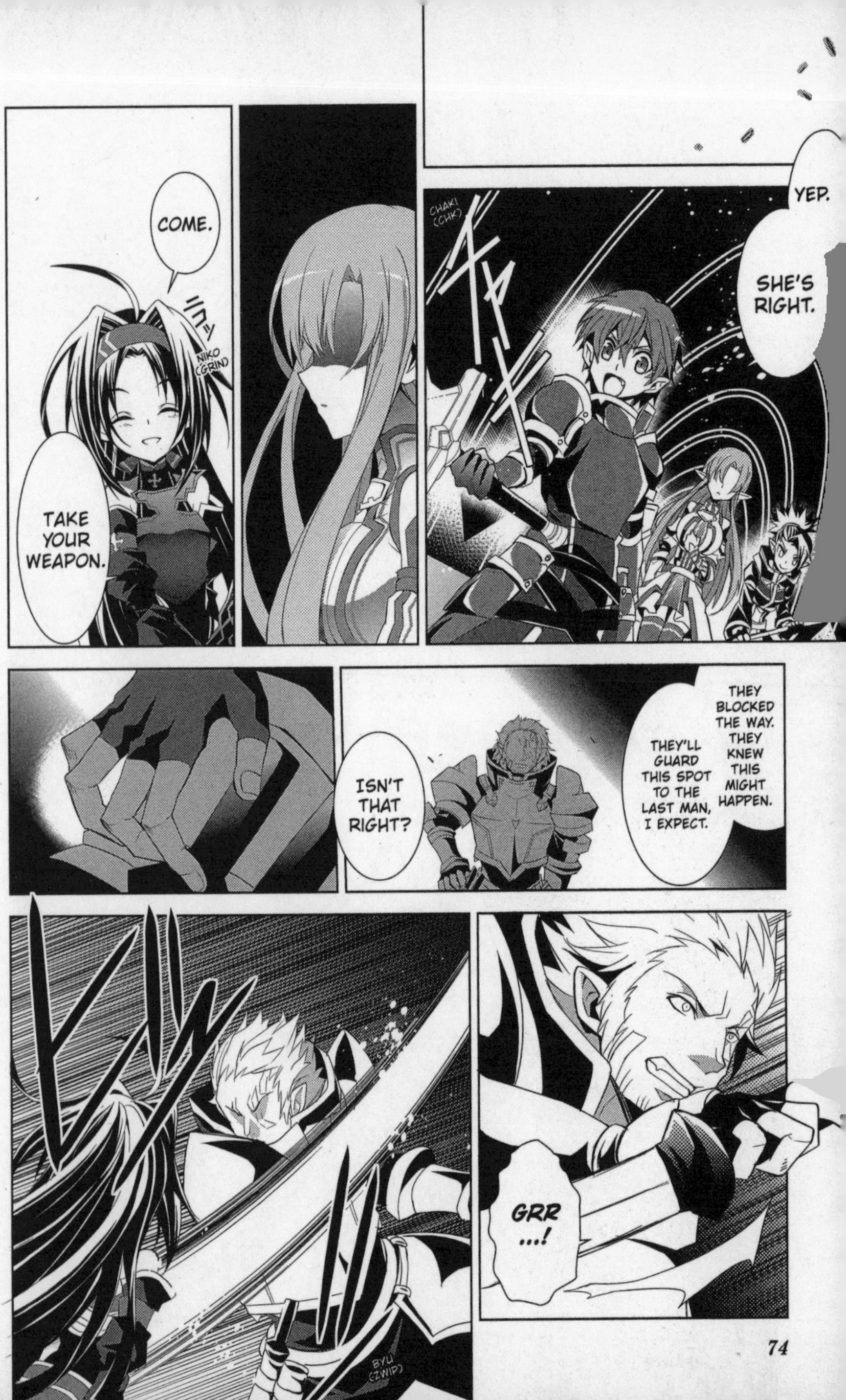
YEP.
SHE'S RIGHT.
CHAKI (CHK)
COME.
NIKO (GRIN)
TAKE YOUR WEAPON.
THEY BLOCKED THE WAY. THEY KNEW THIS MIGHT HAPPEN.
THEY'LL GUARD THIS SPOT TO THE LAST MAN, I EXPECT.
ISN'T THAT RIGHT?
GRR ...!
BYU (ZWIP)

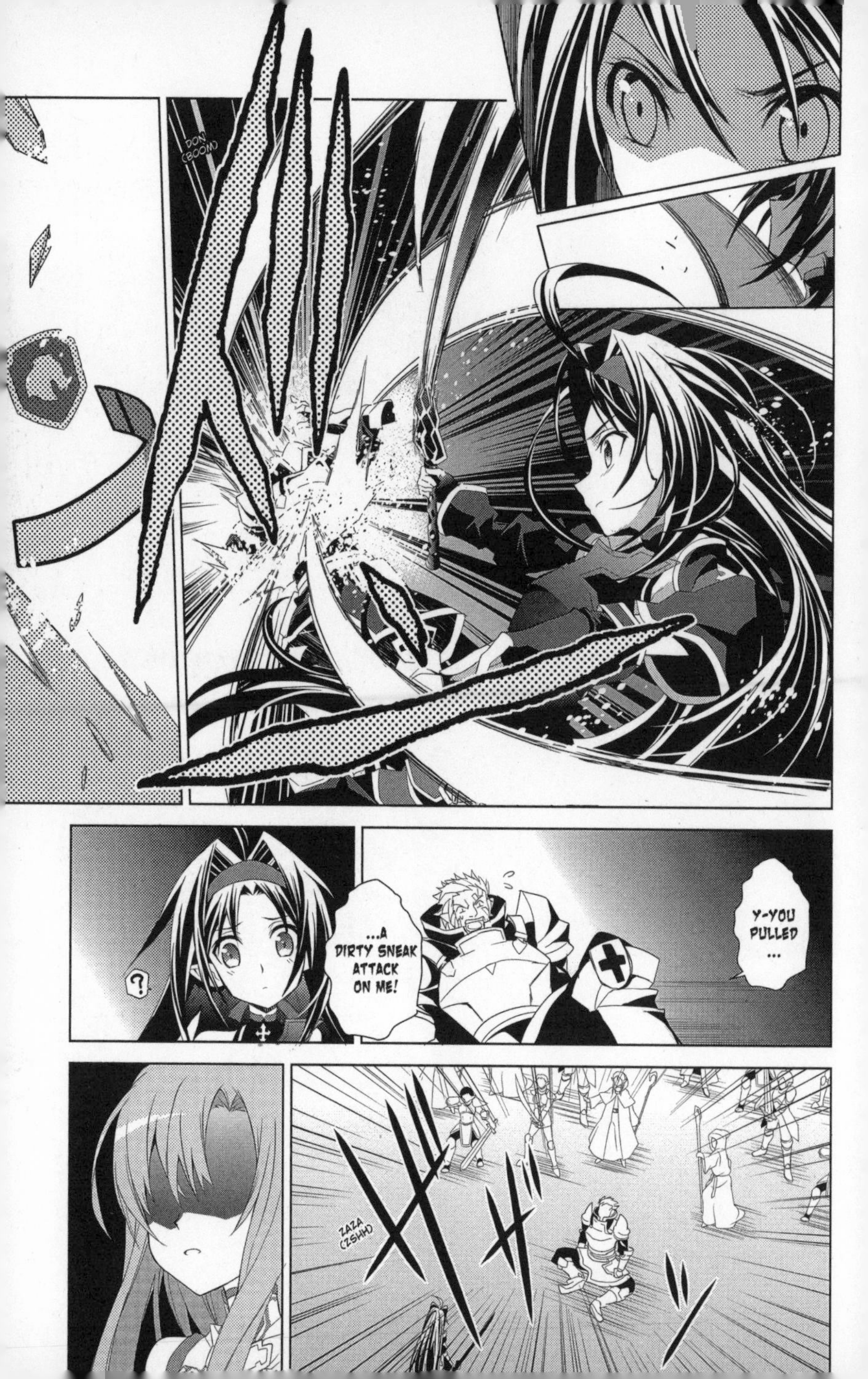
DON (BOOM)
Y-YOU PULLED ...
...A DIRTY SNEAK ATTACK ON ME!
?
ZAZA (ZSHH)

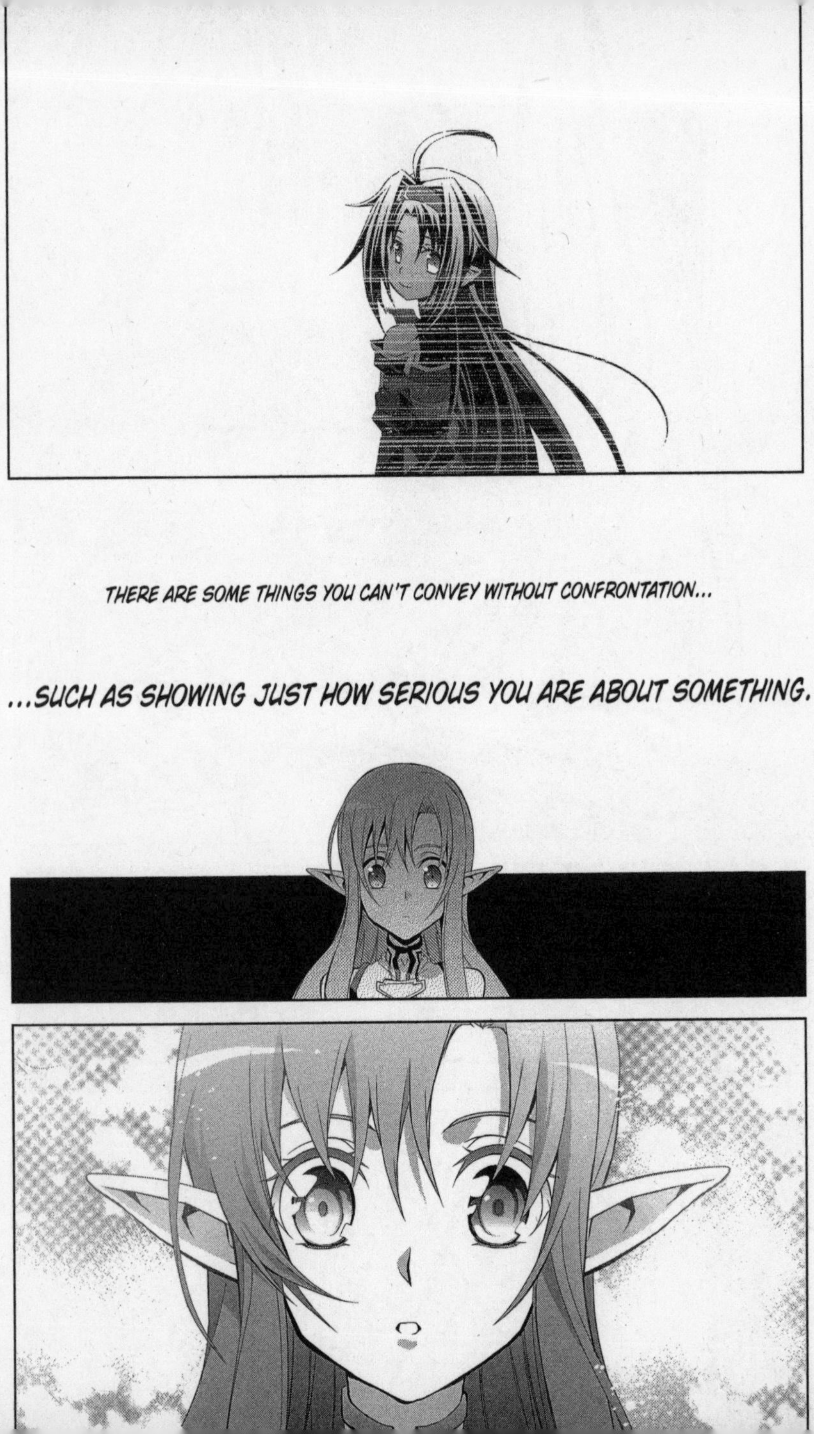
THERE ARE SOME THINGS YOU CAN'T CONVEY WITHOUT CONFRONTATION...
...SUCH AS SHOWING JUST HOW SERIOUS YOU ARE ABOUT SOMETHING.

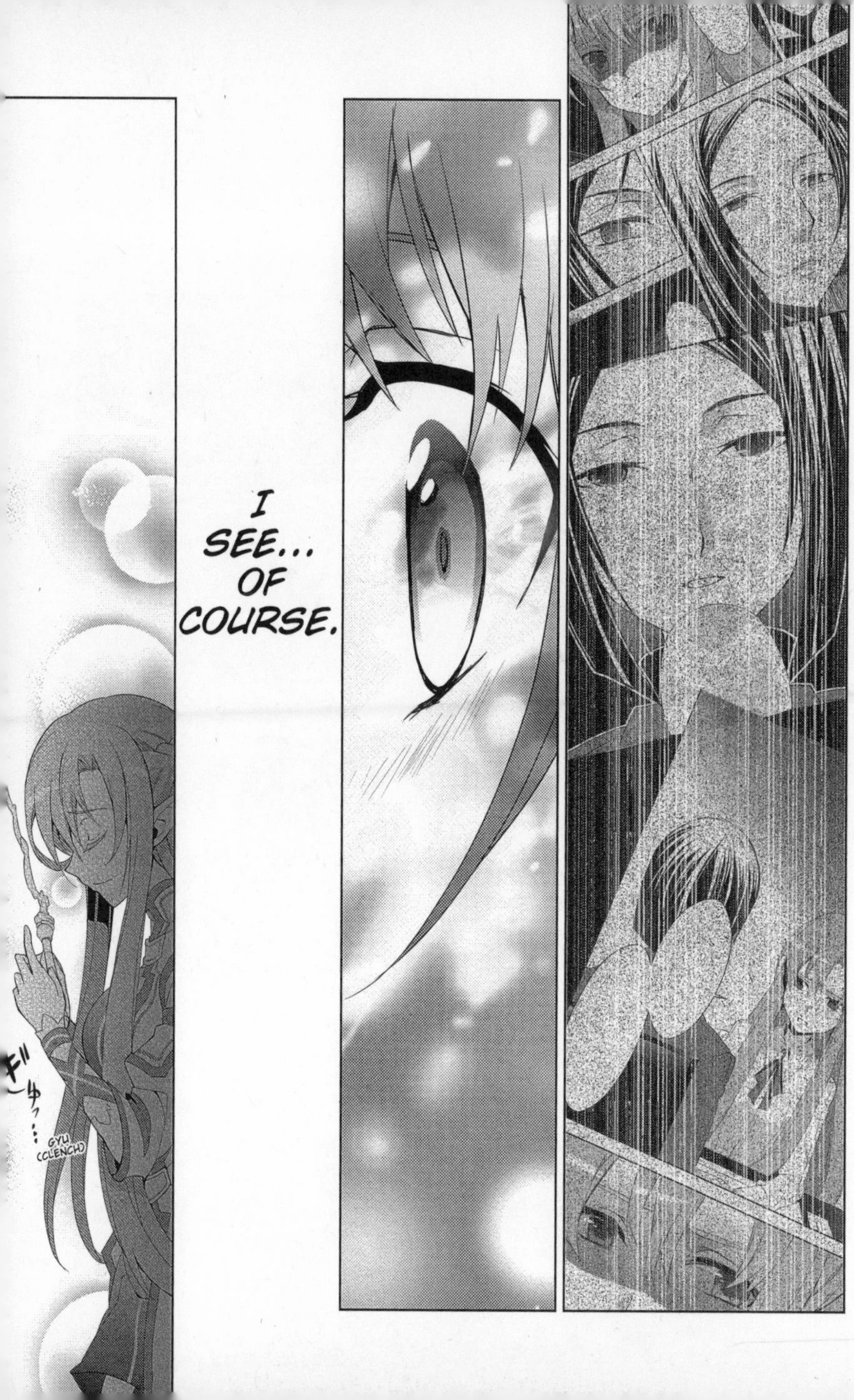
I SEE... OF COURSE.
GYU (CLENCH)

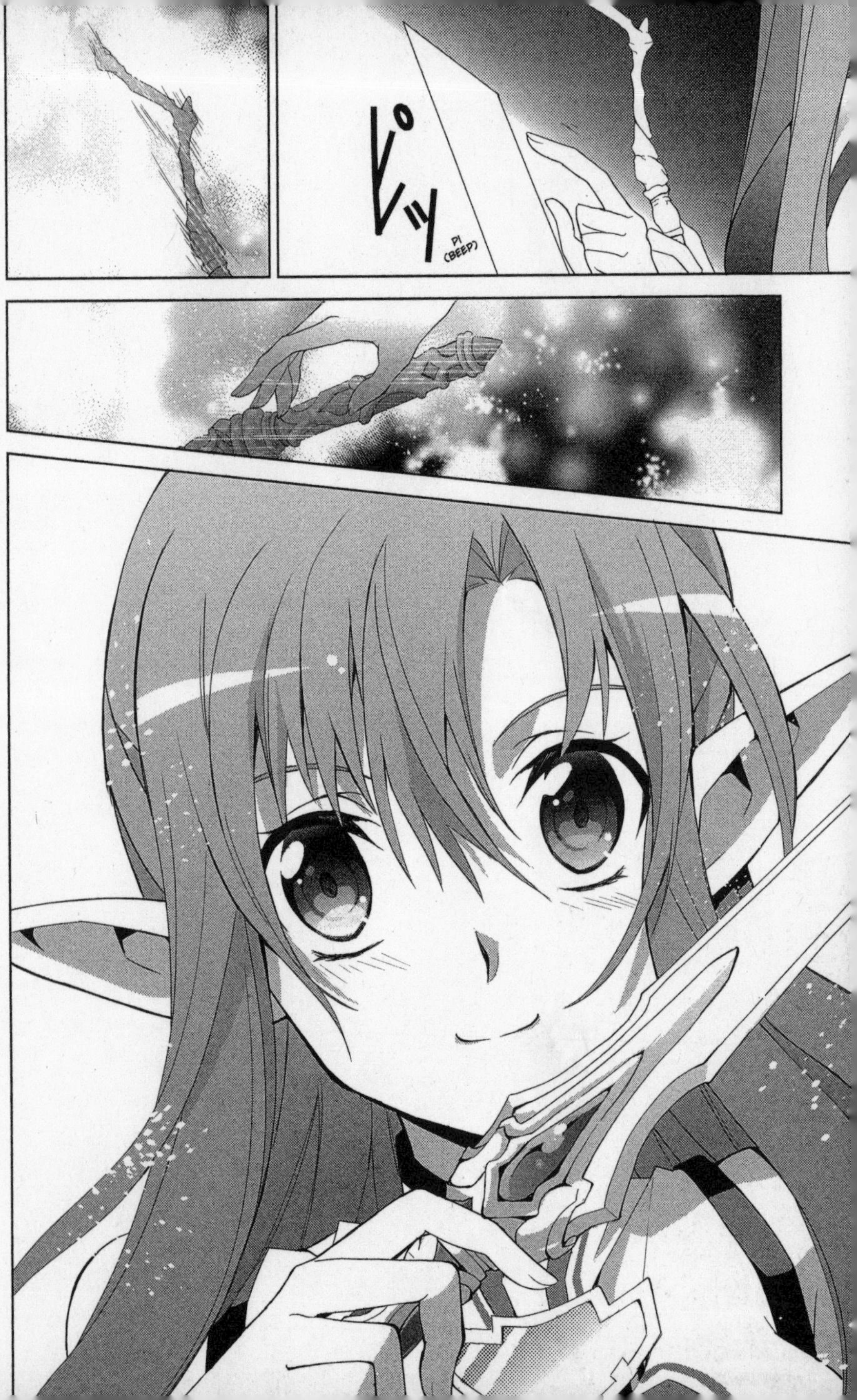
ピピッ
PI
(BEEP)

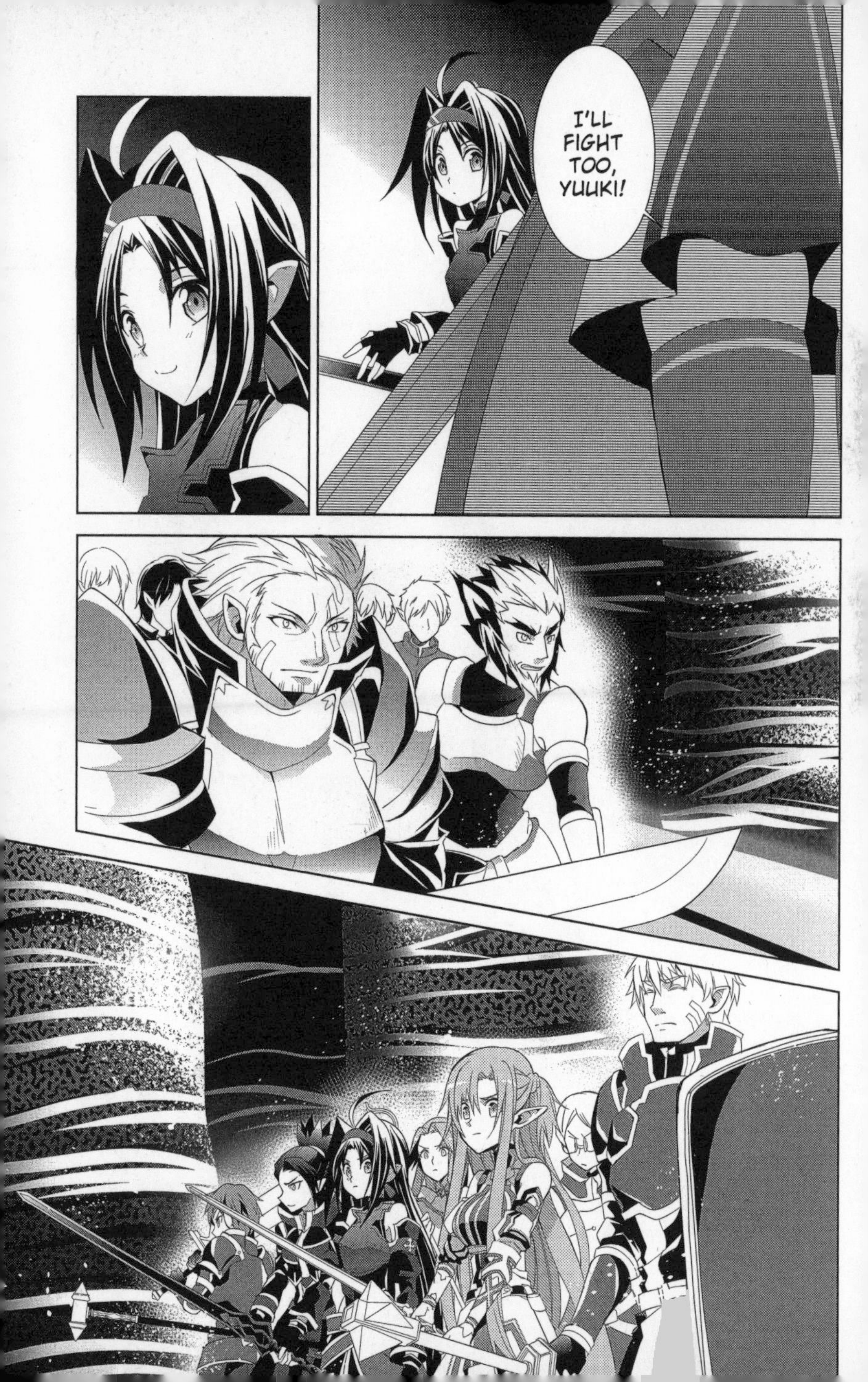
I'LL FIGHT TOO, YUUKI!

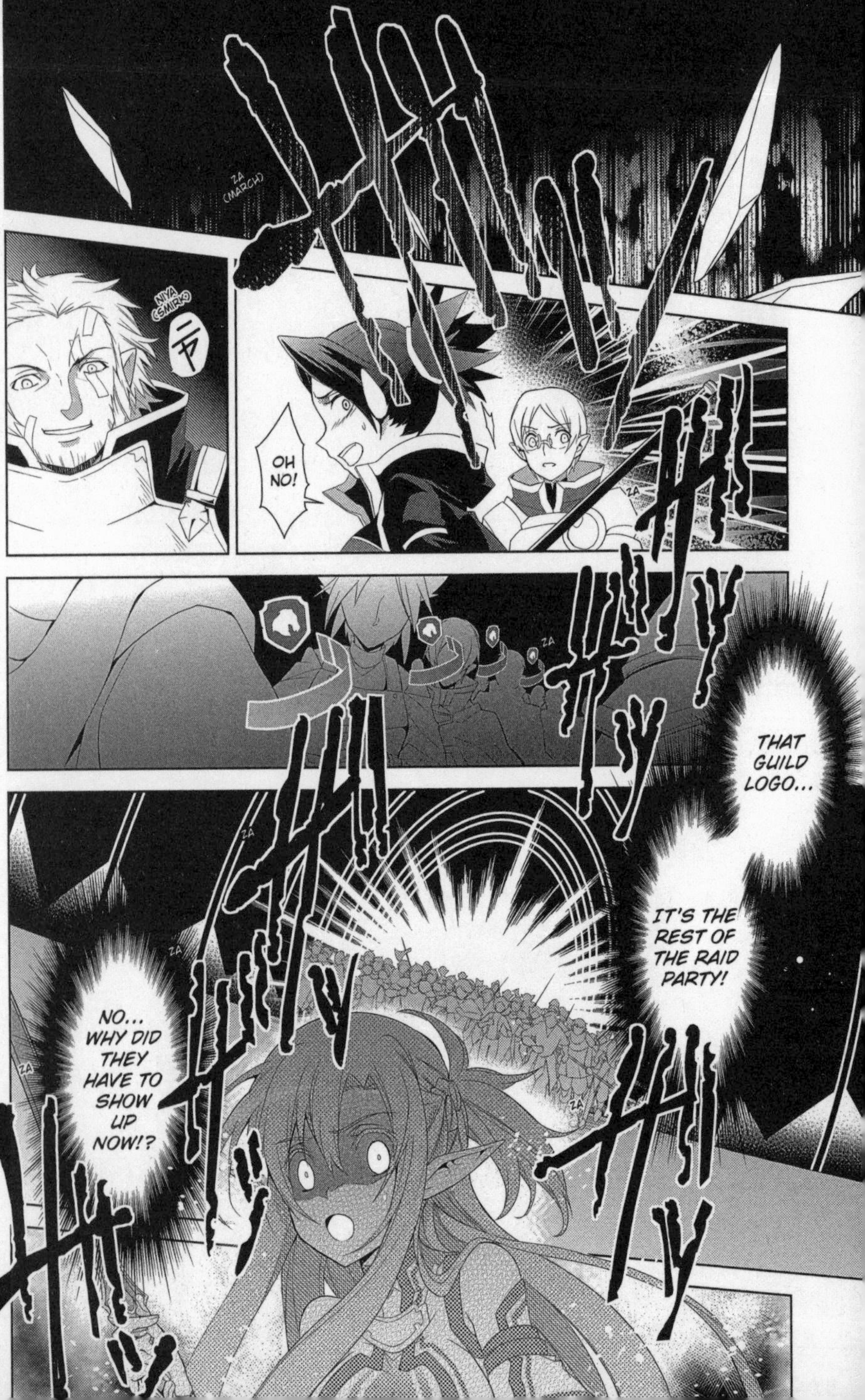
ZA (MARCH)
NIYA (SMIRK)
ニヤ
OH NO!
ZA
ZA
THAT GUILD LOGO...
IT'S THE REST OF THE RAID PARTY!
ZA
ZA
NO... WHY DID THEY HAVE TO SHOW UP NOW!?
ZA
ZA

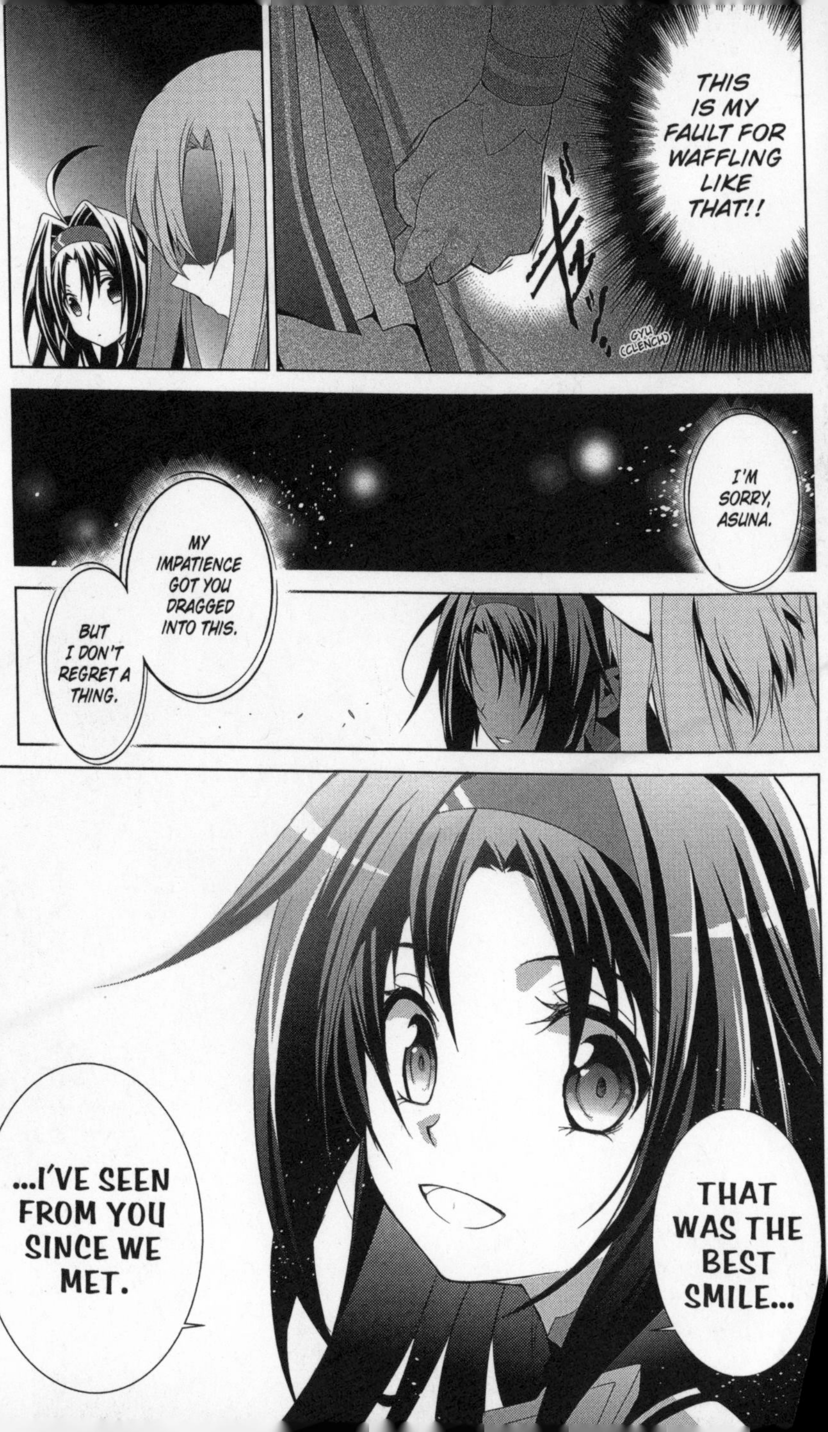
THIS IS MY FAULT FOR WAFFLING LIKE THAT!!
GYU (CLENCH)
I'M SORRY, ASUNA.
MY IMPATIENCE GOT YOU DRAGGED INTO THIS.
BUT I DON'T REGRET A THING.
THAT WAS THE BEST SMILE...
...I'VE SEEN FROM YOU SINCE WE MET.

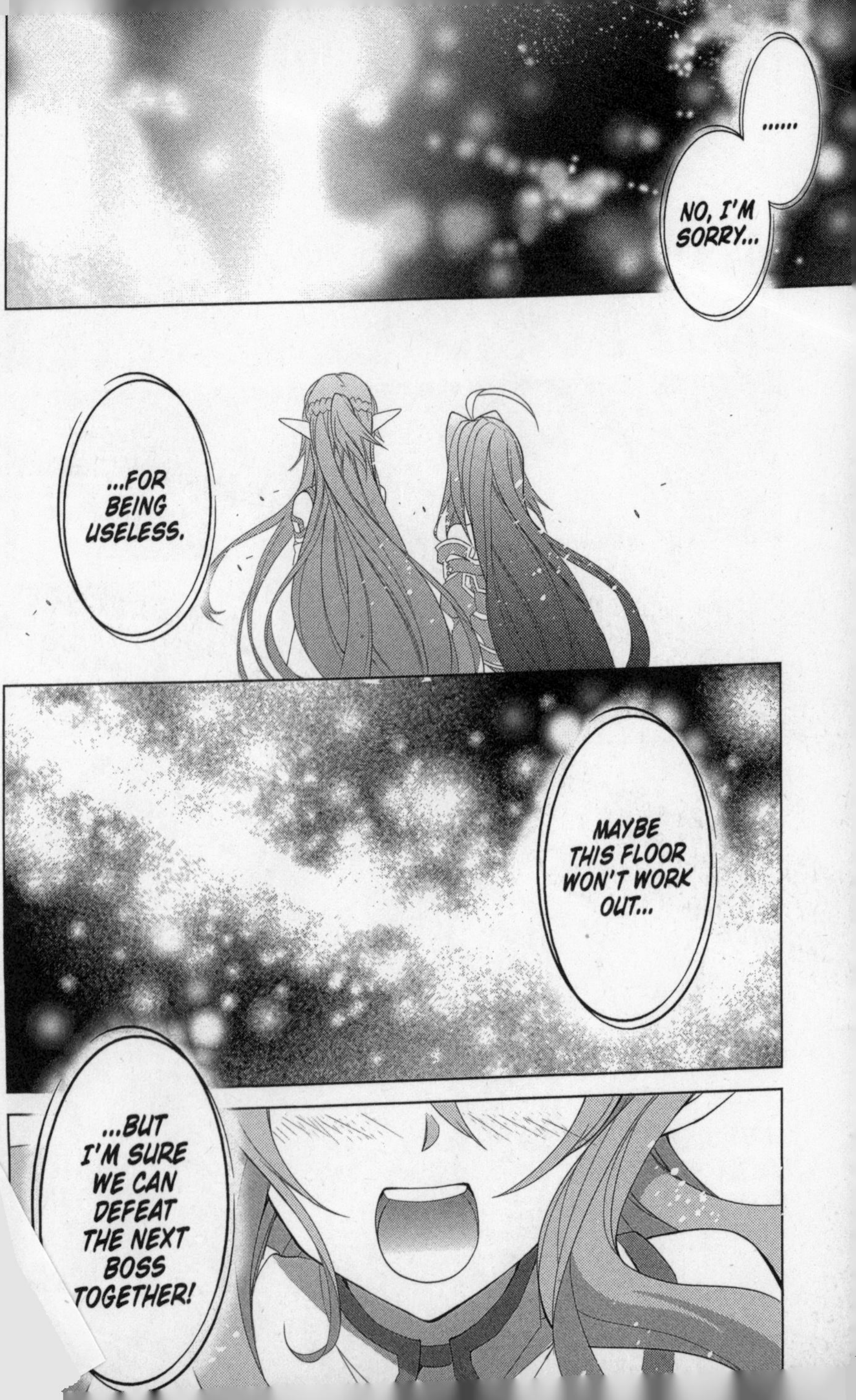
......
NO, I'M SORRY...
...FOR BEING USELESS.
MAYBE THIS FLOOR WON'T WORK OUT...
...BUT I'M SURE WE CAN DEFEAT THE NEXT BOSS TOGETHER!

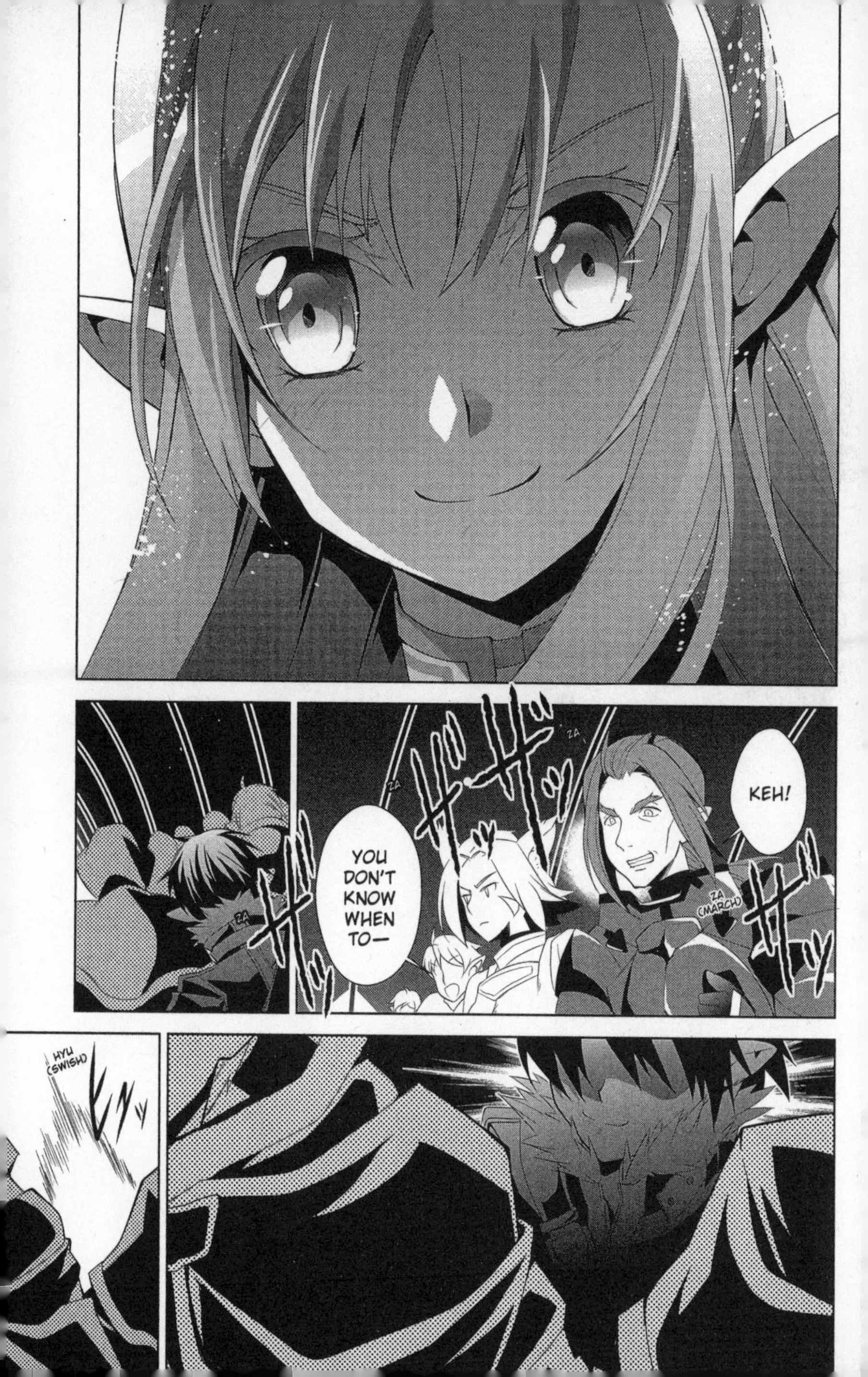
KEH!
ZA
ZA (MARCH)
ZA
YOU DON'T KNOW WHEN TO—
ZA
HYU (SWISH)

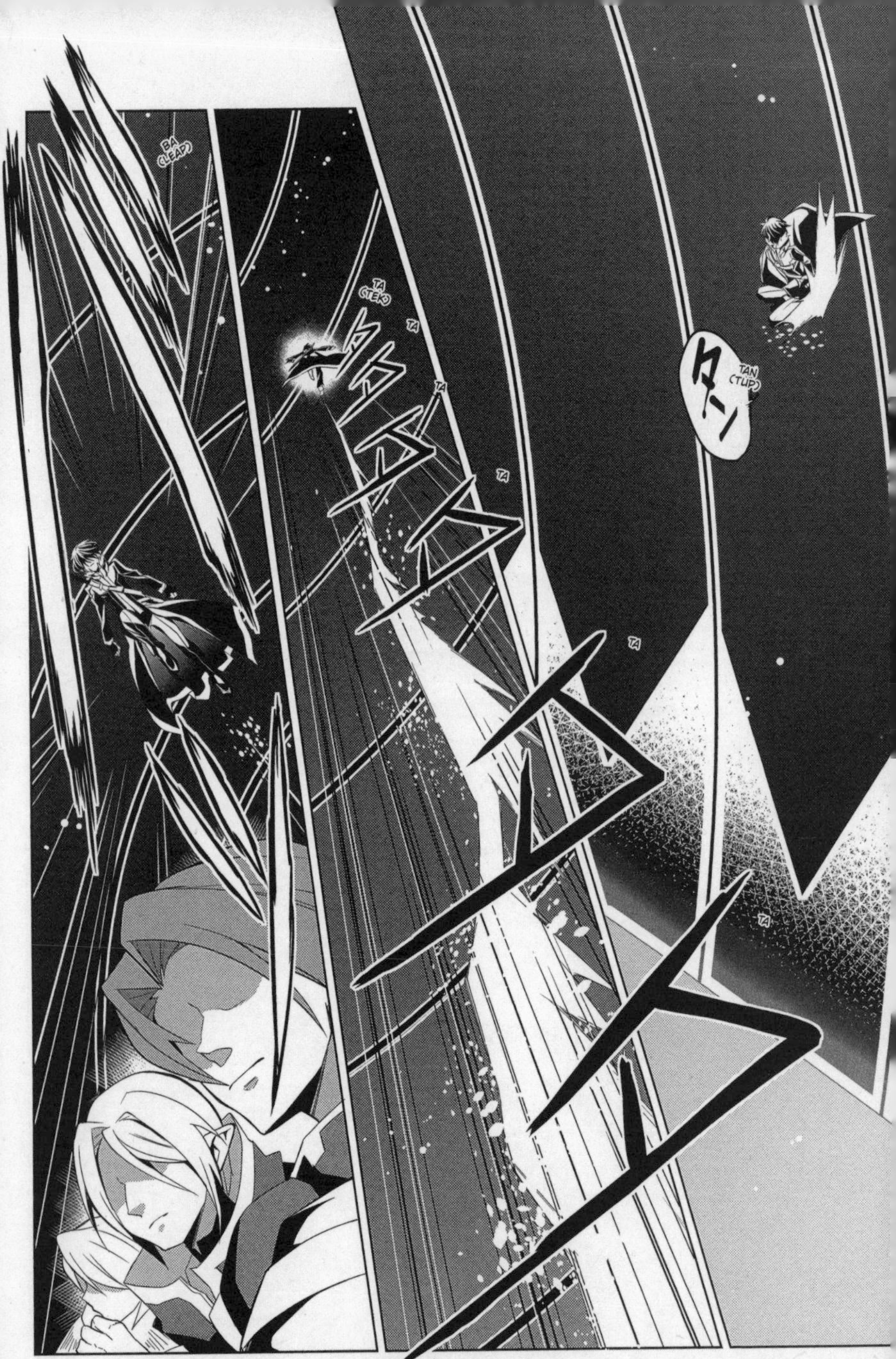
TAN
(TUP)
TA
TA
TA
(TEK)
TA
TA
TA
BA
(LEAP)

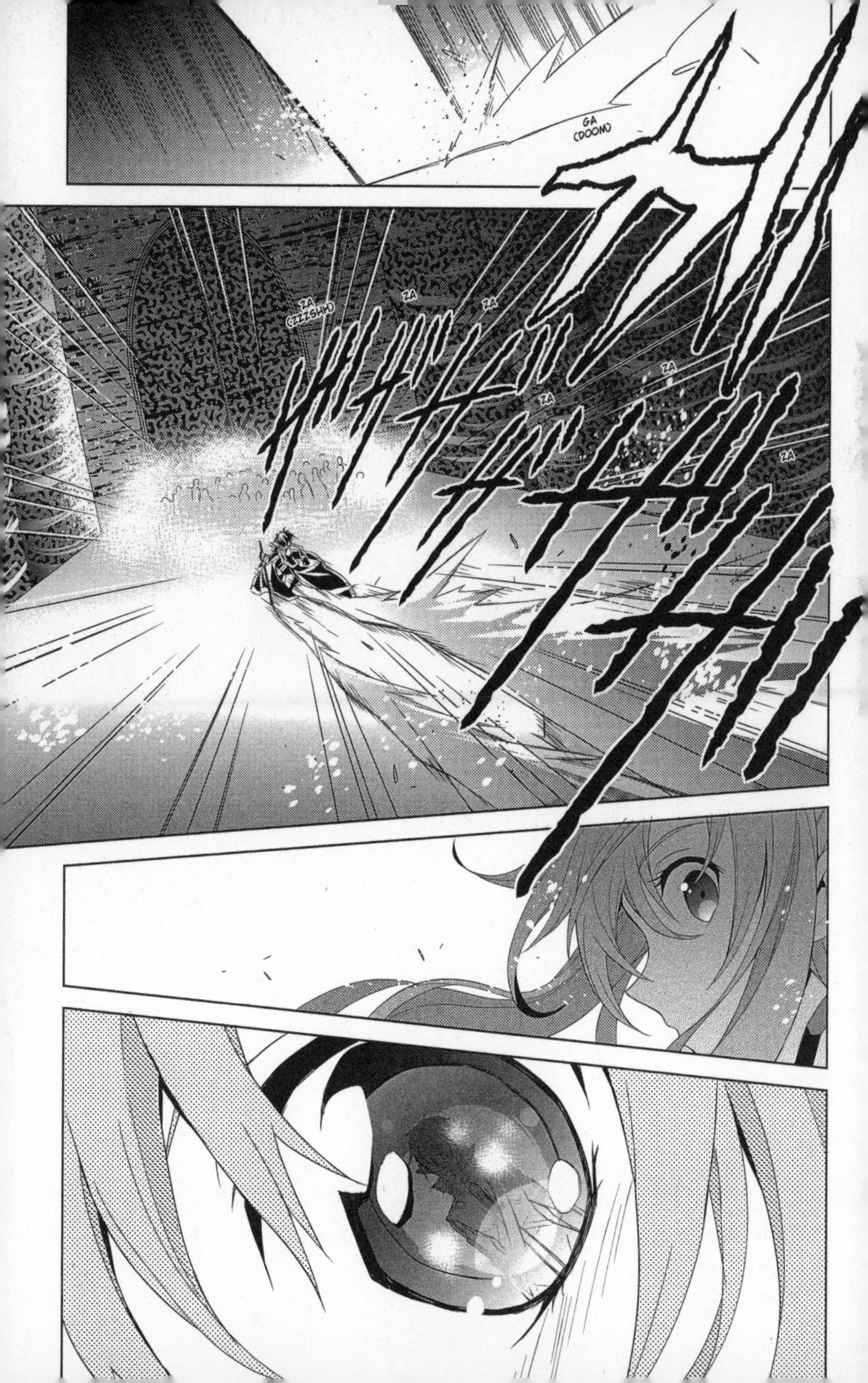
GA (DOOM)
ZA (ZZZSHH)
ZA
ZA
ZA
ZA
ZA

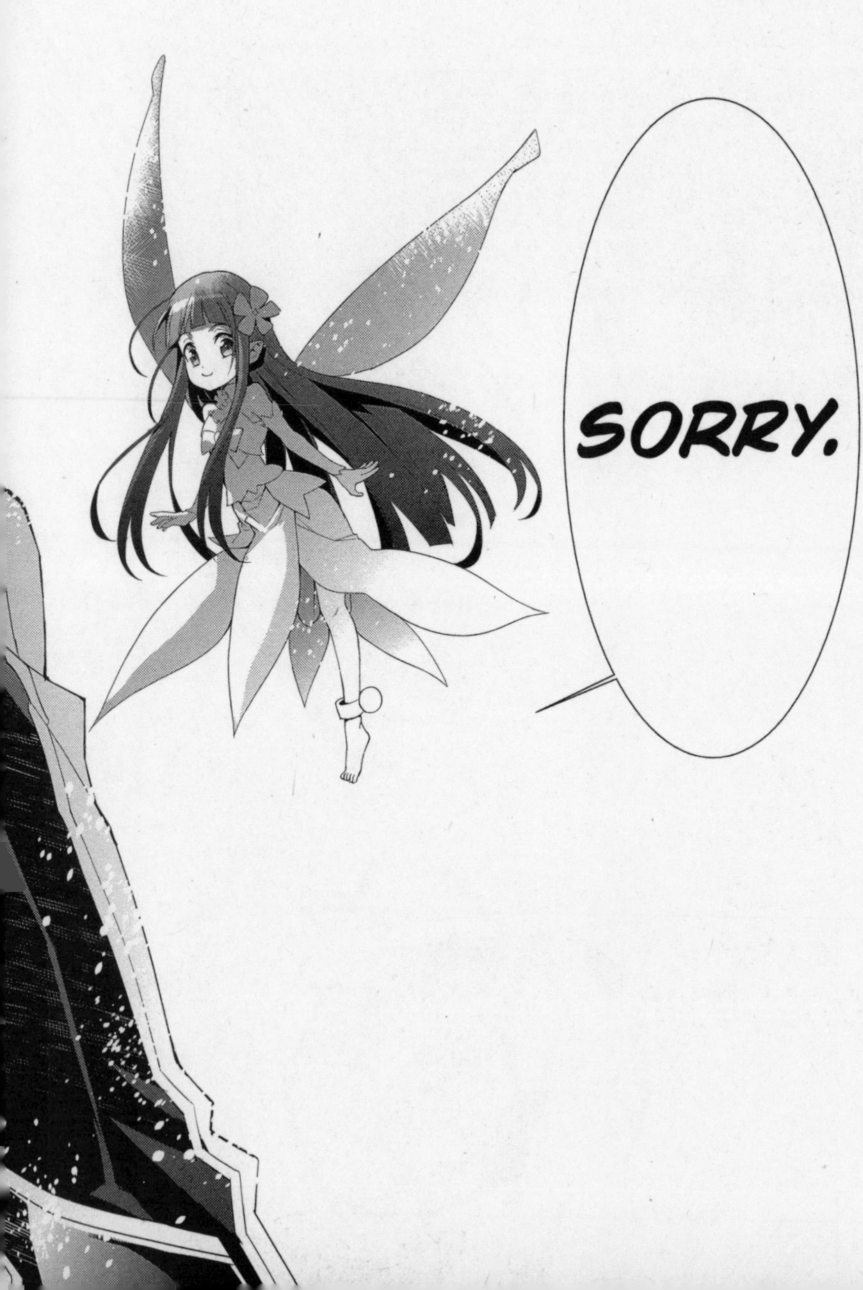
SORRY.

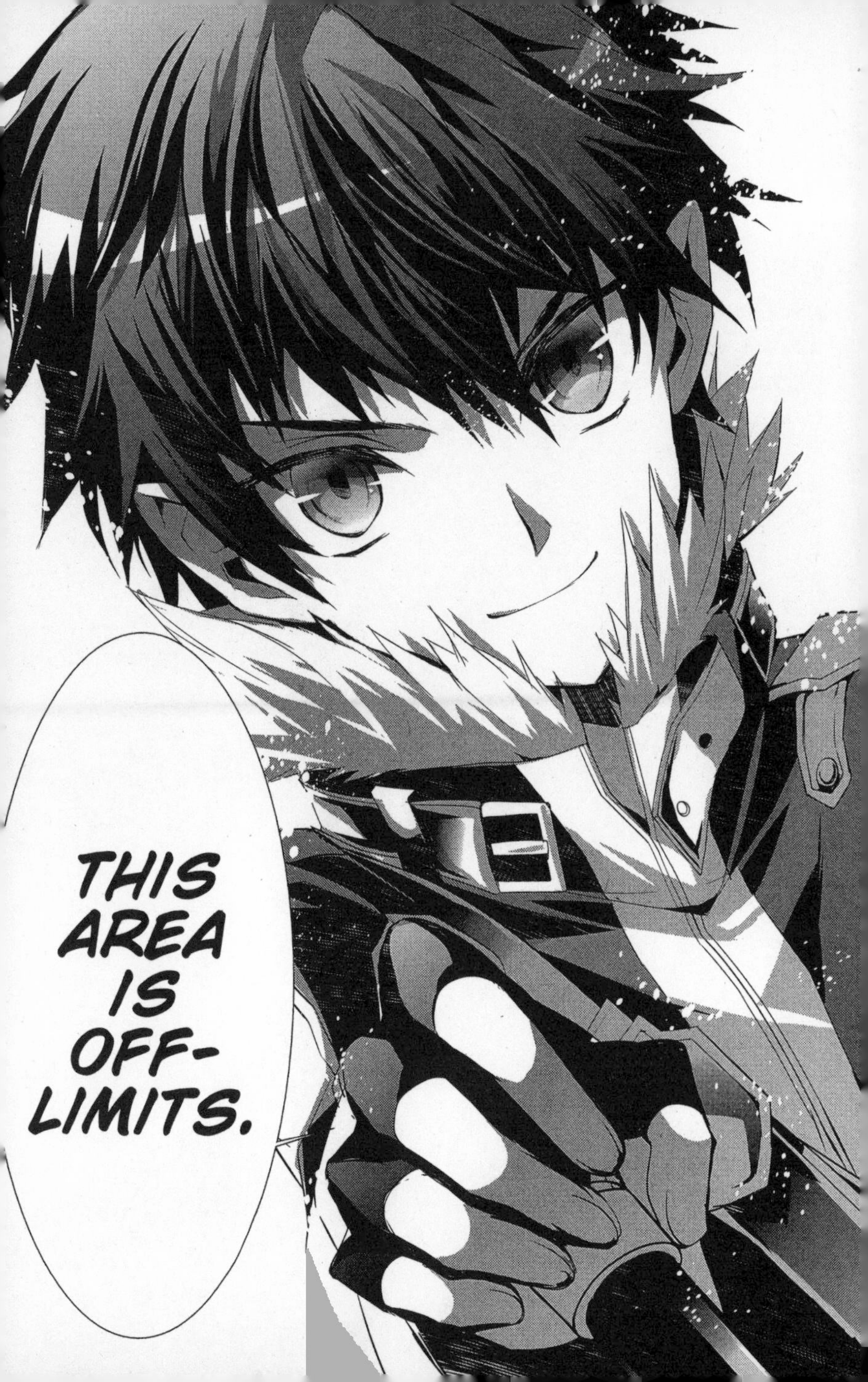
THIS AREA IS OFF-LIMITS.

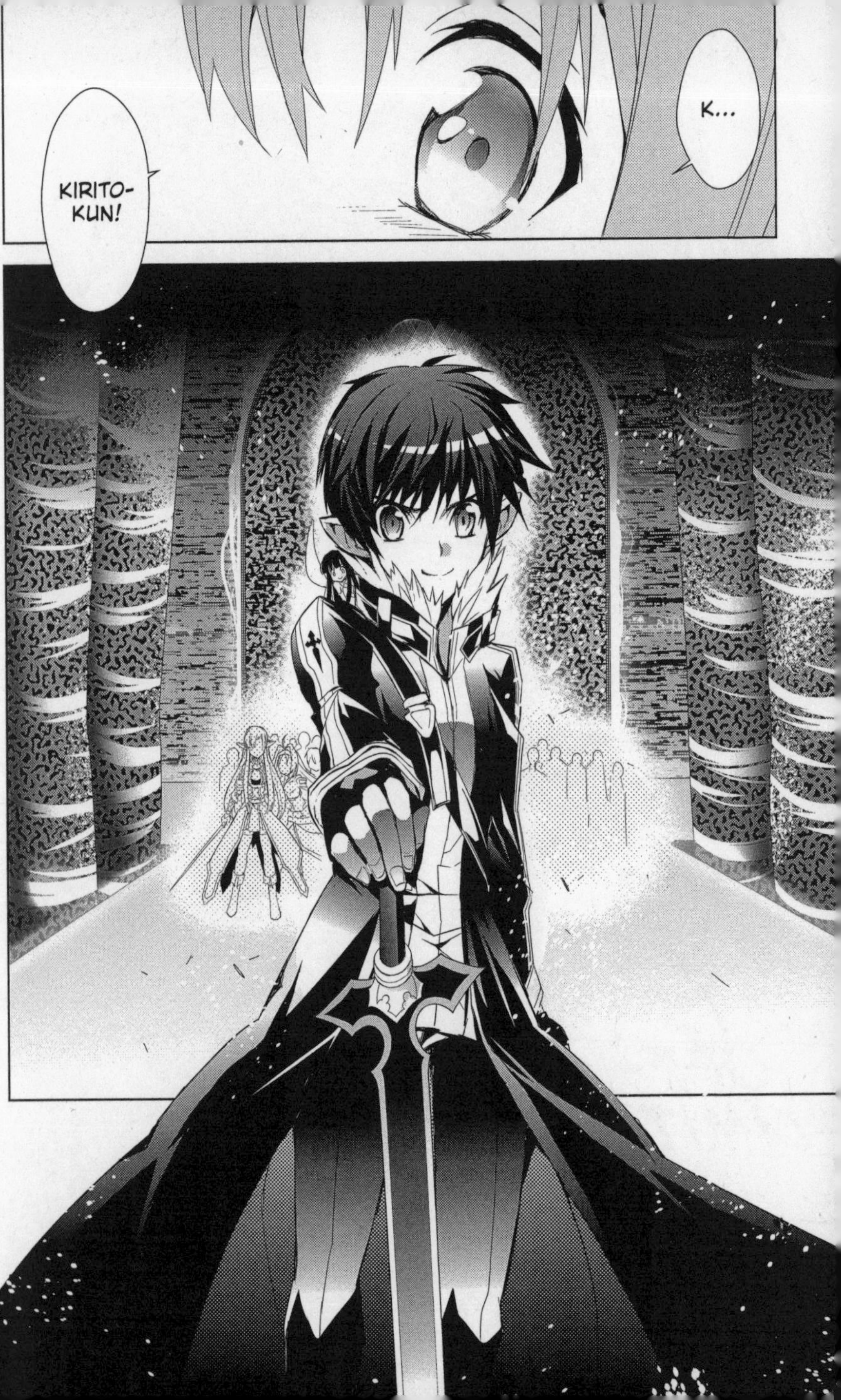
K...
KIRITO-KUN!

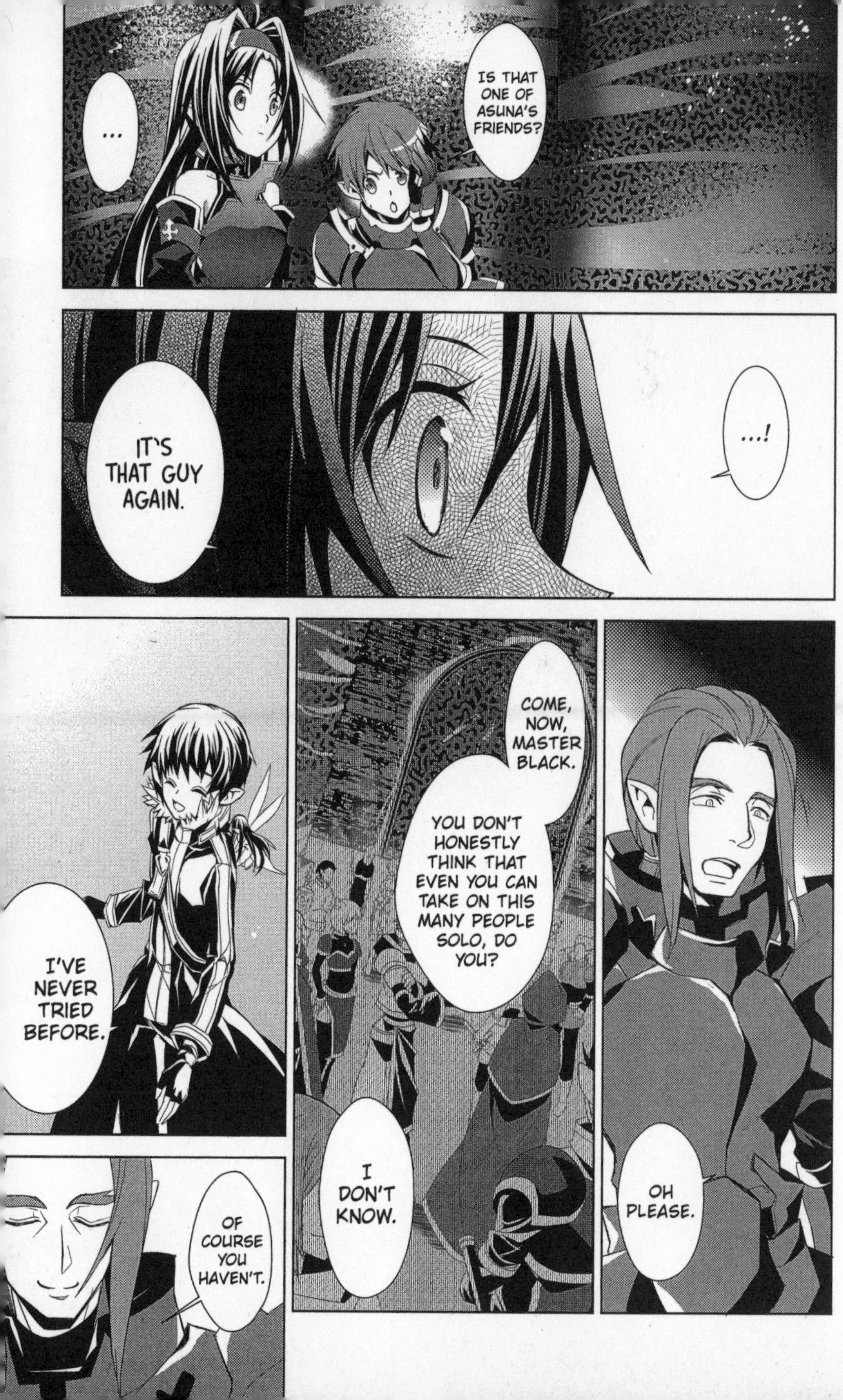
IS THAT ONE OF ASUNA'S FRIENDS?
...
...!
IT'S THAT GUY AGAIN.
COME, NOW, MASTER BLACK.
YOU DON'T HONESTLY THINK THAT EVEN YOU CAN TAKE ON THIS MANY PEOPLE SOLO, DO YOU?
I DON'T KNOW.
I'VE NEVER TRIED BEFORE.
OH PLEASE.
OF COURSE YOU HAVEN'T.

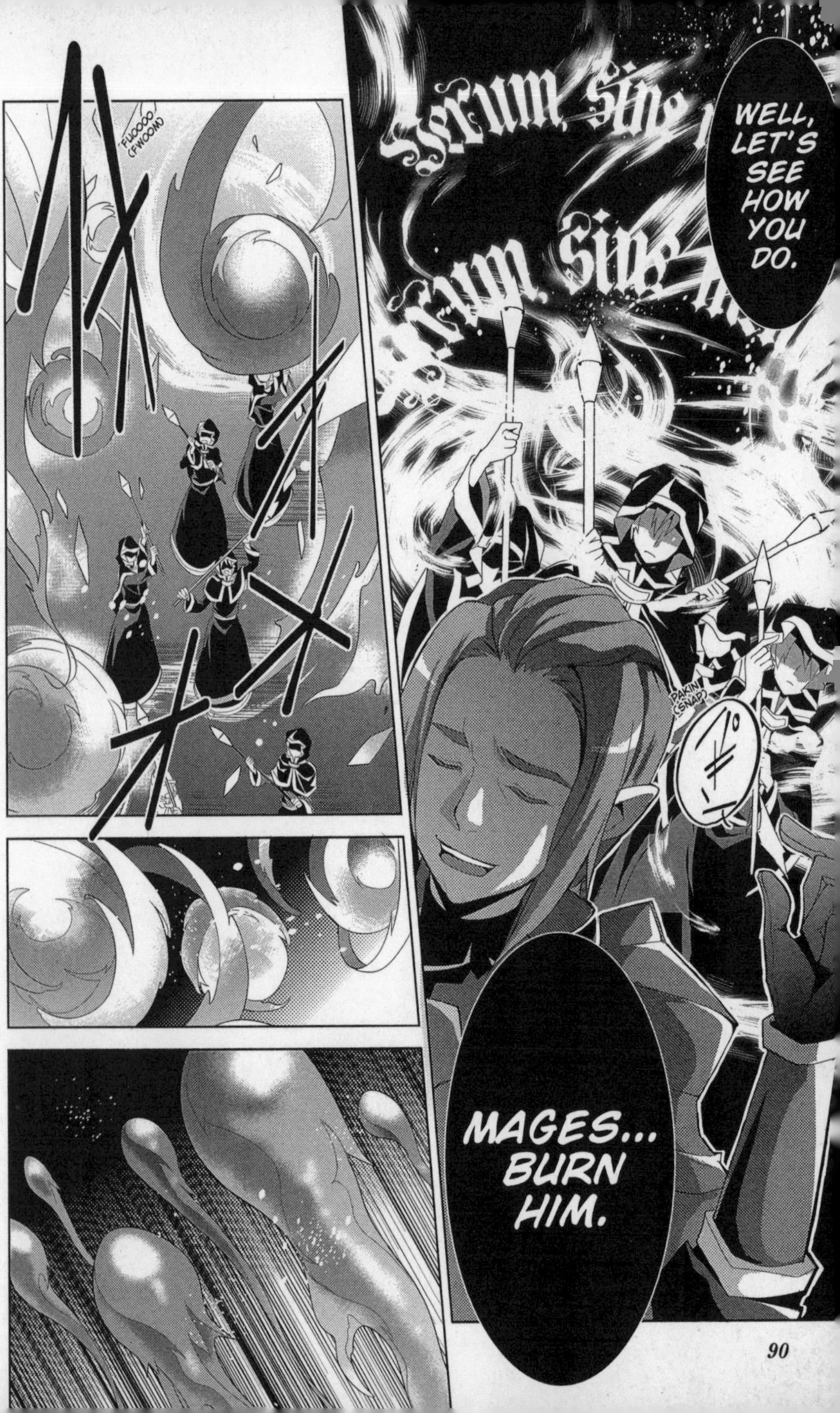
WELL, LET'S SEE HOW YOU DO.
PAKIN (SNAP)
MAGES... BURN HIM.
FUOOOO (FWOOM)

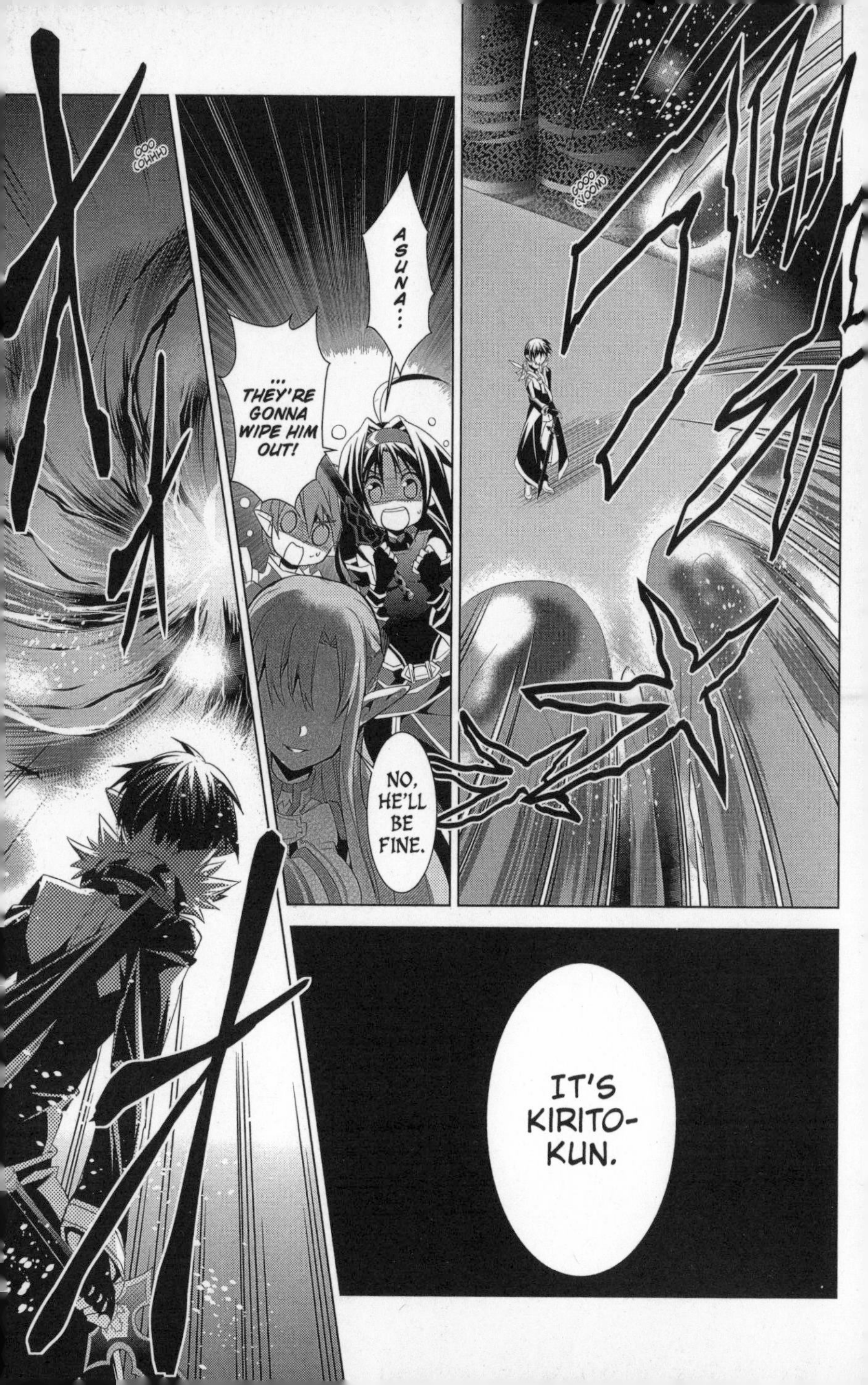
GOOO (VOOM)
ASUNA...!
...THEY'RE GONNA WIPE HIM OUT!
NO, HE'LL BE FINE.
OOO (OHHH)
IT'S KIRITO-KUN.

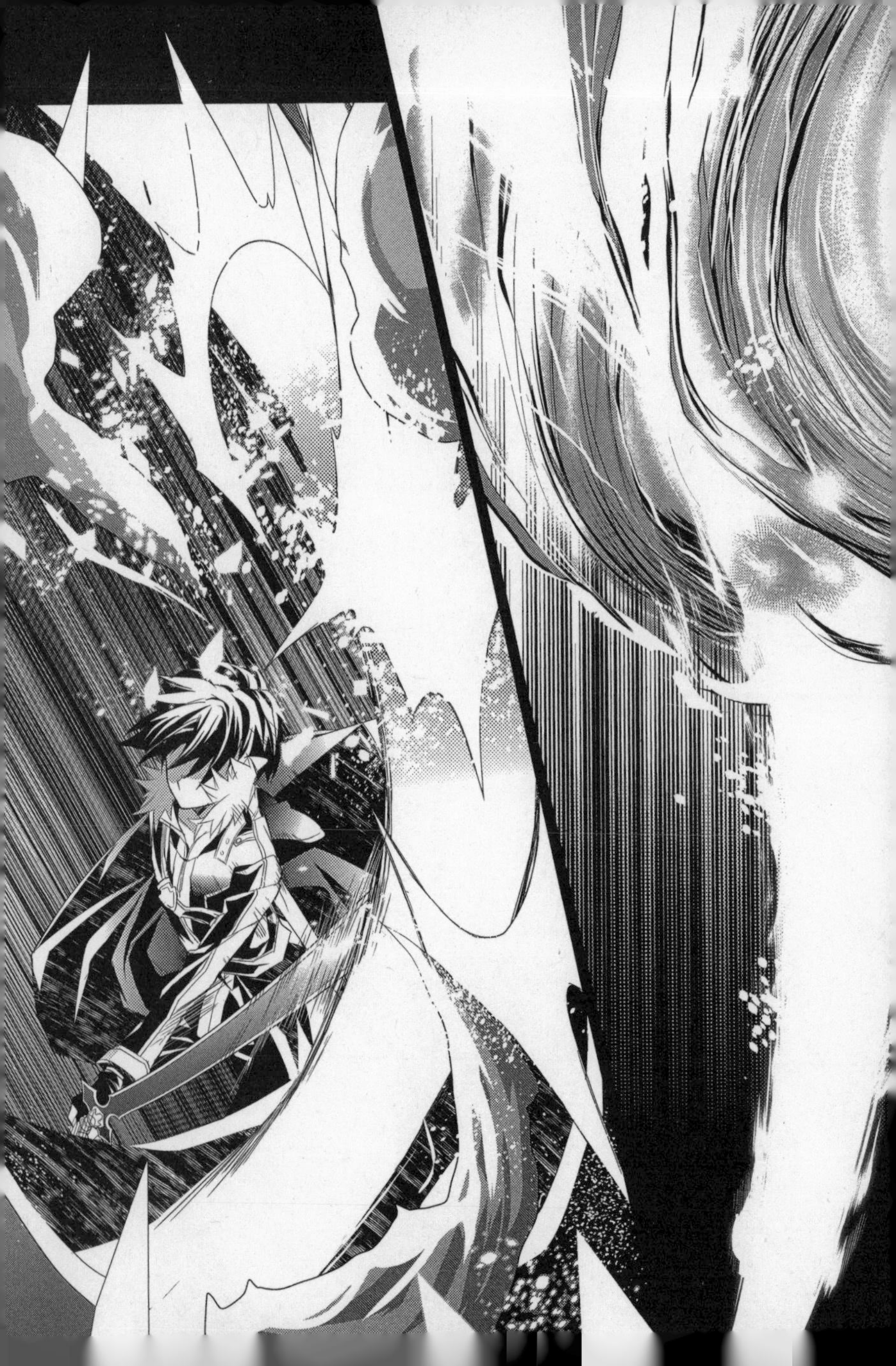

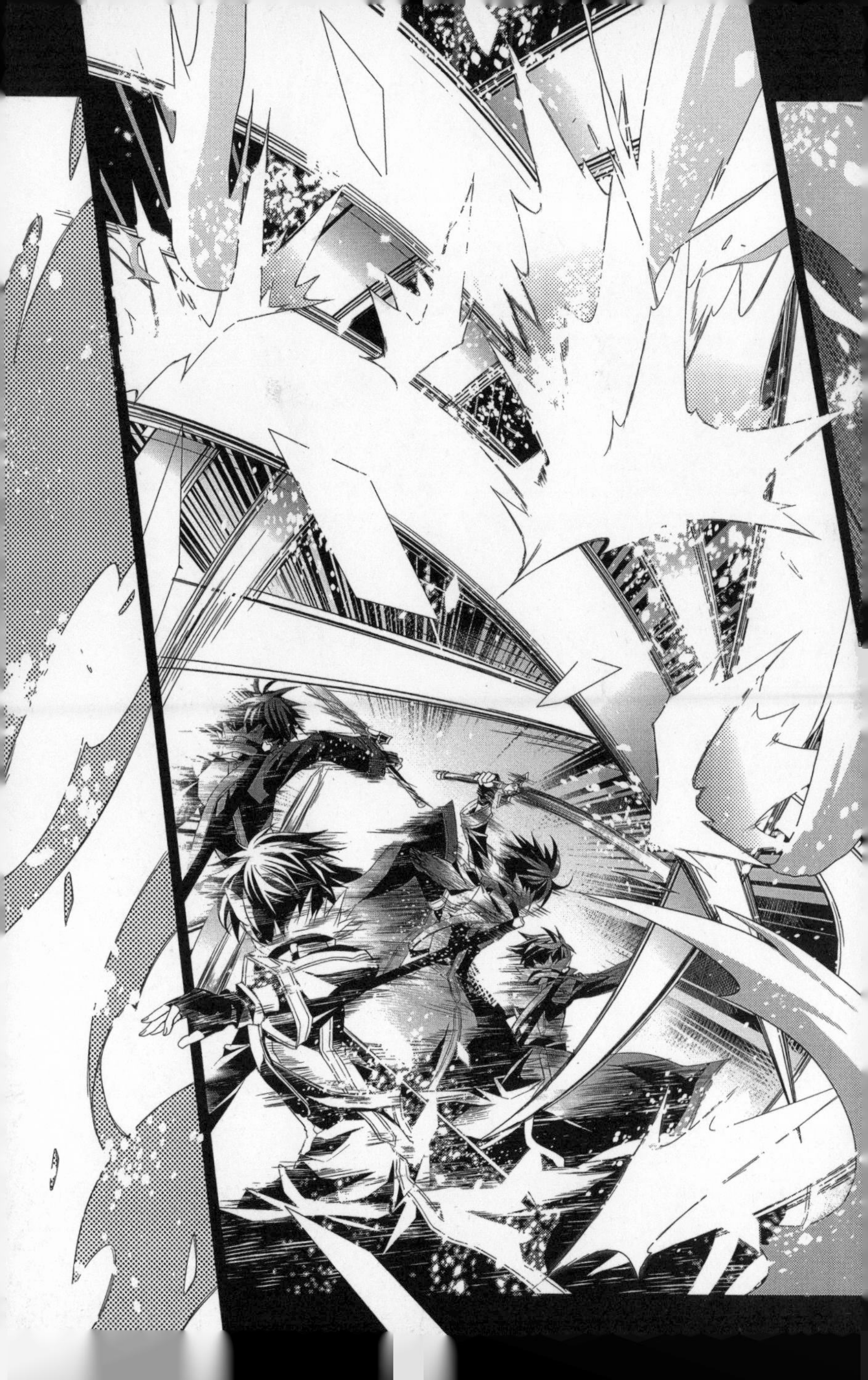

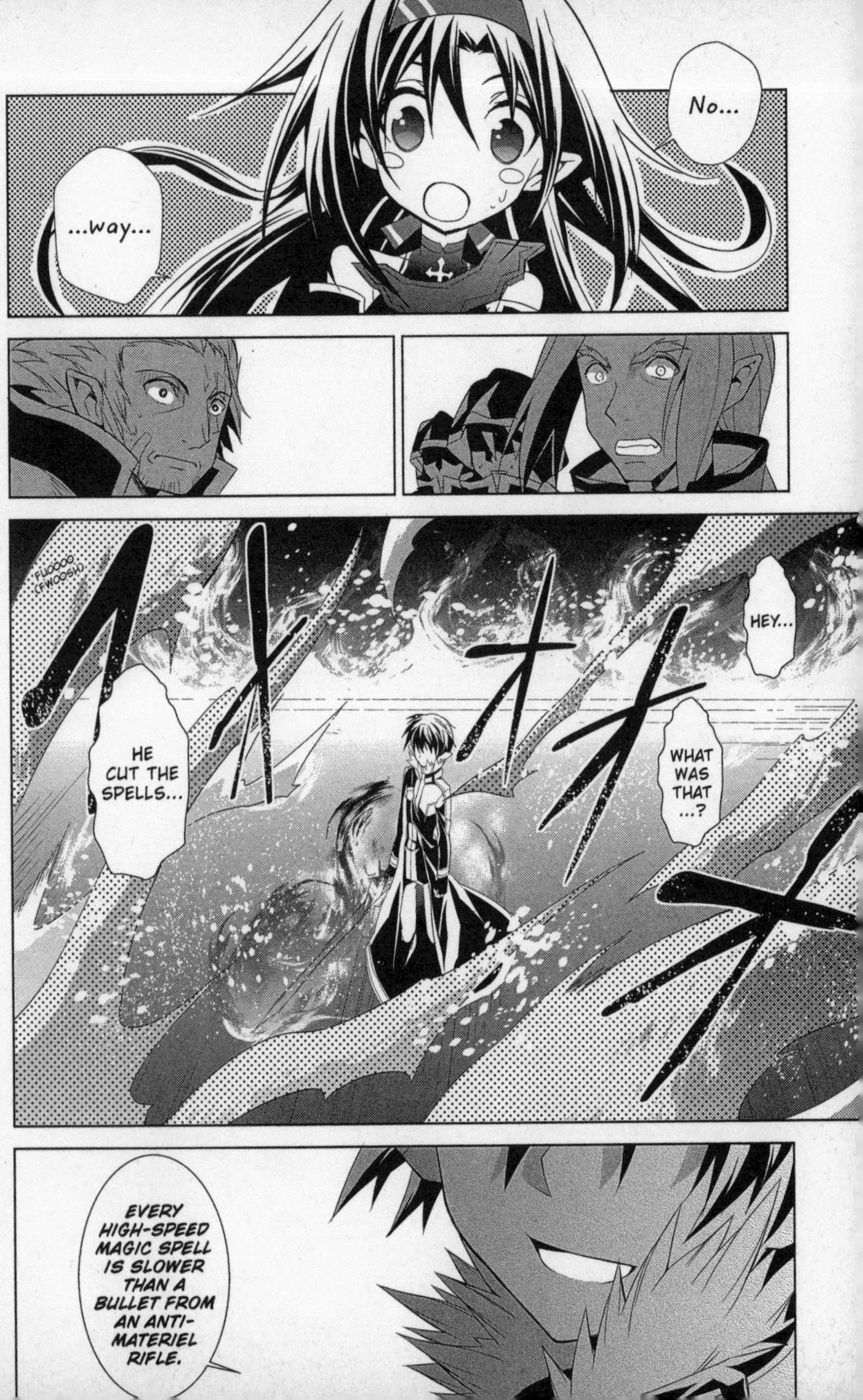
No...
...way...
HEY...
WHAT WAS THAT ...?
FUOOOO (FWOOSH)
HE CUT THE SPELLS...
EVERY HIGH-SPEED MAGIC SPELL IS SLOWER THAN A BULLET FROM AN ANTI-MATERIEL RIFLE.

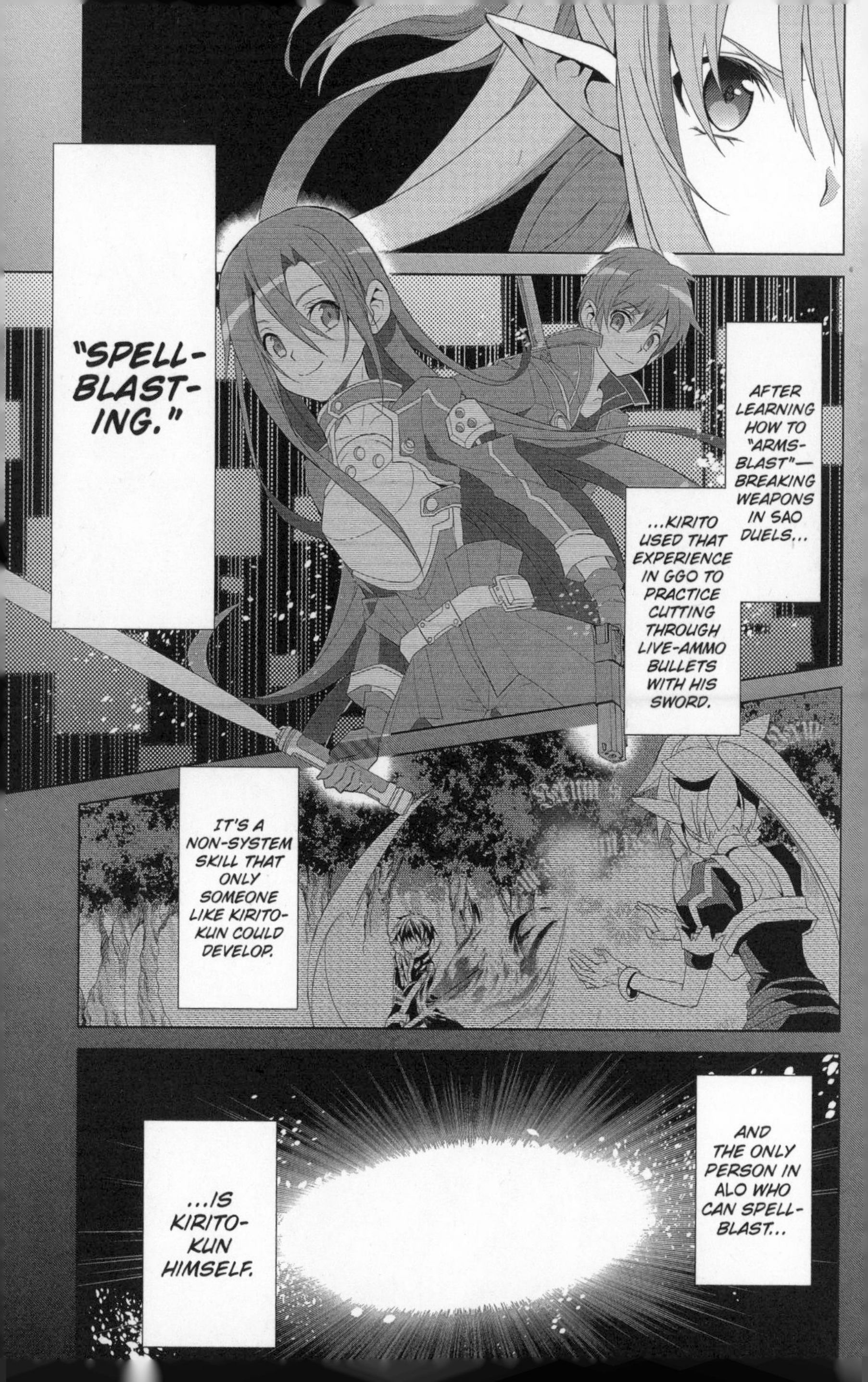
"SPELL-BLASTING."
AFTER LEARNING HOW TO "ARMS-BLAST"—BREAKING WEAPONS IN SAO DUELS...
...KIRITO USED THAT EXPERIENCE IN GGO TO PRACTICE CUTTING THROUGH LIVE-AMMO BULLETS WITH HIS SWORD.
IT'S A NON-SYSTEM SKILL THAT ONLY SOMEONE LIKE KIRITO-KUN COULD DEVELOP.
AND THE ONLY PERSON IN ALO WHO CAN SPELL-BLAST...
...IS KIRITO-KUN HIMSELF.

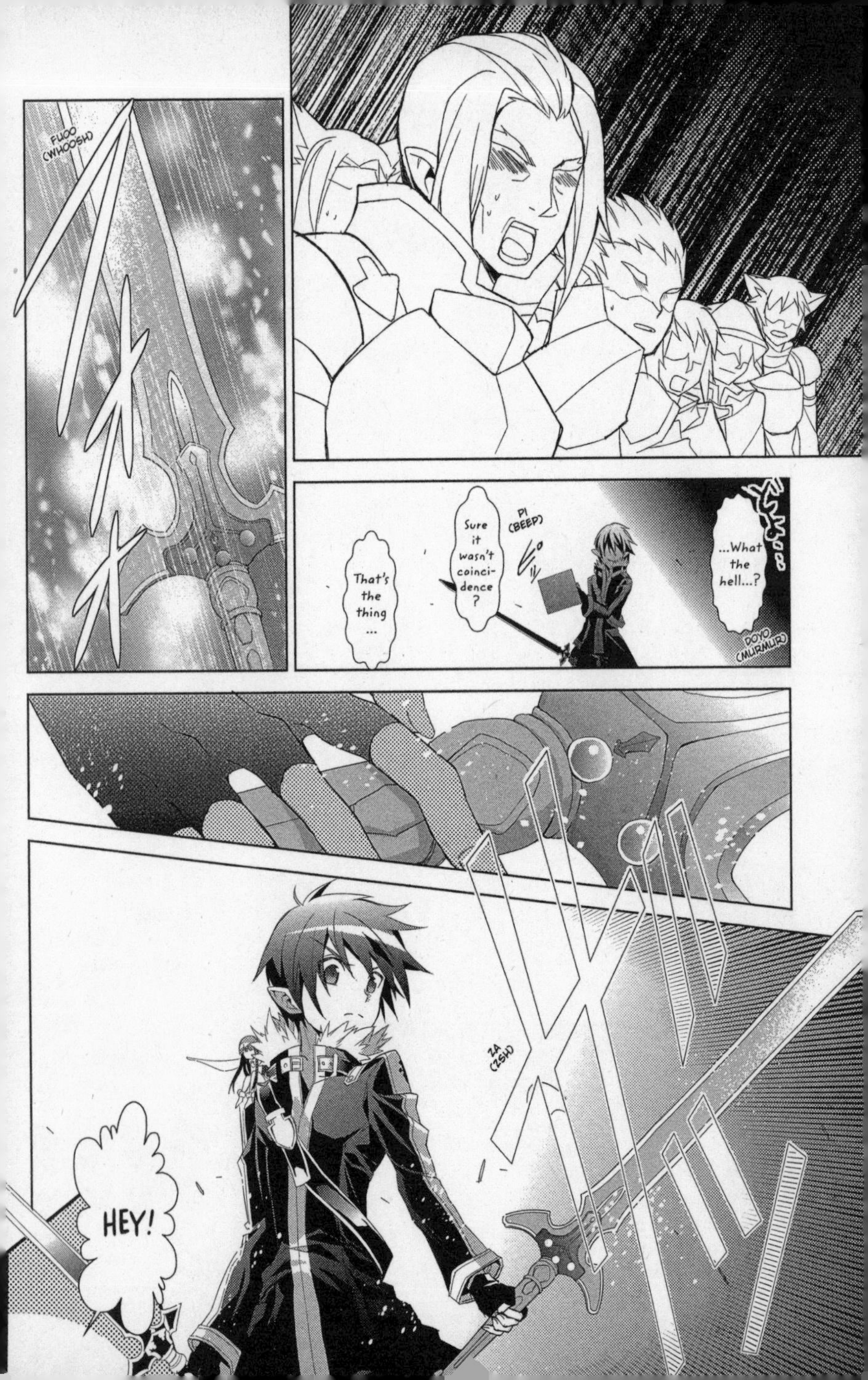
...What the hell...?
DOYO (MURMUR)
PI (BEEP)
Sure it wasn't coinci-dence?
That's the thing...
FUOO (WHOOSH)
ZA (ZSH)
HEY!

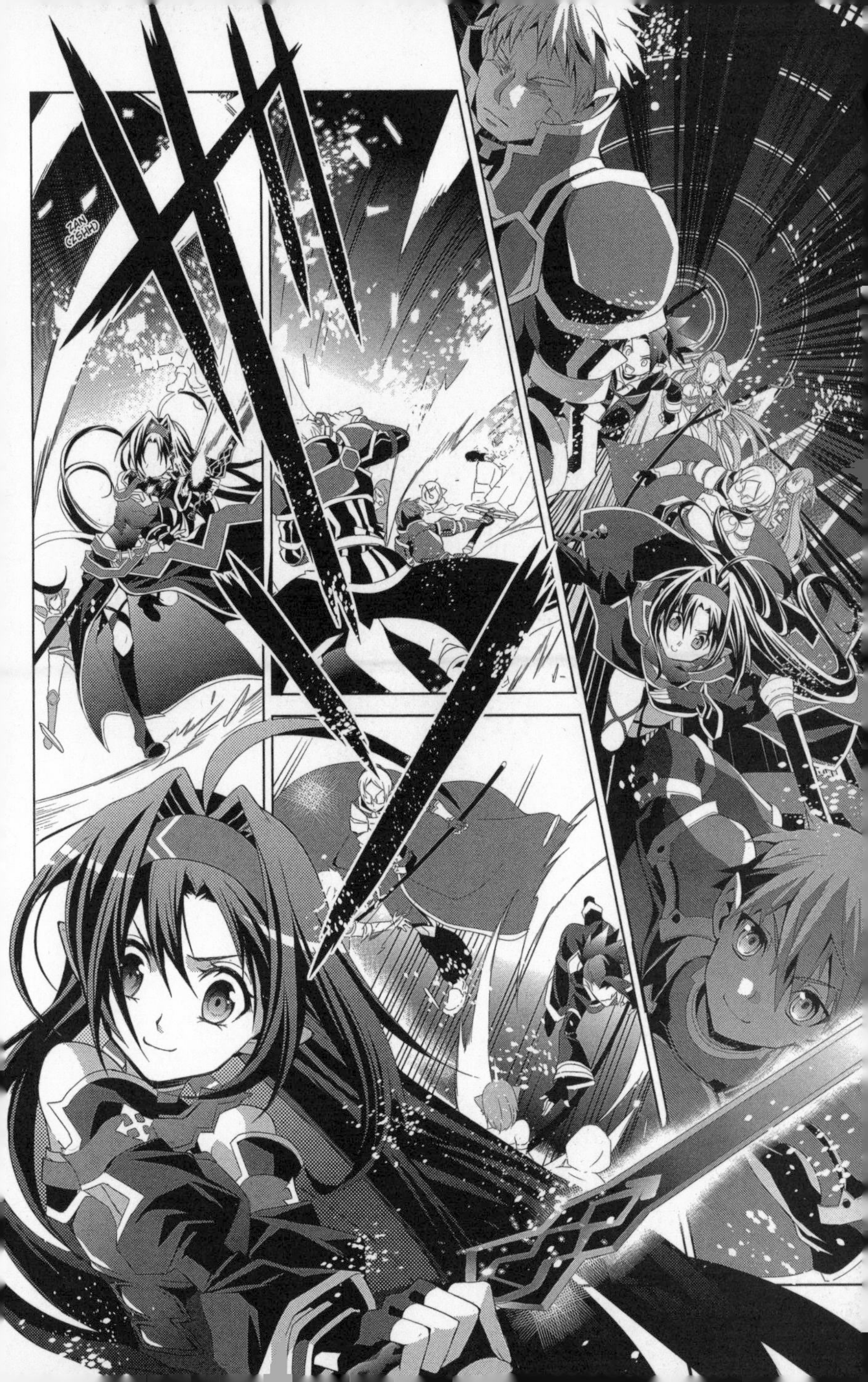
ZAN
(ZSHH)

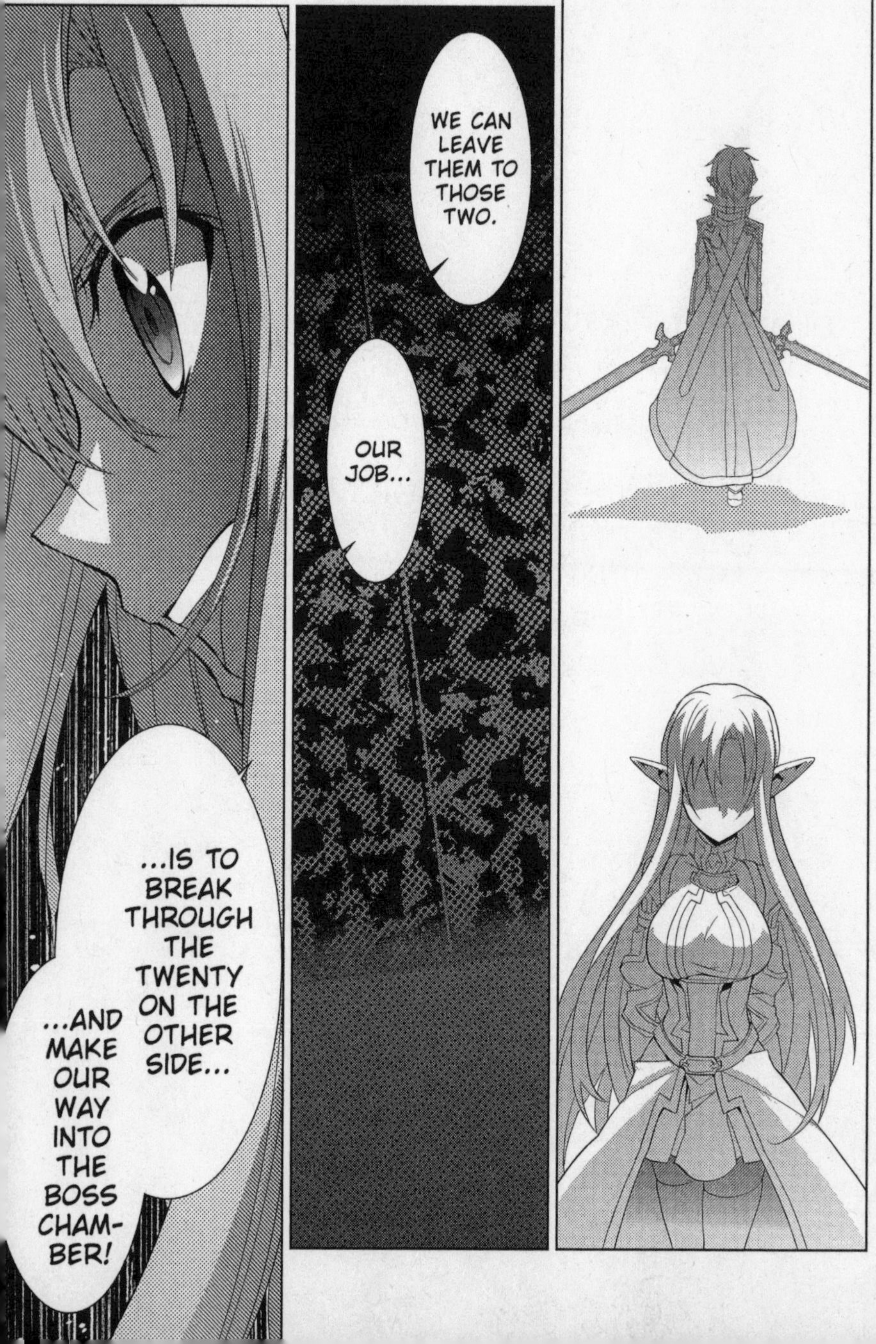
WE CAN LEAVE THEM TO THOSE TWO.
OUR JOB...
...IS TO BREAK THROUGH THE TWENTY ON THE OTHER SIDE...
...AND MAKE OUR WAY INTO THE BOSS CHAMBER!

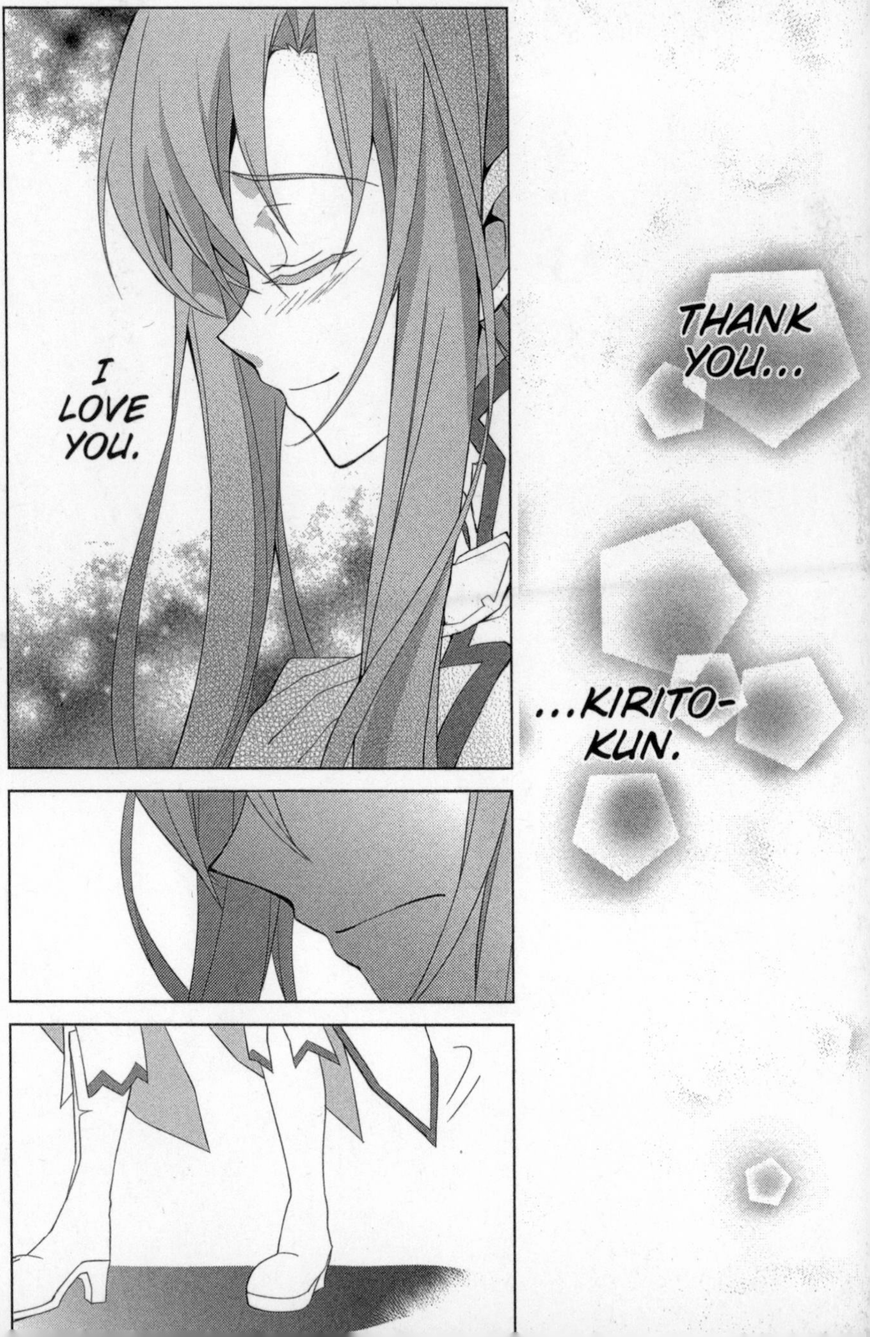
THANK YOU...
...KIRITO-KUN.
I LOVE YOU.

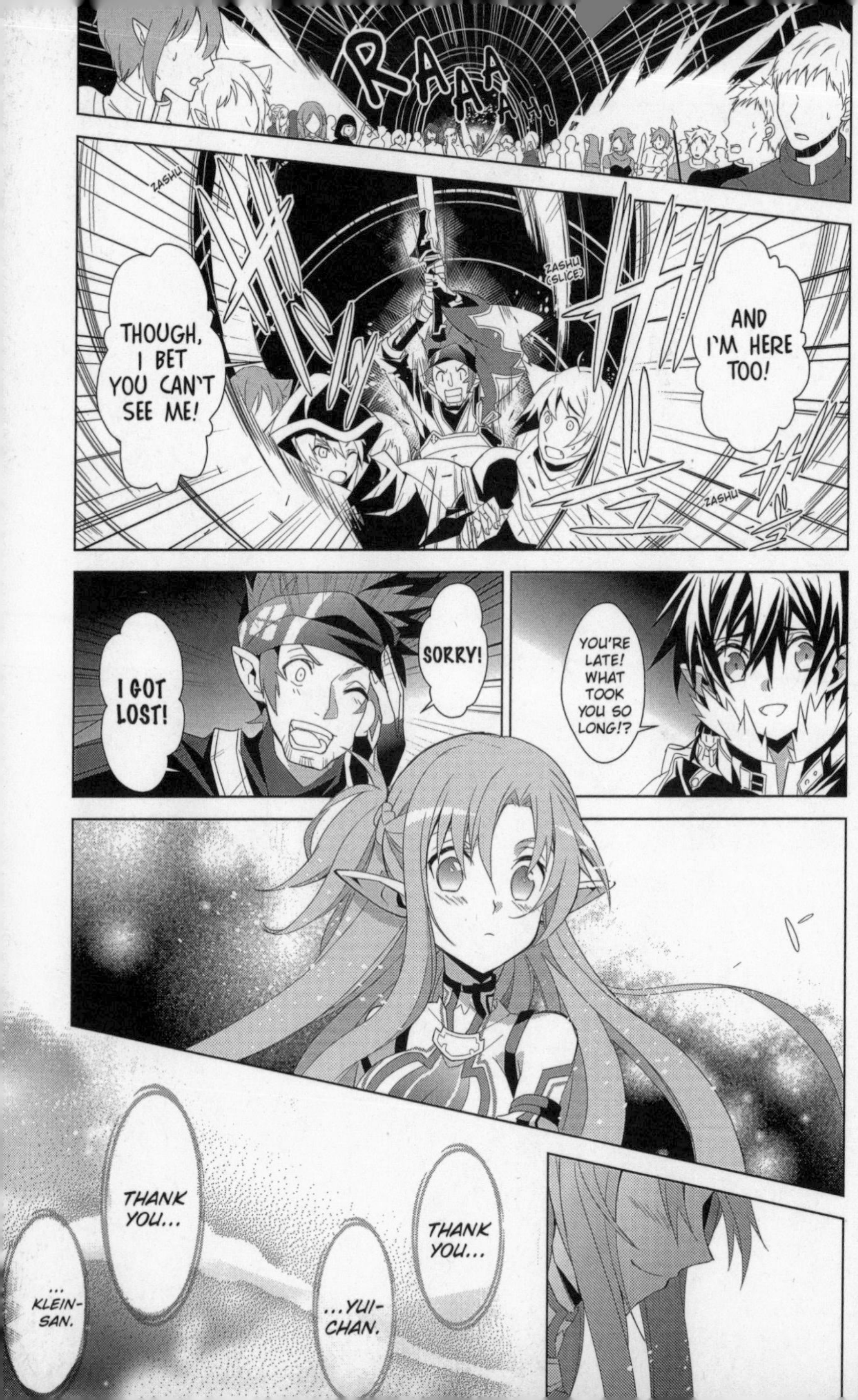
RAAAAH!
ZASHU
AND I'M HERE TOO!
ZASHU (SLICE)
ZASHU
THOUGH, I BET YOU CAN'T SEE ME!
YOU'RE LATE! WHAT TOOK YOU SO LONG!?
SORRY!
I GOT LOST!
THANK YOU...
...YUI-CHAN.
THANK YOU...
...KLEIN-SAN.

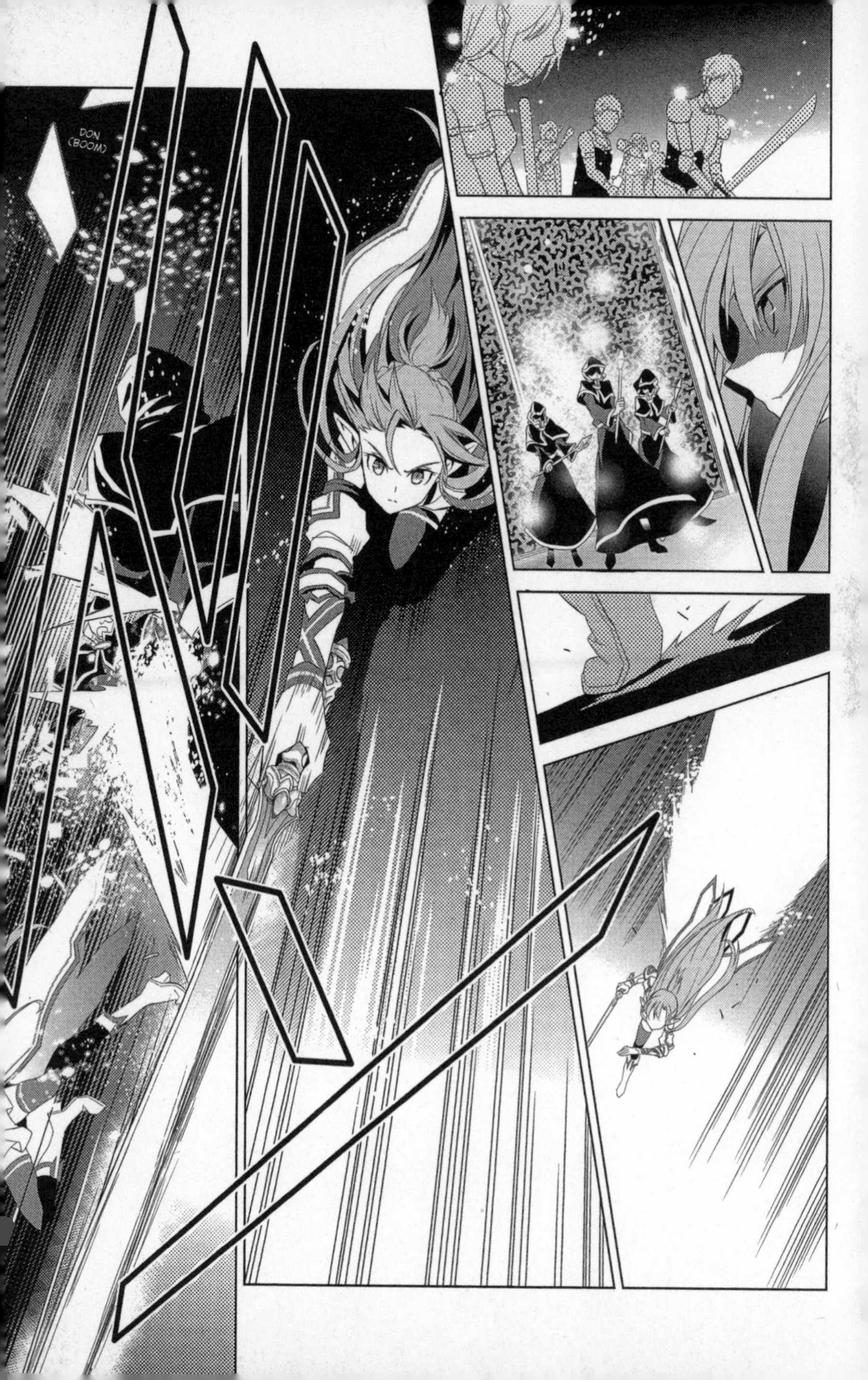
DON
(BOOM)

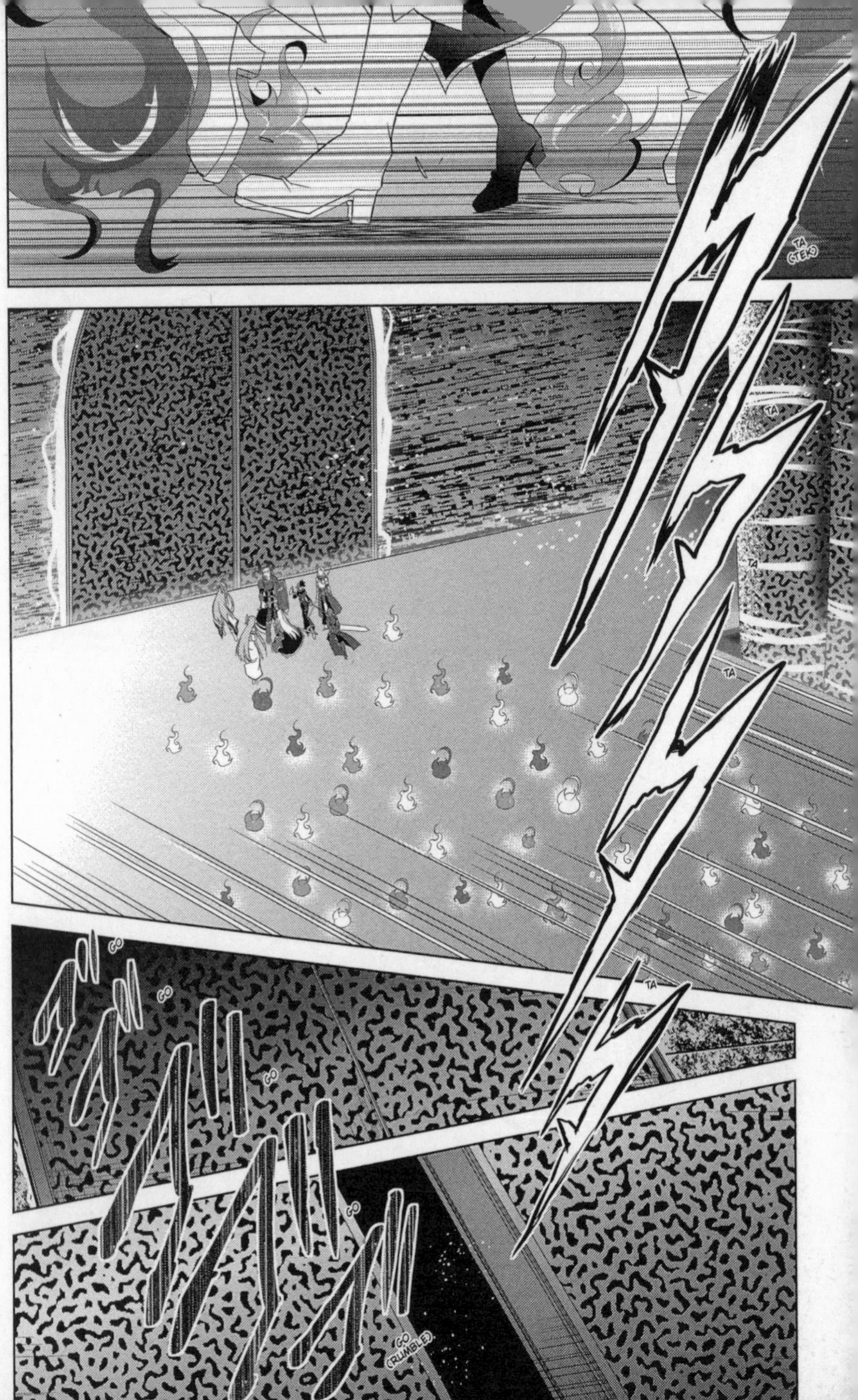
TA
(TEK)
TA
TA
TA
TA
GO
GO
GO
GO
GO
(RUMBLE)

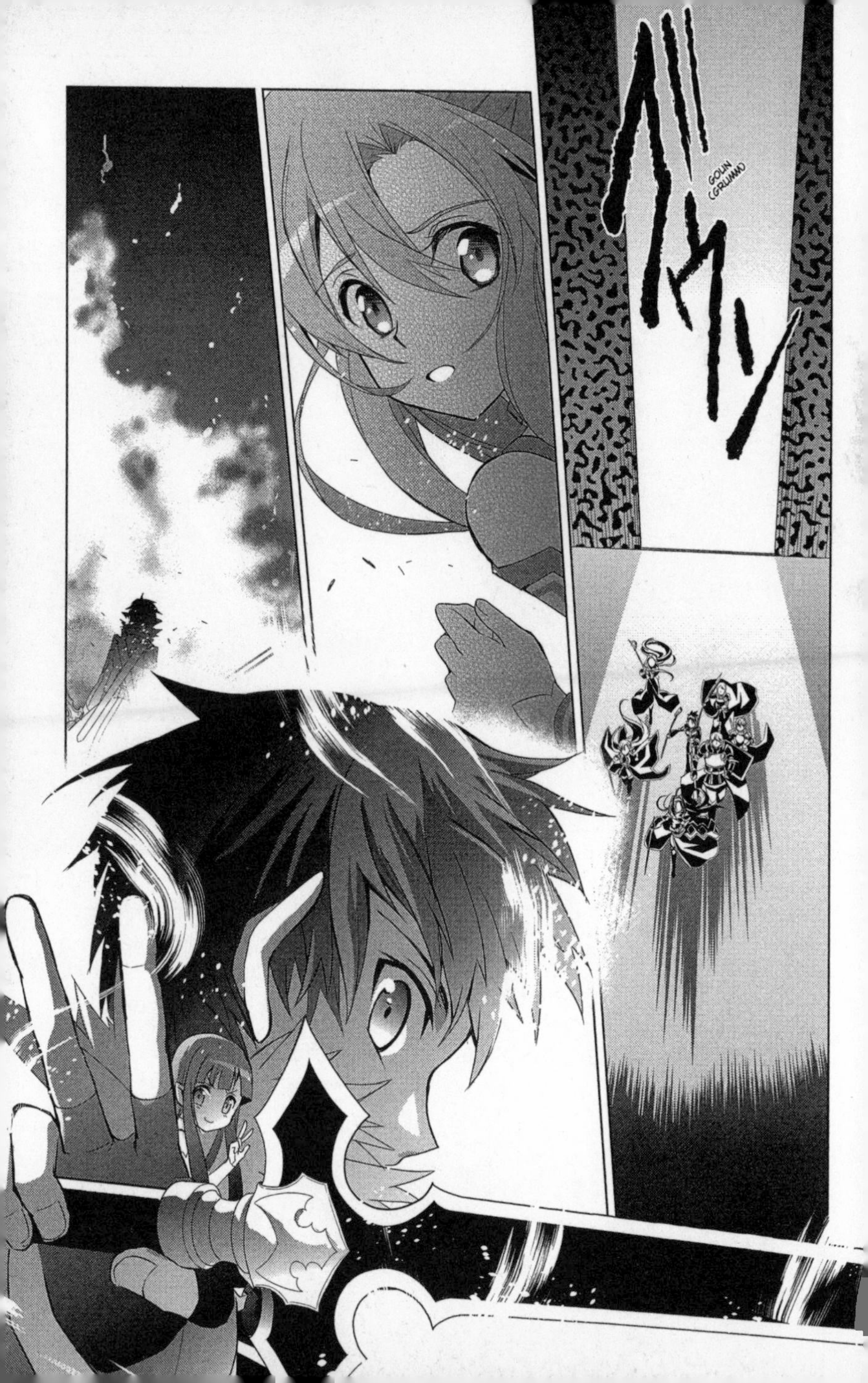
GOUN (GRUMM)

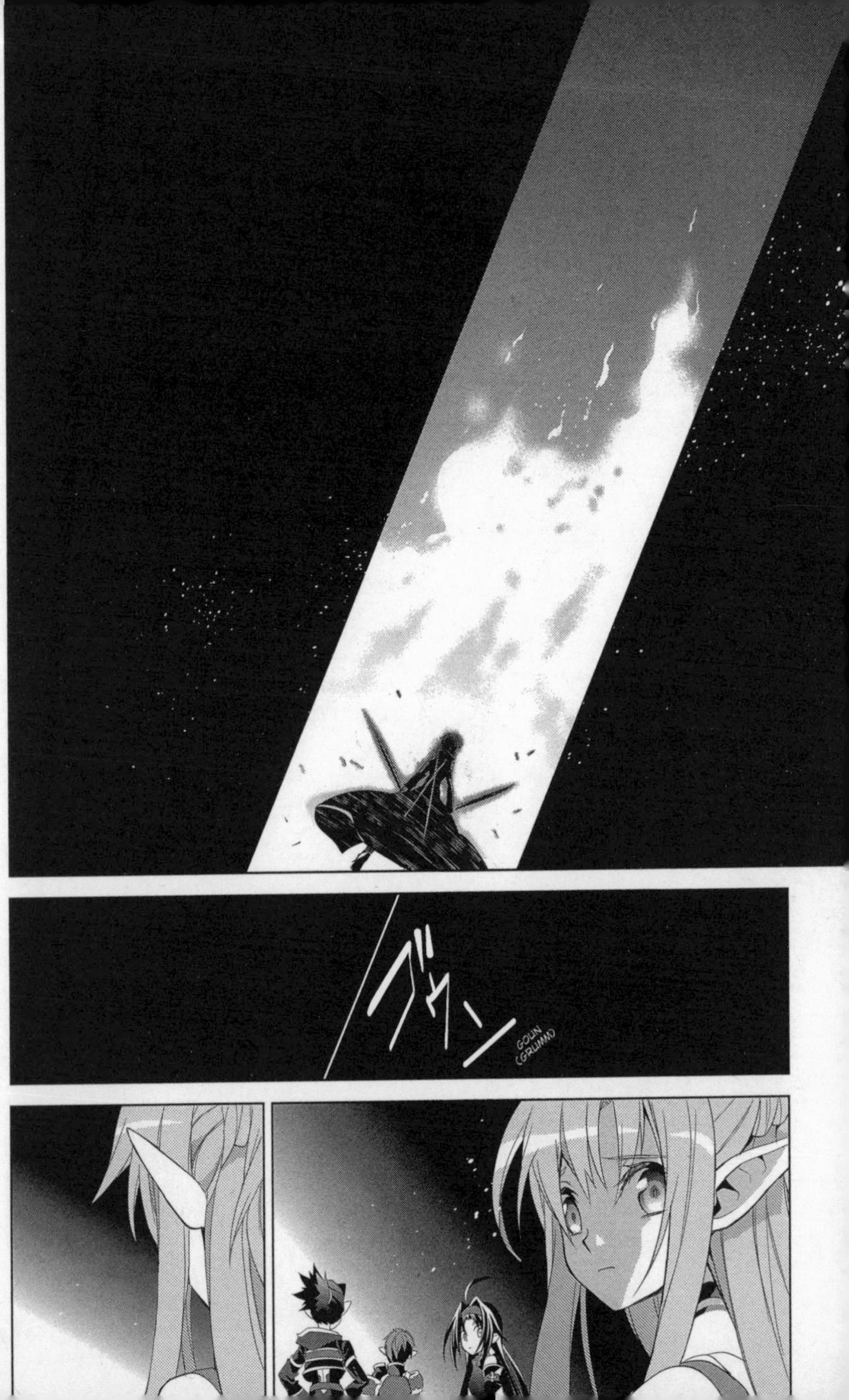
ゴウン
GOUN (GRUMM)

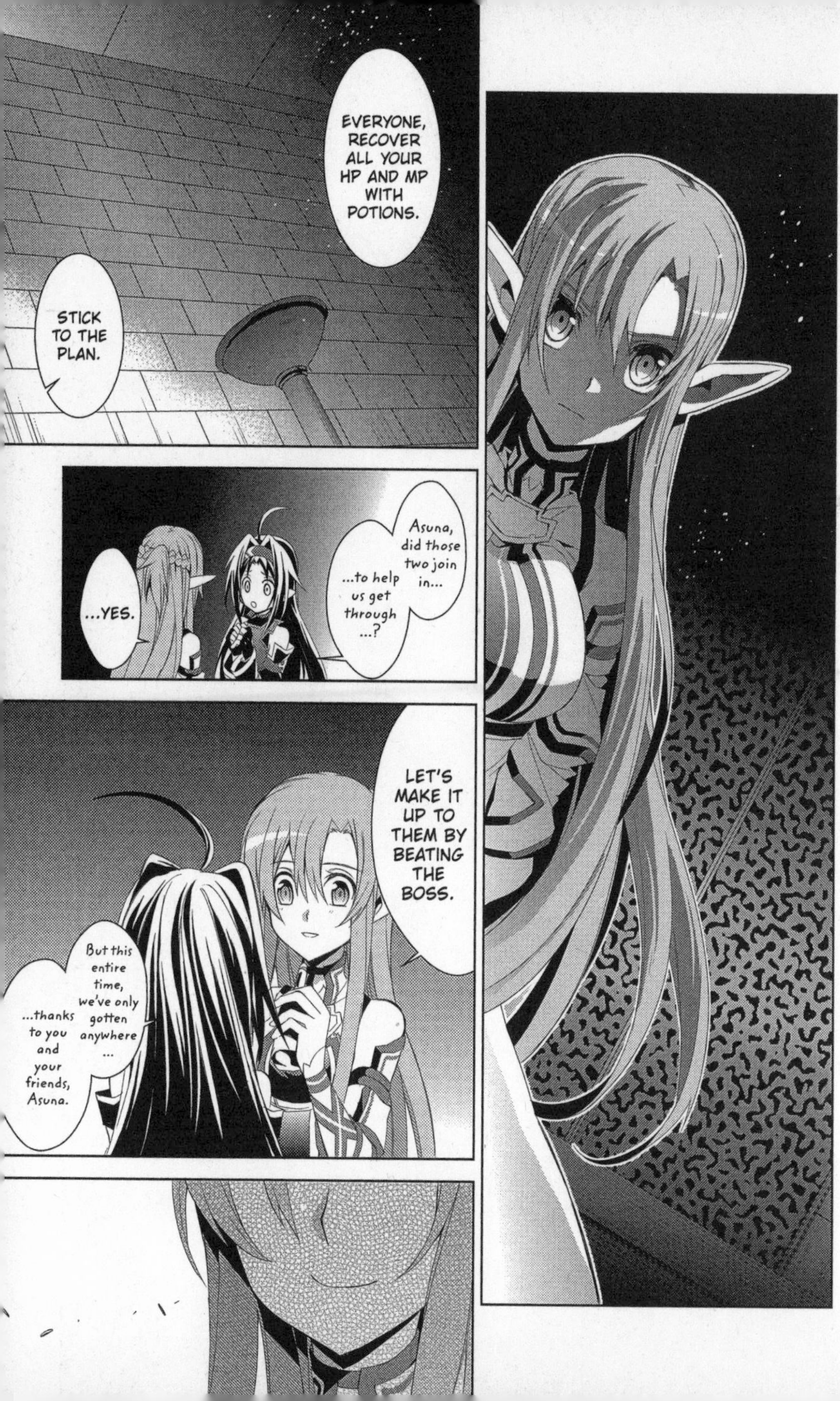
EVERYONE, RECOVER ALL YOUR HP AND MP WITH POTIONS.
STICK TO THE PLAN.
Asuna, did those two join in...
...to help us get through ...?
...YES.
LET'S MAKE IT UP TO THEM BY BEATING THE BOSS.
But this entire time, we've only gotten anywhere ...
...thanks to you and your friends, Asuna.

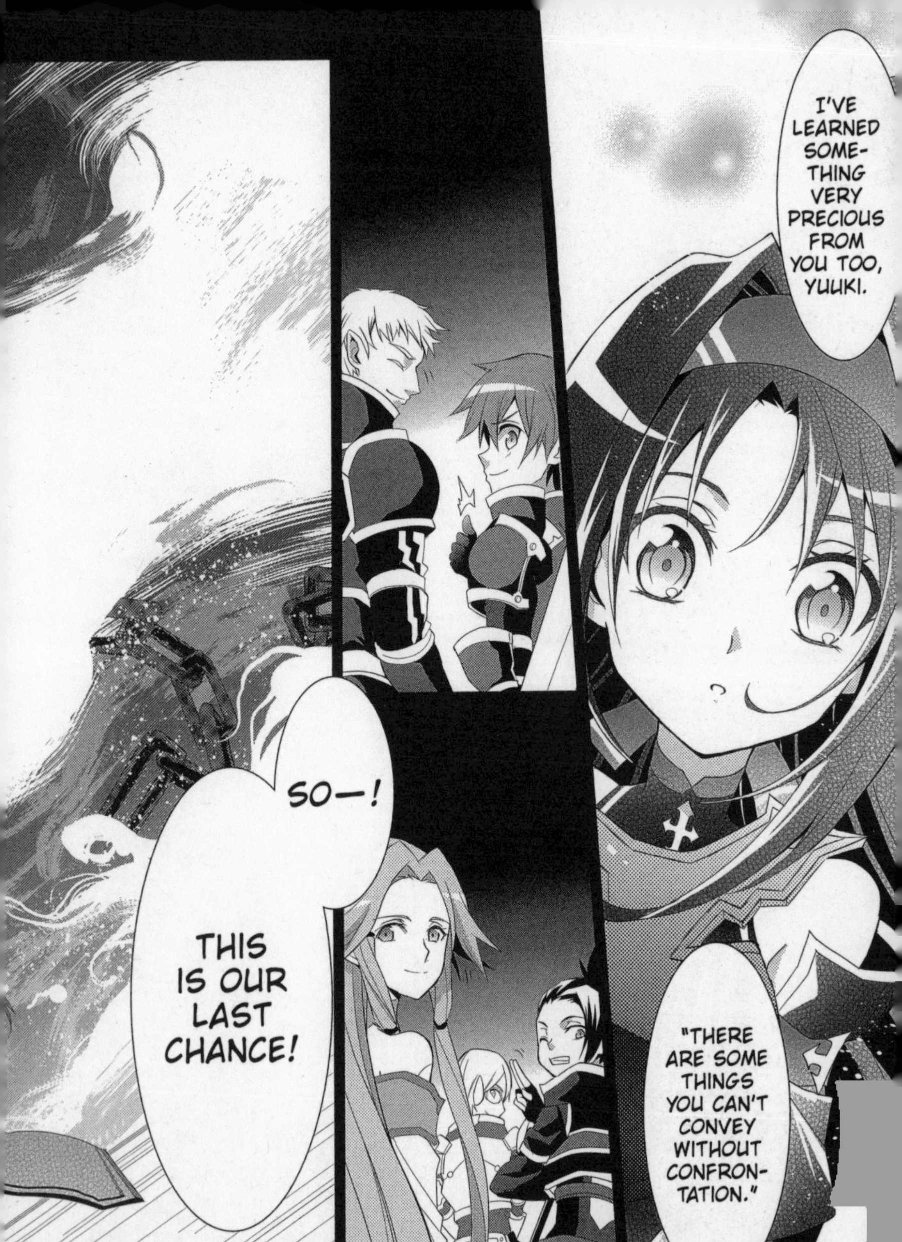
I'VE LEARNED SOMETHING VERY PRECIOUS FROM YOU TOO, YUUKI.
"THERE ARE SOME THINGS YOU CAN'T CONVEY WITHOUT CONFRONTATION."
SO—!
THIS IS OUR LAST CHANCE!

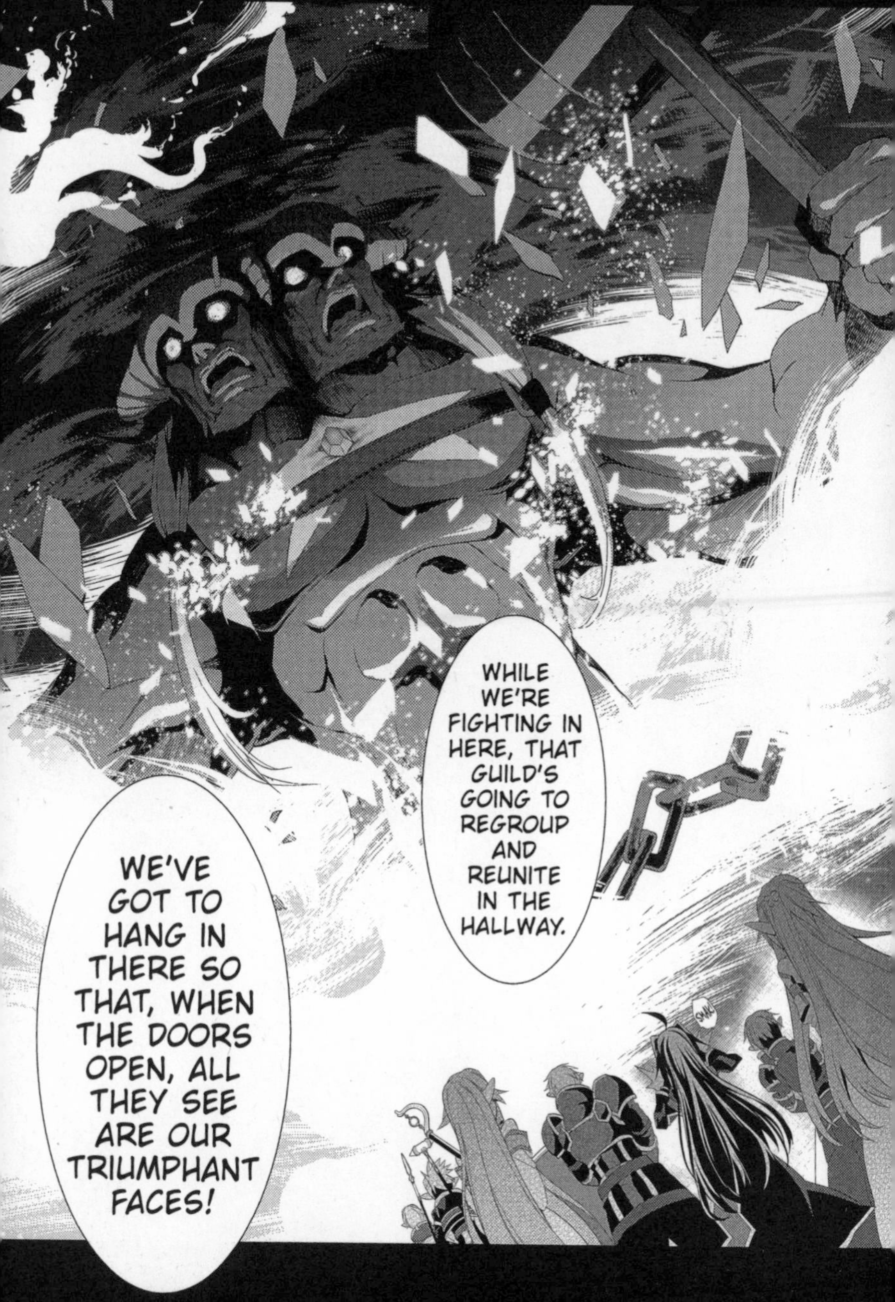
WHILE WE'RE FIGHTING IN HERE, THAT GUILD'S GOING TO REGROUP AND REUNITE IN THE HALLWAY.
WE'VE GOT TO HANG IN THERE SO THAT, WHEN THE DOORS OPEN, ALL THEY SEE ARE OUR TRIUMPHANT FACES!

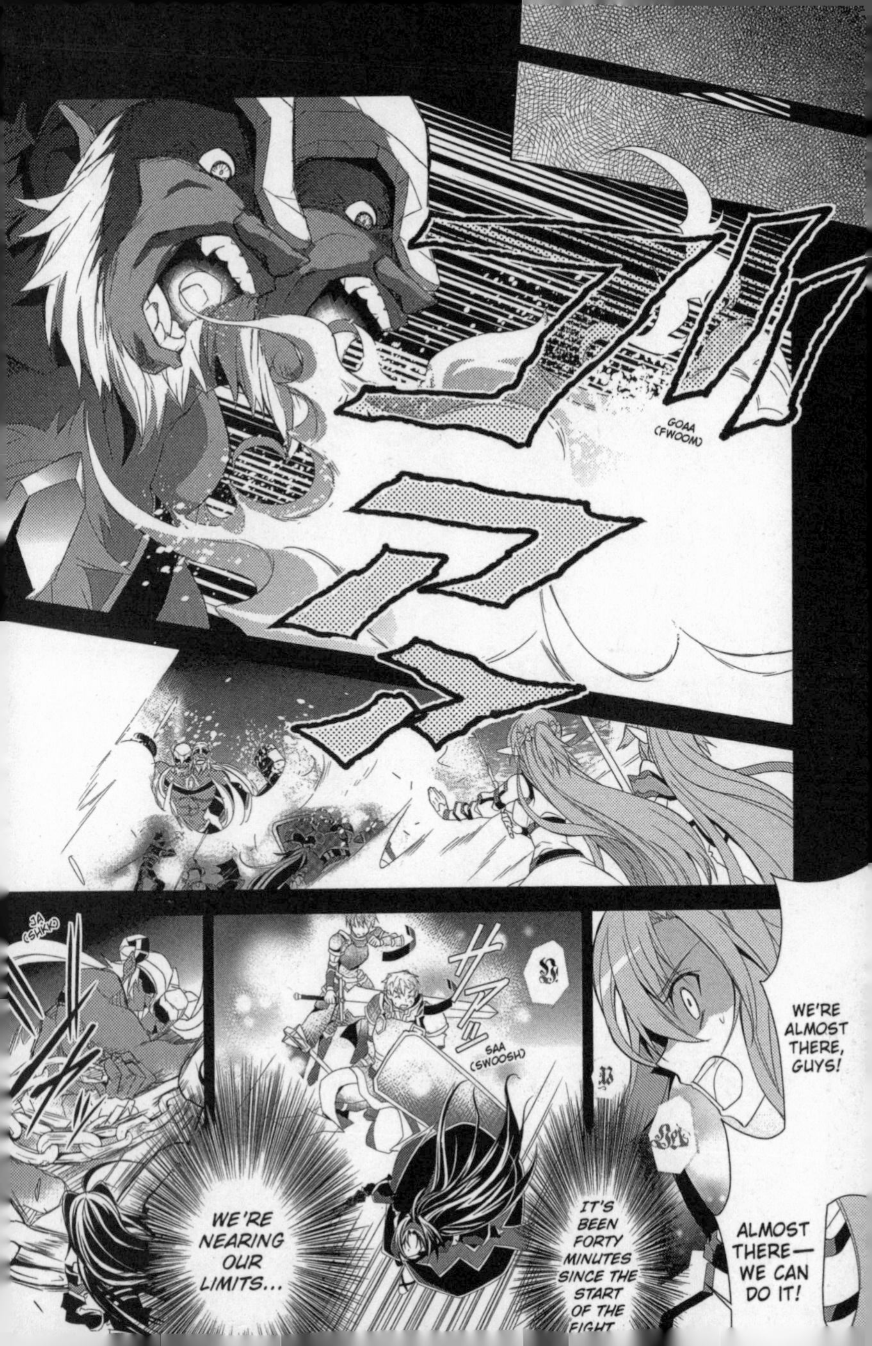
GOAA (FWOOM)
WE'RE ALMOST THERE, GUYS!
ALMOST THERE— WE CAN DO IT!
SAA (SWOOSH)
JA (SHKK)
IT'S BEEN FORTY MINUTES SINCE THE START OF THE FIGHT
WE'RE NEARING OUR LIMITS...

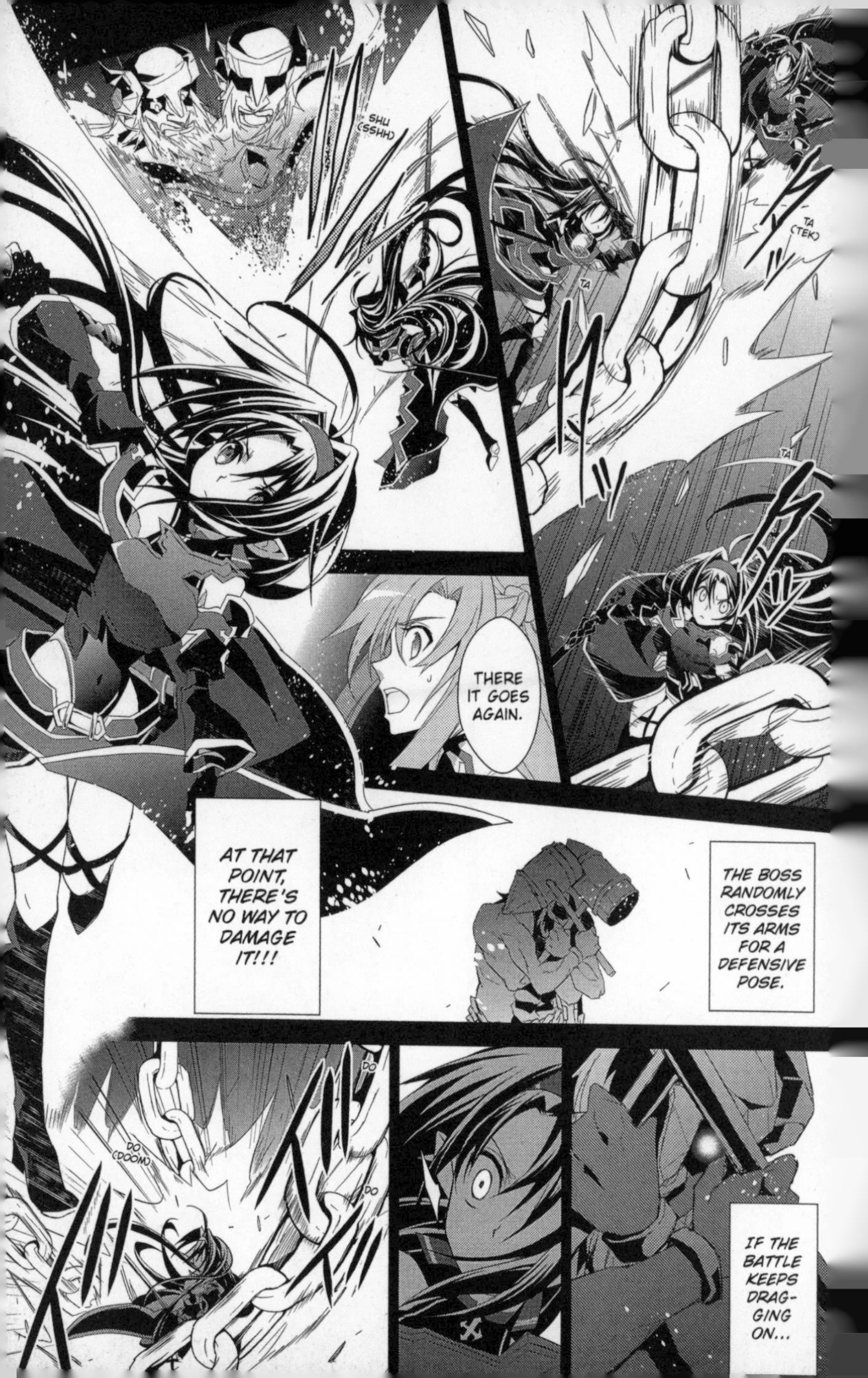
TA (TEK)
TA
TA
SHU (SSHH)
THERE IT GOES AGAIN.
THE BOSS RANDOMLY CROSSES ITS ARMS FOR A DEFENSIVE POSE.
AT THAT POINT, THERE'S NO WAY TO DAMAGE IT!!!
IF THE BATTLE KEEPS DRAG-GING ON...
DO
DO (DOOM)
DO

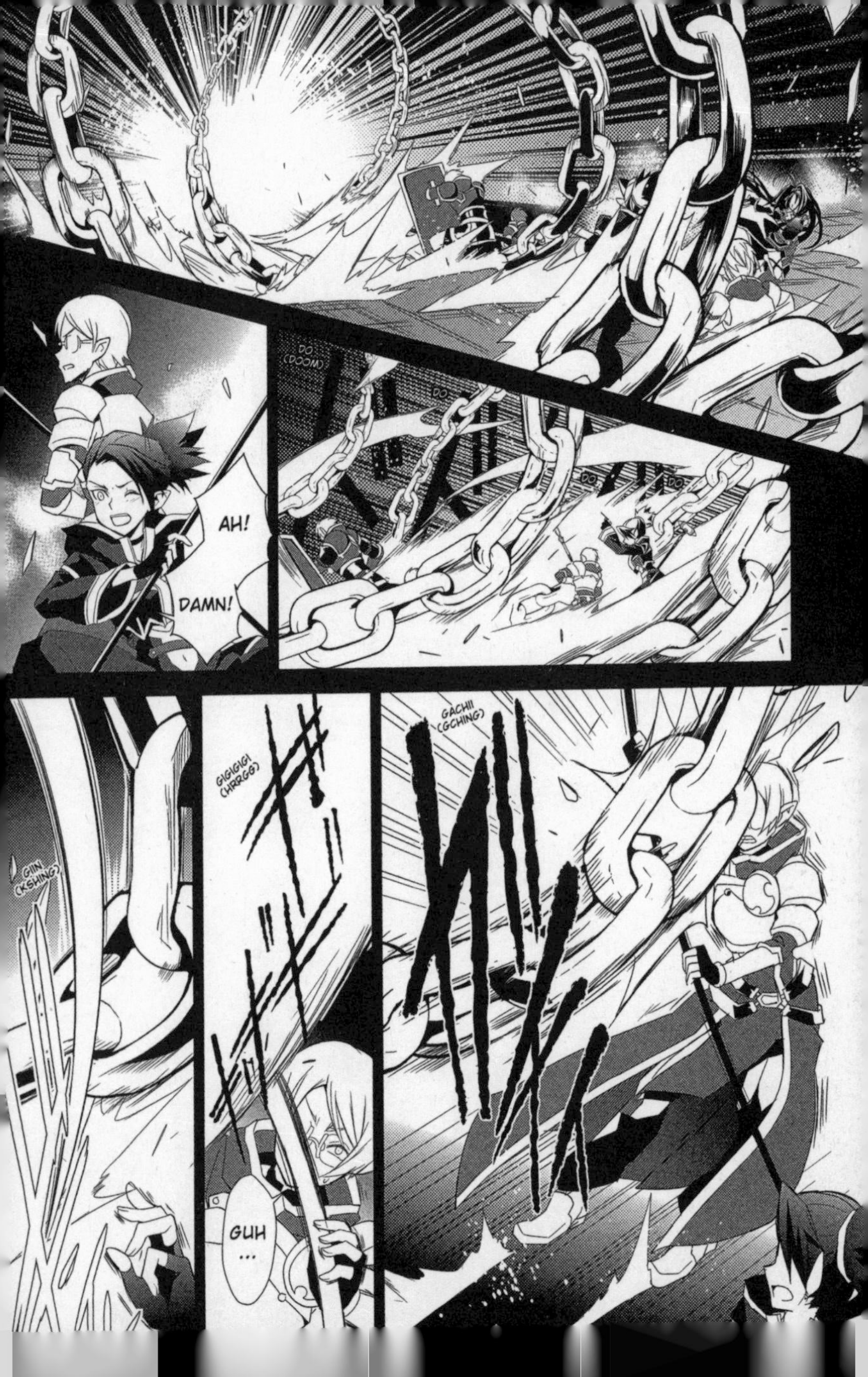
DO
(DOOM)
DO
DO
DO
AH!
DAMN!
GACHII
(GCHING)
GIGIGIGI
(HRRGG)
GUH
...
GIIN
(KSHING)

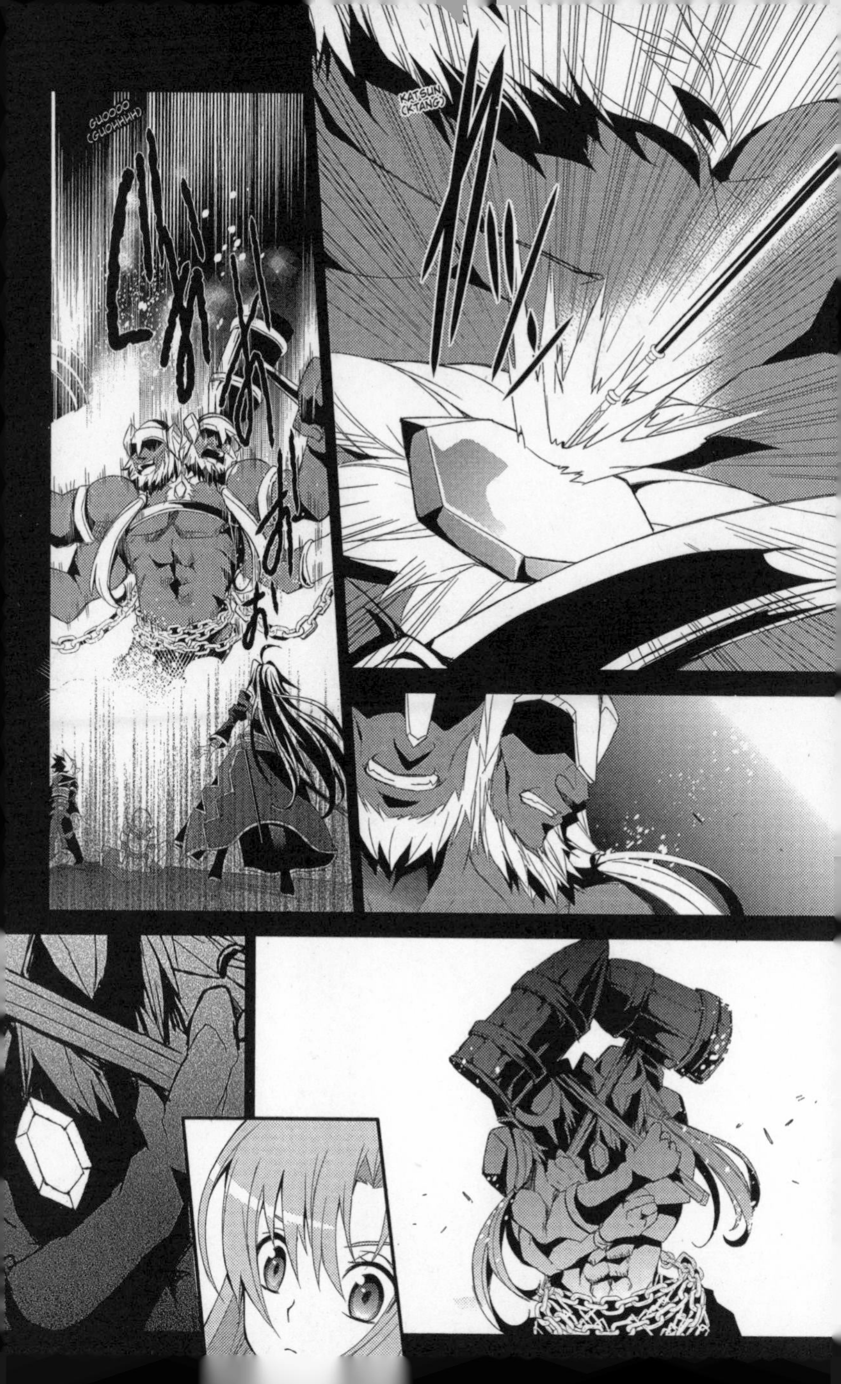
KATSUN (KTANG)
GUOOOO (GUOHHHH)

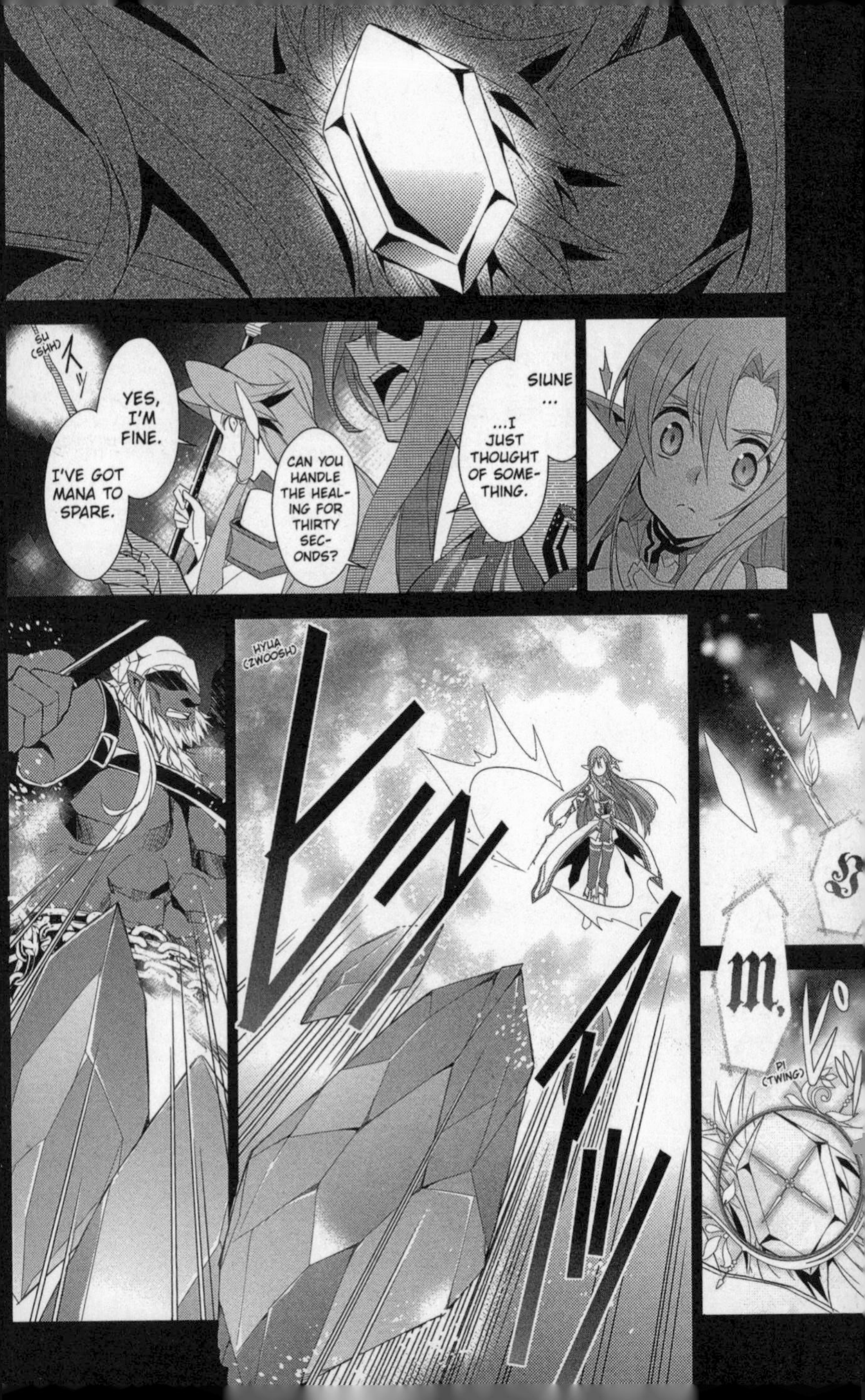
SIUNE ...
...I JUST THOUGHT OF SOME-THING.
CAN YOU HANDLE THE HEAL-ING FOR THIRTY SEC-ONDS?
YES, I'M FINE.
I'VE GOT MANA TO SPARE.
SU (SHH)
PI (TWING)
HYUA (ZWOOSH)

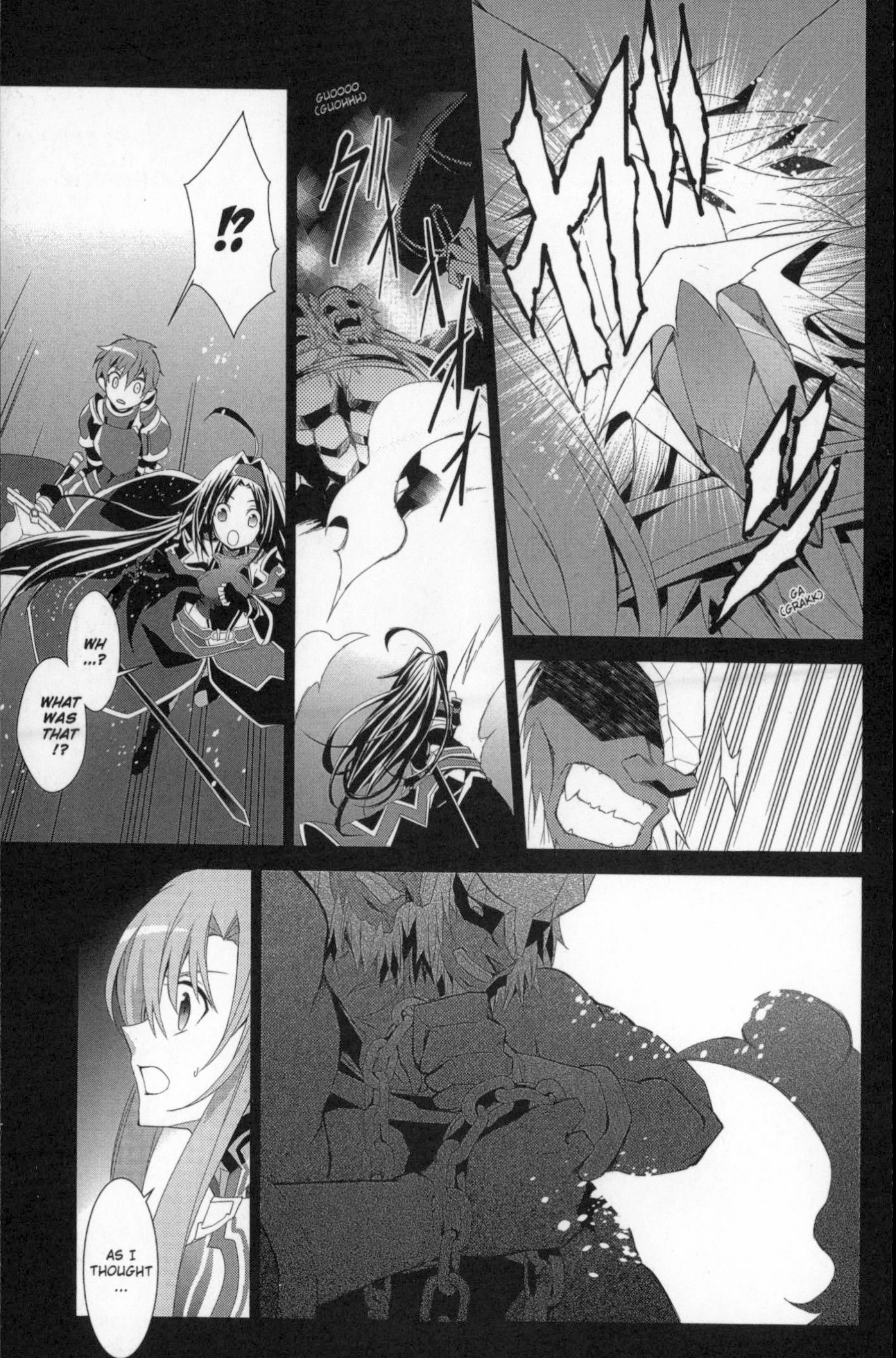
GA (GRAKK)
GUOOOO (GUOHHH)
!?
WH ...?
WHAT WAS THAT !?
AS I THOUGHT ...

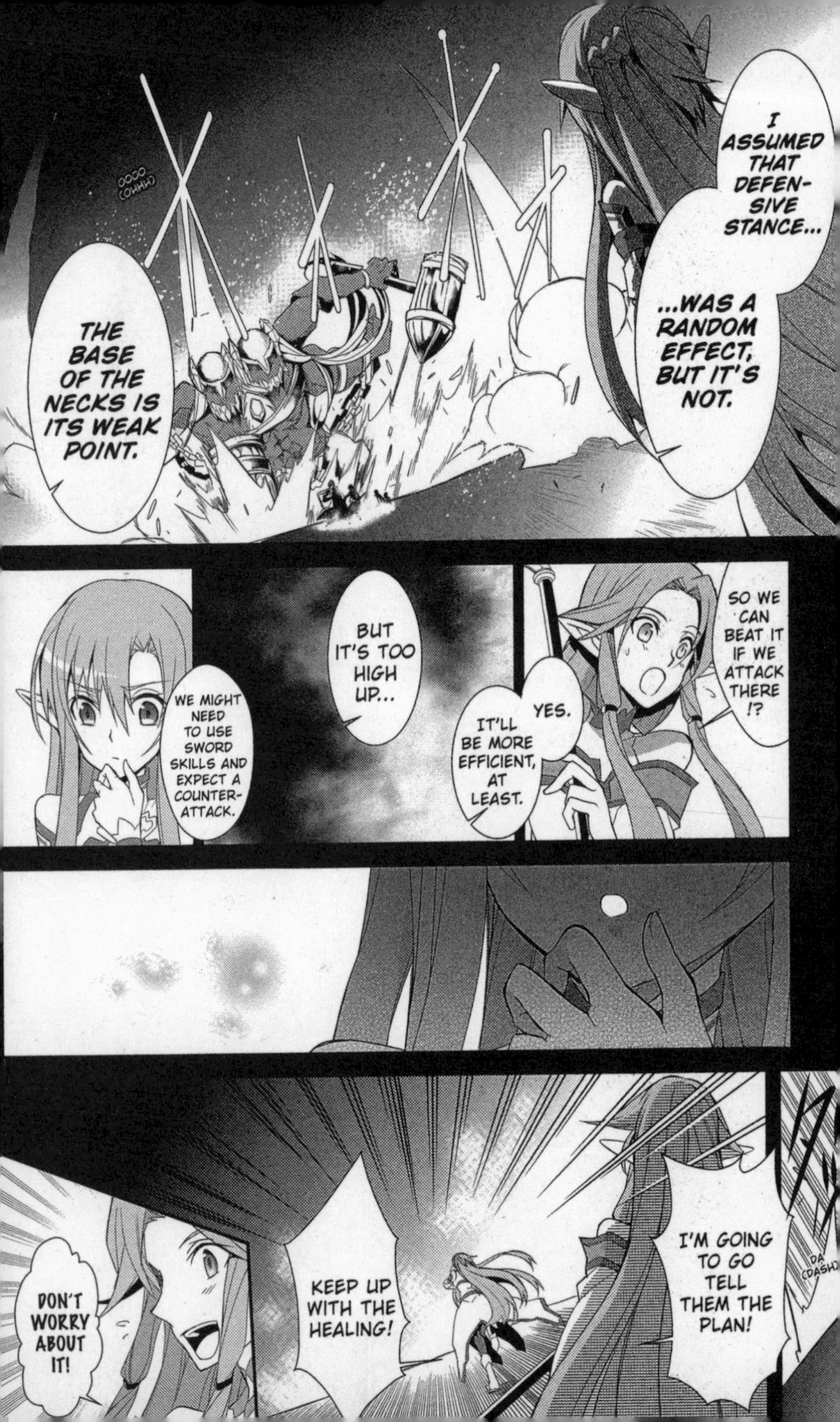
I ASSUMED THAT DEFEN-SIVE STANCE...
...WAS A RANDOM EFFECT, BUT IT'S NOT.
OOOO (OHHH)
THE BASE OF THE NECKS IS ITS WEAK POINT.
SO WE CAN BEAT IT IF WE ATTACK THERE!?
YES.
IT'LL BE MORE EFFICIENT, AT LEAST.
BUT IT'S TOO HIGH UP...
WE MIGHT NEED TO USE SWORD SKILLS AND EXPECT A COUNTER-ATTACK.
DA (DASH)
I'M GOING TO GO TELL THEM THE PLAN!
KEEP UP WITH THE HEALING!
DON'T WORRY ABOUT IT!

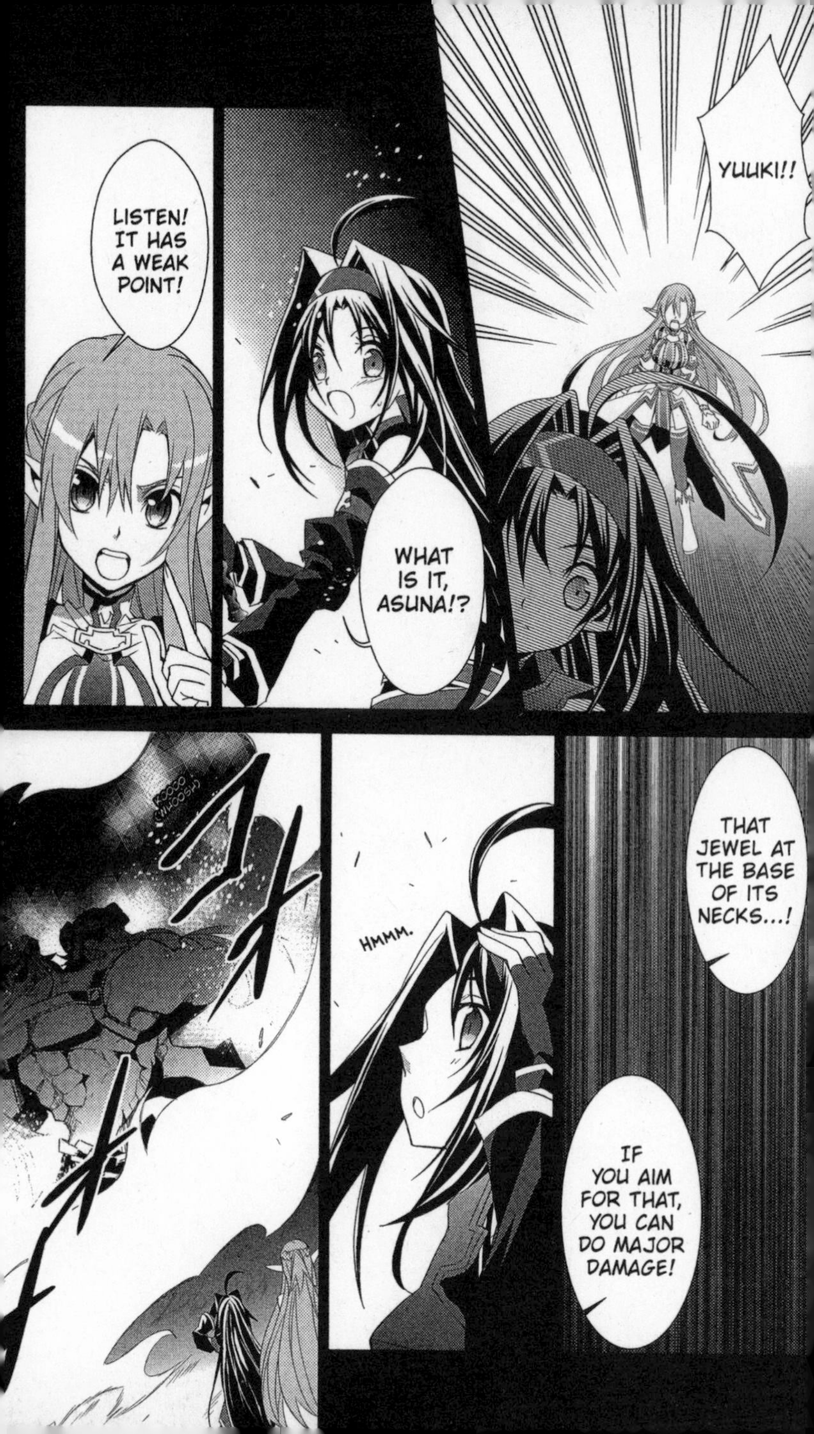
YUUKI!!
WHAT IS IT, ASUNA!?
LISTEN! IT HAS A WEAK POINT!
THAT JEWEL AT THE BASE OF ITS NECKS...!
IF YOU AIM FOR THAT, YOU CAN DO MAJOR DAMAGE!
HMMM.

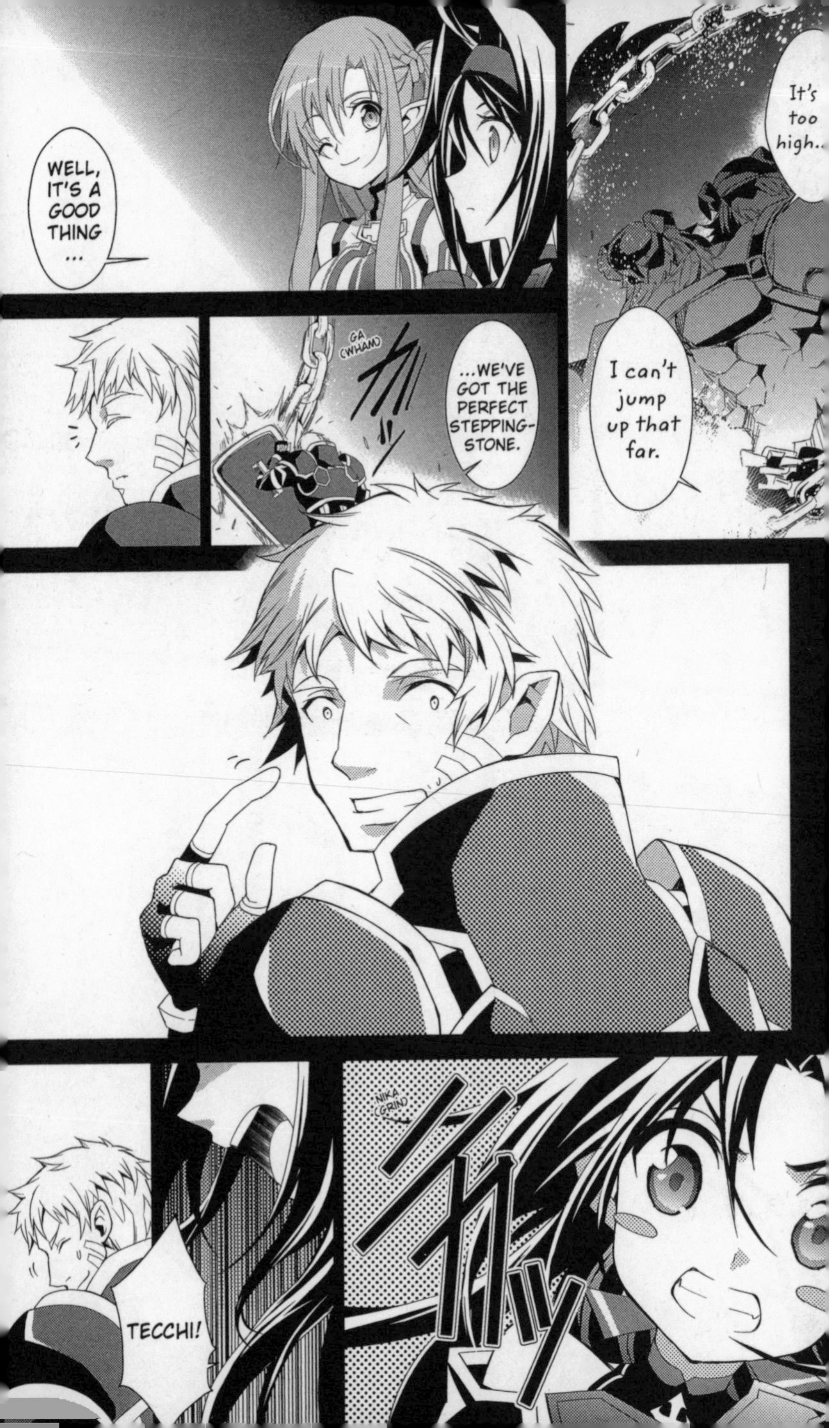

It's too high...
I can't jump up that far.
WELL, IT'S A GOOD THING ...
GA (WHAM)
...WE'VE GOT THE PERFECT STEPPING-STONE.
NIKA (GRIN)
TECCHI!

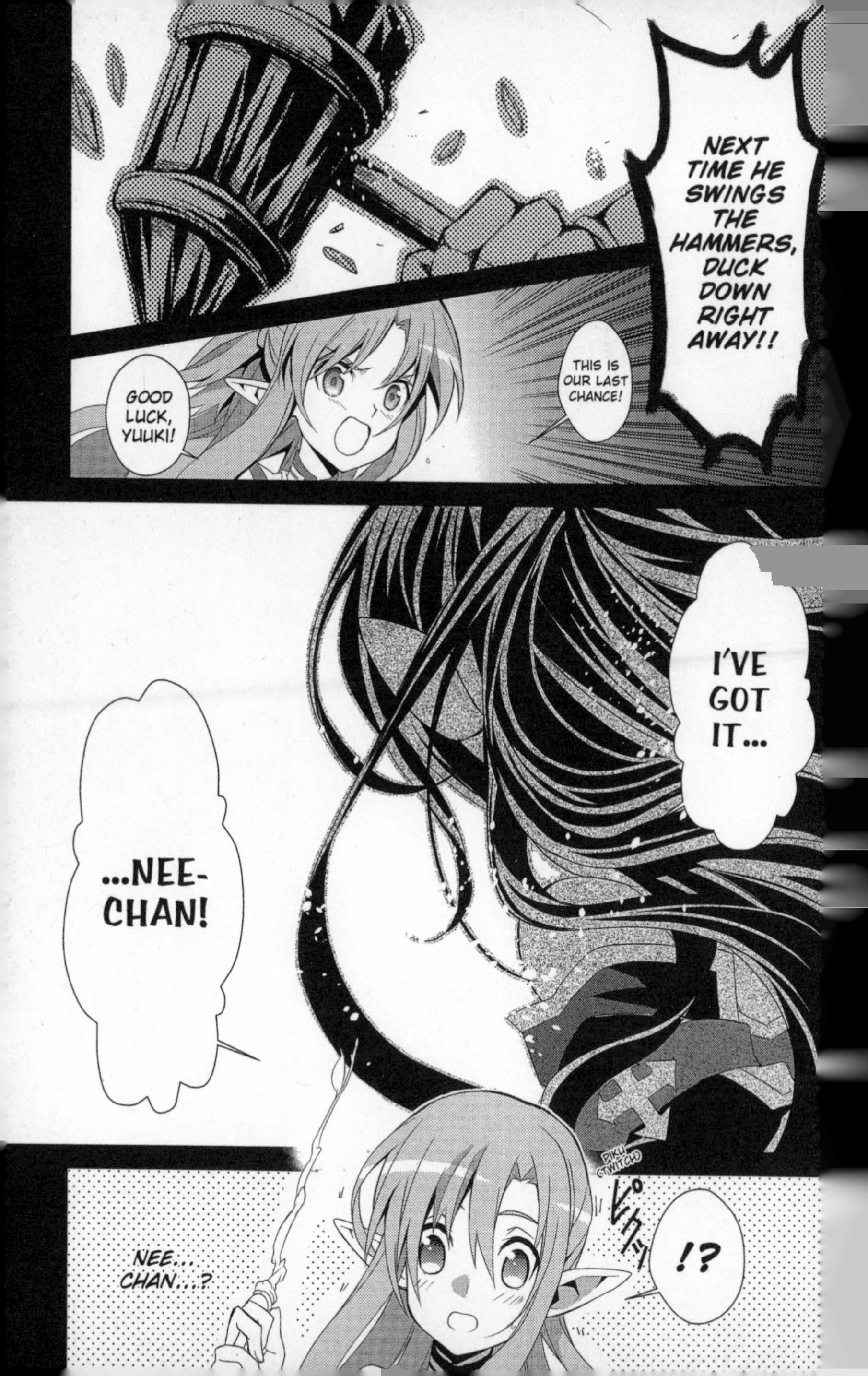
NEXT TIME HE SWINGS THE HAMMERS, DUCK DOWN RIGHT AWAY!!
THIS IS OUR LAST CHANCE!
GOOD LUCK, YUUKI!
I'VE GOT IT...
...NEE-CHAN!
PIKU (TWITCH)
!?
NEE... CHAN...?

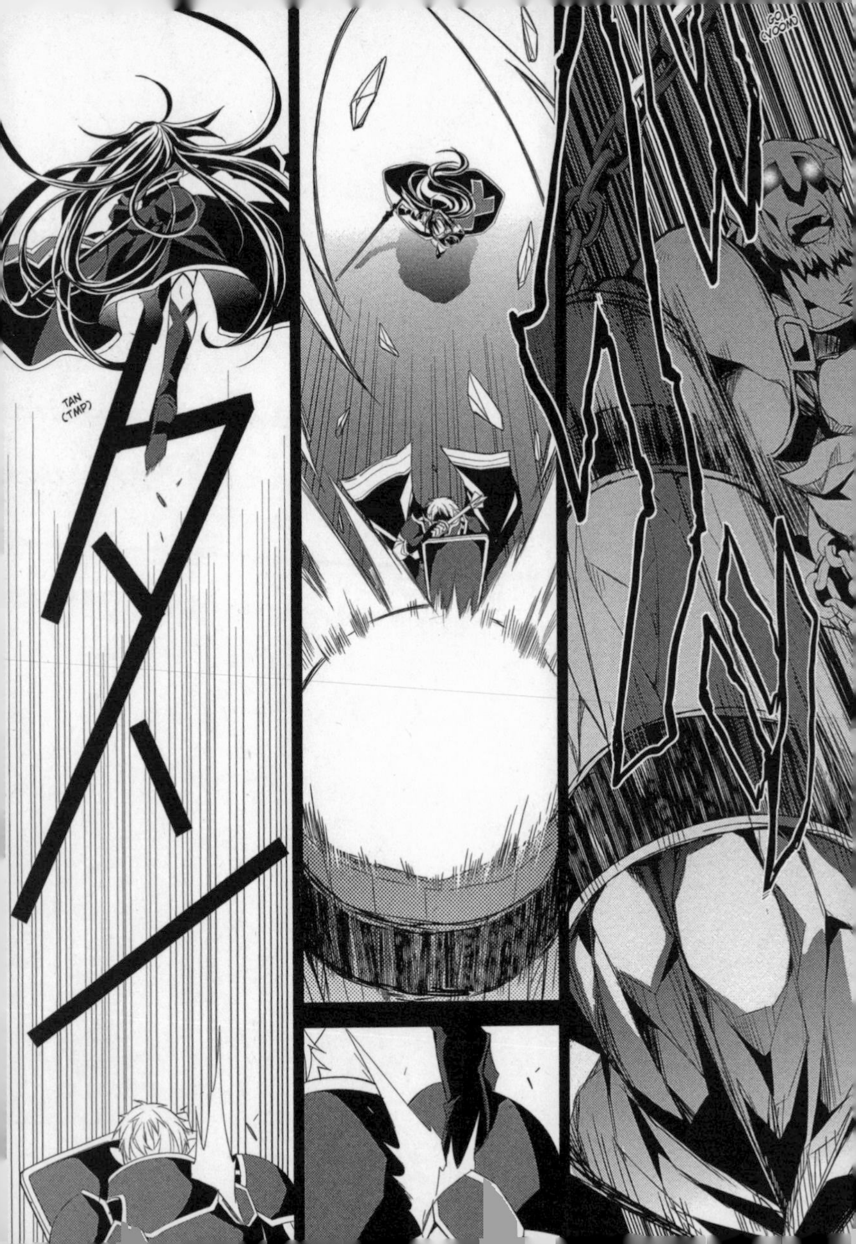
GO
(VOOM)
TAN
(TMP)

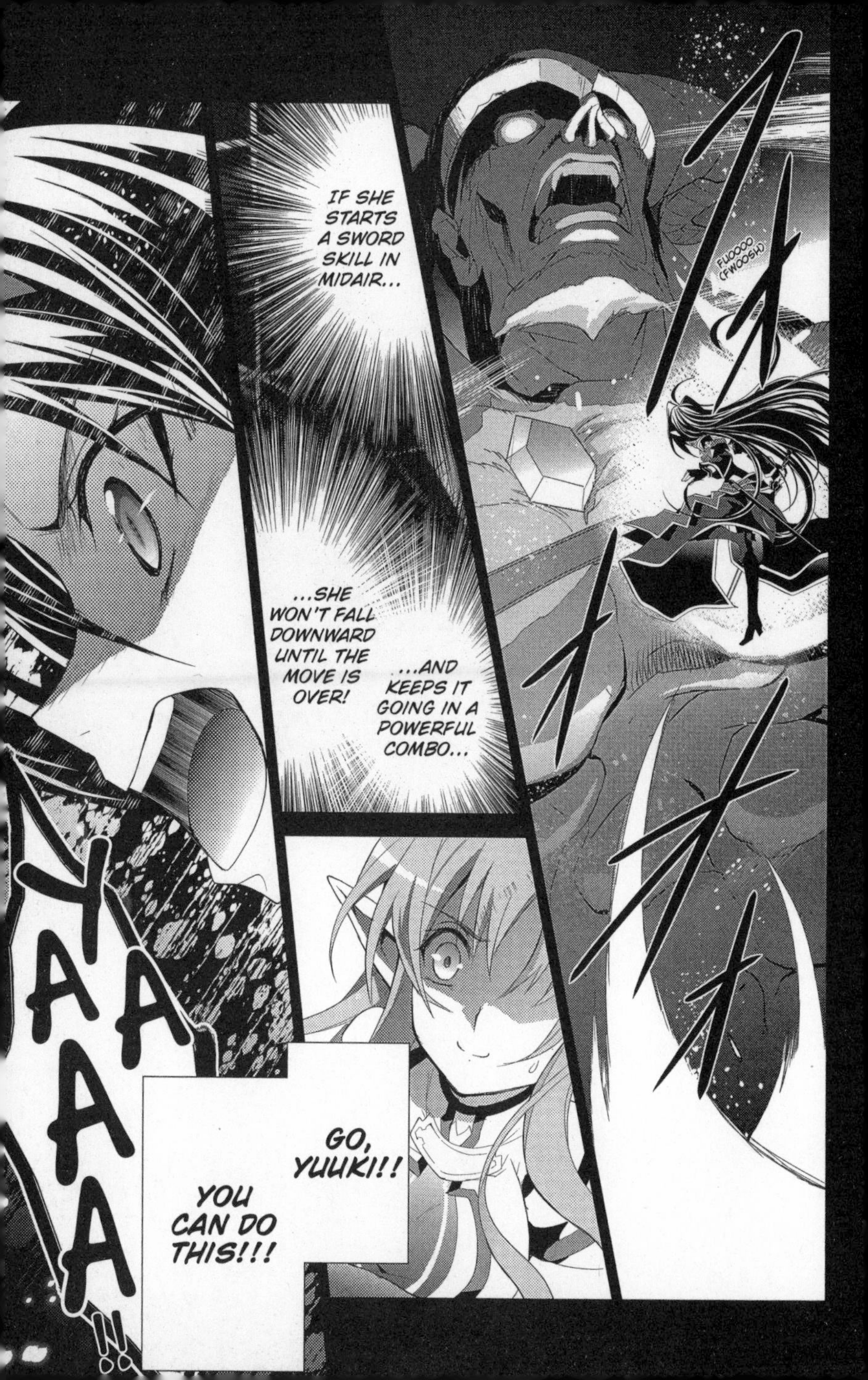
FUOOOO (FWOOSH)
IF SHE STARTS A SWORD SKILL IN MIDAIR...
...AND KEEPS IT GOING IN A POWERFUL COMBO...
...SHE WON'T FALL DOWNWARD UNTIL THE MOVE IS OVER!
GO, YUUKI!!
YOU CAN DO THIS!!!
YAAAAAA!!

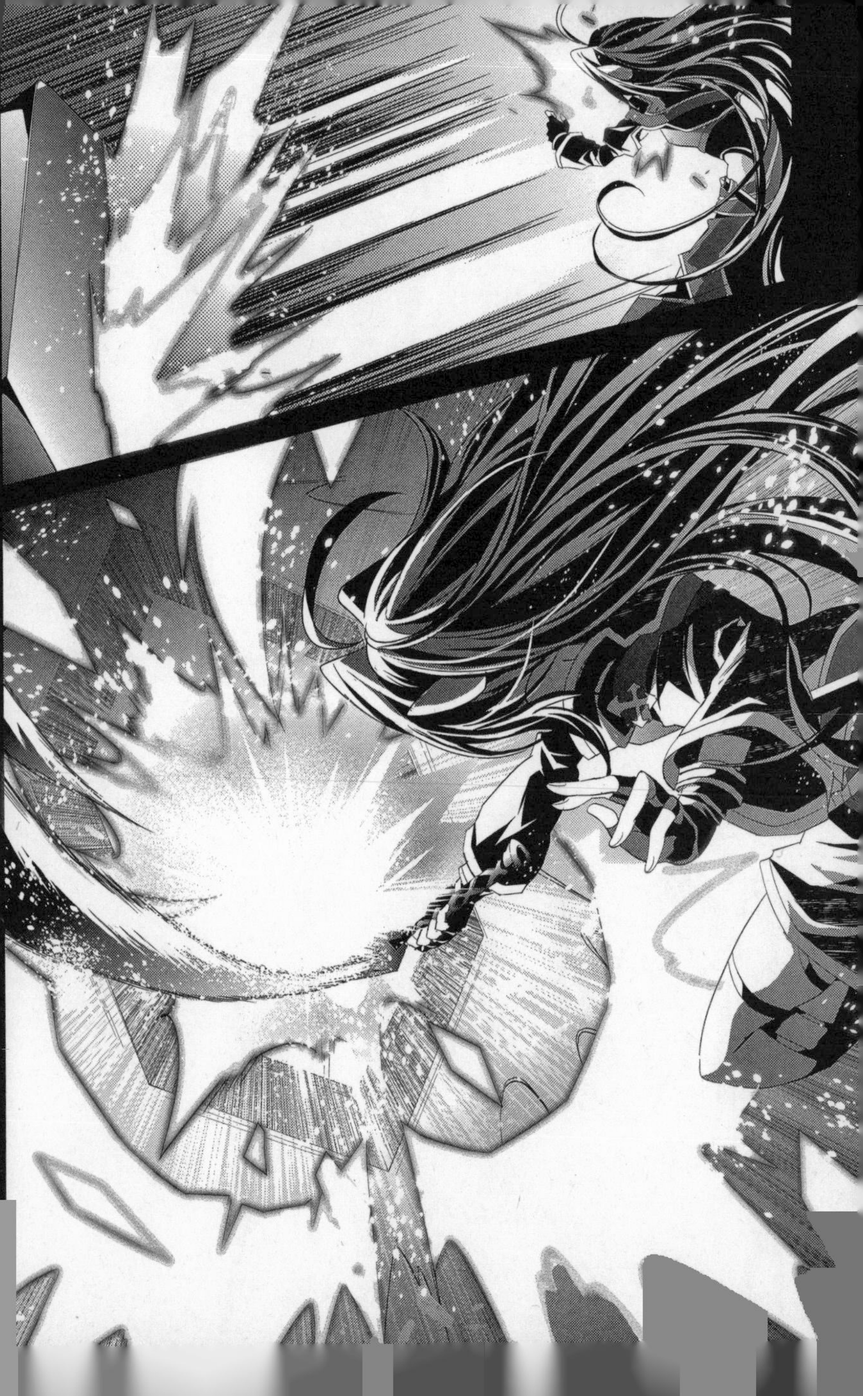

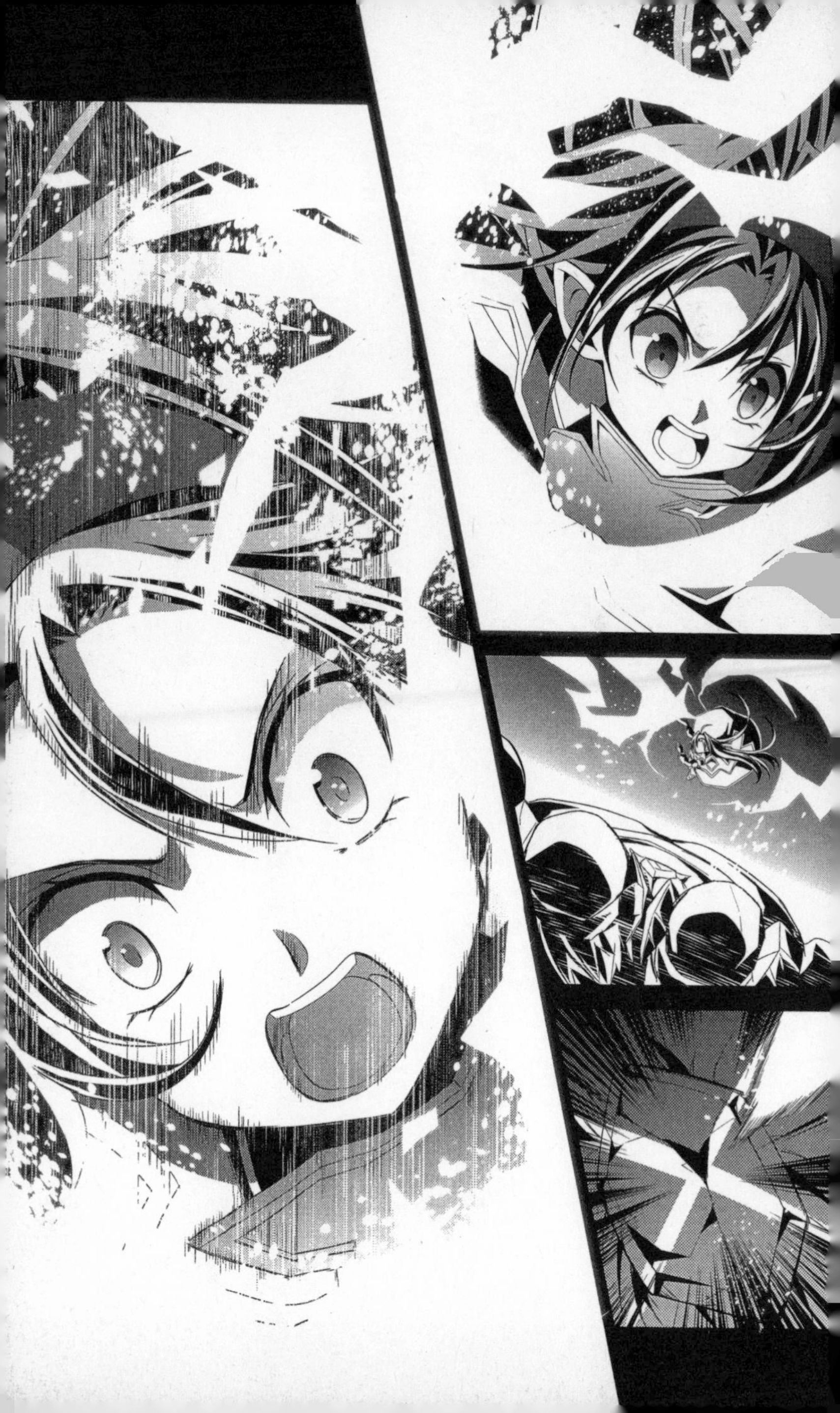

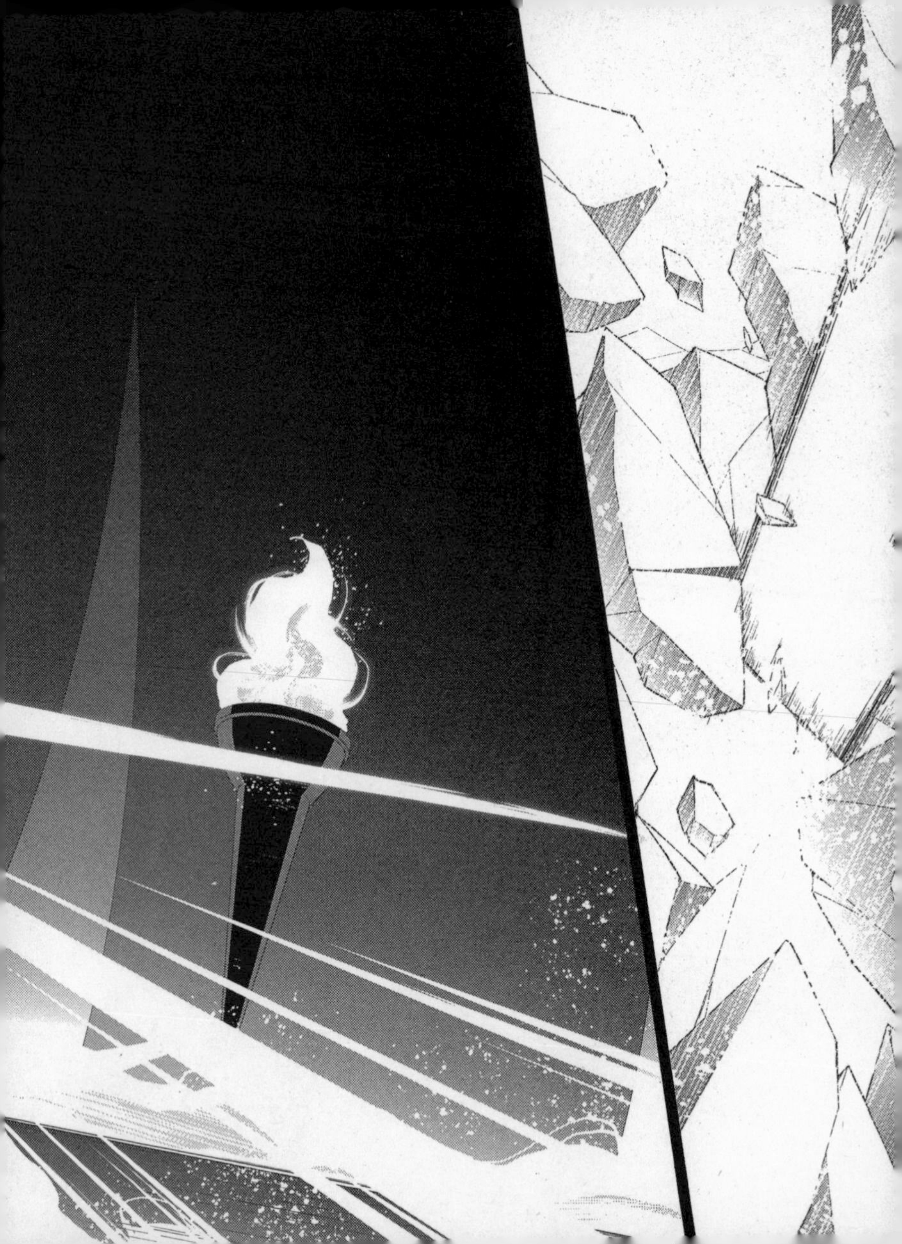

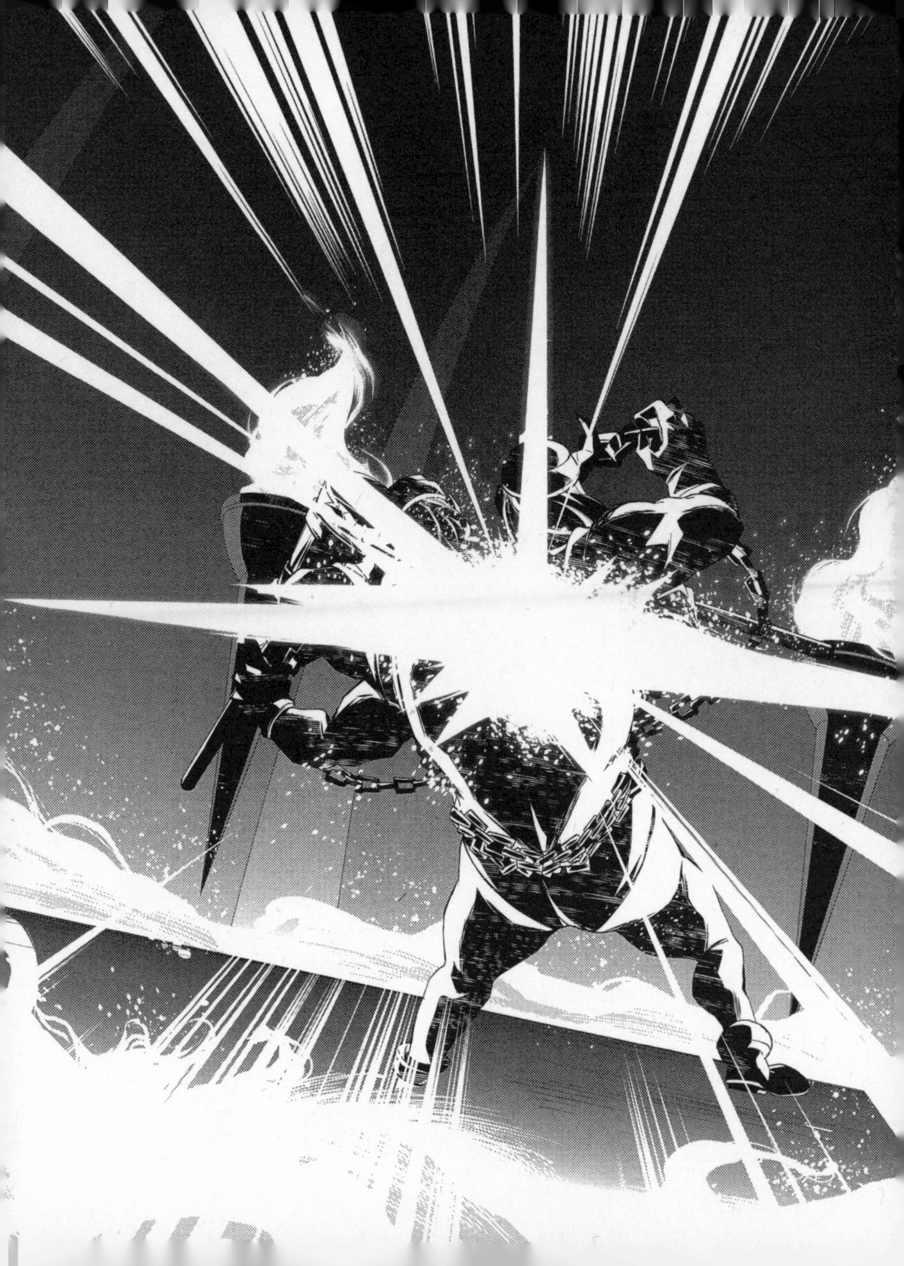

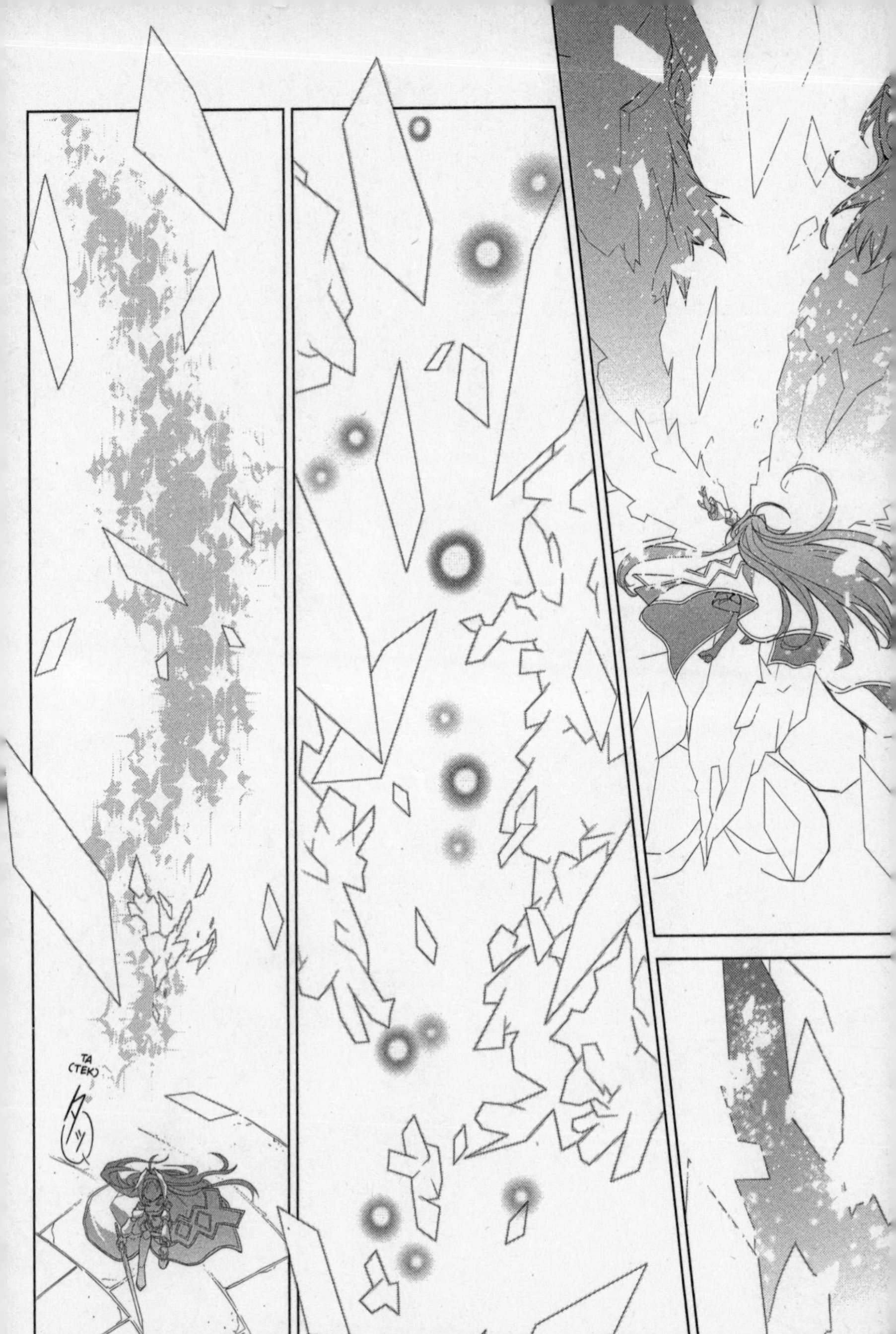
TA
(TEK)

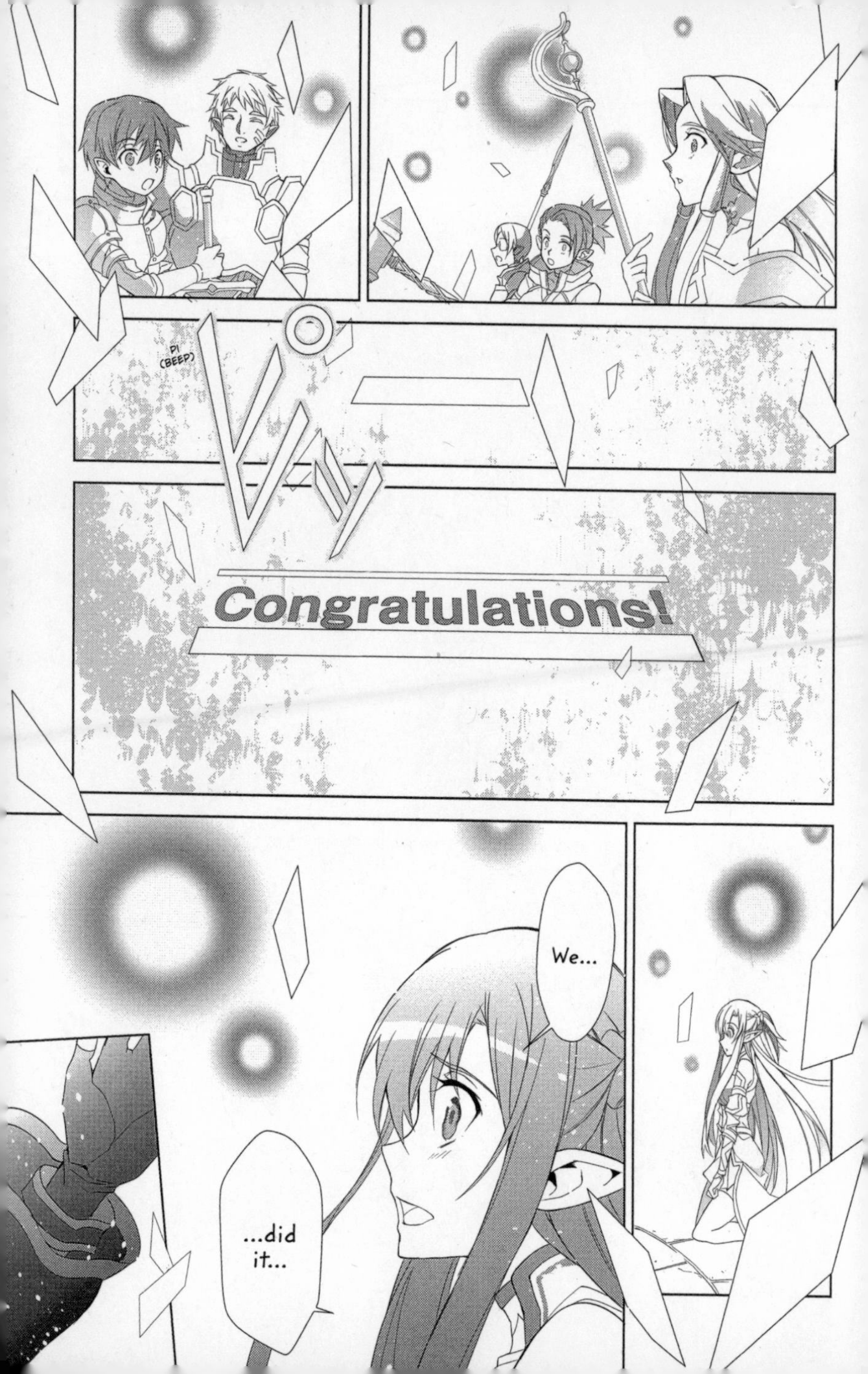
PI
(BEEP)
Congratulations!
We...
...did it...

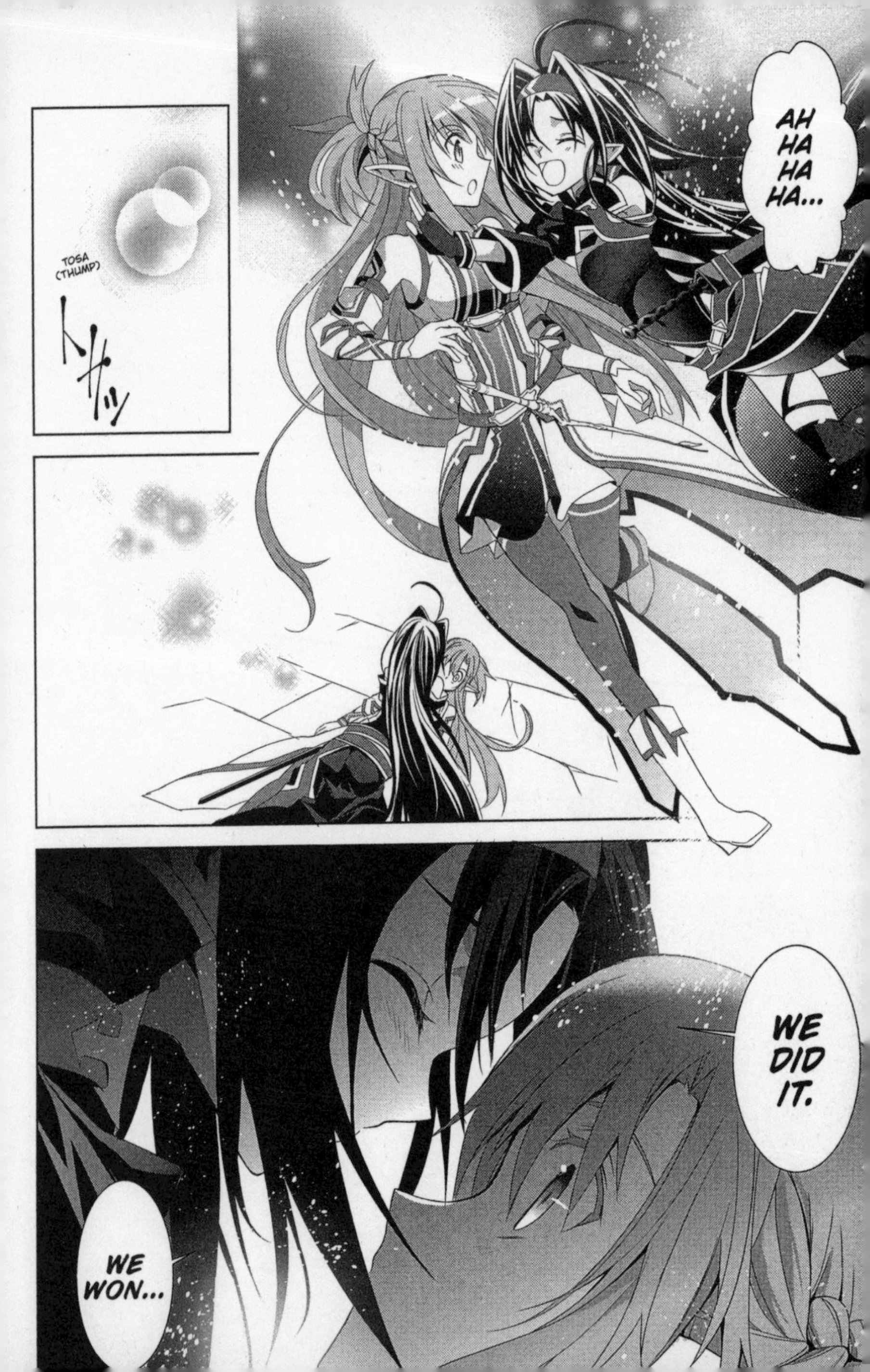
AH HA HA HA...
TOSA (THUMP)
トサッ
WE DID IT.
WE WON...

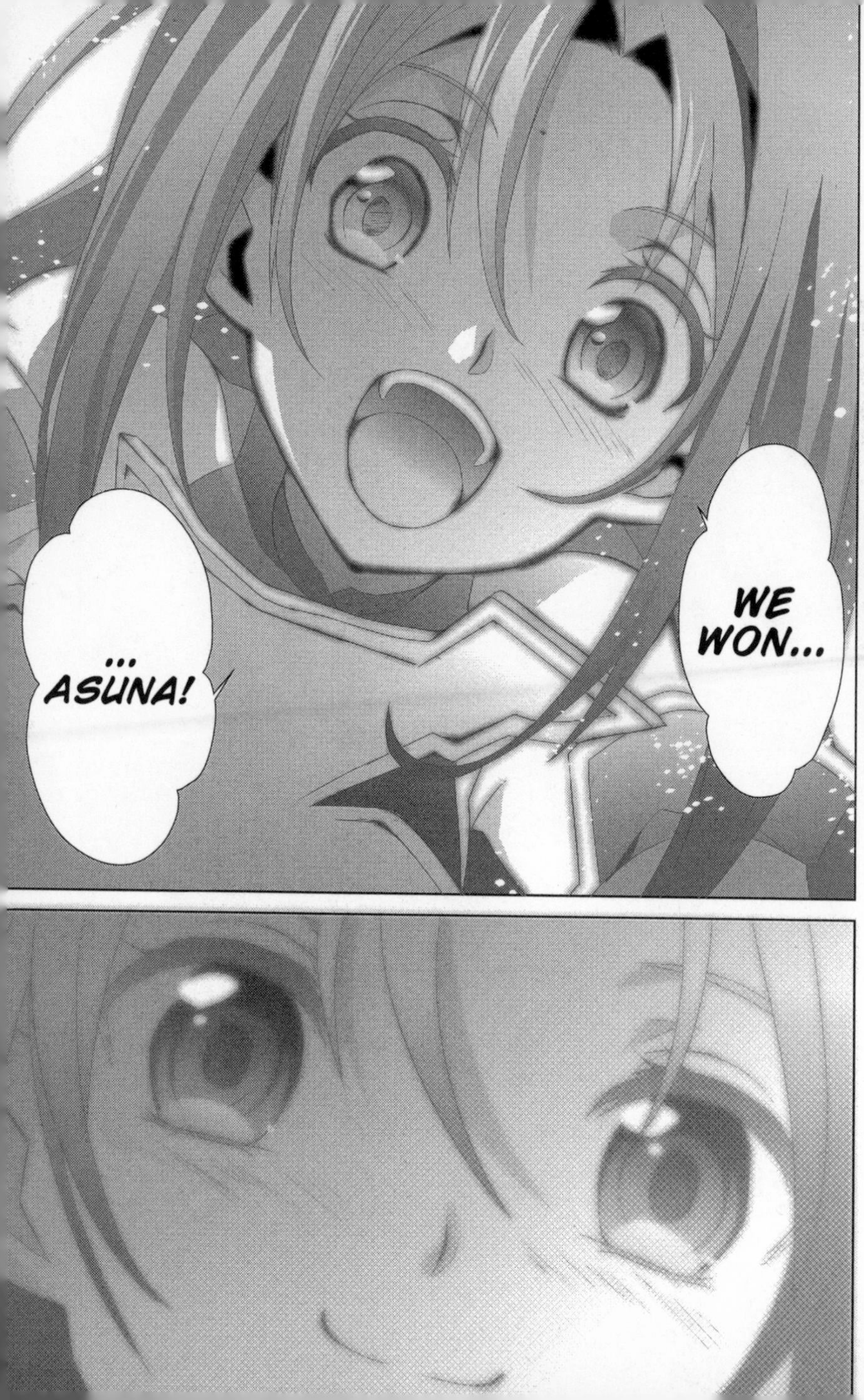
WE WON...
...ASÜNA!

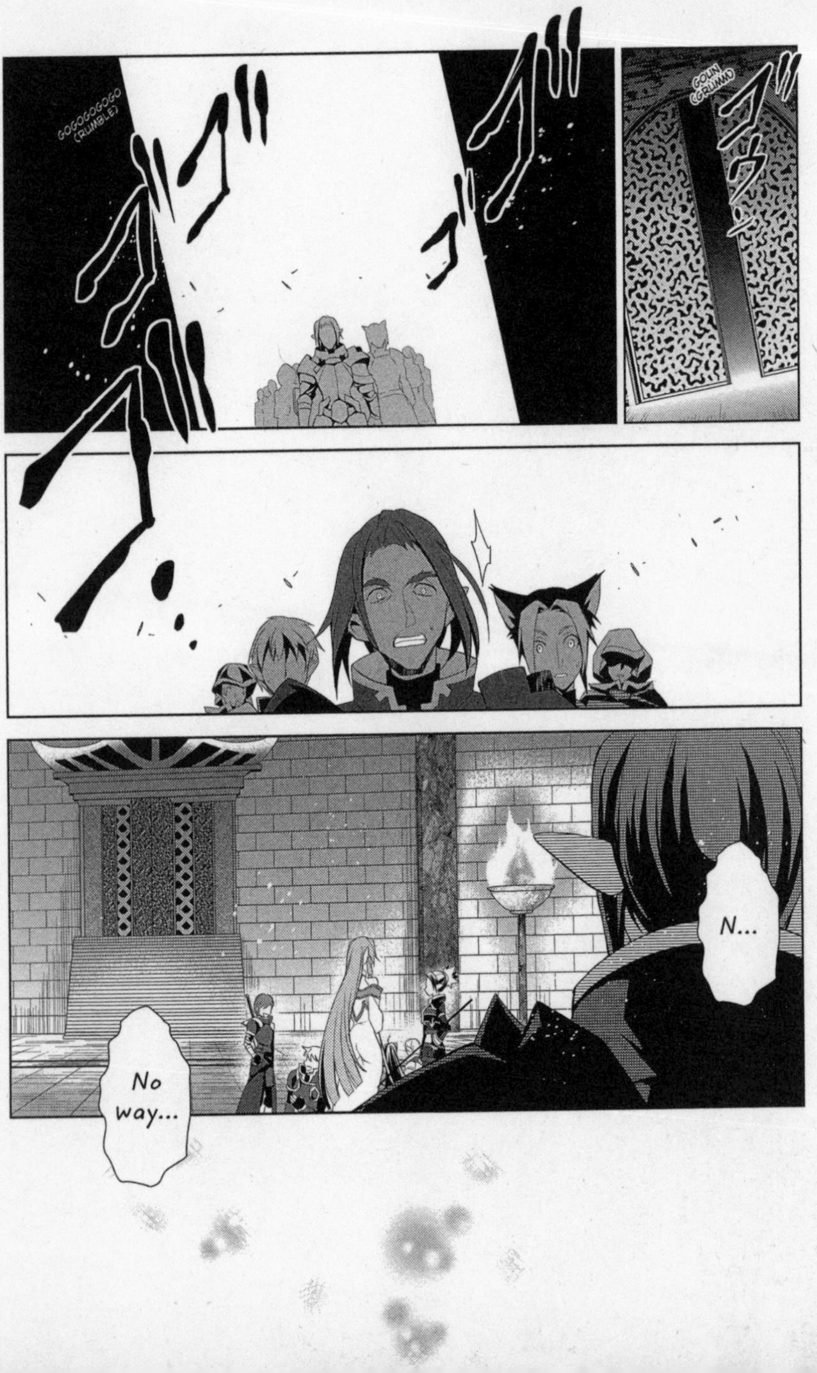
GOUN (GRUMM)
GOGOGOGOGO (RUMBLE)
N...
No way...

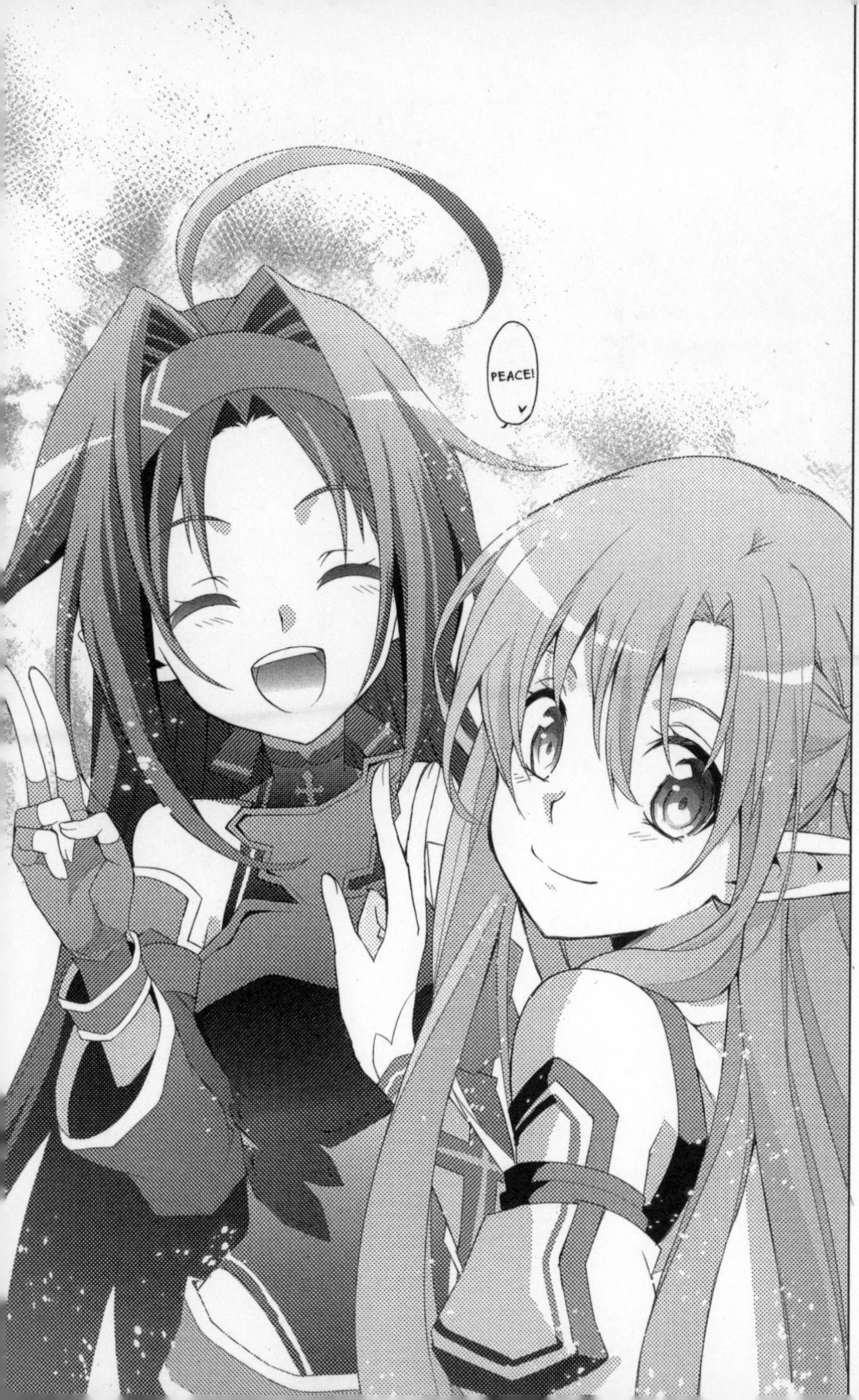
PEACE!

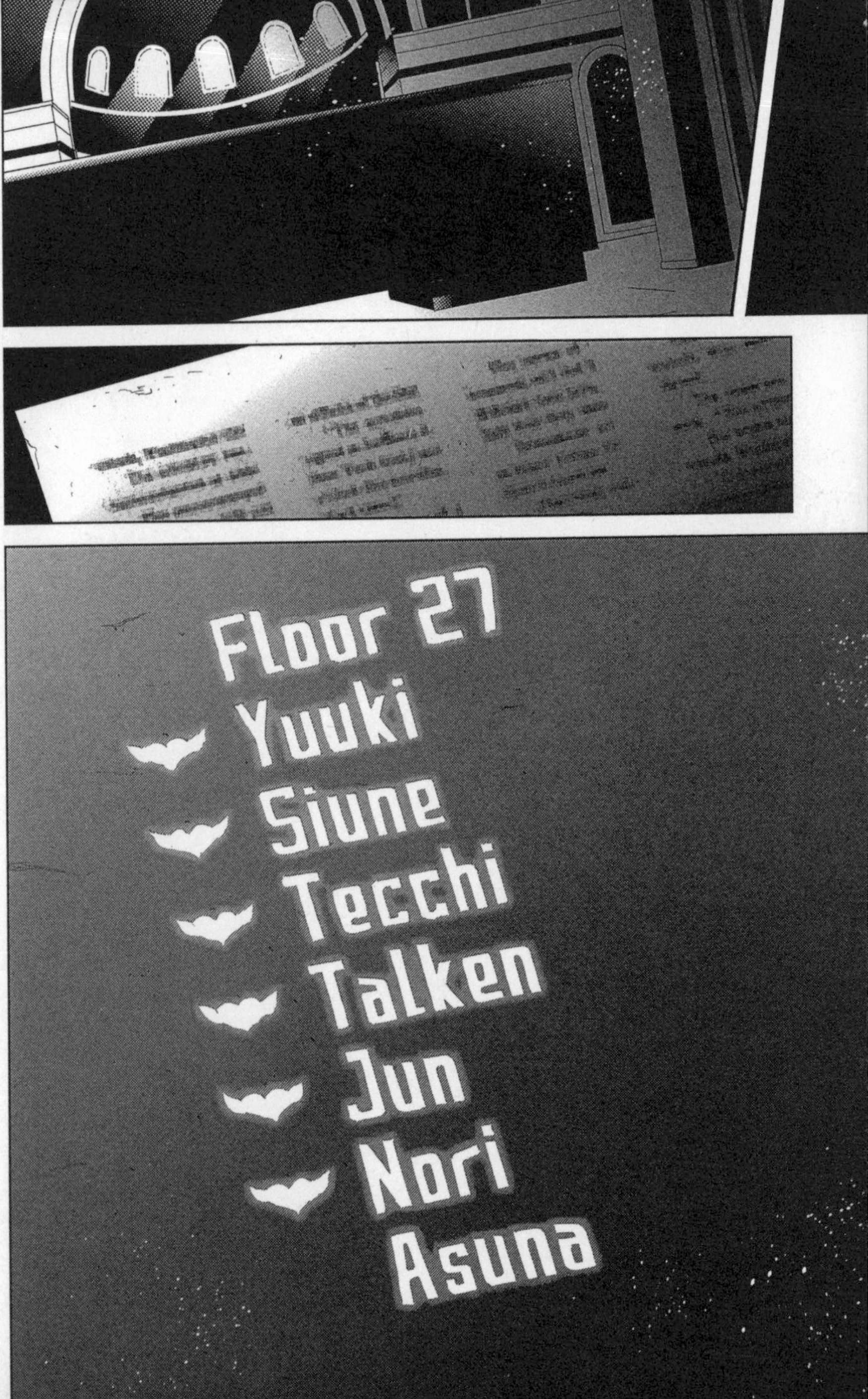
Floor 27
Yuuki
Siune
Tecchi
Talken
Jun
Nori
Asuna

SWORD ART ONLINE
mother's rosary

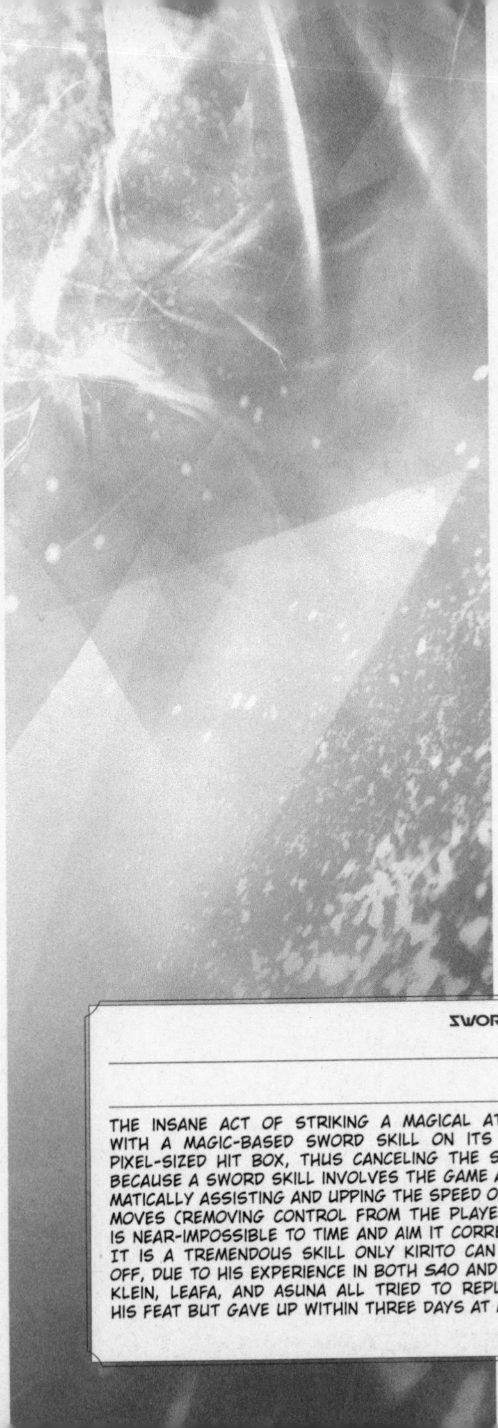

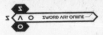

SWORD ART ONLINE mother's ROSARY 03

BACKGROUND GUIDE

SPELL-BLASTING

THE INSANE ACT OF STRIKING A MAGICAL ATTACK WITH A MAGIC-BASED SWORD SKILL ON ITS ONE-PIXEL-SIZED HIT BOX, THUS CANCELING THE SPELL. BECAUSE A SWORD SKILL INVOLVES THE GAME AUTOMATICALLY ASSISTING AND UPPING THE SPEED OF THE MOVES (REMOVING CONTROL FROM THE PLAYER), IT IS NEAR-IMPOSSIBLE TO TIME AND AIM IT CORRECTLY. IT IS A TREMENDOUS SKILL ONLY KIRITO CAN PULL OFF, DUE TO HIS EXPERIENCE IN BOTH SAO AND GGO. KLEIN, LEAFA, AND ASUNA ALL TRIED TO REPLICATE HIS FEAT BUT GAVE UP WITHIN THREE DAYS AT MOST.

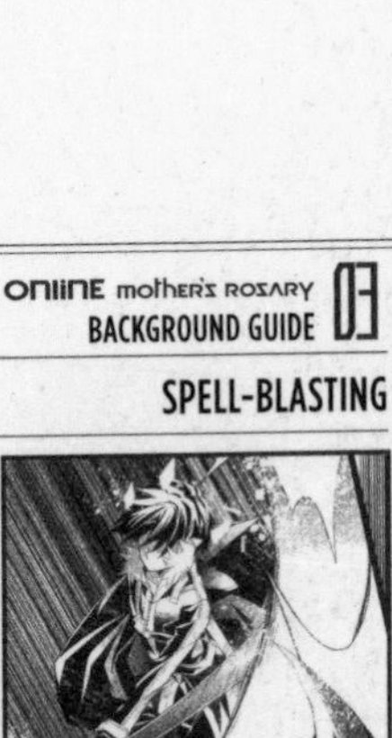

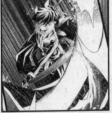

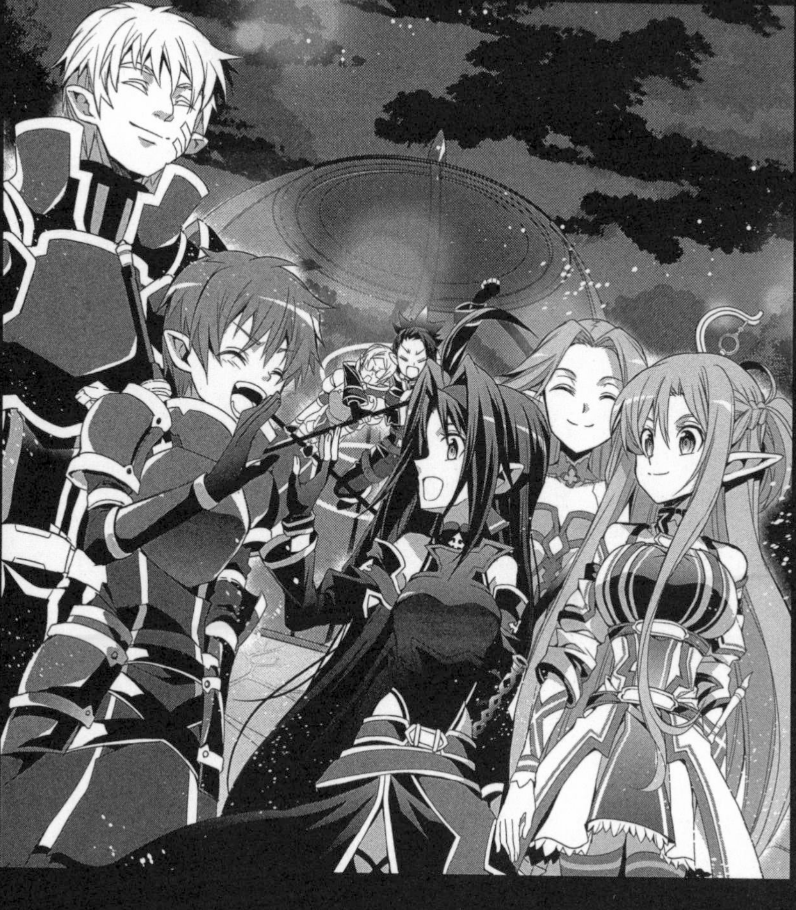

stage.007

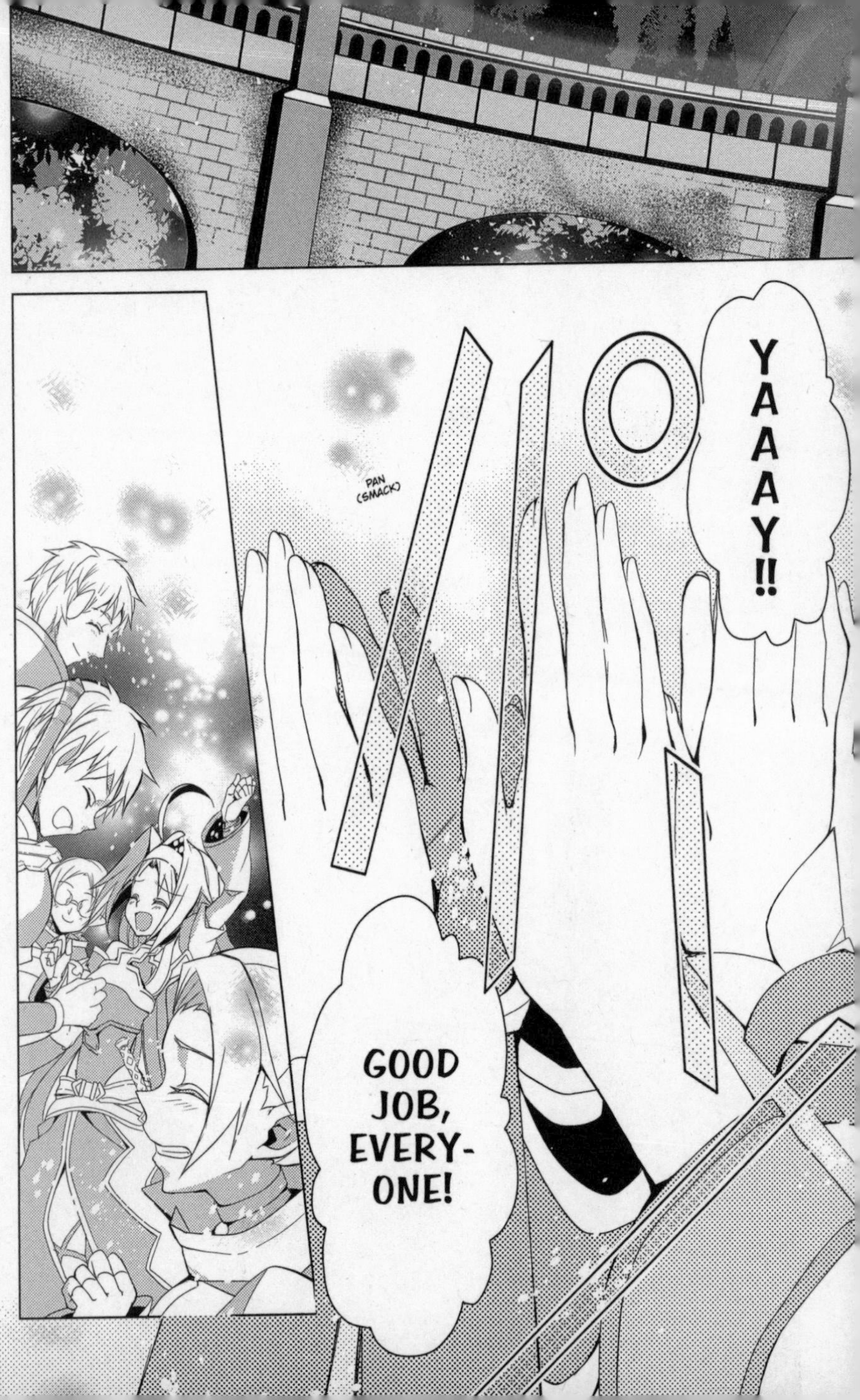
YAAAY!!
PAN (SMACK)
GOOD JOB, EVERY-ONE!

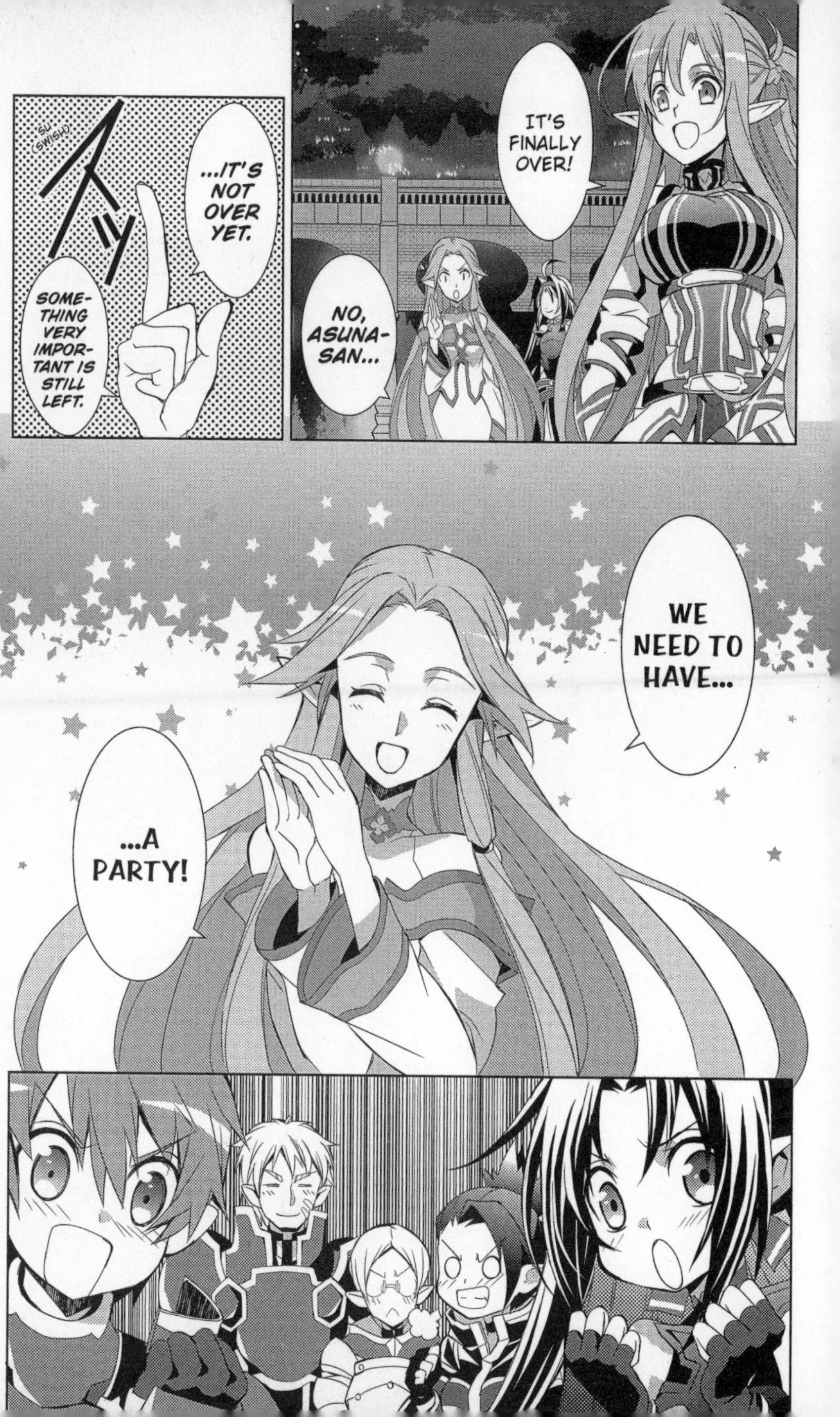
IT'S FINALLY OVER!
NO, ASUNA-SAN...
...IT'S NOT OVER YET.
SU (SWISH)
SOMETHING VERY IMPORTANT IS STILL LEFT.
WE NEED TO HAVE...
...A PARTY!

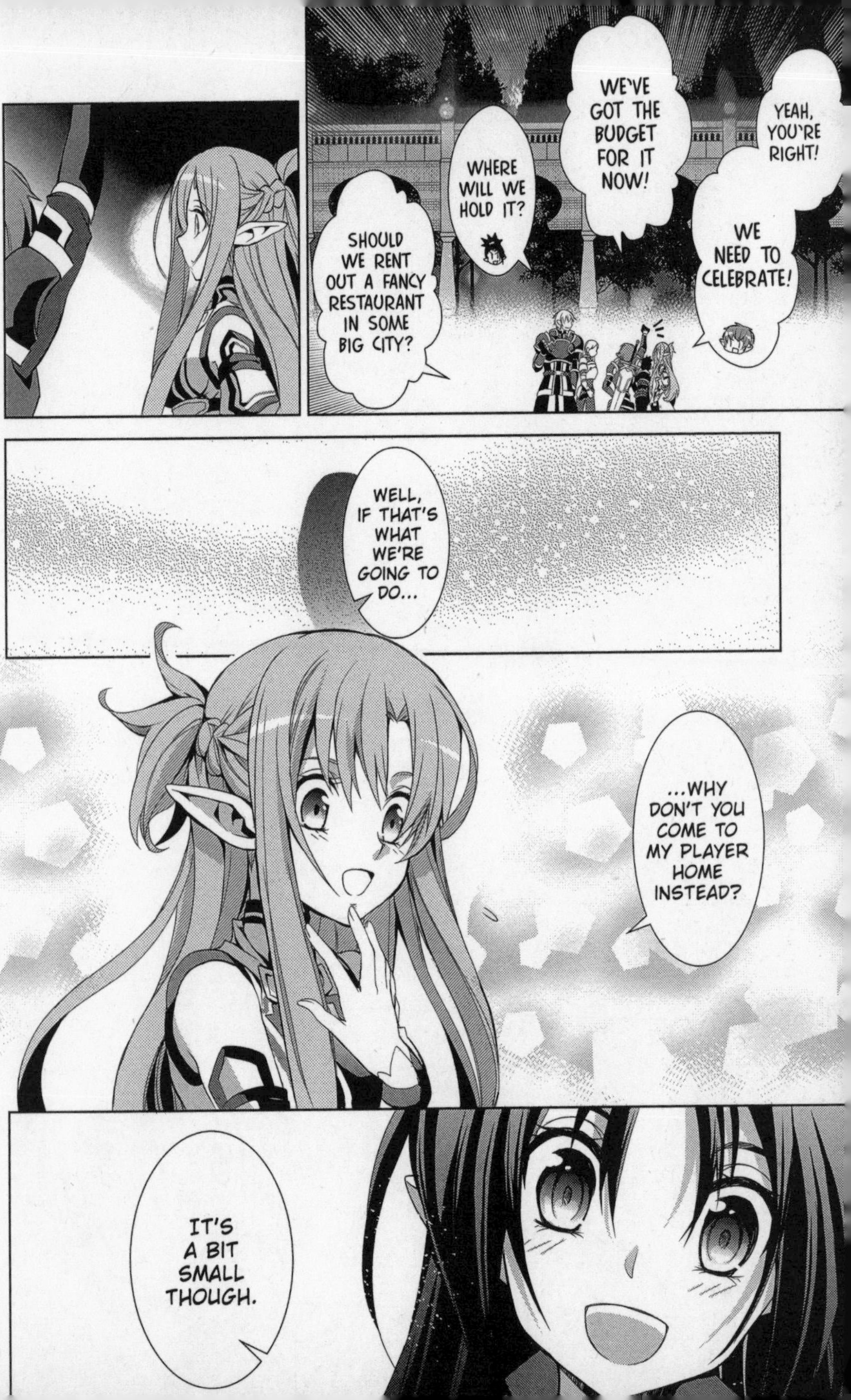
YEAH, YOU'RE RIGHT!
WE NEED TO CELEBRATE!
WE'VE GOT THE BUDGET FOR IT NOW!
WHERE WILL WE HOLD IT?
SHOULD WE RENT OUT A FANCY RESTAURANT IN SOME BIG CITY?
WELL, IF THAT'S WHAT WE'RE GOING TO DO...
...WHY DON'T YOU COME TO MY PLAYER HOME INSTEAD?
IT'S A BIT SMALL THOUGH.

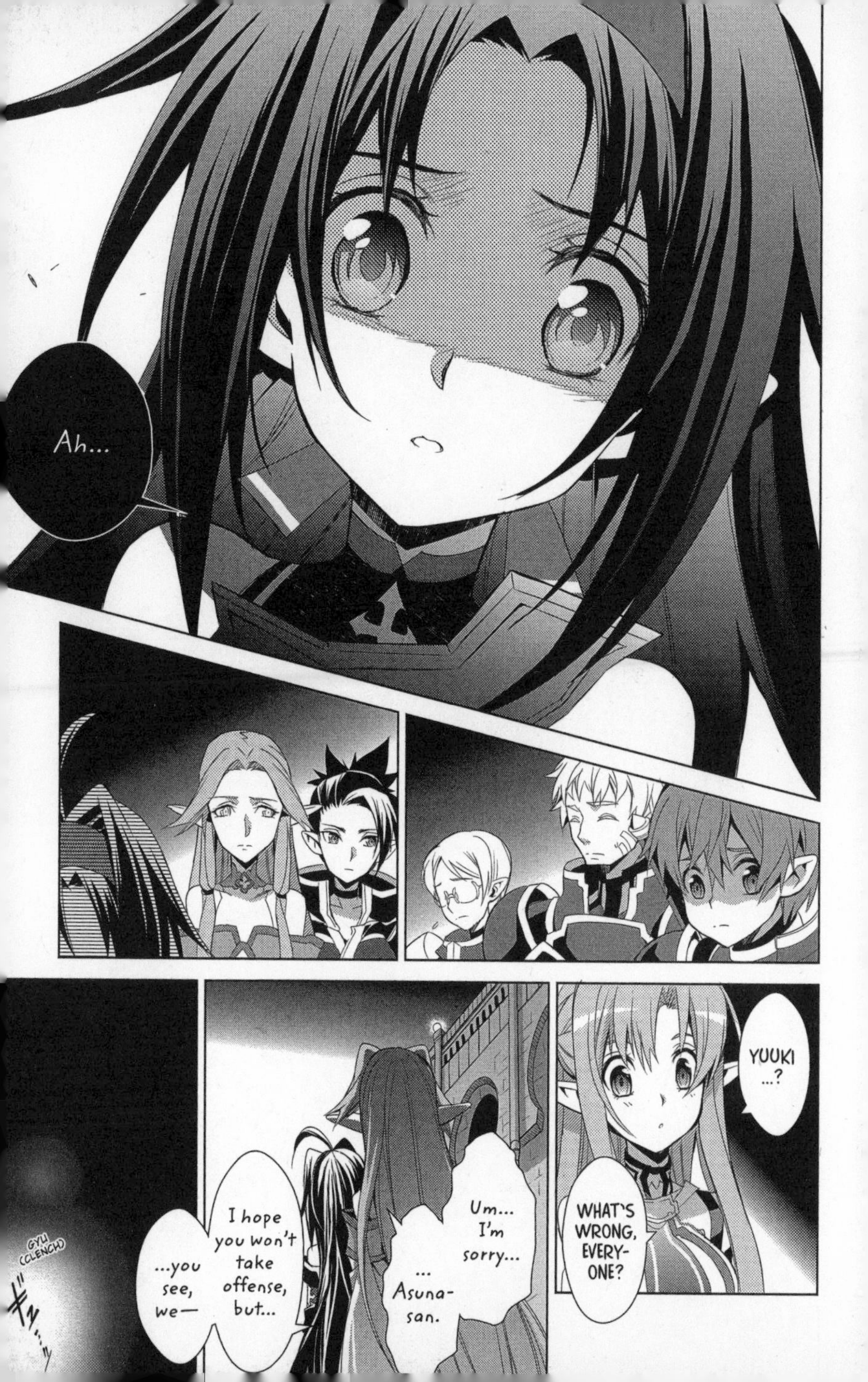
Ah...
YUUKI ...?
WHAT'S WRONG, EVERYONE?
Um... I'm sorry...
... Asuna-san.
I hope you won't take offense, but...
...you see, we—
GYU (CLENCH)

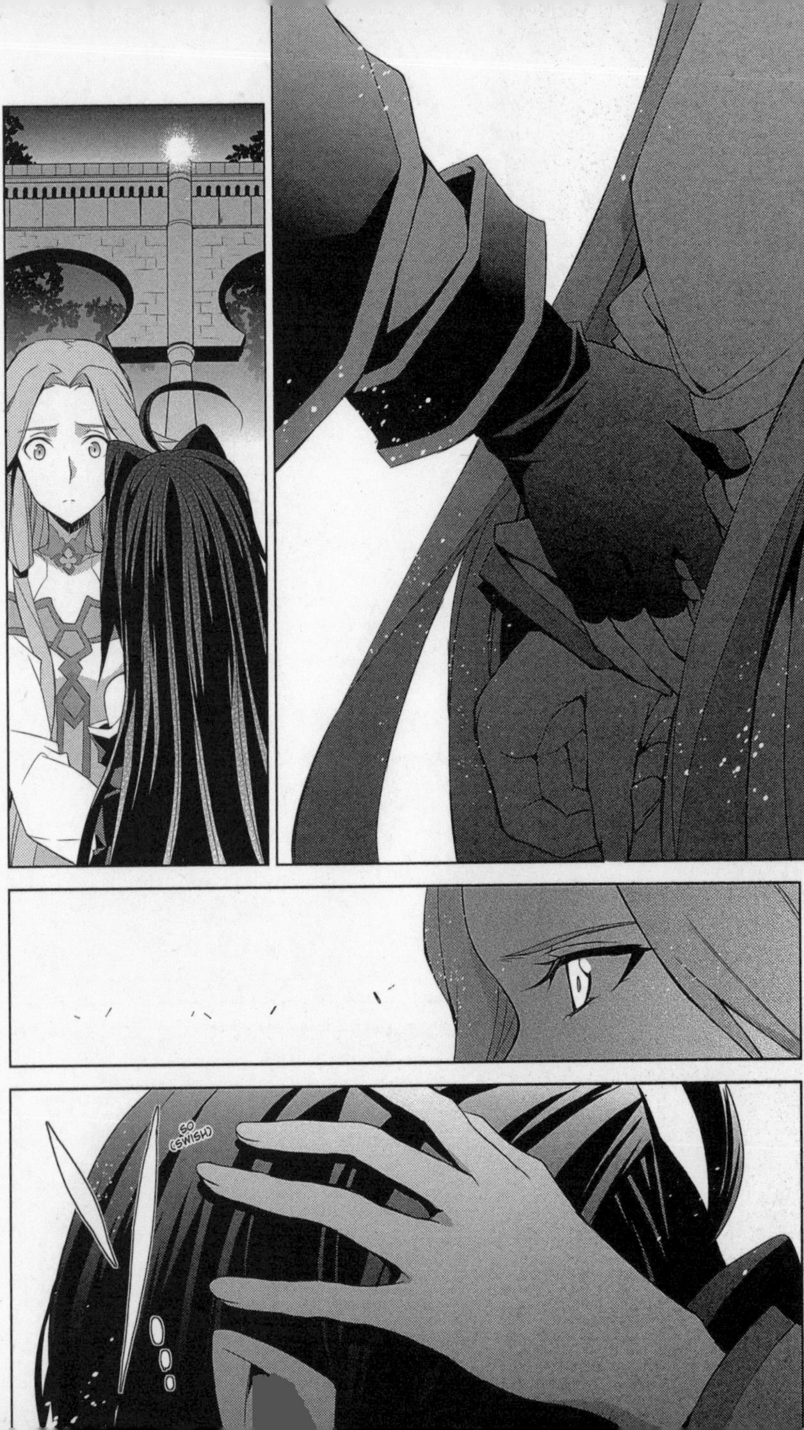
SO
(SWISH)

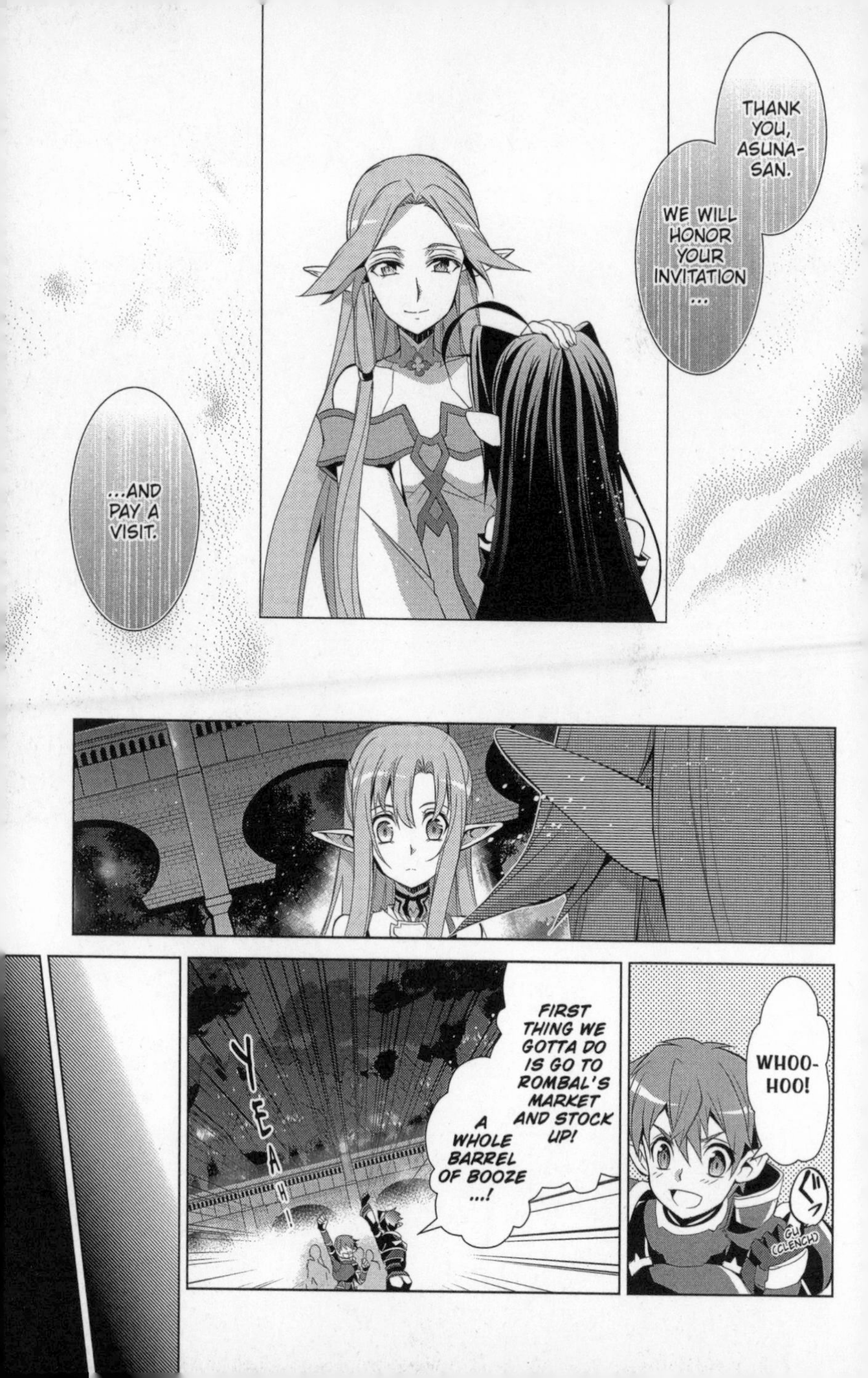
THANK YOU, ASUNA-SAN.
WE WILL HONOR YOUR INVITATION...
...AND PAY A VISIT.
WHOO-HOO!
GU (CLENCH)
FIRST THING WE GOTTA DO IS GO TO ROMBAL'S MARKET AND STOCK UP!
A WHOLE BARREL OF BOOZE...!
YEAAH!

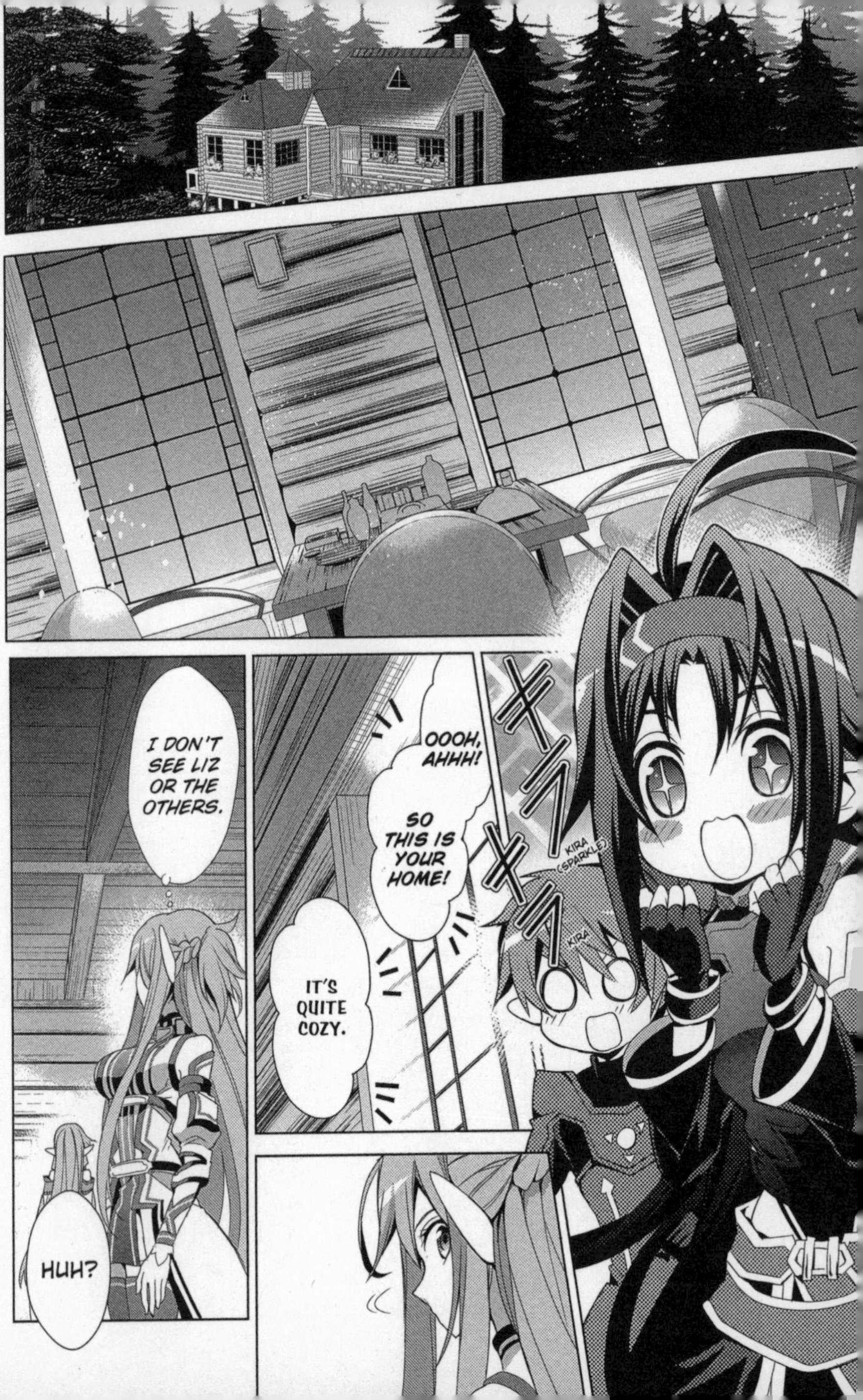
OOOH, AHHH!
SO THIS IS YOUR HOME!
KIRA (SPARKLE)
KIRA
IT'S QUITE COZY.
I DON'T SEE LIZ OR THE OTHERS.
HUH?

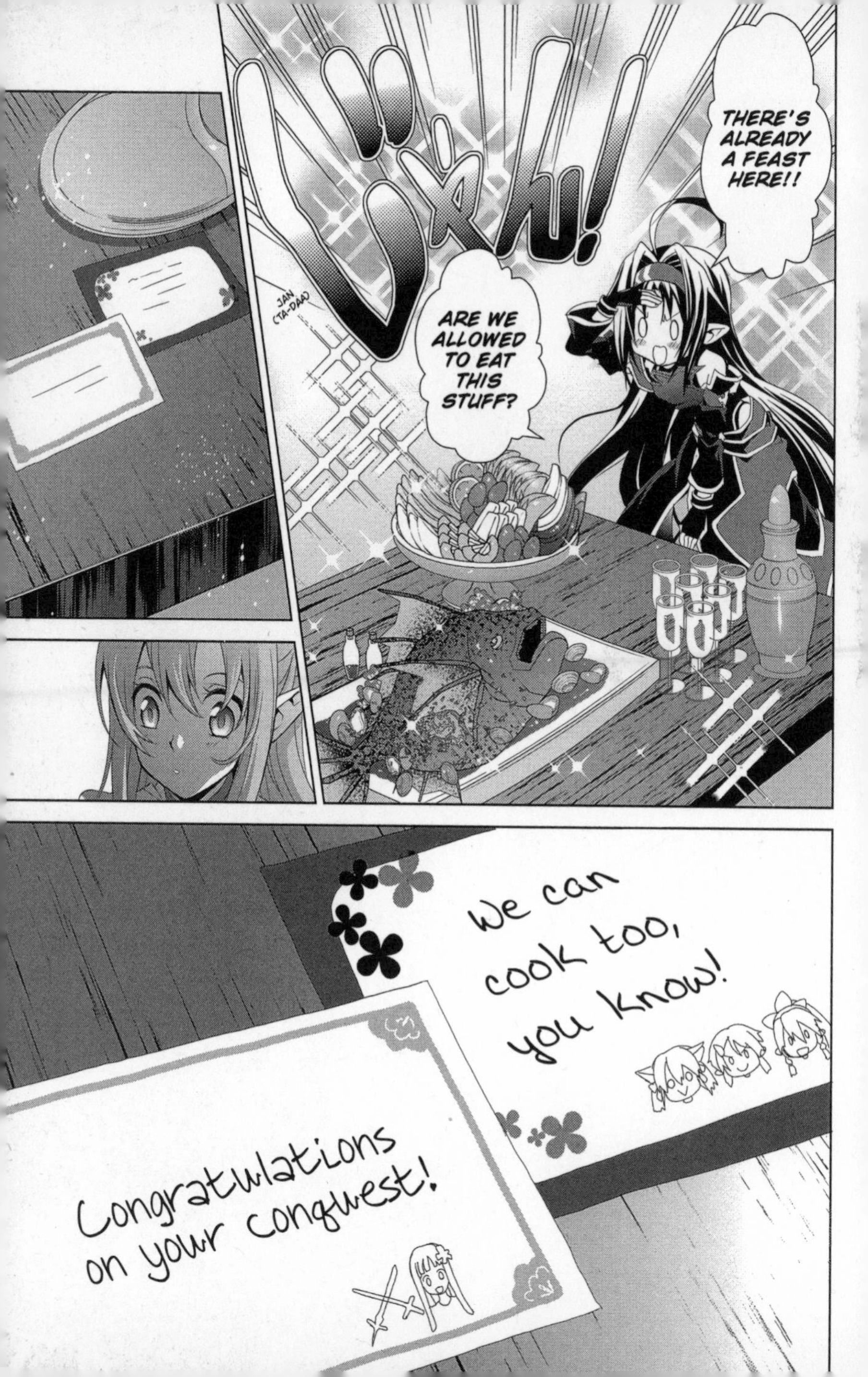
THERE'S ALREADY A FEAST HERE!!
JAN (TA-DAA)
ARE WE ALLOWED TO EAT THIS STUFF?
We can cook too, you know!
Congratulations on your conquest!

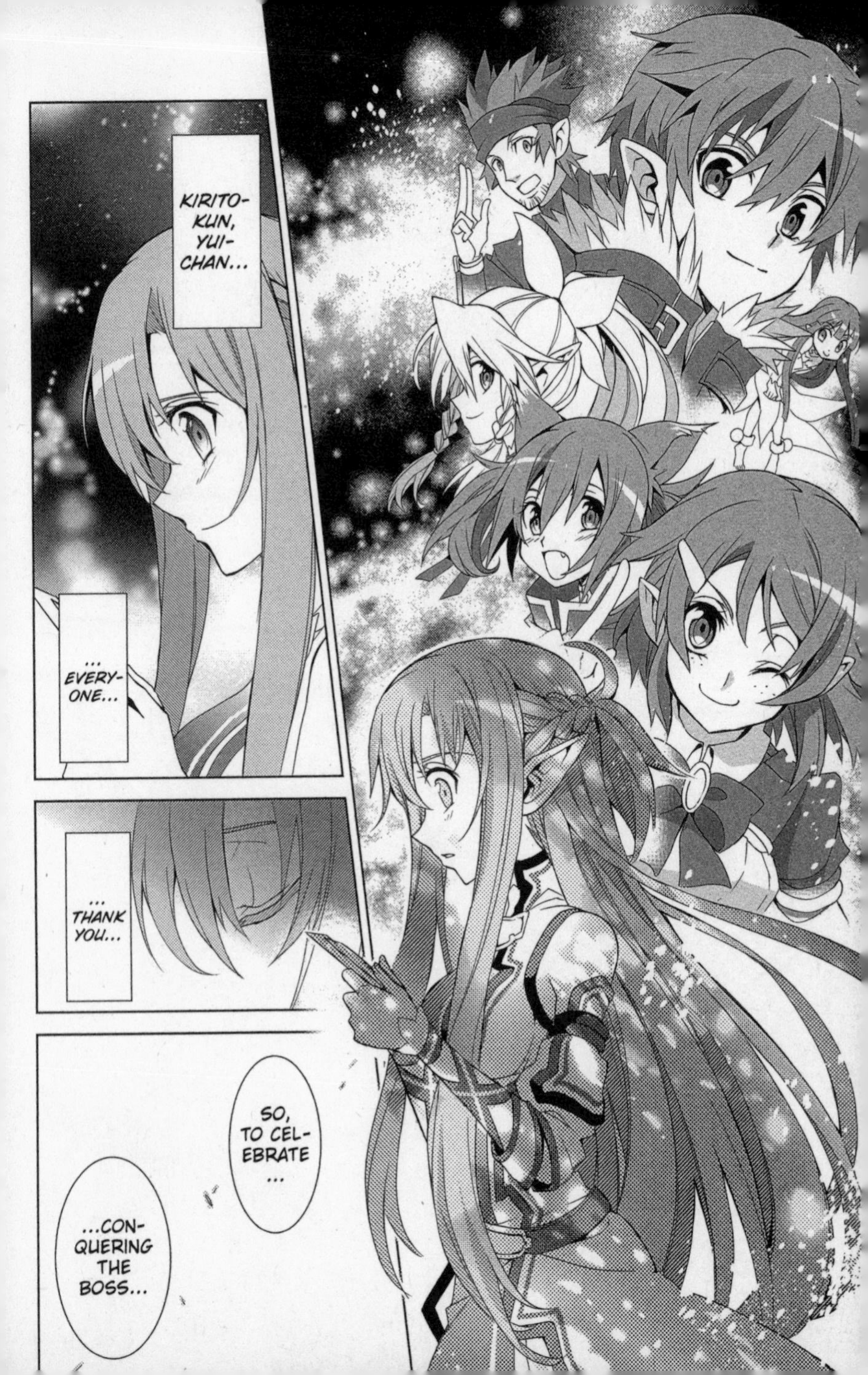
KIRITO-KUN, YUI-CHAN...
...EVERY-ONE...
...THANK YOU...
SO, TO CEL-EBRATE...
...CON-QUERING THE BOSS...

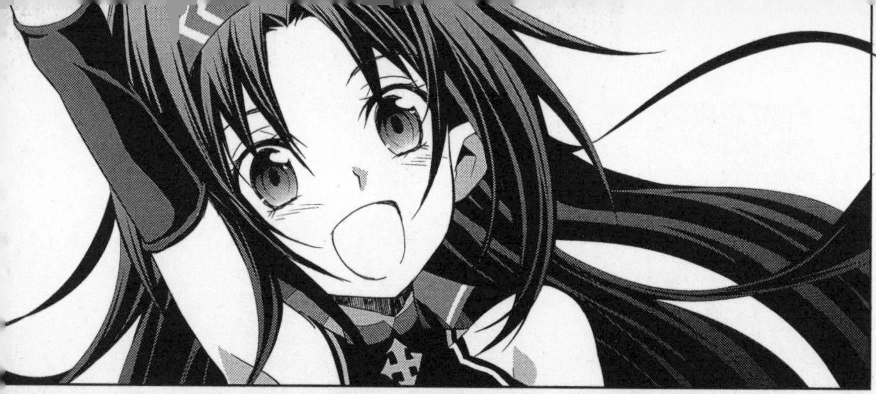
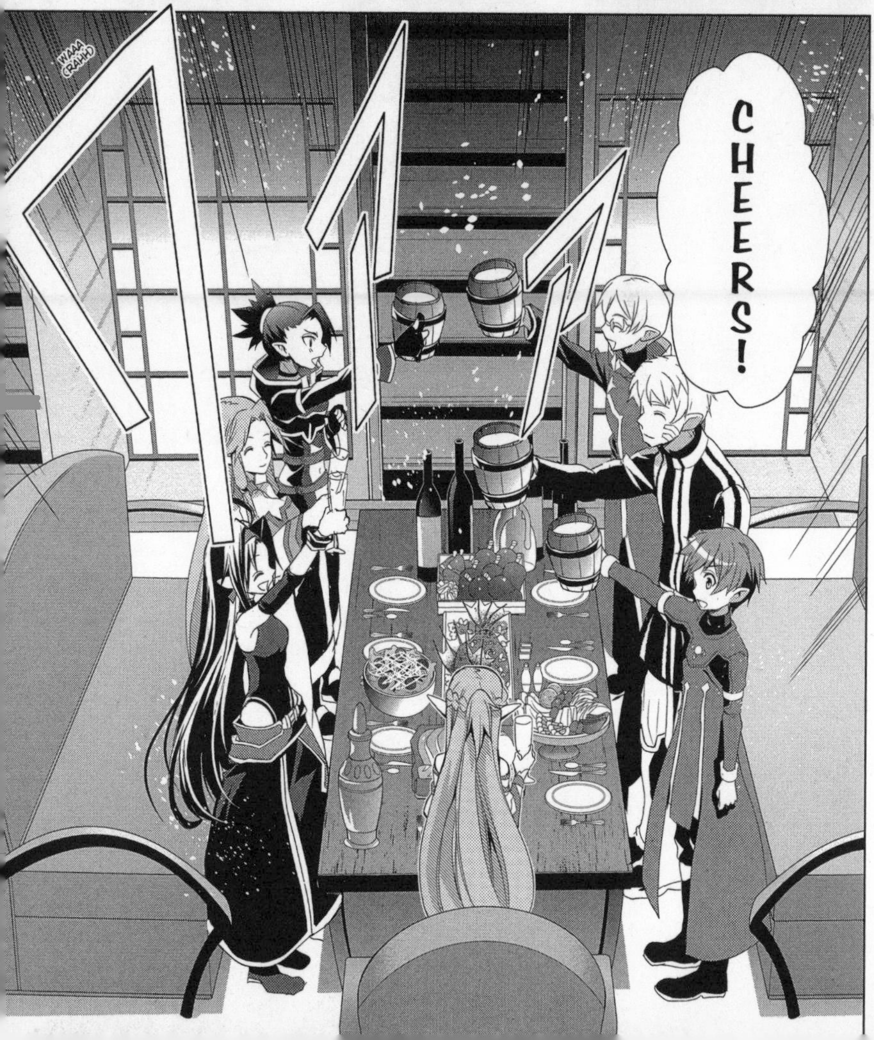
CHEERS!
WAAA CRAHHD

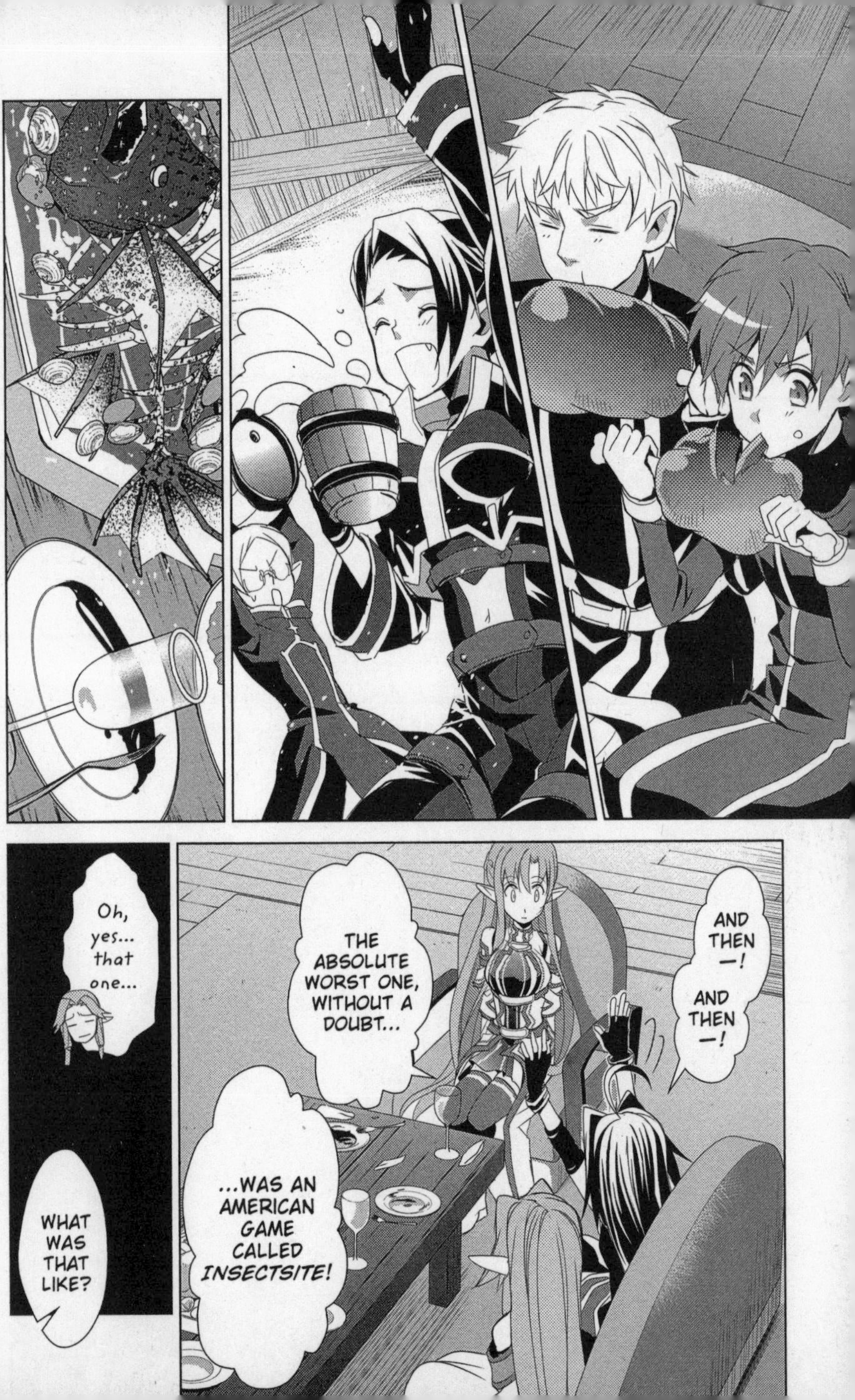
AND THEN—!
AND THEN—!
THE ABSOLUTE WORST ONE, WITHOUT A DOUBT...
...WAS AN AMERICAN GAME CALLED *INSECTSITE*!
Oh, yes... that one...
WHAT WAS THAT LIKE?

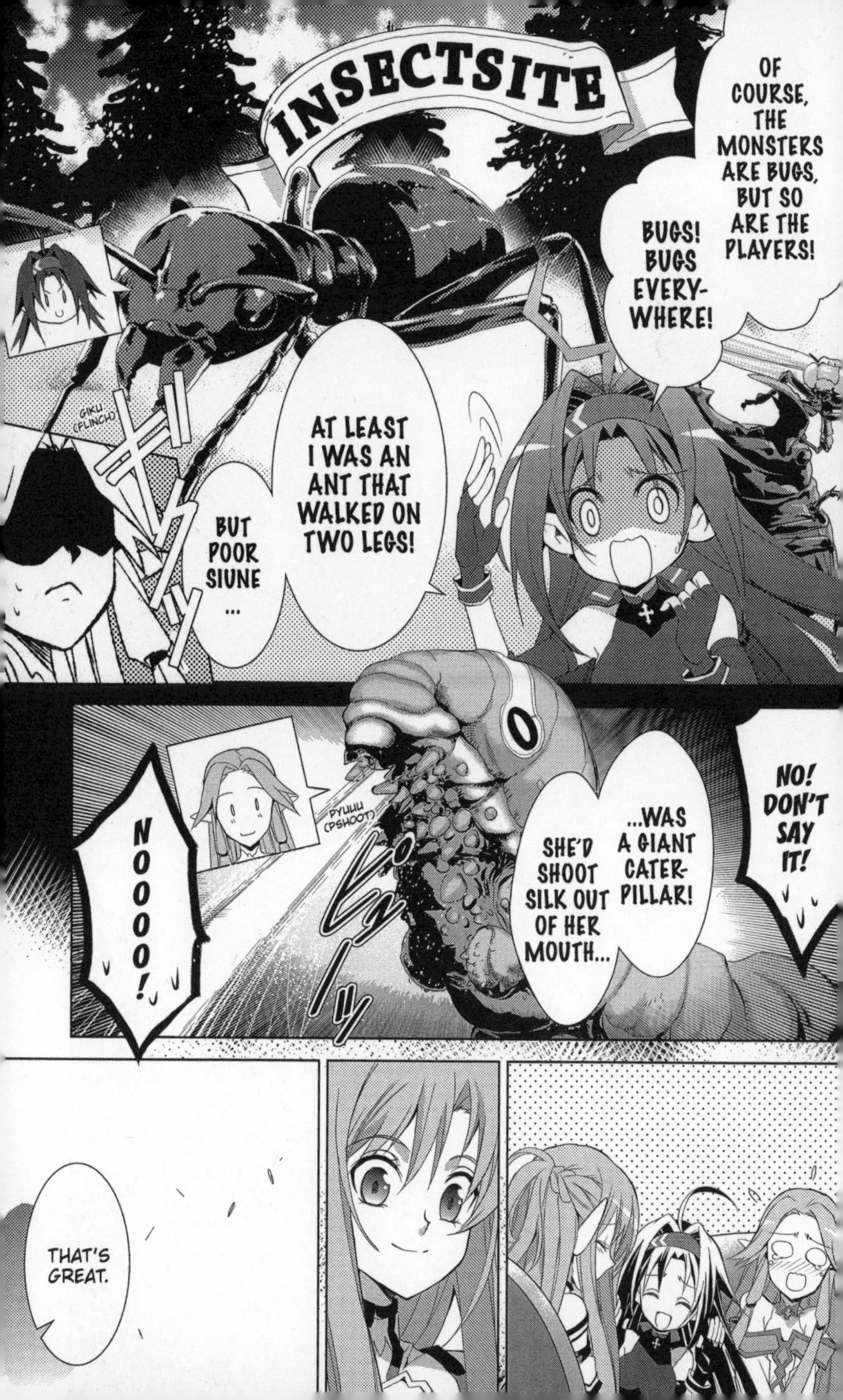
INSECTSITE
OF COURSE, THE MONSTERS ARE BUGS, BUT SO ARE THE PLAYERS!
BUGS! BUGS EVERY-WHERE!
AT LEAST I WAS AN ANT THAT WALKED ON TWO LEGS!
GIKU (FLINCH)
BUT POOR SIUNE ...
NO! DON'T SAY IT!
...WAS A GIANT CATER-PILLAR!
SHE'D SHOOT SILK OUT OF HER MOUTH...
PYUUU (PSHOOT)
NOOOOO!
THAT'S GREAT.

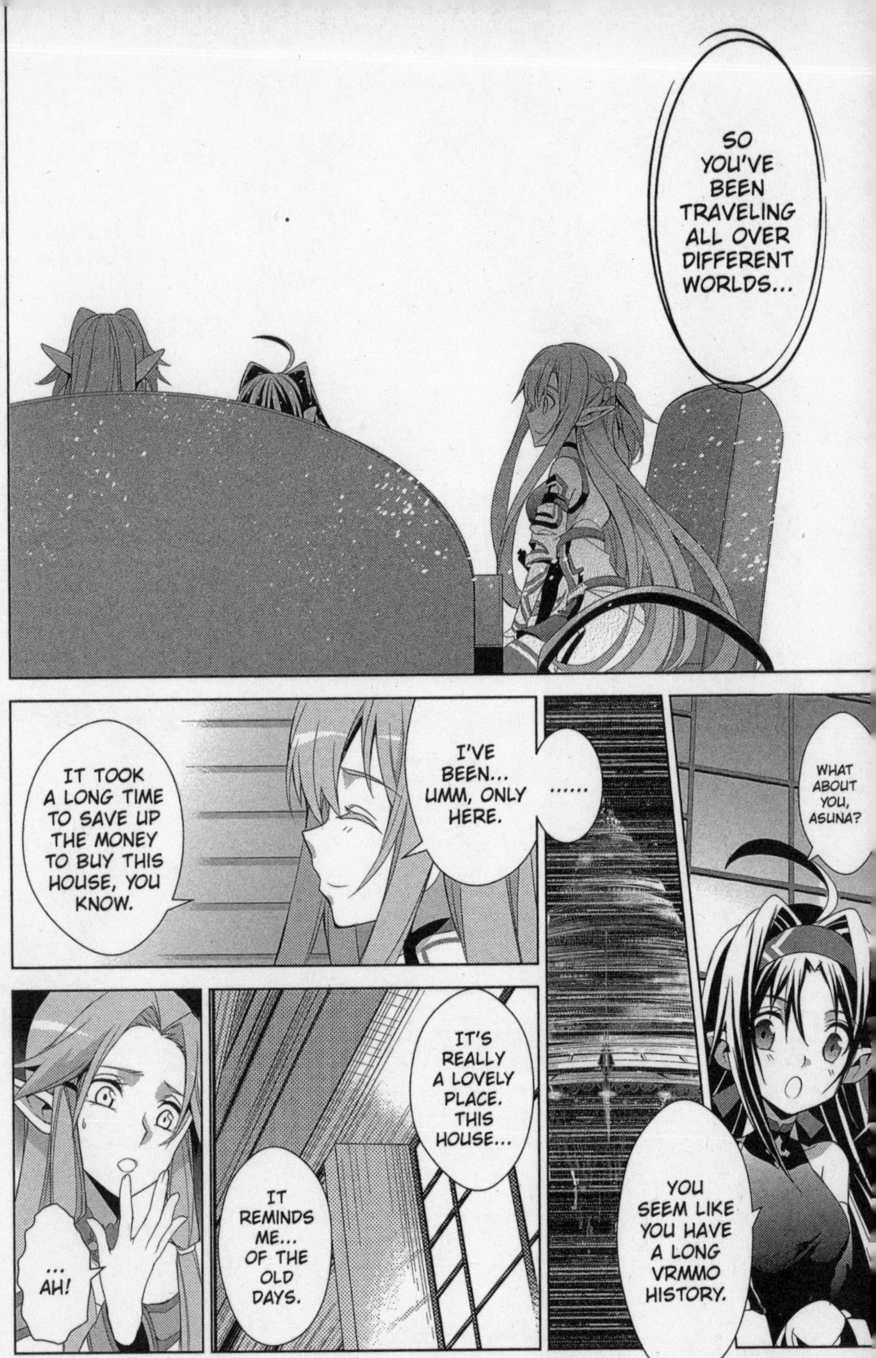
SO YOU'VE BEEN TRAVELING ALL OVER DIFFERENT WORLDS...
WHAT ABOUT YOU, ASUNA?
YOU SEEM LIKE YOU HAVE A LONG VRMMO HISTORY.
......
I'VE BEEN... UMM, ONLY HERE.
IT TOOK A LONG TIME TO SAVE UP THE MONEY TO BUY THIS HOUSE, YOU KNOW.
IT'S REALLY A LOVELY PLACE. THIS HOUSE...
IT REMINDS ME... OF THE OLD DAYS.
... AH!

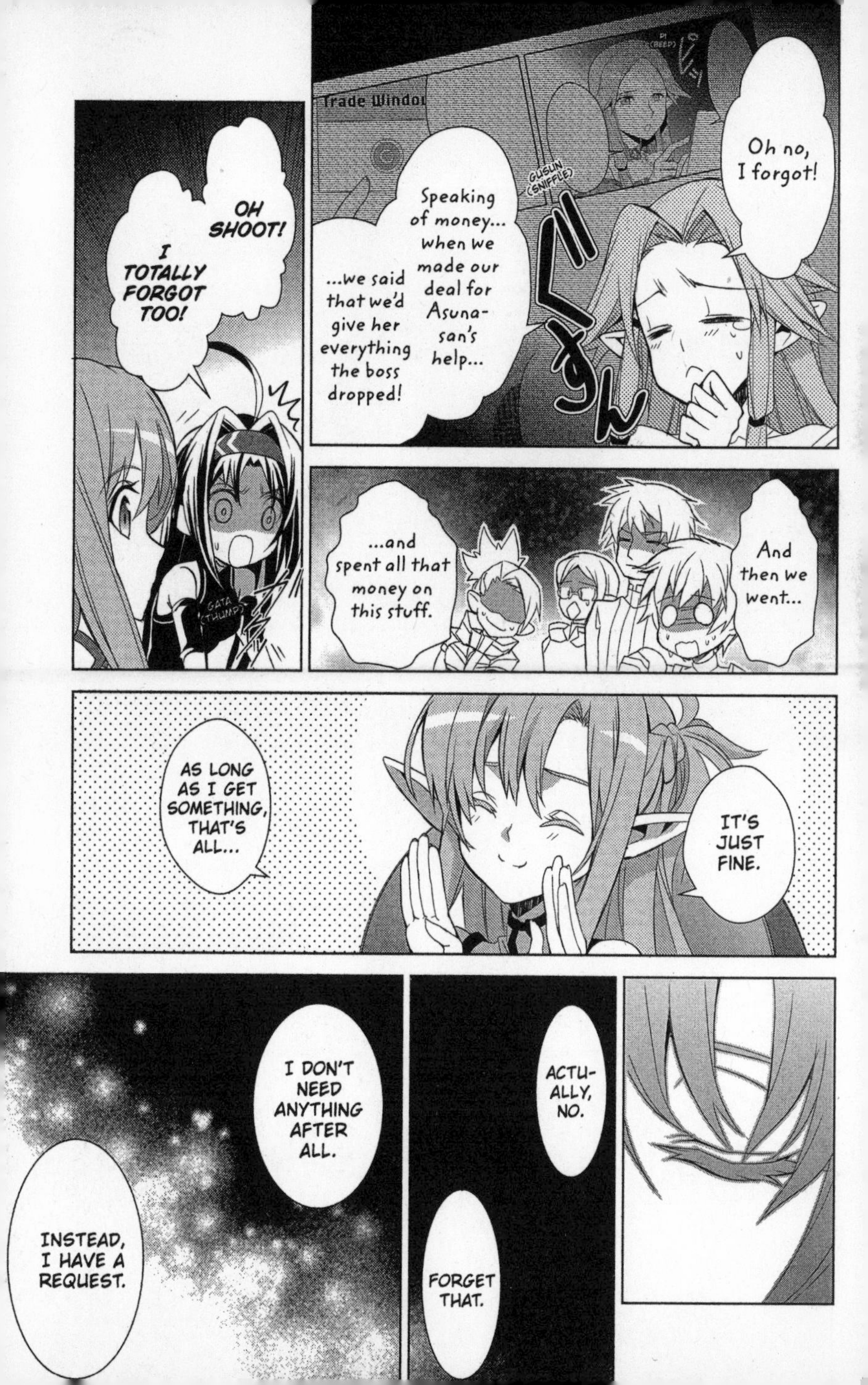
Oh no, I forgot!
PI (BEEP)
Trade Windo
GUSUN (SNIFFLE)
Speaking of money... when we made our deal for Asuna-san's help...
...we said that we'd give her everything the boss dropped!
And then we went...
...and spent all that money on this stuff.
OH SHOOT! I TOTALLY FORGOT TOO!
GATA (THUMP)
IT'S JUST FINE.
AS LONG AS I GET SOMETHING, THAT'S ALL...
ACTU-ALLY, NO.
FORGET THAT.
I DON'T NEED ANYTHING AFTER ALL.
INSTEAD, I HAVE A REQUEST.

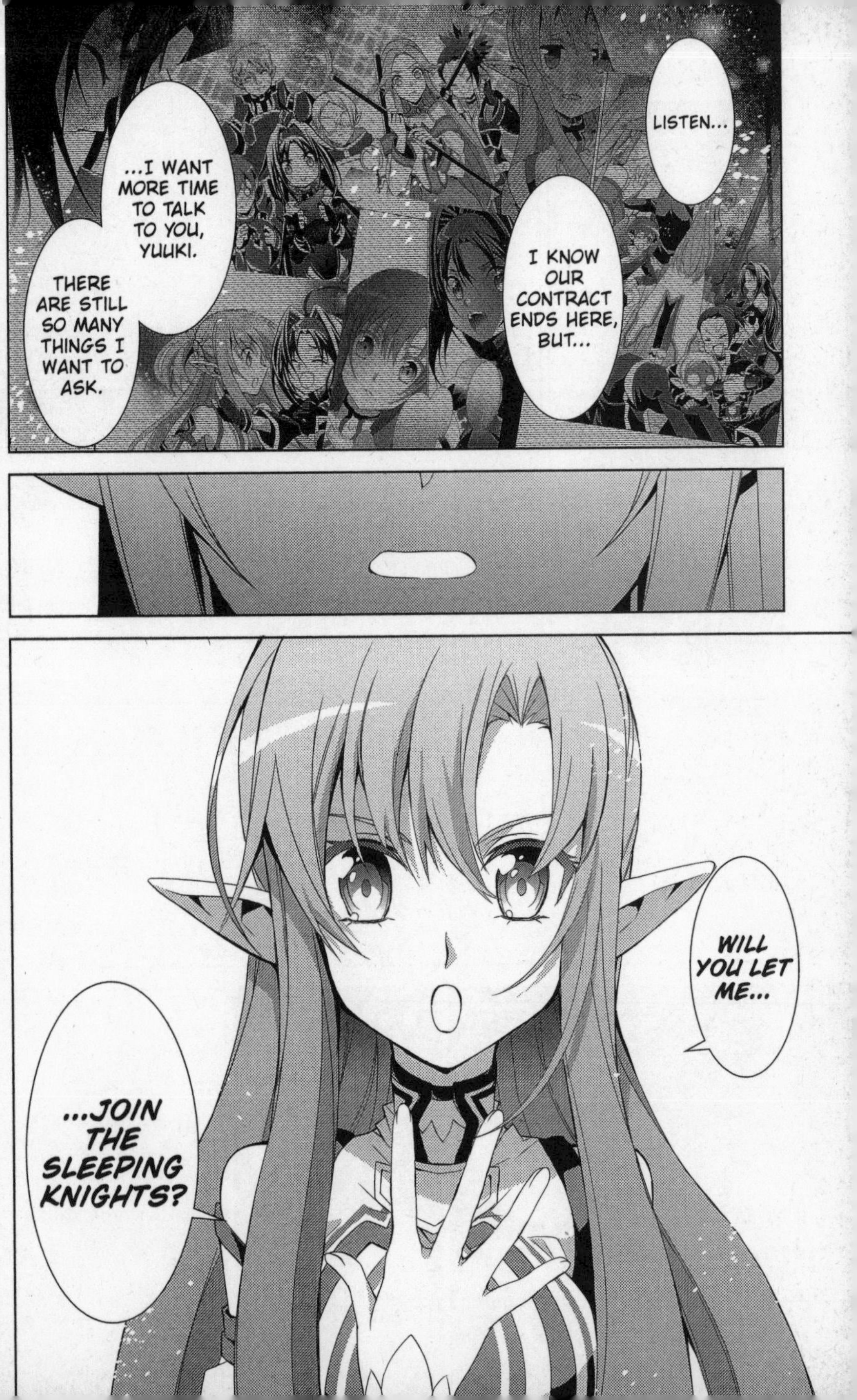
LISTEN...
I KNOW OUR CONTRACT ENDS HERE, BUT...
...I WANT MORE TIME TO TALK TO YOU, YUUKI.
THERE ARE STILL SO MANY THINGS I WANT TO ASK.
WILL YOU LET ME...
...JOIN THE SLEEPING KNIGHTS?

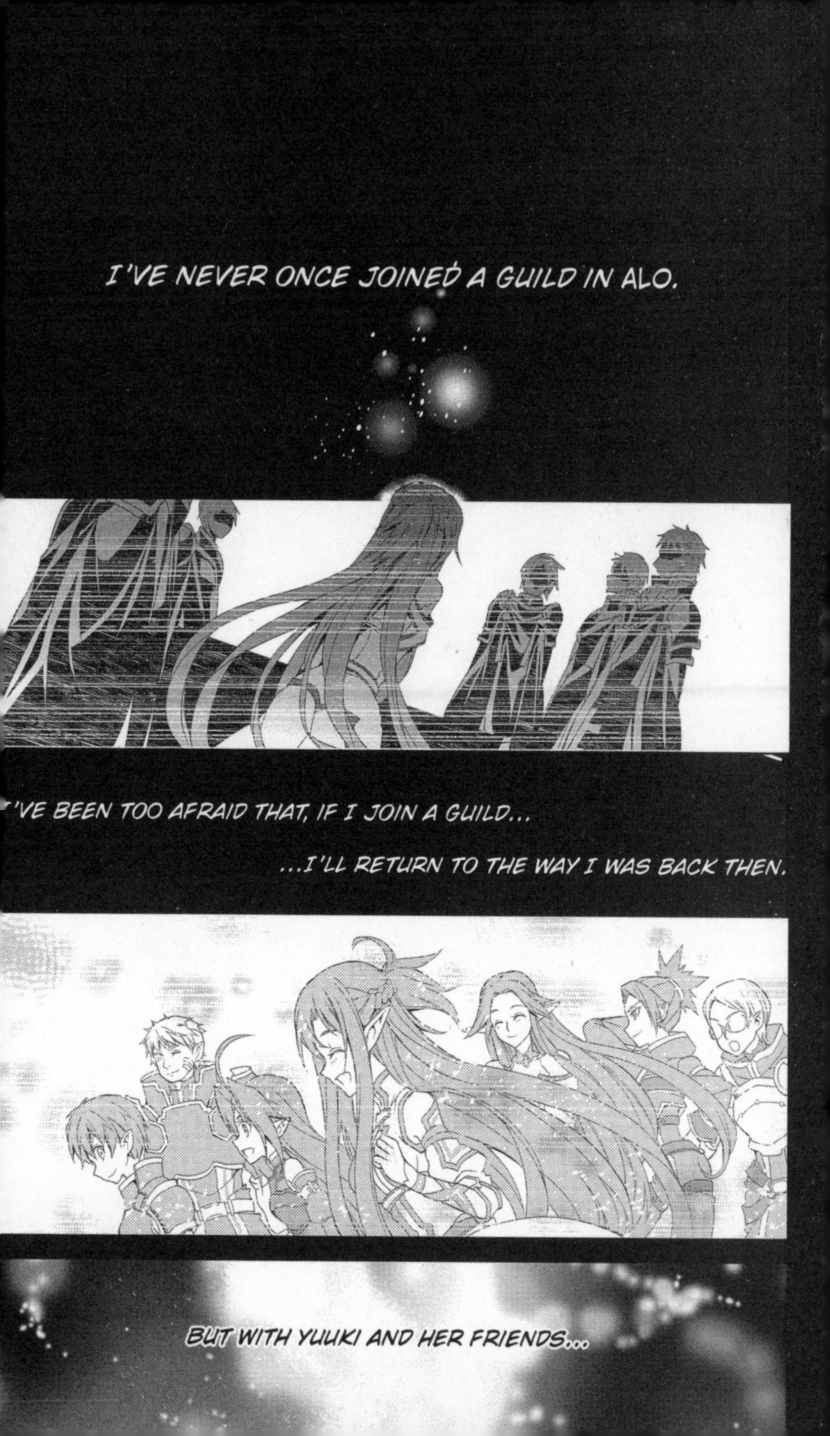
I'VE NEVER ONCE JOINED A GUILD IN ALO.
'VE BEEN TOO AFRAID THAT, IF I JOIN A GUILD...
...I'LL RETURN TO THE WAY I WAS BACK THEN.
BUT WITH YUUKI AND HER FRIENDS...

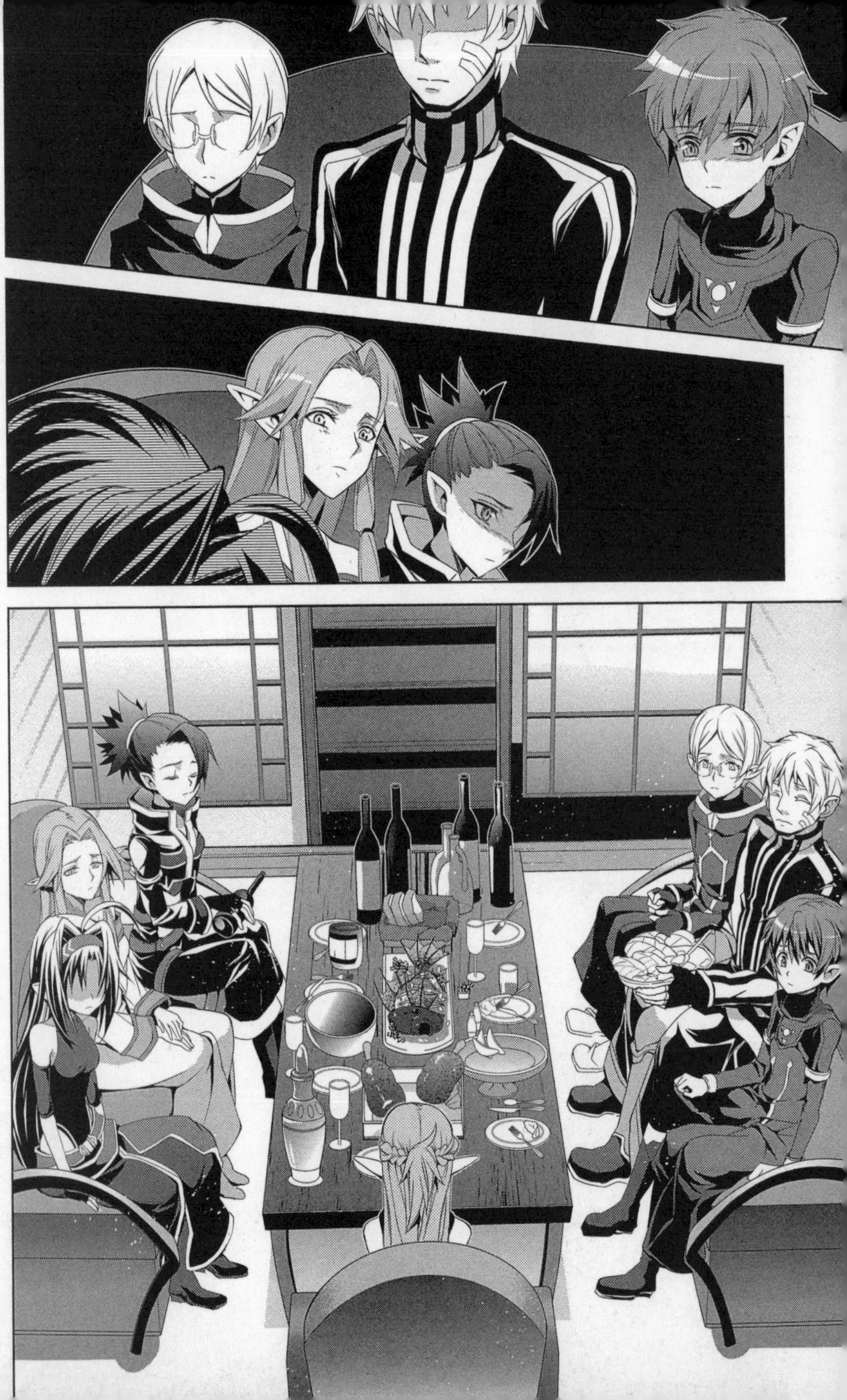

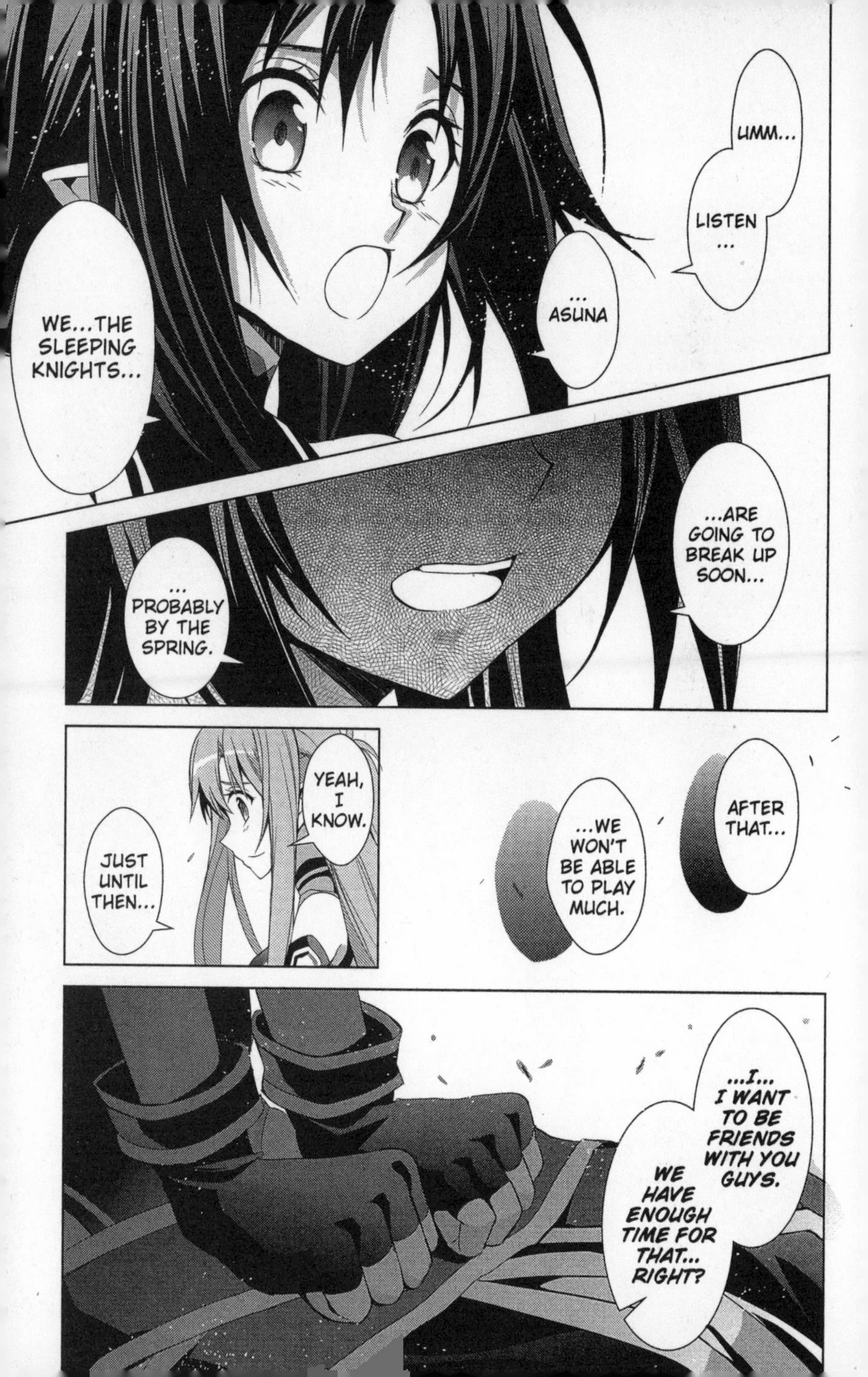
UMM...
LISTEN ...
... ASUNA
WE...THE SLEEPING KNIGHTS...
...ARE GOING TO BREAK UP SOON...
... PROBABLY BY THE SPRING.
AFTER THAT...
...WE WON'T BE ABLE TO PLAY MUCH.
YEAH, I KNOW.
JUST UNTIL THEN...
...I... I WANT TO BE FRIENDS WITH YOU GUYS.
WE HAVE ENOUGH TIME FOR THAT... RIGHT?

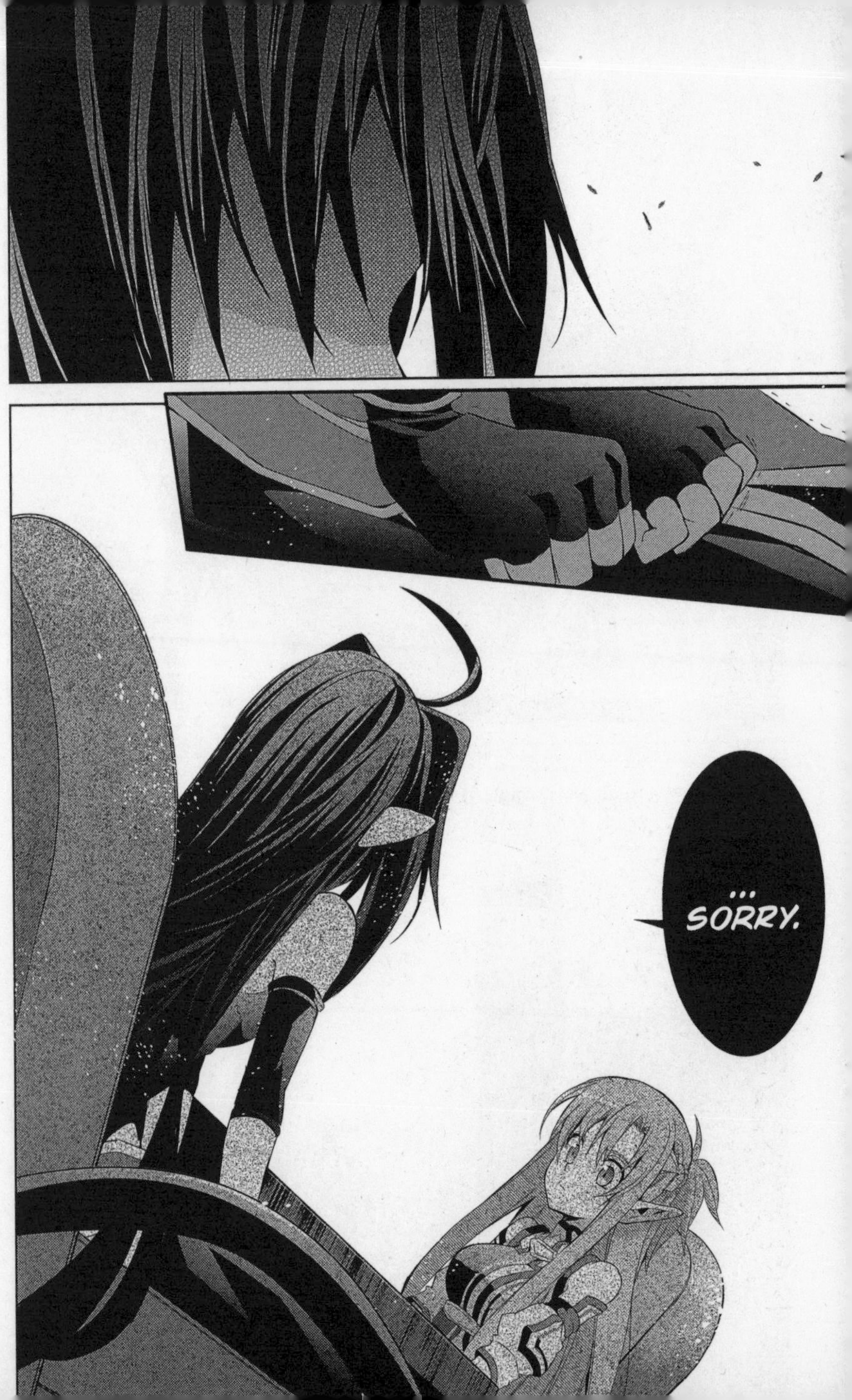
...
SORRY.

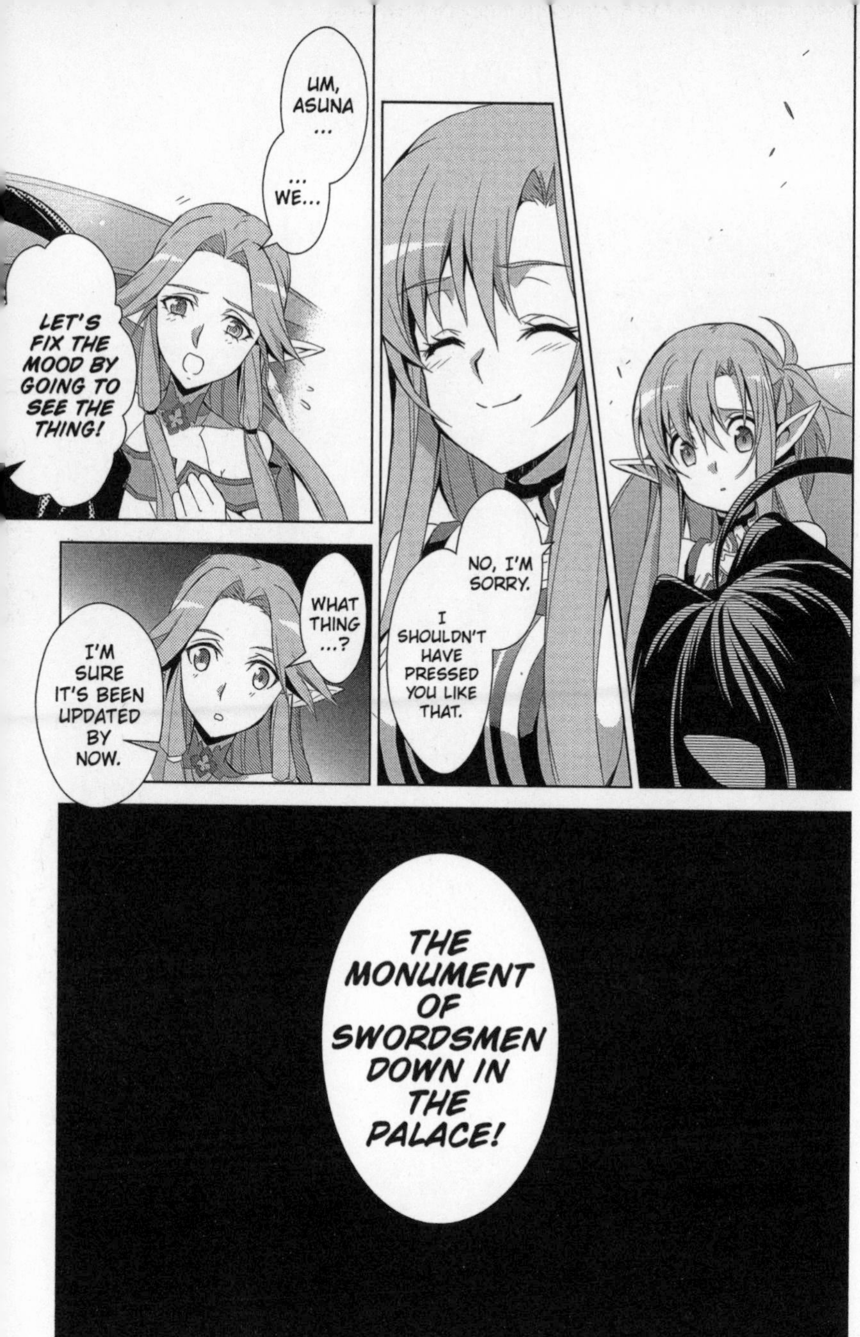
NO, I'M SORRY.
I SHOULDN'T HAVE PRESSED YOU LIKE THAT.
UM, ASUNA...
...WE...
LET'S FIX THE MOOD BY GOING TO SEE THE THING!
WHAT THING...?
I'M SURE IT'S BEEN UPDATED BY NOW.
THE MONUMENT OF SWORDSMEN DOWN IN THE PALACE!

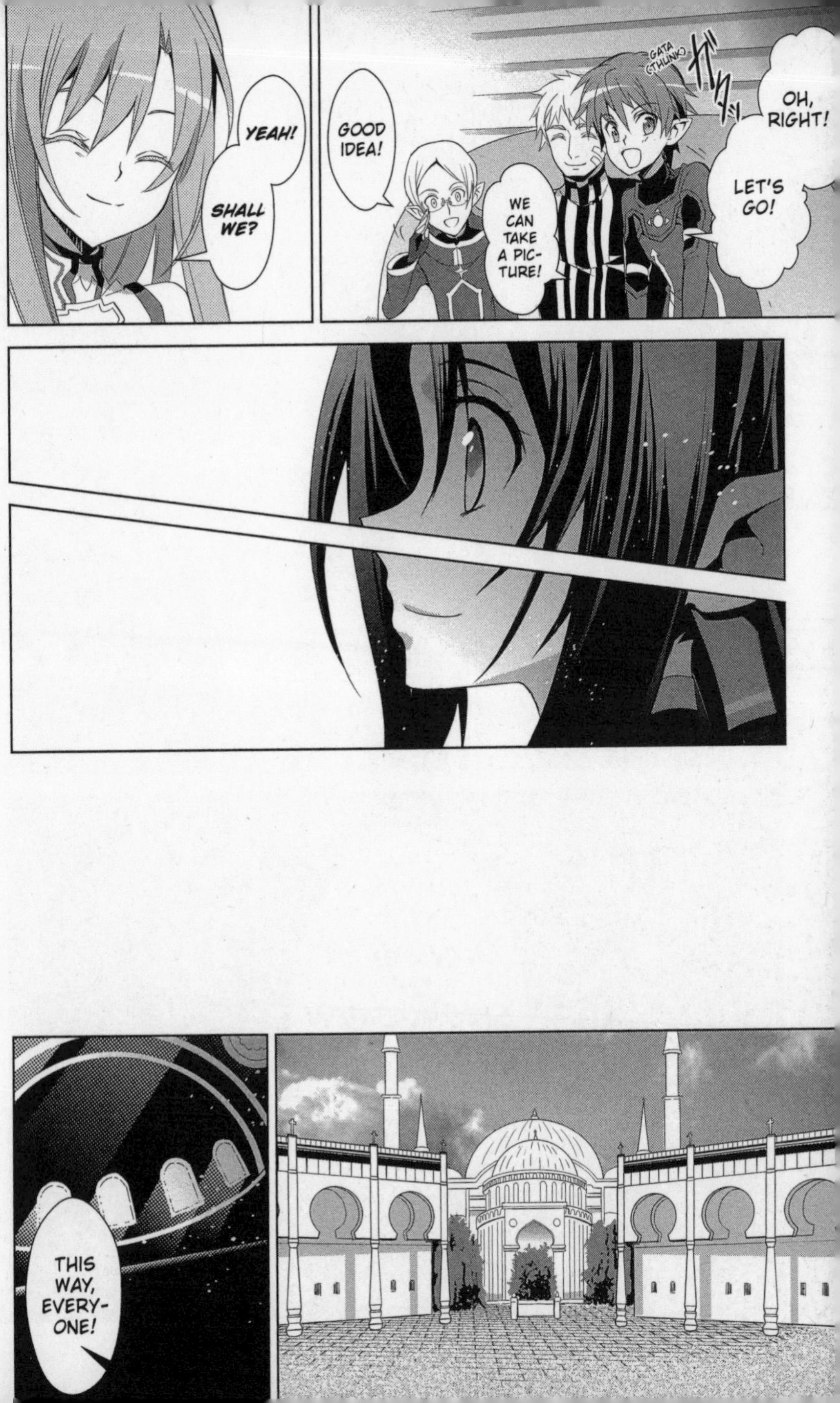
GATA (THUNK)
OH, RIGHT!
LET'S GO!
WE CAN TAKE A PIC-TURE!
GOOD IDEA!
YEAH!
SHALL WE?
THIS WAY, EVERY-ONE!

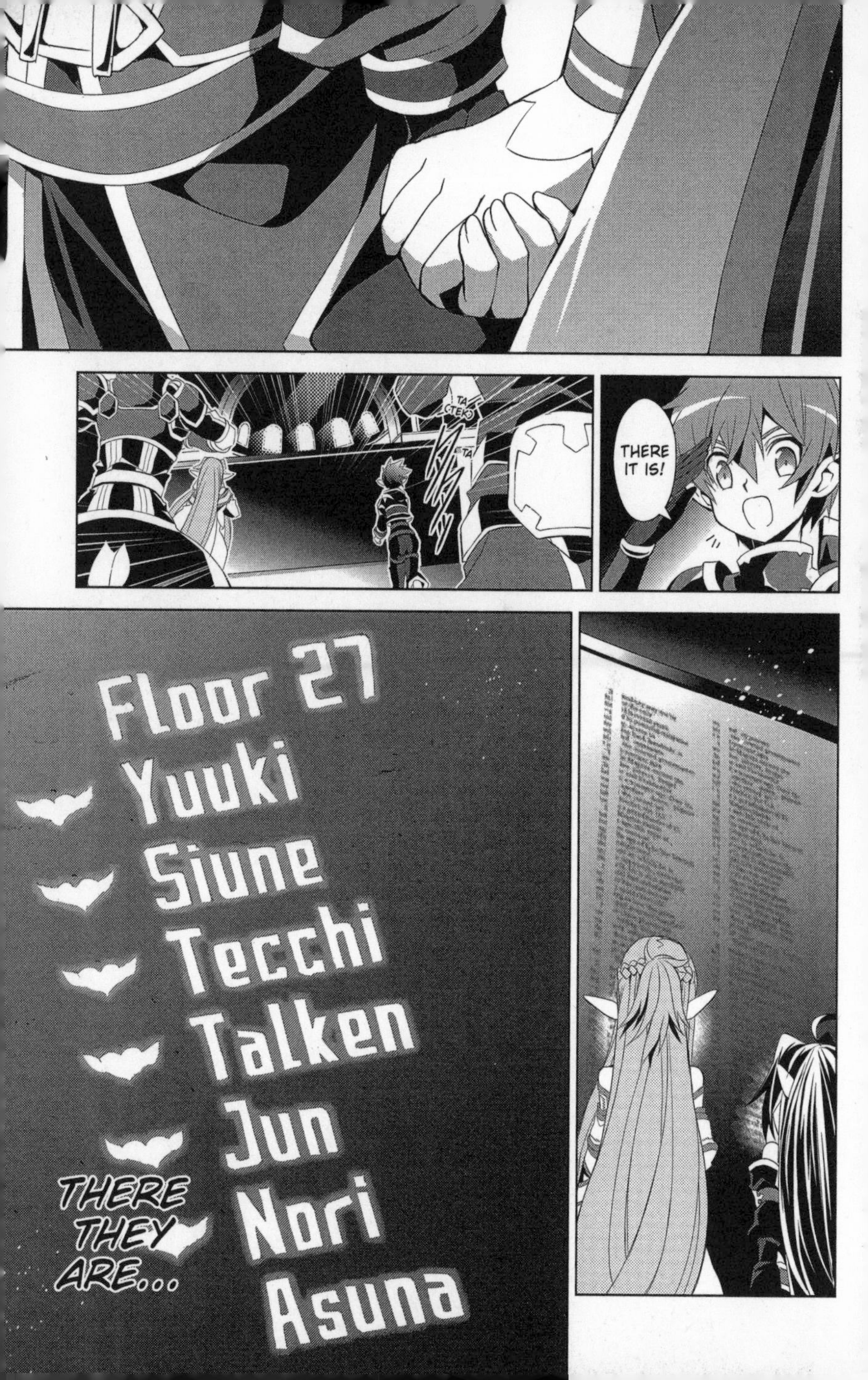
THERE IT IS!
TA (TEK)
TA
Floor 27
Yuuki
Siune
Tecchi
Talken
Jun
Nori
Asuna
THERE THEY ARE...

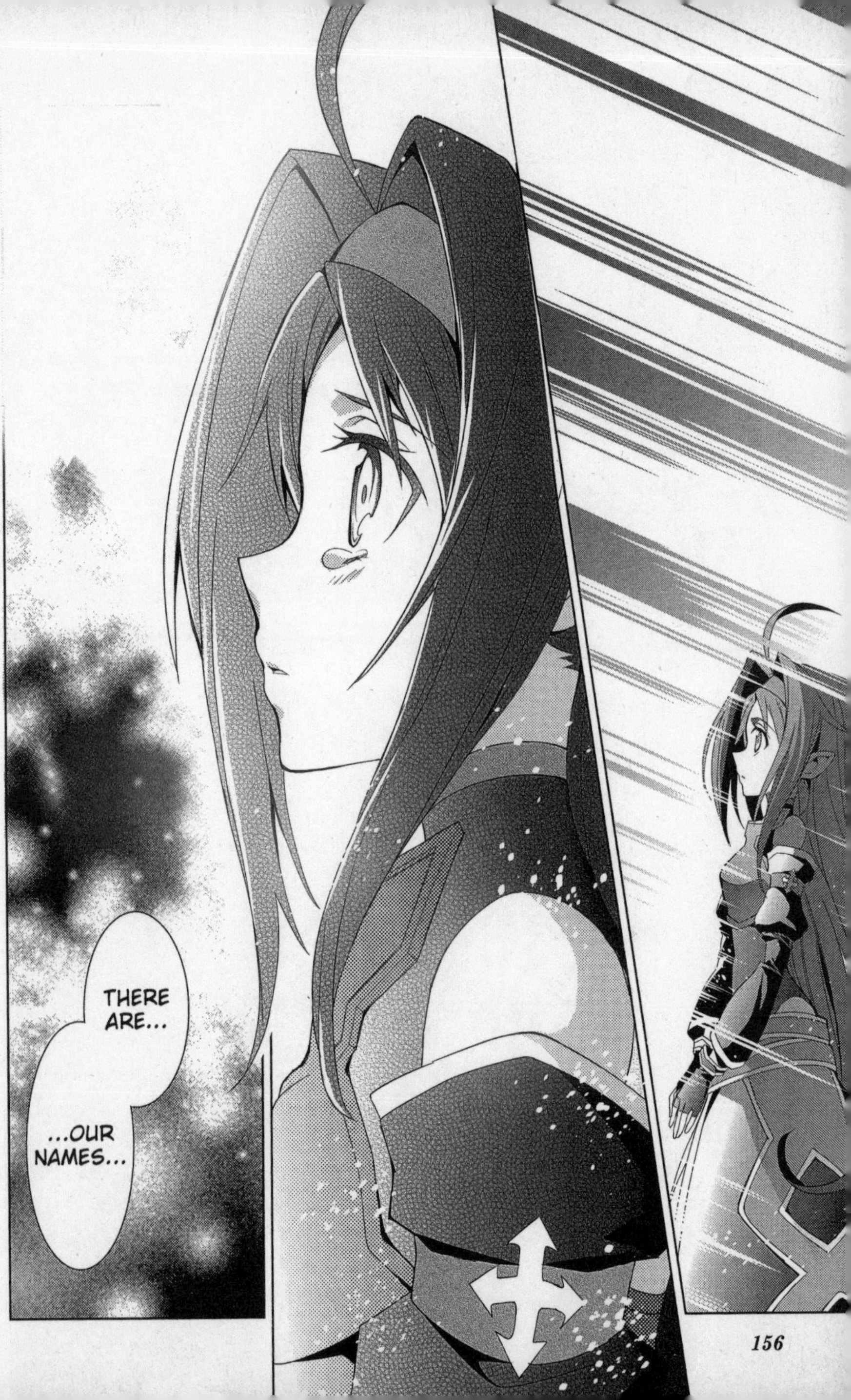
THERE ARE...
...OUR NAMES...

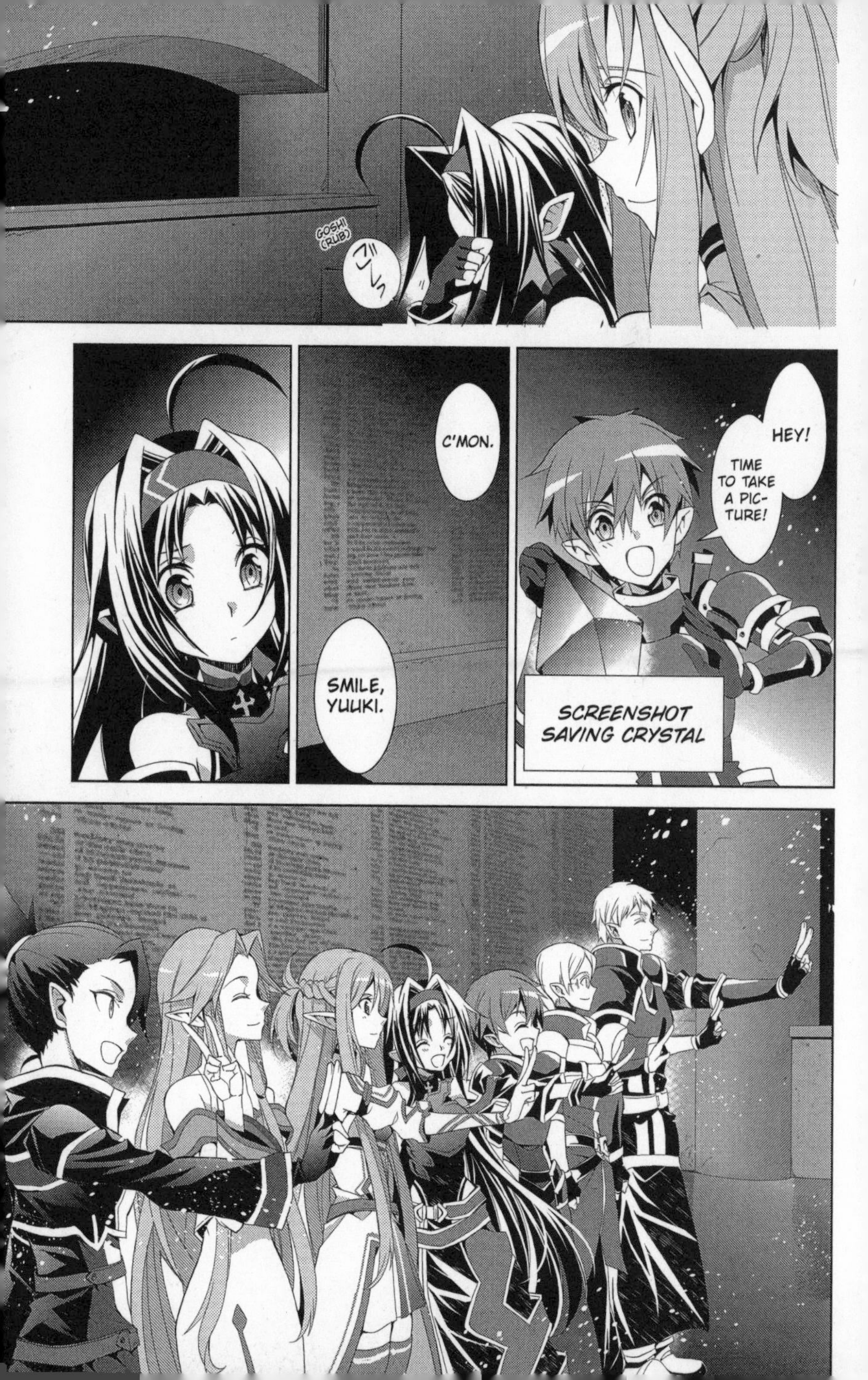
GOSHI (RUB)
HEY! TIME TO TAKE A PICTURE!
SCREENSHOT SAVING CRYSTAL
C'MON.
SMILE, YUUKI.

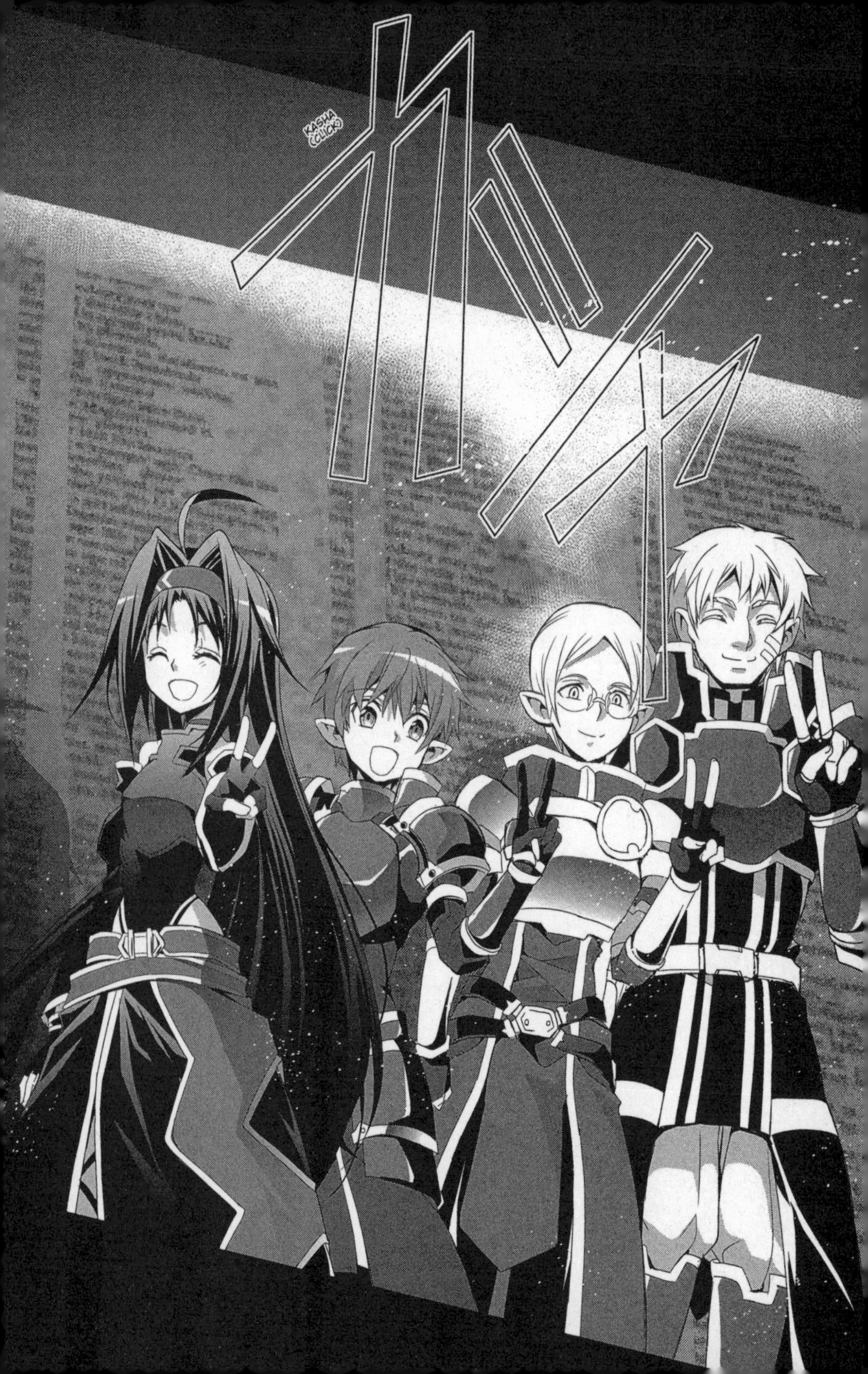
KASHA
(CLICK)

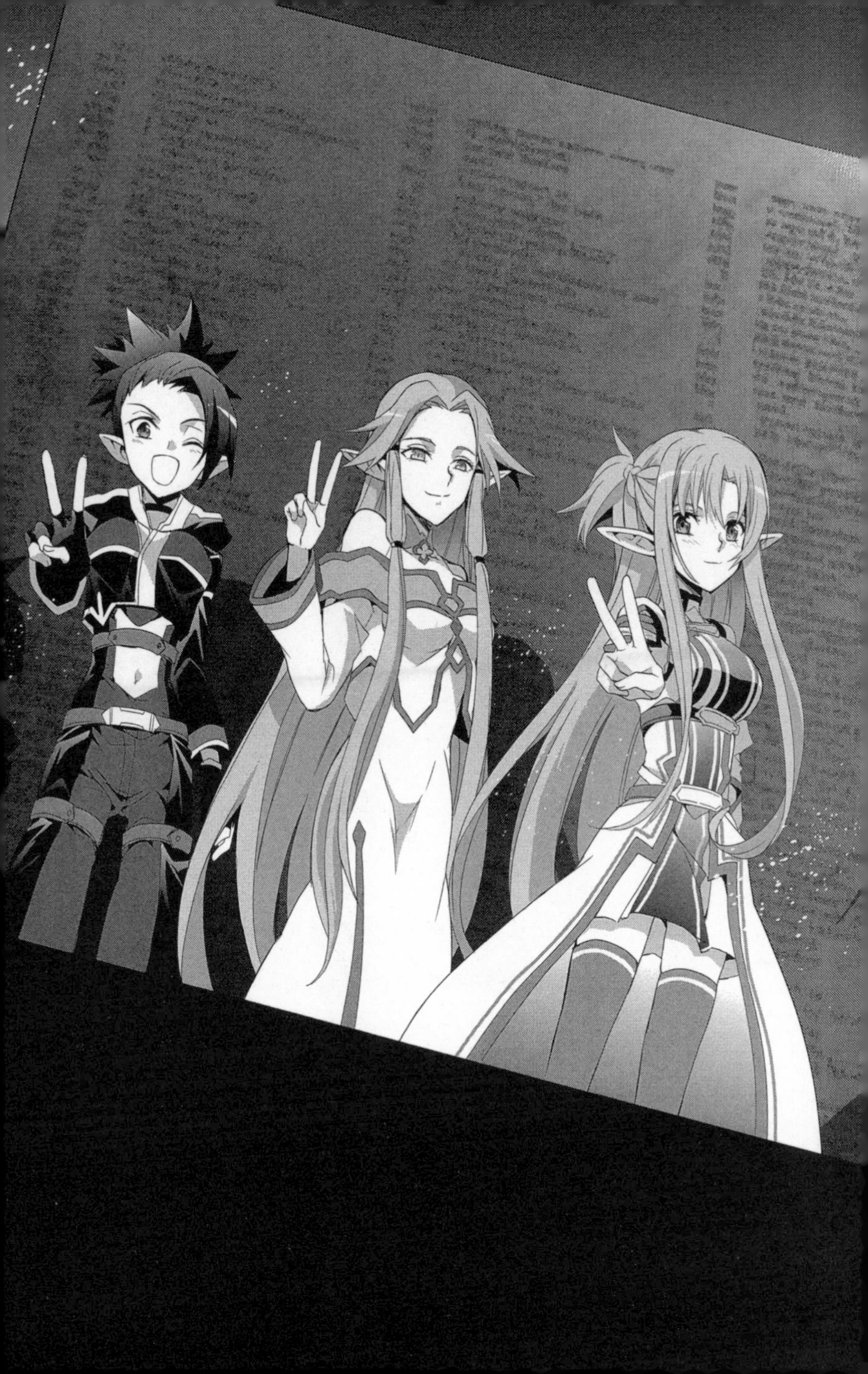

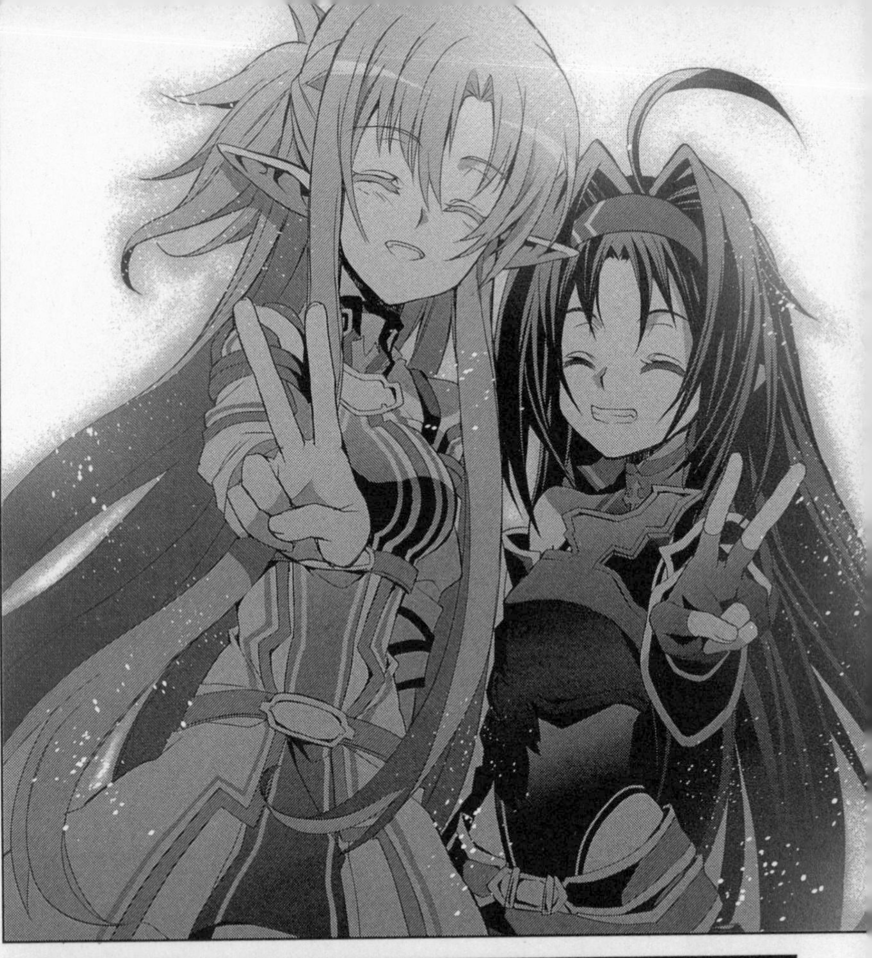

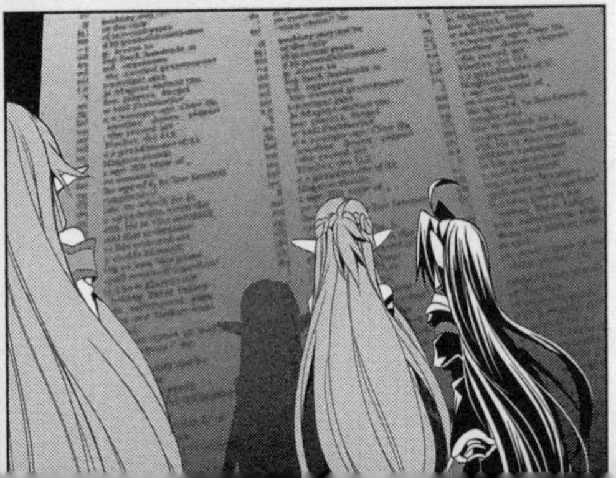

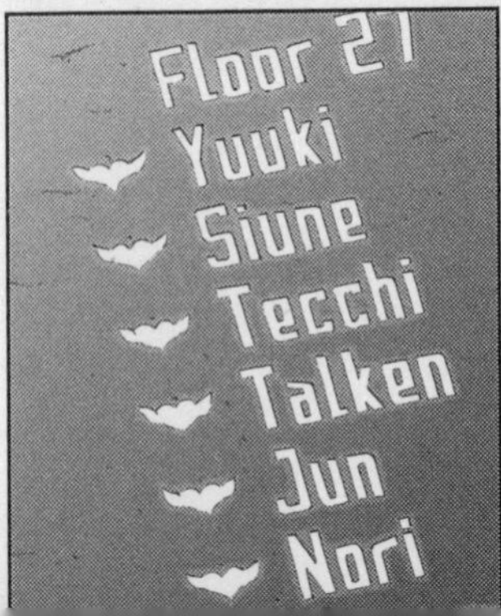
Floor 27
Yuuki
Siune
Tecchi
Talken
Jun
Nori

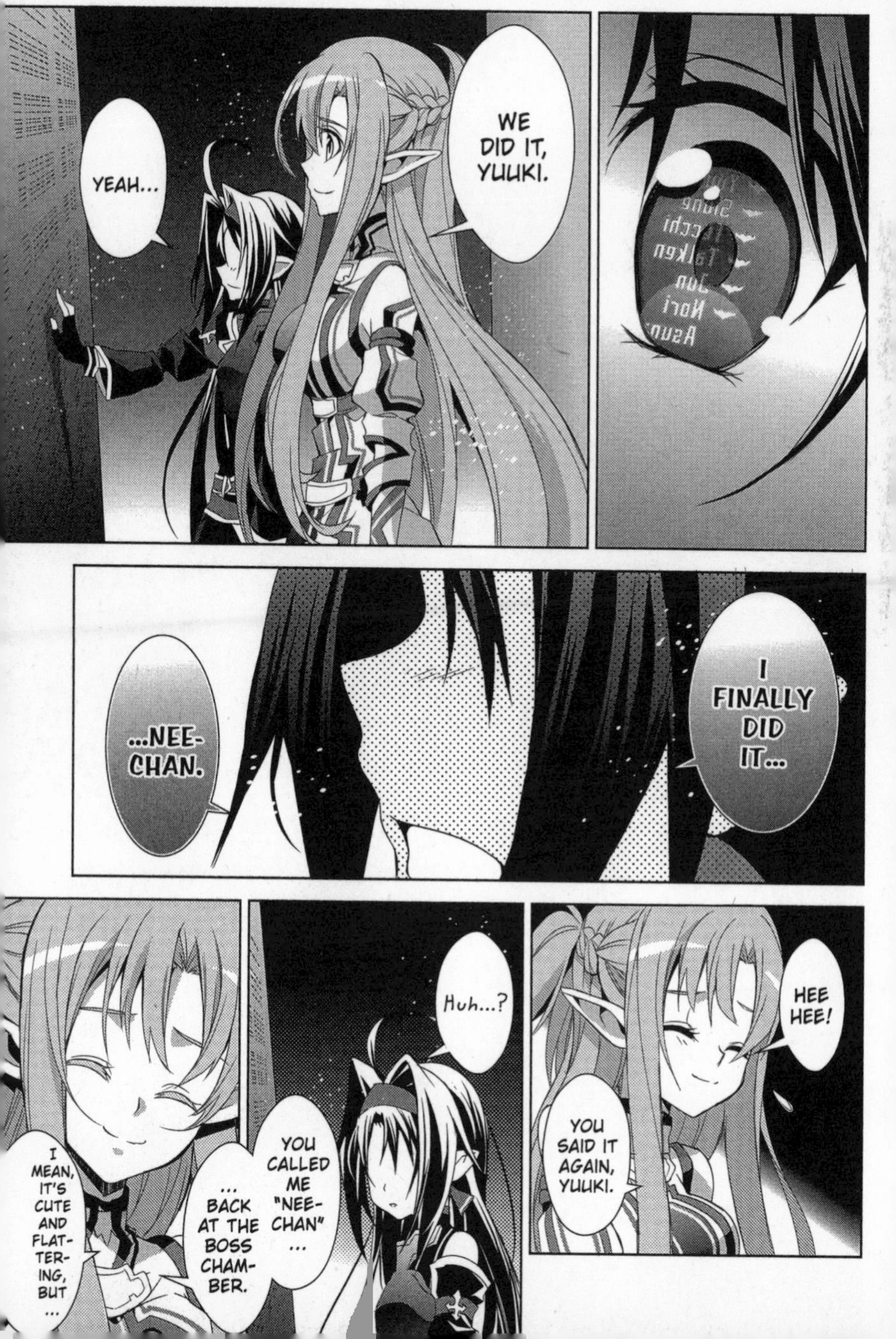
WE DID IT, YUUKI.
YEAH...
I FINALLY DID IT...
...NEE-CHAN.
HEE HEE!
YOU SAID IT AGAIN, YUUKI.
Huh...?
YOU CALLED ME "NEE-CHAN"...
... BACK AT THE BOSS CHAMBER.
I MEAN, IT'S CUTE AND FLATTERING, BUT...

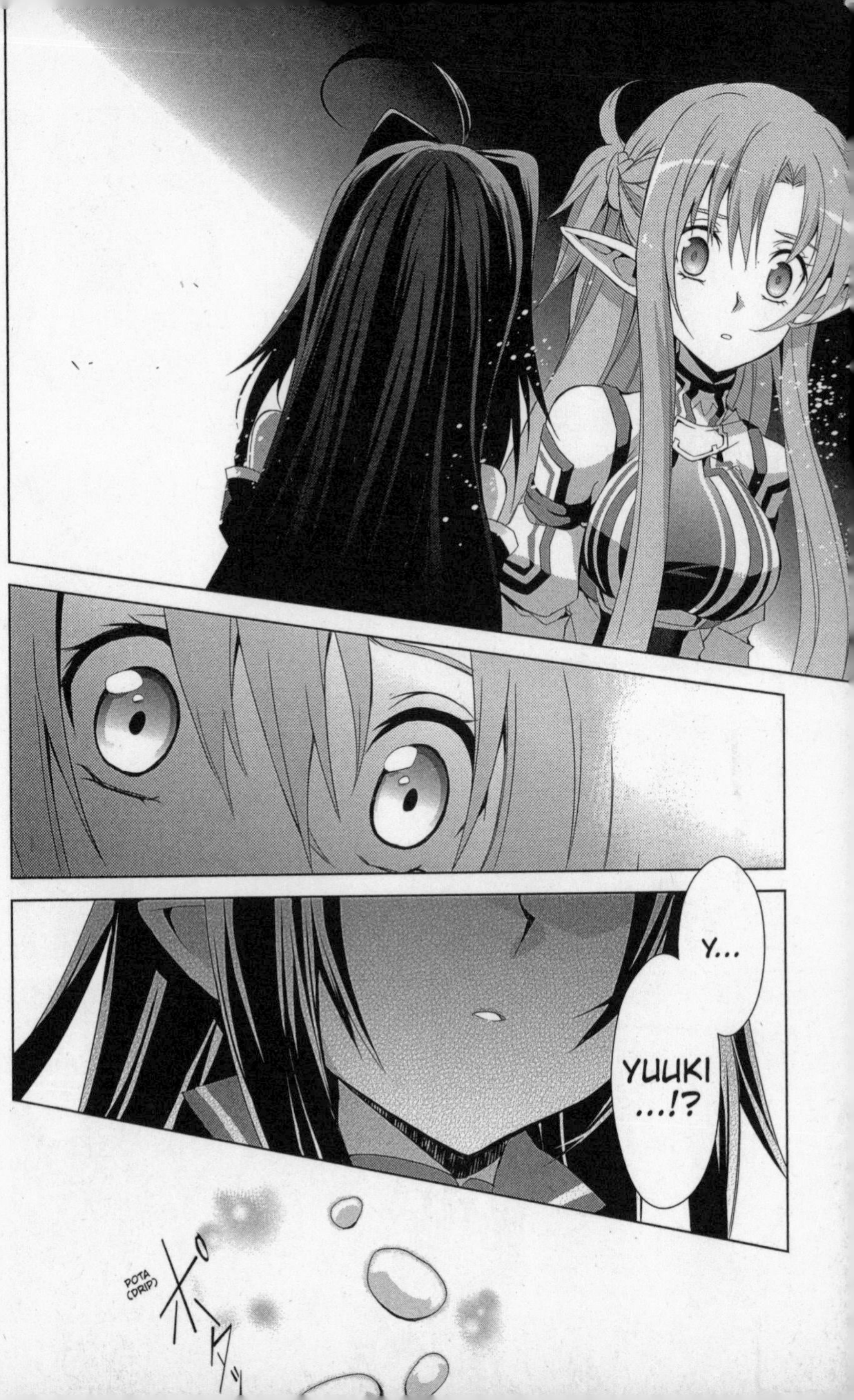
Y...
YUUKI ...!?
POTA (DRIP)

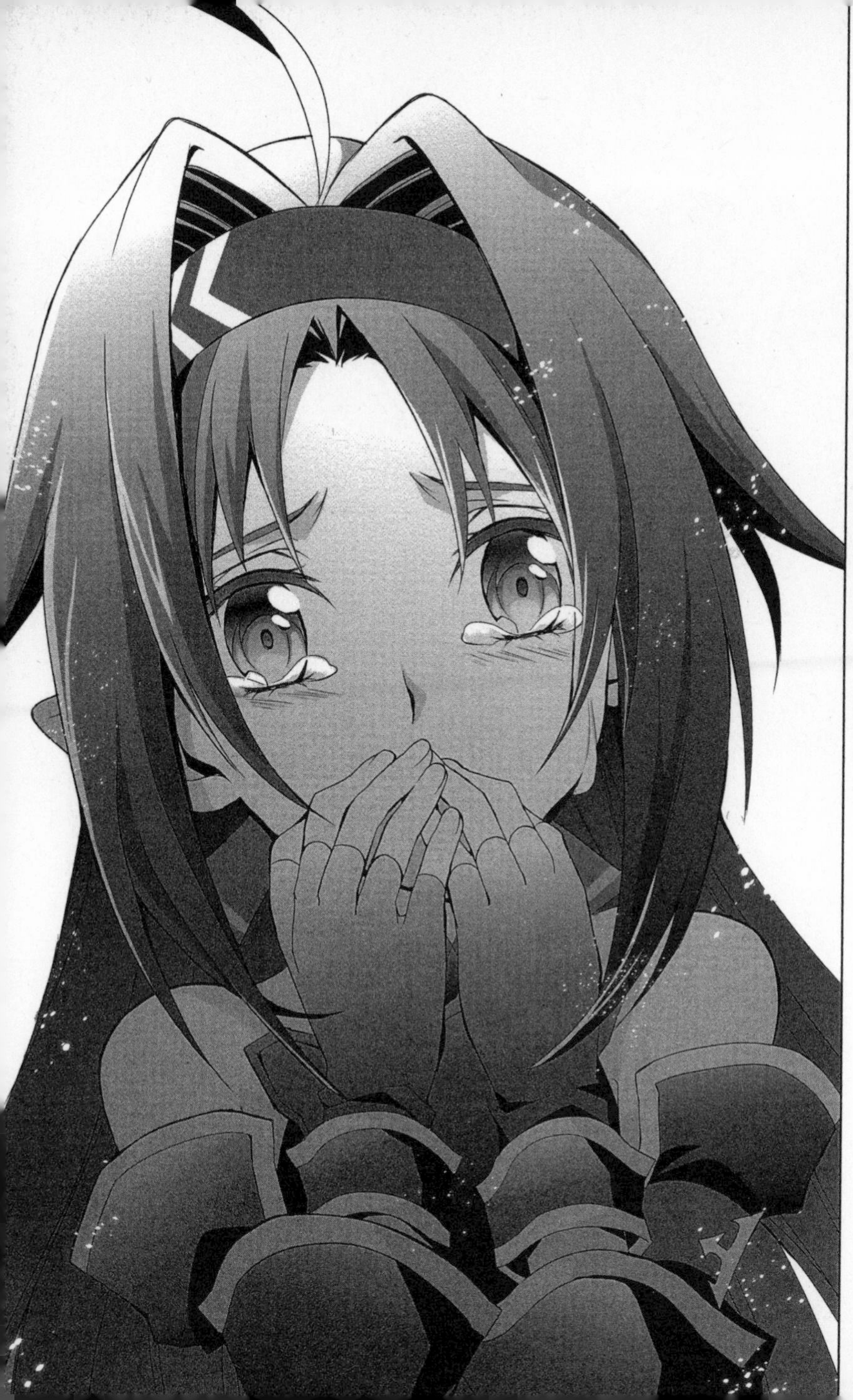

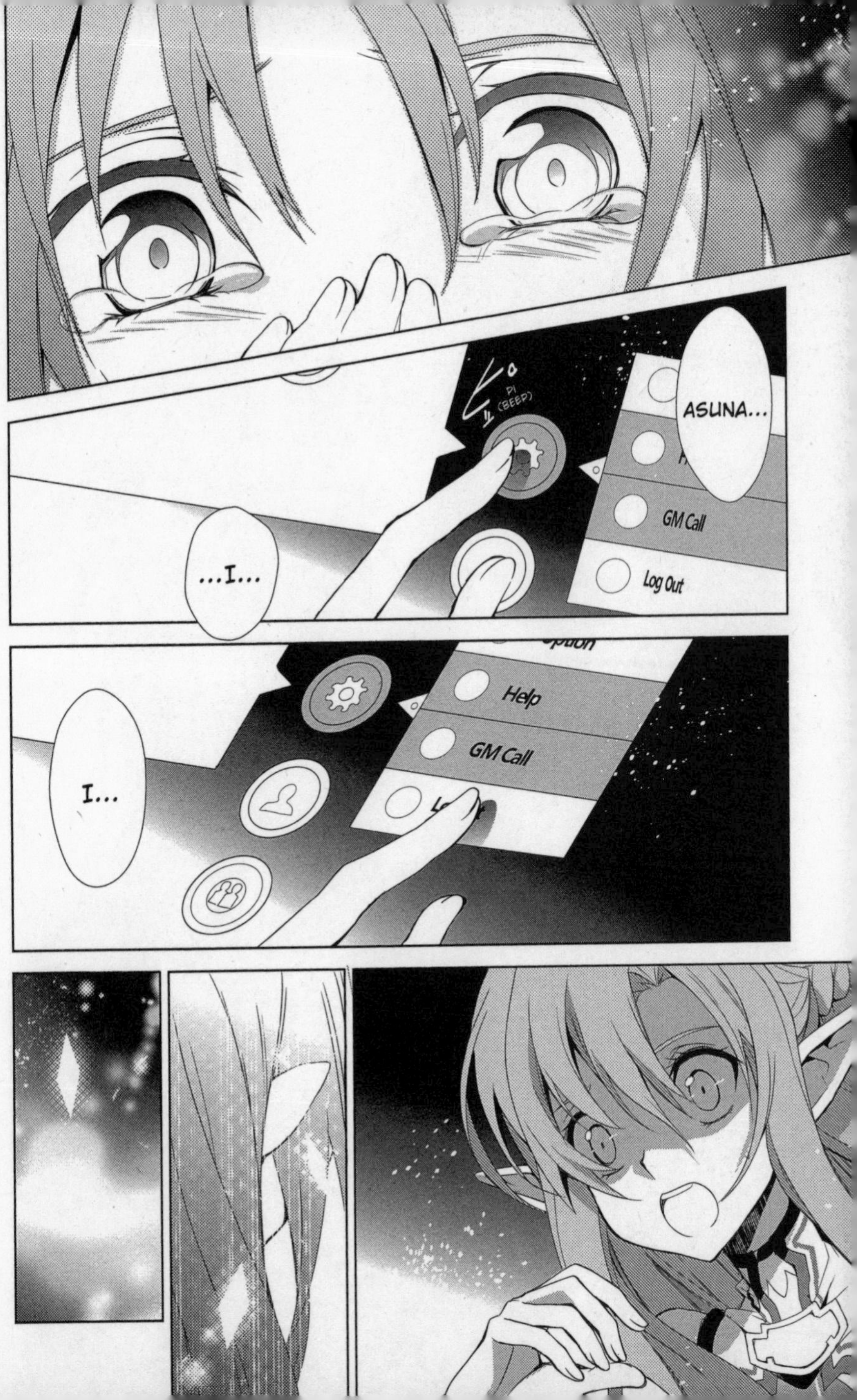
ASUNA...
PI (BEEP)
GM Call
Log Out
...I...
Help
GM Call
I...

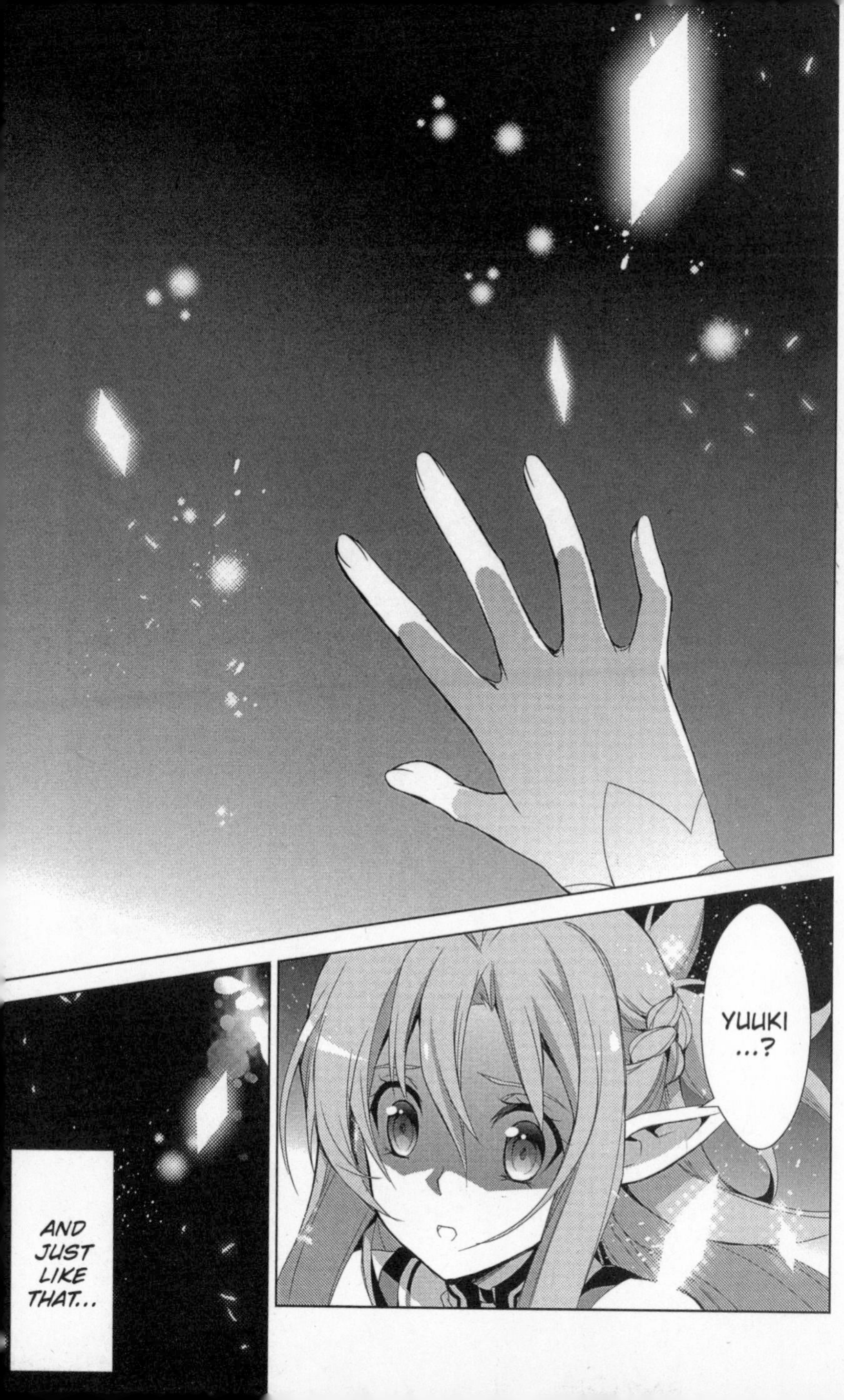
YUUKI ...?
AND JUST LIKE THAT...

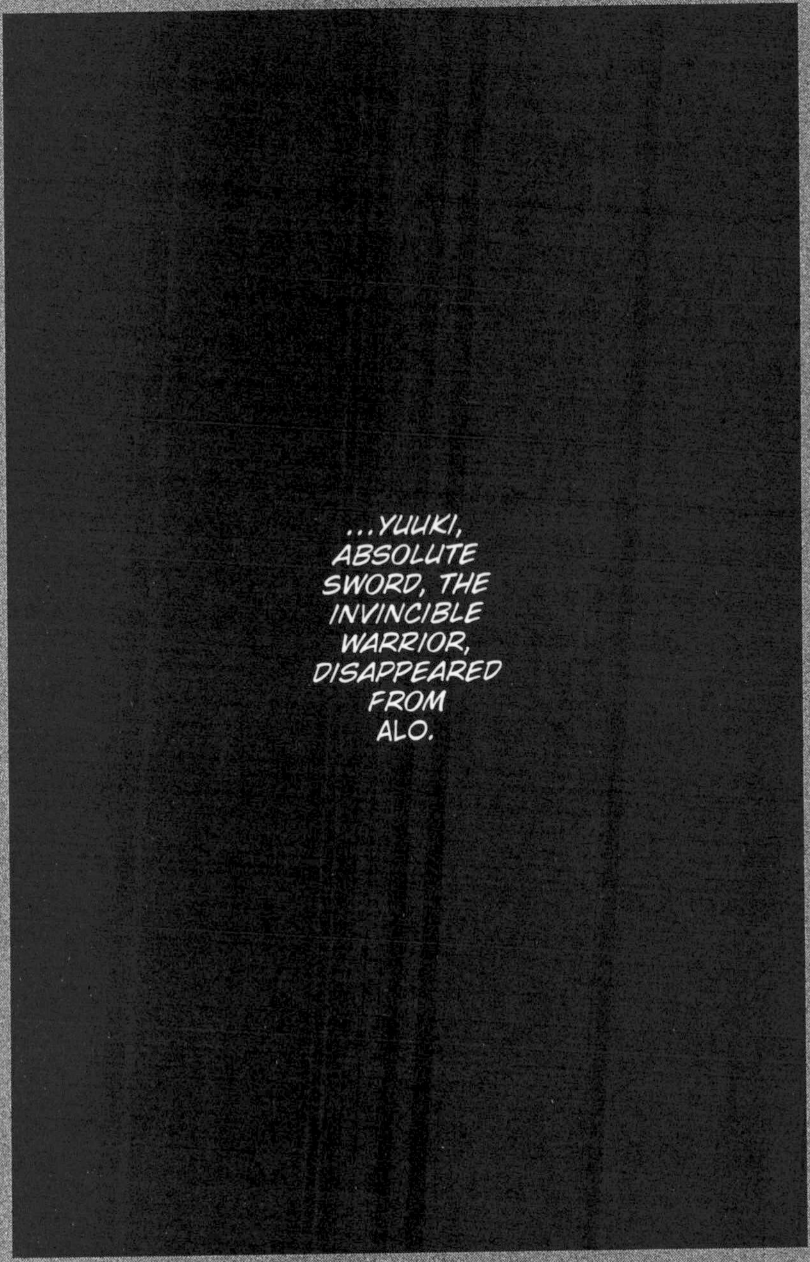
...YUUKI, ABSOLUTE SWORD, THE INVINCIBLE WARRIOR, DISAPPEARED FROM ALO.

Sword Art Online
mother's rosary

To Be Continued in the Next Stage...!!

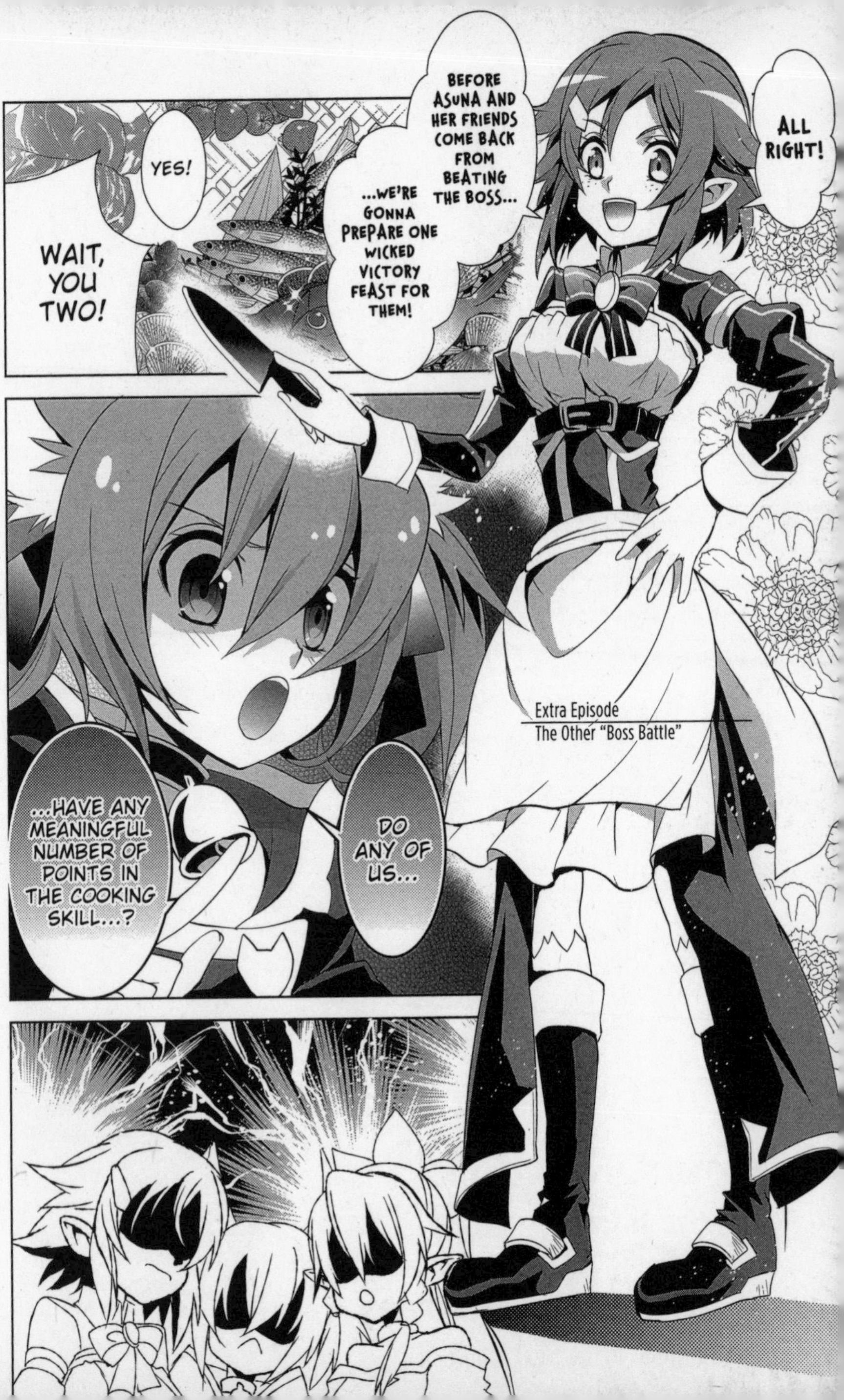
ALL RIGHT!
BEFORE ASUNA AND HER FRIENDS COME BACK FROM BEATING THE BOSS...
...WE'RE GONNA PREPARE ONE WICKED VICTORY FEAST FOR THEM!
YES!
WAIT, YOU TWO!
Extra Episode
The Other "Boss Battle"
DO ANY OF US...
...HAVE ANY MEANINGFUL NUMBER OF POINTS IN THE COOKING SKILL...?

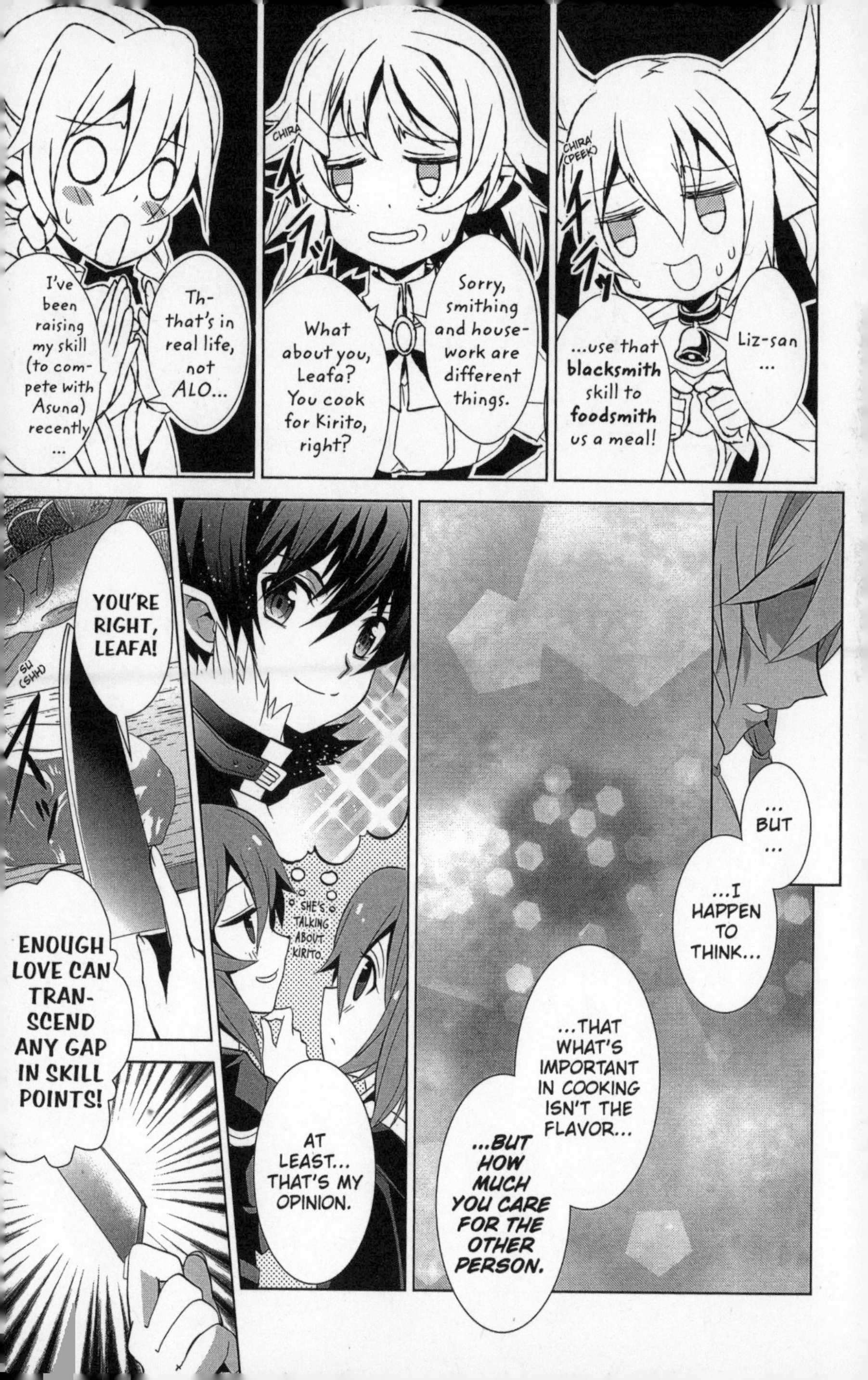
CHIRA (PEEK)
Liz-san ...
...use that blacksmith skill to foodsmith us a meal!
CHIRA
Sorry, smithing and house-work are different things.
What about you, Leafa? You cook for Kirito, right?
Th-that's in real life, not ALO...
I've been raising my skill (to compete with Asuna) recently ...
... BUT ...
...I HAPPEN TO THINK...
...THAT WHAT'S IMPORTANT IN COOKING ISN'T THE FLAVOR...
...BUT HOW MUCH YOU CARE FOR THE OTHER PERSON.
SHE'S TALKING ABOUT KIRITO.
AT LEAST... THAT'S MY OPINION.
YOU'RE RIGHT, LEAFA!
SU (SHH)
ENOUGH LOVE CAN TRANSCEND ANY GAP IN SKILL POINTS!

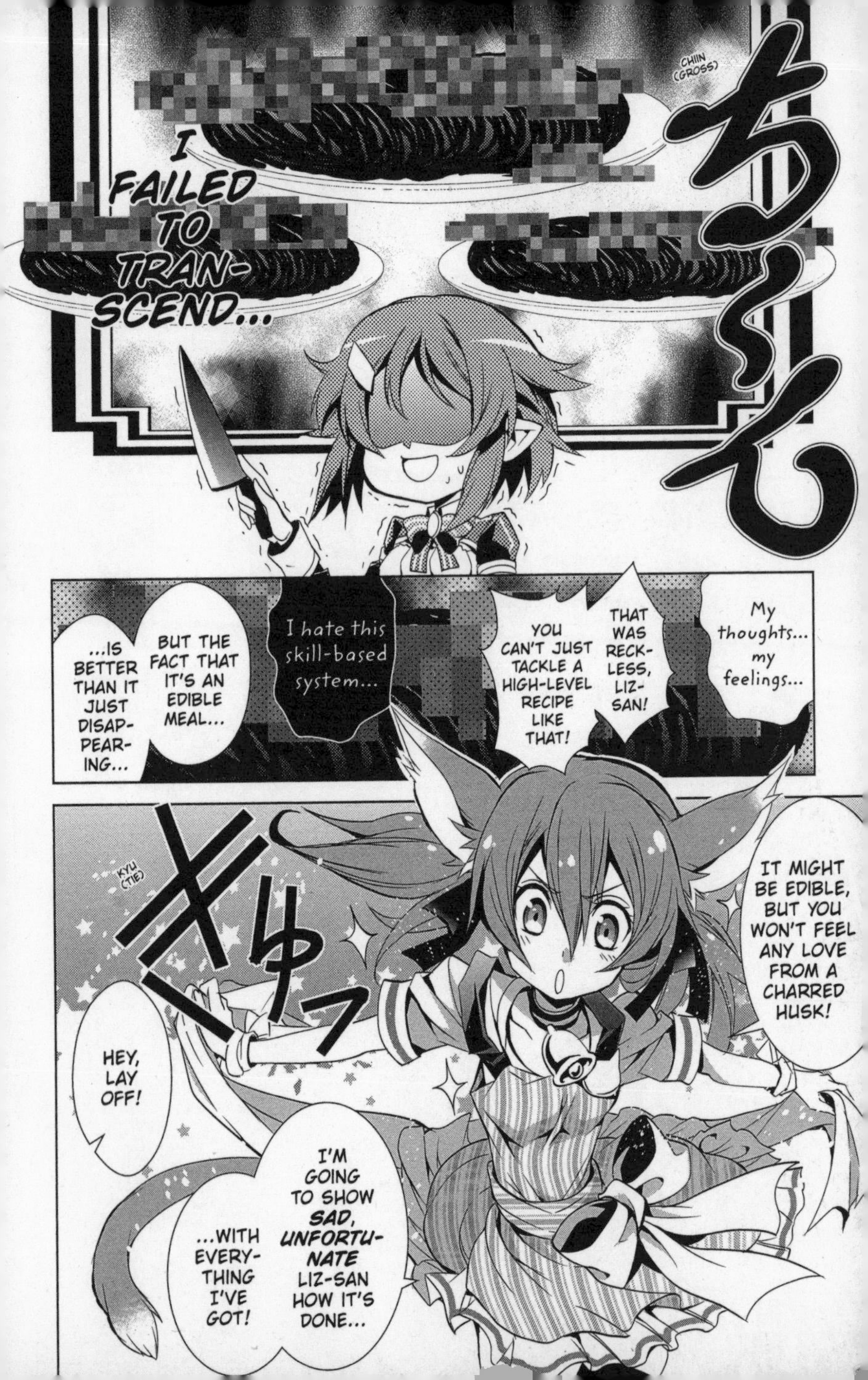
CHIIN (GROSS)
I FAILED TO TRAN-SCEND...
My thoughts... my feelings...
THAT WAS RECK-LESS, LIZ-SAN!
YOU CAN'T JUST TACKLE A HIGH-LEVEL RECIPE LIKE THAT!
I hate this skill-based system...
BUT THE FACT THAT IT'S AN EDIBLE MEAL...
...IS BETTER THAN IT JUST DISAP-PEAR-ING...
IT MIGHT BE EDIBLE, BUT YOU WON'T FEEL ANY LOVE FROM A CHARRED HUSK!
KYU (TIE)
HEY, LAY OFF!
I'M GOING TO SHOW SAD, UNFORTU-NATE LIZ-SAN HOW IT'S DONE...
...WITH EVERY-THING I'VE GOT!

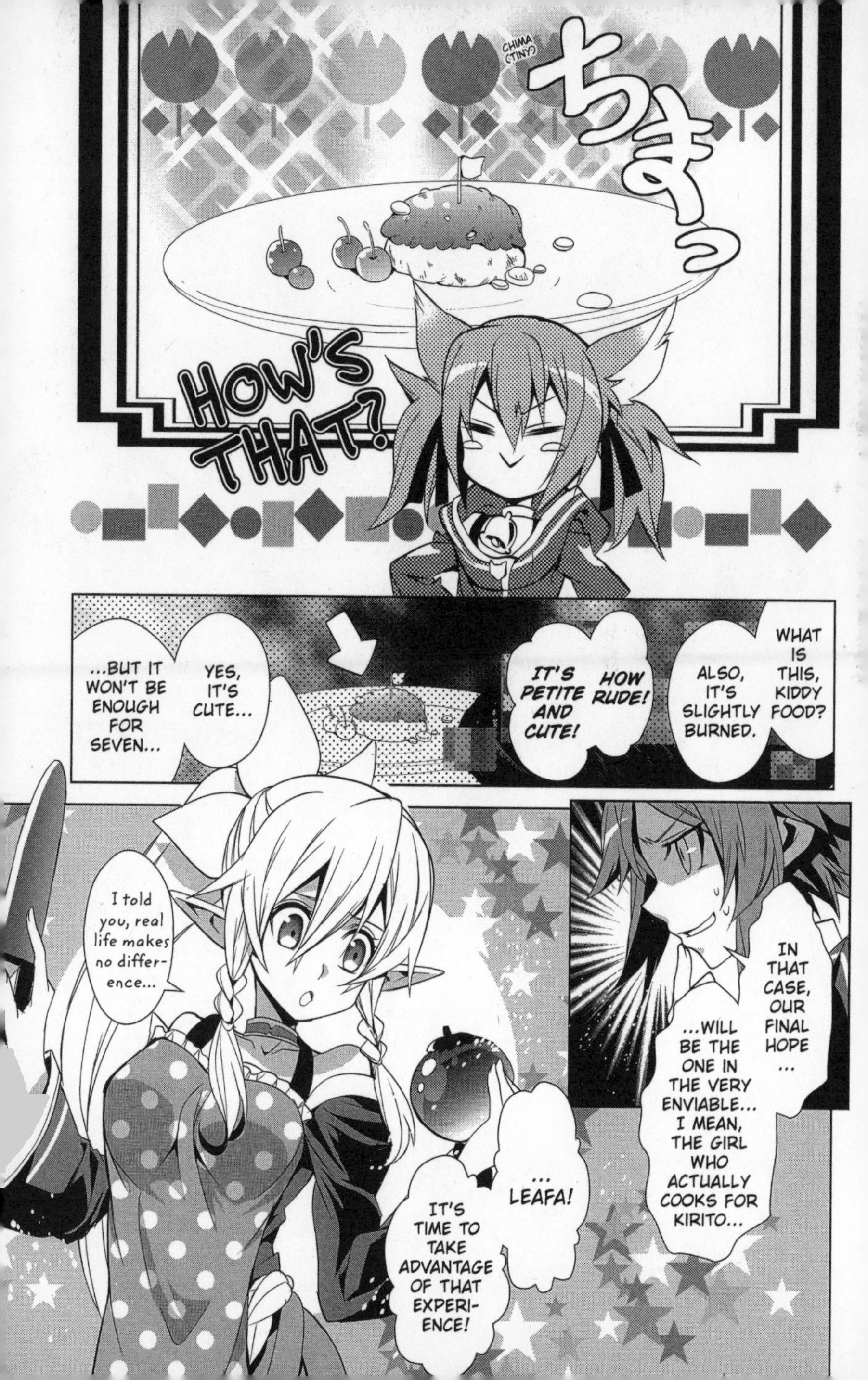
CHIMA (TINY)
ちまっ
HOW'S THAT?
WHAT IS THIS, KIDDY FOOD?
ALSO, IT'S SLIGHTLY BURNED.
HOW RUDE!
IT'S PETITE AND CUTE!
YES, IT'S CUTE...
...BUT IT WON'T BE ENOUGH FOR SEVEN...
IN THAT CASE, OUR FINAL HOPE ...
...WILL BE THE ONE IN THE VERY ENVIABLE... I MEAN, THE GIRL WHO ACTUALLY COOKS FOR KIRITO...
... LEAFA!
IT'S TIME TO TAKE ADVANTAGE OF THAT EXPERIENCE!
I told you, real life makes no difference...

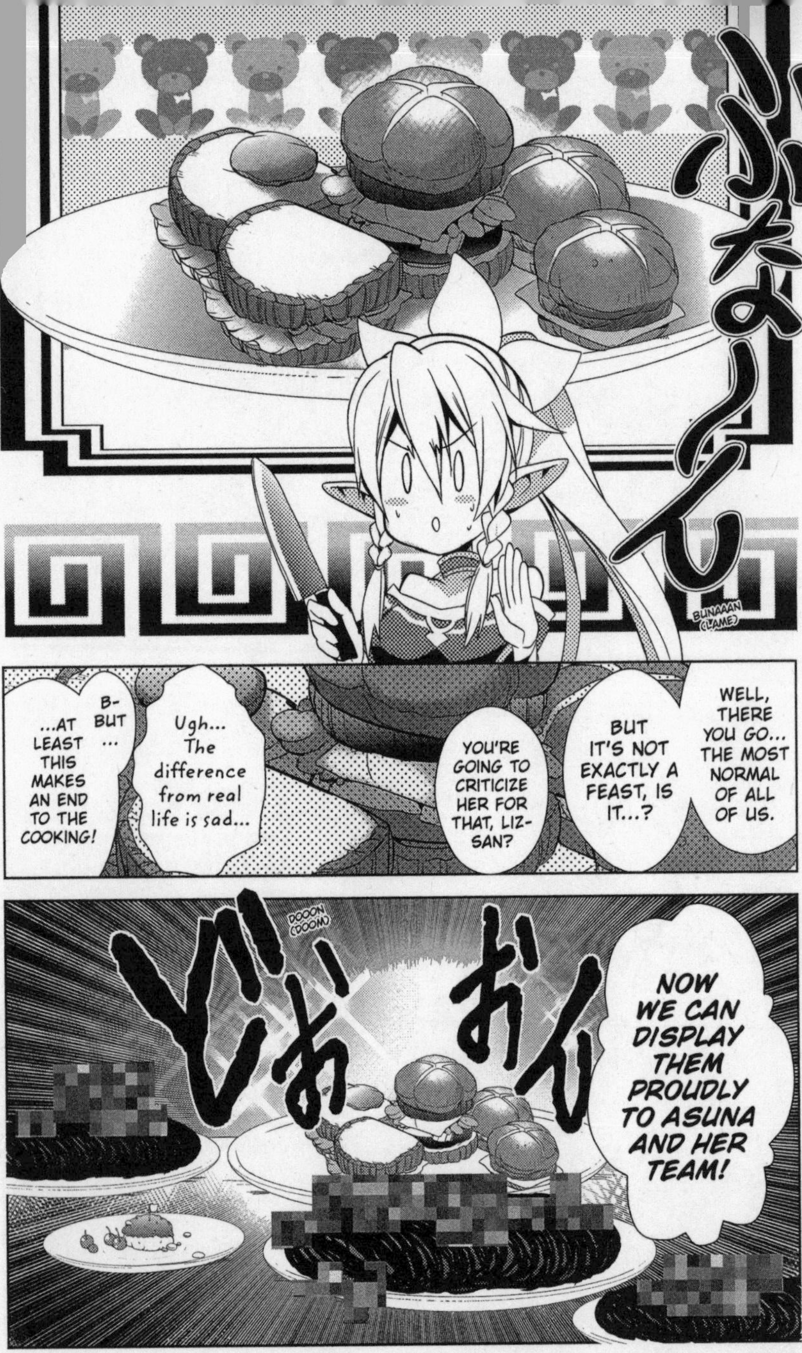
ぶなぁ〜ん
BUNAAAN (LAME)
WELL, THERE YOU GO... THE MOST NORMAL OF ALL OF US.
BUT IT'S NOT EXACTLY A FEAST, IS IT...?
YOU'RE GOING TO CRITICIZE HER FOR THAT, LIZ-SAN?
Ugh... The difference from real life is sad...
B-BUT...
...AT LEAST THIS MAKES AN END TO THE COOKING!
NOW WE CAN DISPLAY THEM PROUDLY TO ASUNA AND HER TEAM!
DOOON (DOOM)

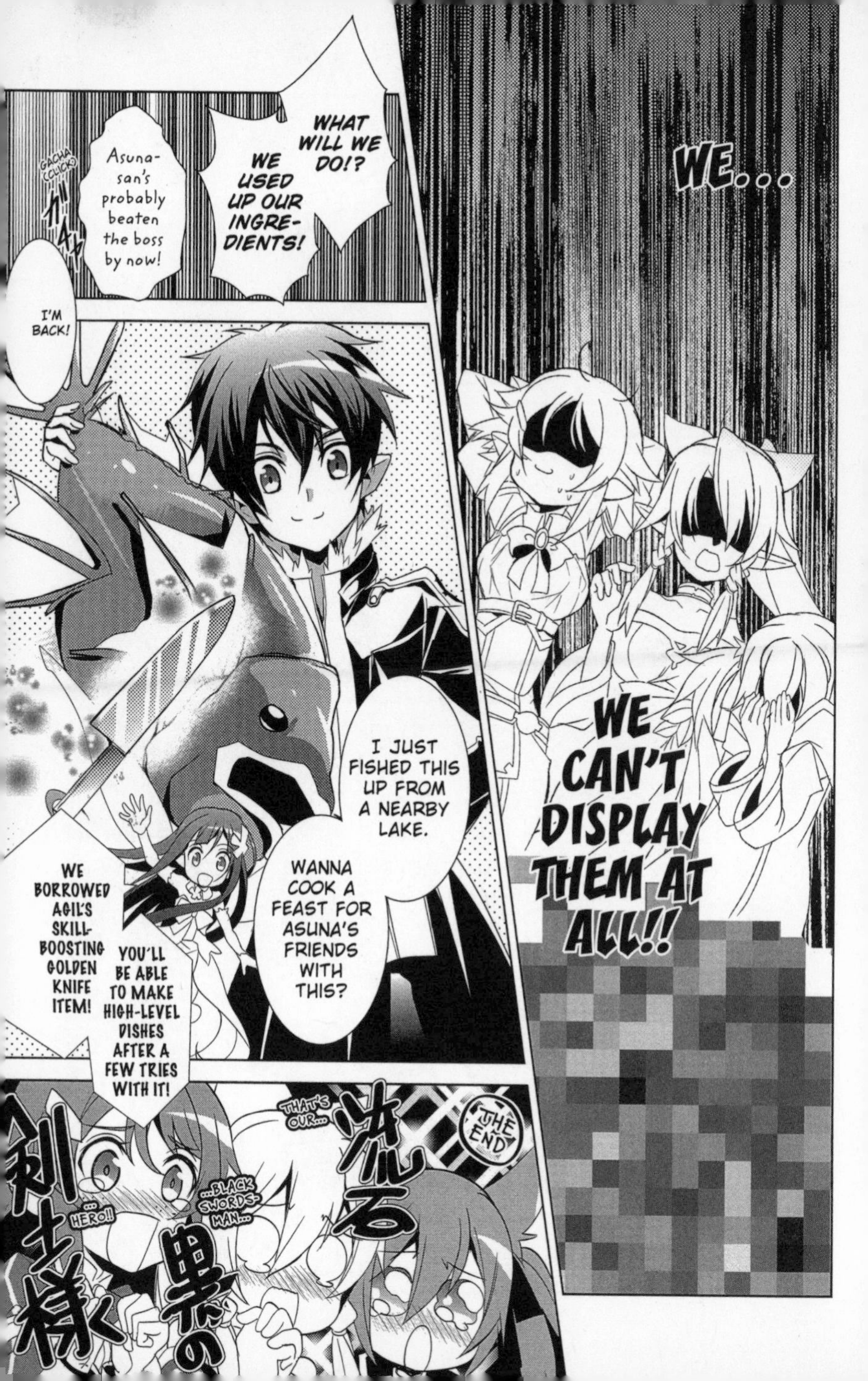
WE...
WE CAN'T DISPLAY THEM AT ALL!!
WHAT WILL WE DO!?
WE USED UP OUR INGREDIENTS!
Asuna-san's probably beaten the boss by now!
GACHA (CLICK)
I'M BACK!
I JUST FISHED THIS UP FROM A NEARBY LAKE.
WANNA COOK A FEAST FOR ASUNA'S FRIENDS WITH THIS?
WE BORROWED AGIL'S SKILL-BOOSTING GOLDEN KNIFE ITEM!
YOU'LL BE ABLE TO MAKE HIGH-LEVEL DISHES AFTER A FEW TRIES WITH IT!
THE END
THAT'S OUR...
...BLACK SWORDSMAN...
黒の
...HERO!!
剣士様

AFTERWORD MANGA

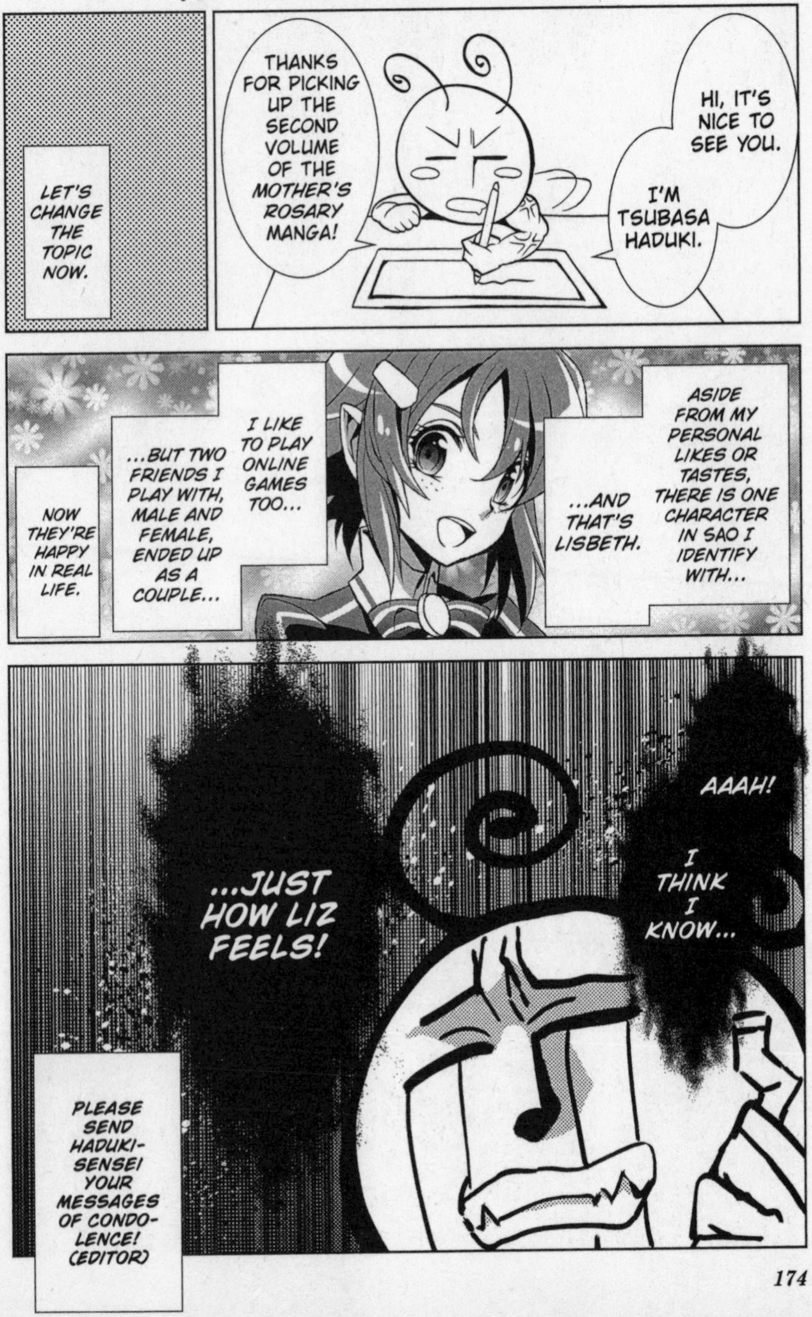
HI, IT'S NICE TO SEE YOU.
I'M TSUBASA HADUKI.
THANKS FOR PICKING UP THE SECOND VOLUME OF THE MOTHER'S ROSARY MANGA!
LET'S CHANGE THE TOPIC NOW.
ASIDE FROM MY PERSONAL LIKES OR TASTES, THERE IS ONE CHARACTER IN SAO I IDENTIFY WITH...
...AND THAT'S LISBETH.
I LIKE TO PLAY ONLINE GAMES TOO...
...BUT TWO FRIENDS I PLAY WITH, MALE AND FEMALE, ENDED UP AS A COUPLE...
NOW THEY'RE HAPPY IN REAL LIFE.
AAAH!
I THINK I KNOW...
...JUST HOW LIZ FEELS!
PLEASE SEND HADUKI-SENSEI YOUR MESSAGES OF CONDOLENCE! (EDITOR)

SPECIAL THANKS

RIONA
CORAL

MITSUHIRO ONODA
SAORI MIYAMOTO
TAKASHI SAKAI
EMIRI NIHEI
NICOE

REKI KAWAHARA
ABEC

KAZUMA MIKI
TOMOYUKI TSUCHIYA

THE STAFF OF THE *SWORD ART ONLINE* ANIME SERIES

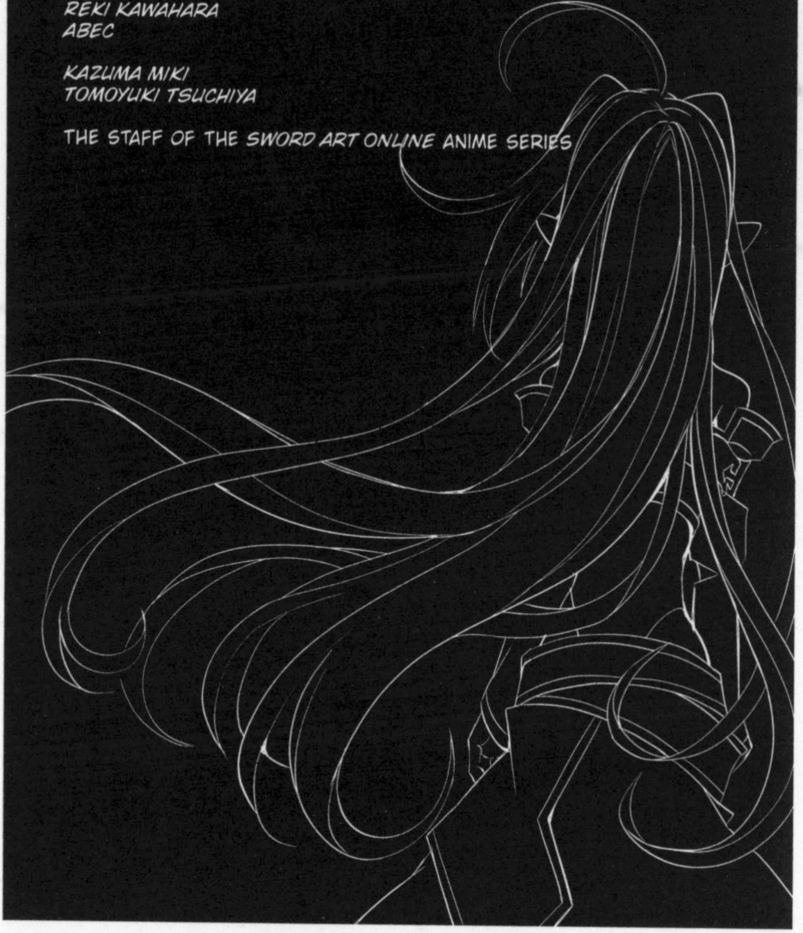